University of Ulster

Interpreting the CMMI®

A Process Improvement Approach

Second Edition

Interpreting the CMMI®

A Process Improvement Approach

Second Edition

MARGARET K. KULPA
KENT A. JOHNSON

CRC Press
Taylor & Francis Group
Boca Raton   London   New York

CRC Press is an imprint of the
Taylor & Francis Group, an **informa** business

AN AUERBACH BOOK

Auerbach Publications
Taylor & Francis Group
6000 Broken Sound Parkway NW, Suite 300
Boca Raton, FL 33487-2742

© 2008 by Taylor & Francis Group, LLC
Auerbach is an imprint of Taylor & Francis Group, an Informa business

No claim to original U.S. Government works
Printed in the United States of America on acid-free paper
10 9 8 7 6 5 4 3 2 1

International Standard Book Number-13: 978-1-4200-6052-2 (Hardcover)

Library of Congress Cataloging-in-Publication Data

Kulpa, Margaret K.
Interpreting the CMMI : a process improvement approach / Margaret K. Kulpa and Kent A. Johnson. -- 2nd ed.
p. cm.
Includes bibliographical references and index.
ISBN 978-1-4200-6052-2 (alk. paper)
1. Capability maturity model (Computer software) 2. Computer software--Development. I. Johnson, Kent A. II. Title.

QA76.758.K85 2008
005.1068'5--dc22   2007041375

Visit the Taylor & Francis Web site at
http://www.taylorandfrancis.com

and the Auerbach Web site at
http://www.auerbach-publications.com

Contents

SECTION III IMPLEMENTATION

SECTION IV MEASUREMENT

SECTION VI ODDS AND ENDS

SECTION VII APPENDICES

About the Authors

 **Margaret K. Kulpa** is the chief operating officer for AgileDigm, Incorporated. She is an internationally known author, presenter, and consultant in the areas of management, software engineering, and process improvement. With over 30 years of diverse system and software experience, Kulpa has primarily concentrated her efforts in the process improvement arena. She provides oversight and additional assistance where needed for clients, both domestic and international. Services provided include training in CMMI concepts and implementation, measurement strategies, acquisition, mentoring, consulting, and appraisal (SCAMPI) assistance. Services are provided to both low-maturity organizations beginning process improvement and to organizations struggling with high-maturity goals and objectives, from Maturity Level 1 through Maturity Level 5. Kulpa works with organizations to establish and maintain organizational infrastructures capable of initiating and generating software and systems engineering process improvement initiatives. She is a recognized expert in managing offshore software development.

Kulpa has developed and taught courses in software quality assurance, project management, peer reviews, requirements development and management, process baselines and modeling, safety and security, and other software engineering-related subjects. She has developed courses in the Staged and Continuous representation of the CMMI, and has served as an external member on SCAMPI^{SM} Appraisals (the latest SEI appraisal method). She is the primary author of *Interpreting the CMMI: A Process Improvement Approach* (Auerbach, 2003). She has been a reviewer and editor for the Institute for Electronics and Electrical Engineers (IEEE) magazine and enjoys acting as a featured speaker at conferences.

Kulpa can be reached via email at margaret.kulpa@agiledigm.com.

Kent A. Johnson is the chief technical officer for AgileDigm, Incorporated. Johnson is a proven leader and skilled troubleshooter with solid business and technical acumen. He has successfully worked with executives, managers, and engineering staff to improve their organizations in industries including aviation, naval, telecommunications, utilities, automotive, defense, government, software product development, and medical devices.

Johnson is an SEI-authorized SCAMPI^{SM} Lead Appraiser, an SEI-certified SCAMP-I^{SM} High Maturity Lead Appraiser, an SEI-authorized CMMI® instructor, and an experienced process improvement consultant. He has been involved in process improvement with the SEI since 1987.

He has helped clients move from Maturity Level 1 to Level 5 using both the CMM and CMMI. He has conducted more than 50 formal appraisals, including four high maturity (ML 4/5) SCAMPI A appraisals. He is coauthor of *Interpreting the CMMI: A Process Improvement Approach* (Auerbach, 2003) and *Ada 95 Quality and Style* (Springer, 1997).

Internationally, Johnson has helped clients in more than 20 countries to improve their systems and software processes. He is past chairman of the International Council on Systems Engineering (INCOSE) Systems Architecture Working Group and he has conducted presentations and tutorials to audiences exceeding 500 attendees at conferences including US SEPG conferences, European SEPG conferences, Software Engineering Systems Analysis and Modeling Conference (SESAM–Stockholm), INCOSE Conferences (USA), Java and Object Orientation Conference (JAOO–France), Software Technology Conference (USA), and various SPINs.

Johnson can be reached via e-mail at kent.johnson@agiledigm.com.

AgileDigm, Incorporated

AgileDigm, Incorporated, is an international, woman-owned, veteran-owned process improvement and management consulting firm. AgileDigm has been named as a Partner of the Software Engineering Institute (SEI) at Carnegie Mellon University. SEI Partners and their staff undergo a rigorous selection, training, and authorization process. Successful candidates are licensed by the SEI to deliver the institute's technologies. AgileDigm is licensed and has all rights and responsibilities associated with delivering the CMMI® Product Suite and the People CMM® Product Suite worldwide. AgileDigm is at the Web at www.agiledigm.com.

INTRODUCTION

1

Chapter 1

Introduction

What Is the CMMI*®?

CMMI is an acronym (it is not a four-letter word). The acronym stands for Capability Maturity Model Integration**SM. Some people would say the CMMI is a model, while others would describe it as a set of models. But most will agree that the CMMI is a merger of process improvement models for systems engineering, software engineering, hardware engineering, and integrated teams.

Some of the goals of the CMMI are to provide a common vocabulary across the set of models and to provide clarification on how these areas interrelate. The integrated model has both a continuous and staged perspective.

Why Did We Write This Book?

We wrote this book because we were tired of explaining the same things over and over and over again, and tired of fighting the same battles over and over and over again. Sometimes, the people we were explaining concepts and features of process improvement to were nice; but frankly, many times they were not. Whenever change might be introduced into an organization, most people feel threatened and

---

* ® CMMI is registered in the U.S. Patent and Trademark Office by Carnegie Mellon University.
** SM Capability Maturity Model Integration, and SCAMPI are service marks of Carnegie Mellon University.

act accordingly. They are afraid of losing what power and control they may have over their work lives and afraid of appearing foolish, out-of-date, or incompetent. That is not the purpose of process improvement, nor of the CMMI. In this book we hope to show you some possible benefits of using the CMMI and some possible problems to be overcome when using the CMMI. We try to present a balanced viewpoint.

This is the second version of our book *Interpreting the CMMI*. One thing that surprised us from the first version of our book was the criticism we received concerning our concentration on the CMMI and *not* the CMM. We thought that most organizations that had used the CMM were in the process of transitioning over to the CMMI. Apparently, this was not true. Now, five years later, most organizations that began the transition from CMM to CMMI have finished their effort. For those readers, we have included examples of where the current version of the CMMI (version 1.2) differs from the original version, version 1.1. There are still some organizations, however, that:

- Are very new to model-based improvement
- Have never used a model
- Are considering using the CMMI
- Have some very basic experience using the older CMM as their model for improvement

For those organizations and individuals who have some knowledge of the CMM way of doing things, we have kept our discussions of the CMM in this book.

After using the CMMI with organizations in different parts of the world, we found that the model is difficult for most people to pick up and use right away. Two of the problems in the CMMI include interpretation and organizational decisions. The model itself was written to cover many different organizational and project situations. An ambiguous style was intentionally chosen by the authors of the CMMI to fit these many situations. This ambiguity results in the need for a lot of interpretation and decision making by the model users. We hope to help identify these decisions for you and provide a positive influence in your decision making.

How to Read This Book

We have tried to write this book for the widest audience possible—that is, for the experienced process improvement practitioner, the inexperienced practitioner, the CMMI expert, and the CMMI novice. This book is divided into six sections. Section 1 includes this chapter, up to and including Chapter 4. Chapter 1 introduces the reader to the purpose of this book, provides some clarification as to what process improvement really is, and answers some questions in very general terms as to why to use the CMMI and how to use it. Chapters 2 through 4 discuss the structure of the CMMI. Section 2 includes Chapters 5 through 8. These chapters provide an overview of the Process Areas, arranged according to the structure of the Staged Representation of the CMMI. Section 3 includes Chapters 9 through 15. Chapters 9 through 15 go more into the process improvement area and offer some of our suggestions and hints on how to apply the concepts proposed in the CMMI to your organization. These chapters display tables, templates, and charts that may prove applicable in your improvement efforts. Section 4 consists of Chapters 16 through 19. These chapters address measurement issues, from basic metrics to collect as part of normal CMMI implementation, to statistical process control and high maturity concerns. Section 5 is about appraisals and consists of Chapters 20 through 22. This section contains chapters on SCAMPI[SM] appraisal types, the steps in the most formal appraisal (SCAMPI A), and required SCAMPI documentation (PIIDs). Section 6 is our wrap-up section. There is a chapter on incorporating Agile Methods into CMMI process improvement and a chapter containing our closing thoughts. We have also included appendices. These appendices contain interesting bits of information. So, readers new to process improvement and the CMMI should first concentrate on Chapters 2 through 8. The CMMI "expert" may wish to skip Chapters 2 through 8. The reader seeking help in process improvement techniques (whether using the CMMI or not) should focus on Chapters 9 through 15. Those of you interested in measurement issues and techniques should read Chapters 16 through 19; and those of you interested in SCAMPI appraisals should read Chapters 20 through 22. Chapter 23 is for the Agile Methods's "inquiring minds." Of course, everyone should read Chapter 1. If you have gotten this far, you are so good. Give yourself a star. We thank you for buying this book. If you didn't buy the book but just borrowed it, hey, we are happy about that too. At least you are reading something we sweated over. We hope you like it, and we hope it helps you.

Why Use CMMI?

A lot of readers will already know why they want to start using the CMMI in their organizations to drive their process improvement programs, but some of the reasons we have heard include:

- You want to be on the cutting edge of process improvement.
- CMMI must be better than CMM because it is newer.
- You have tried other process improvement strategies and have not liked the outcome, or have grown tired of that approach.
- You have a customer that is making you use CMMI.
- Your previous model has been superseded by another, so you might as well try the latest version of the CMMI.

Some readers are looking for other reasons to invest in this model, such as:

- This model includes help/direction/ideas about software engineering, systems engineering, hardware engineering, and integrated team development.
- One of the primary goals of the CMMI is to allow organizations to reduce the cost and confusion incurred from multiple assessments and multiple process improvement programs to cover both their systems and software engineering activities.

Family of CMMs

Most readers will come to this book with knowledge of the Capability Maturity Model also known as the CMM for Software. So in order to describe concepts within the CMMI, we will often compare the approaches taken in the CMMI to a similar topic in the CMM for Software. In some cases, we may describe the concept within the CMMI as it relates to other models, such as the Systems Engineering CMM (SE-CMM) or Systems Engineering Capability Model Electronic Industries Association (EIA) 731. But for the most part we will stay within what some call the family of CMMs. Some readers would of course want us to consider other models and evaluation approaches in our discussions including, to name a few, the Software Development Capability Evaluation (SDCE), International Organization for Standardization (ISO) 9000 series, Six Sigma, and ISO 2000; however, that is not what this book is about.

Terminology

This book uses the language that has become a part of the process improvement community. This community has grown up around the family of CMMs. The community includes process practitioners, process improvement specialists, evaluators, assessors, appraisers, project managers, and executives that have spent significant effort to implement, evaluate, and improve processes in a wide variety of domains. Unfortunately, not all the sources that make up the overall process improvement body of knowledge are consistent in their use of terms. For that reason, we have defined a number of terms throughout this book. In some cases these definitions will come from a specific reference and we will note that reference in the text. In other cases, we will just give you our definition.

People first coming to model-based process improvement can misunderstand the term *model*. These models are not intended to be architectural type plans for your organization's processes. You don't just follow these steps and you will have a good process. Models are more a yardstick or guideline to determine what might be missing from your processes. The CMMI is referred to as a reference model. The term *reference model* is used to indicate this idea of a yardstick or guideline for your processes.

The term *organization* is used in a general sense throughout the book to mean the group that the process improvement initiative covers. In some cases, an organization is an entire company, in some cases a division or department within a company, and in some cases it might be a group responsible for developing a specific product.

During our work with clients we have also found it useful to discuss the differences between the CMMI, a process model, a process, a process description, a procedure, and an appraisal.

Initially, some people have a problem because they think CMMI is a process or a set of processes. It is neither. CMMI is a process *model*. The CMMI cannot just be copied as is and serve as an organization's processes. CMMI is a collection of best practices from highly functioning organizations collected to help you improve your processes by describing *what* things or activities should be done in your organization.

So what is a process? Well, a process is what you *really* do in your organization. The process is written down as the activities or steps you go through to perform work. Your organization's processes must be documented to be real, to be performed consistently, and to be improved. If your organization has undocumented processes and you believe that these processes are used consistently then you are living in a world of denial.

Although, the CMMI uses the term *process description* to refer to processes that are documented, in normal conversation you will often hear people using just the term *process*. The CMMI recommends certain attributes that are necessary when documenting processes—we cover those recommendations in more detail in later chapters. So what is a process description? Well, a process description is a "documented expression of a set of activities to achieve a given purpose." The process description documents the steps of the process performed, that is, *what* you do when you perform a task. Closely related are procedures that describe the step-by-step instructions on *how* to perform the steps in the process.

So what is an appraisal? Well, just because an organization has process descriptions and procedures, it does not mean they are being followed or even contain "the right stuff." An appraisal is a way to evaluate the organization's processes and procedures, how they were implemented, to what extent they are followed, and to what extent they map to the CMMI practices. In the CMMI world, SCAMPI (Standard CMMI Appraisal Method for Process Improvement) is a set of appraisal methods that differ in their intent and rigor. The SCAMPI can be used for internal process improvement, supplier selection, process monitoring, and for maturity or capability level ratings for contract awards—more on that later.

So, how are these terms related? Figure 1.1 shows the relationship between these key terms.

The CMMI is used as a guideline to create processes and procedures. CMMI is used as the reference model for the SCAMPI appraisal method to examine the organization's processes and procedures.

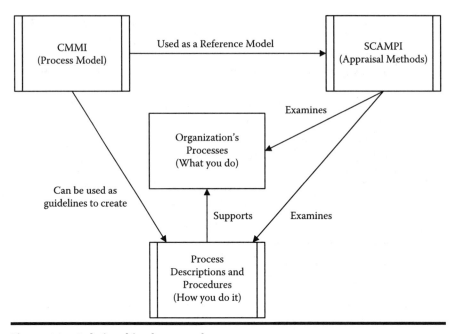

Figure 1.1   Relationships between key terms.

One more thing: *Data* are plural. Although most folks generally say, "the data is not yet available," proper grammar is to say, "the data are not yet available." So it may sound a little funny when you read it.

History of the CMMI

Here is a very short history of the CMMI. Short because most readers of this book will already know this and because other sources can give you much more detail on the story.

People were successfully using the Capability Maturity Model, which was designed for improving software processes and measuring the maturity of software processes in an organization. This success brought more and more attention to model-based process improvement in other areas. This resulted in a number of other models being developed, including the:

- Systems Engineering CMM (SE-CMM)
- Software Acquisition Capability Maturity Model (SA-CMM)
- Integrated Product Development Team Model (IPD-CMM)
- Systems Engineering Capability Assessment Model (SECAM)
- Systems Engineering Capability Model (SECM)

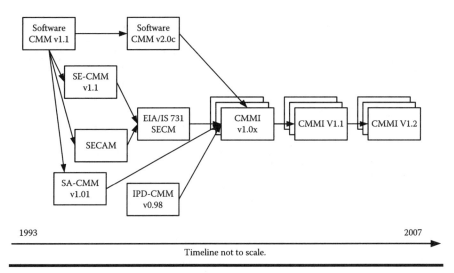

Figure 1.2   Models directly influencing CMMI.

Figure 1.2 shows the relative timeline for the primary models directly influencing the CMMI. It may be of interest to note that, as shown, the SECM is actually an integrated model in its own right; that is, an integration of two systems engineering models (the SE-CMM and SECAM) as shown by the two arrows coming into SECM. CMMI version 1.1 was most directly influenced by CMM v2.0c for software, SECM for systems engineering, SA-CMM for acquisition, and IPD-CMM for integrated teaming. Of course, CMMI version 1.2 was most directly influenced by CMMI version 1.1.

Some organizations that wanted to use this collection of models were confused because each model was slightly different. The new model—CMMI—is designed to integrate the plethora of models created throughout the years by the Software Engineering Institute (SEI) and other organizations. The idea of reconciling these models with other methodologies and standards—ISO 9001 and 15504, among others—was introduced. Several adopters of the SEI's software process improvement mantra, including the Department of Defense (DOD), requested a halt to the generation of more models, and instead recommended that the SEI integrate the concepts expressed in these disparate models into one model. Hence, the journey toward CMMI began.

Some readers will take us to task for starting our history with the CMM for Software. They will be right to say that the CMM is based on years and years of quality and process improvement performed by many great and wonderful people. Since we don't think merely mentioning Walter Shewhart, W. Edwards Deming, Joseph Juran, and Philip Crosby helps the reader understand the CMMI, we have left them out of our history; but clearly the CMMI would not be here without their significant contributions in this area.

Appraisal View versus Improvement View

It is often the case while working with organizations that we encounter two distinctly different views on how to use the CMMI. We call these views:

■ The appraisal view
■ The process improvement view

The appraisal view is more focused on what's the minimum required to satisfy the model and what's needed to pass the test (assessment, appraisal, evaluation, or SCAMPI). The process improvement view is more focused on what's best for your organization and what's needed to improve the organization.

An example of how these different views would address a CMMI practice can be seen in the area of how an organization would "Objectively Evaluate Adherence to the plans, processes, procedures and methods" within a process area. This is a concept contained within a process area of the CMMI called Process and Product Quality Assurance.

Taking an appraisal view, an organization might decide to have developers and engineers perform a review of each other's work. This approach looks like a quick way to get independent verification until you realize that these developers and engineers will still need to be trained in evaluation and will need additional budget and schedule to perform the evaluations. A dysfunctional appraisal view might go as far as having one person reviewing an entire large program or project (clearly an overwhelming job for just one person) in order to get the check mark during an appraisal.

Taking a process improvement view, an organization would realize the need for clear responsibility defined for quality-related activities. Establishing an independent quality group staffed with trained and experienced professionals would go a long way toward ensuring that the organization continues to perform the processes as written. This group would need to be staffed at a sufficient level to be effective. In many cases this means 3 percent to 5 percent of the technical staff or more.

We have worked with many organizations and our experience tells us that organizations that focus on an appraisal view will fail. They fail to truly satisfy the model mainly because of a lack of institutionalization, but also will fail to provide any real business value to their organization in return for the expense.

Those organizations taking the process improvement view will succeed in providing business value and also will do much better in an appraisal—yes, sometimes this requires hard work, but this is the only truly successful path that we have seen. This book will most often take the process improvement view. We have, however, added a lot of information concerning what is important when preparing for and facing a formal appraisal of your process improvement efforts.

Changes from CMMI Version 1.1 to CMMI Version 1.2

Many changes were made to the CMMI. Some of the changes boil down to wording changes, especially in the practices, subpractices, and examples. In some cases, information was restructured and moved to different chapters. However, the major changes can be summarized as follows:

- The name of the model was changed to CMMI for Development. Even though the name has been changed to "Development," maintenance activities also pertain to this model. Maintenance, not just new development, requires developing requirements, managing changes, planning and monitoring activities, ensuring quality, and so on.
- Both the staged and continuous representations are now in one document (hooray!).
- More information was added relating to amplifications, generic practices, examples, and hardware engineering.
- Common features were eliminated.
- Advanced practices used in the continuous representation were eliminated. In some cases, base practices and advanced practices were combined into specific practices. Because of this consolidation, the numbering system for specific practices follows that of the staged representation, not that of the continuous representation.
- Supplier Sourcing as a separate discipline was eliminated; its concepts now reside in the Supplier Agreement Management (SAM) process area. Integrated Supplier Management was also removed, with its concepts incorporated into SAM.
- Guidelines for declaring a process area as "not applicable" were clarified. SAM is the only process area that can be considered "not applicable."
- The overview and glossary were changed. New definitions were added to the glossary, with some older definitions either reworded or deleted.
- Integrated Product and Process Development (IPPD) material was simplified and consolidated. IPPD is considered an "addition," not reflected as separate process areas. The process areas Organizational Environment for Integration and Integrated Teaming were removed. IPPD concepts, (such as work environment material), were added to Organizational Process Definition (OPD) and Integrated Project Management (IPM).
- Material was added to ensure that standard processes are deployed to new projects at their startup (see IPM and Organizational Process Focus).

The changes to the specific practices and material in the individual process areas have been incorporated into our discussions of the different maturity levels later in this book.

Changes to Our Book, *Interpreting the CMMI,* from First Edition to Second Edition

So what's new with the book you are reading? The big news for us—the authors—is that we negotiated with our publisher to get the price down. We did this by not including a CD-ROM.

The primary change is to use CMMI version 1.2 as the basis for this book. CMMI version 1.2 was released by the SEI in late August 2006. This change has had an impact throughout our book, including the definitions and wording of the process areas and their supporting practices, as well as the changed structure and integration of the continuous with the staged representation of the model.

We have added much more information concerning the SCAMPI Appraisal Method, to include what this appraisal method is, what its official purpose is, how it can help an organization's process improvement program, and what to focus on in order to pass an appraisal. We have added information describing the most rigorous appraisal method (the SCAMPI A) and how to complete the PIIDs (Practice Implementation Indicator Descriptions). This new emphasis on the appraisal is really the main concern of organizations that begin a process improvement program. There is also a chapter on incorporating Agile Methods into CMMI process improvement activities.

We have incorporated lessons learned from our work with various organizations—what worked, what didn't, and what organizations have told us about the pros and cons of using the CMMI.

We have updated our measurement chapters. We have developed some new ideas in measurement that have been well received at various client sites and international conferences.

We have also had considerable experience in high maturity organizations worldwide. We have therefore updated our high-maturity chapters based on our participation with process improvement initiatives and high-maturity SCAMPIs (appraisals). We have also added more instructions on reading and interpreting statistical control charts and performance models.

Summary

The CMMI builds on a history of process improvement. The CMMI by its nature can impact a large part of your organization since it combines concepts and models from systems engineering, software engineering, hardware engineering, and integrated teaming.

Two of the problems in CMMI include interpretation and organizational decisions. The model itself was written to cover many different organizational and project situations. An ambiguous style was intentionally chosen by the authors of the

CMMI to fit these many situations. This ambiguity results in the need for a lot of interpretation and decision making by the model users. We hope to help identify these decisions for you and provide a positive influence in your decision making.

Chapter 2

Beginning the Journey

Introduction

This chapter is for those individuals who are just beginning a process improvement program. This chapter focuses on defining what a process is and why it is important; gives a brief comparison of improvement models; offers suggestions of where and how to start your program; and discusses some of the problems you can expect to encounter. This chapter also contains information on different types of process improvement approaches. This chapter should be considered introductory only. For more information, please read later chapters that delve into how to write processes and procedures, and how to set up your process improvement program.

What Is Process Improvement?

Have you ever tried to tell your mother exactly what you do for a living? Have you ever sat next to someone on an airplane and tried to explain what your job is? Have you ever gotten into a long discussion with the immigration police after an international flight and tried to describe what your business is and why you had to leave the country to do it? Well, this section of the book is for you.

When we tell someone that we do process improvement for a living, everyone thinks they know what that is. If they decide to be "helpful," they will start sending us articles via e-mail that they have picked up from the Internet. It rapidly becomes clear that these people have no idea what process improvement is. That is not their fault. There are different types of process improvement approaches out there. So, this section of the book tries to discuss what some of them are.

We believe that most approaches to improving processes can be summarized by the following categories (the terminology used is mostly ours):

1. Business Process Reengineering (BPR)
2. Benchmarking
3. Process Engineering/Workflow Management
4. Reverse Engineering
5. Model-based process improvement

Business Process Reengineering was a method promoted by Michael Hammer and James Champy in their book *Reengineering the Corporation* and quite common in the early 1990s. Its definition (from their book) is "the fundamental rethinking and radical redesign of business processes to achieve dramatic improvements in critical measures of performance, such as cost, quality, service, and speed." This type of improvement was *radical* improvement and focused on *core business processes at the enterprise-level* of a business. Core business processes could be such areas or functions as customer engagement, customer support, manufacturing, distribution, market to collection, integrated supply chain, time to market, and corporate governance. The criteria for selection of these processes as a core business process were such things as size (usually large), strategic importance, cross-organizational boundaries, and customer impact. The italics demonstrate the basic values of BPR and the differences between BPR and CMMI process improvement.

Some of the steps involved in BPR are:

1. Establish a reengineering team
2. Analyze the organization's culture for health and tolerance for change
3. Identify core processes to determine criticality and "pain points"
4. Document the process using block diagrams and flowcharts
5. Analyze the direction of the business regarding its mission, vision, values, goals, and objectives for discrepancies
6. Invent a new process by pretending that the organization has been destroyed and no longer exists
7. Deploy the "best" solution (through piloting and evaluation)

Benchmarking involves finding and implementing best practices that lead to superior performance. The best practices usually come from another part of your organization or a completely different external business. For example, there is a benchmarking study that was done by a defense contractor who benchmarked his distribution system against that of a cosmetics company. The steps in benchmarking can be summarized as:

1. Identify the benchmark subject—that is, which process or processes need to be improved
2. Identify benchmark partners (internal or external)
3. Collect data (surveys, site visits, research)
4. Document the gap (what works, what doesn't work)
5. Determine what to do and what the effect will be in the organization (quantified)
6. Deploy the changes

Benchmarking can be used as an input to CMMI process improvement. It is not unusual for CMMI process improvement teams to visit other sites or to attend conferences to learn from other process improvement teams and organizations.

Process Engineering/Workflow Management is the type of process improvement that most people understand and confuse with CMMI process improvement. Basically, this type of process engineering looks at functions in the workplace, or the flow of work, and tries to identify where the bottlenecks are. Usually, the steps are loaded into a tool that uses animation to show the steps in the work flow. Where can we speed up this process? Where is the hole in this process? Who or what is causing the problem? The best example we can think of is the airline baggage-handling system. In this scenario, the passenger approaches the check-in counter. He shows his identification. The airline representative asks him some questions, reviews his ID, hands him his boarding pass, and places his luggage on the luggage belt with an appropriate tag. The luggage belt takes the luggage to the back room where it is scanned and then proceeds to be loaded onto the plane. The plane takes off and lands at the appropriate airport at the appointed time. The luggage is placed on the luggage belt and delivered to the owner of the luggage.

OK, those of you who travel frequently know we are being kind. We will not discuss what some of the problems are or why we have selected some of the wording we used in this scenario. As for our example, in process/workflow management, an analysis would be done to measure the throughput of this sequence of events. Usually, the steps in this series of events would be input into a tool that would graphically demonstrate the time it takes for each step to occur and where any problems (such as slower speeds) occur. The results would be reviewed and the bottlenecks studied to see how to improve performance.

What is reverse engineering? Reverse engineering is when you look at the results of something and then you take it apart to figure out how it was made or how it works. Then, you either put it back together the same way or you design a new, improved way and put it back together that way. So, you are working backward. Let's say we are trying to figure out how to make a watch. We take it apart to see how all of the pieces fit together, and then we (try) to put it back together. Or, let's say we have an old, legacy system; perhaps a payroll system. We need to incorporate the latest tax deduction strategy implemented by the federal government or some other sort of law or regulation. The payroll system is very old and very complicated, not well documented, and not well managed when it comes to changes. So, we know how the tax change is supposed to work. We know the output of the payroll system is a correct paycheck for the correct person. We begin by identifying what we think are the appropriate programs to update with our mandated tax change; we review and analyze what the inputs, processing, and outputs are of each program; we identify and analyze the interfaces with each identified program, other programs in the payroll system, and any external programs or processing that might interact or be affected by the change; we make the change; and we test it. And those of you who have done this know it blows up because it is impossible to do all of the aforementioned steps correctly with such a difficult, poorly documented system. The point is, we tried to decompose the existing system into its parts, and then tried to figure out how those parts worked together. Then, we defined how the change would affect the old way of calculating payroll. This is reverse engineering. We figured out how to make something work based on how it worked before. We worked backward from the output (the paycheck) to the processing (the programs) to the input (the tax change).

The last approach for improving processes to discuss is called model-based process improvement. This is the type of approach that the CMMI uses. There are many models available for process improvement —ISO and Malcolm Baldridge to name just two. The difference between the previous types of improvement approaches and model-based improvement is on which processes are selected for improvement. BPR selects high-level business processes (like corporate governance or time to market). Benchmarking selects any process that is causing problems (like distribution and delivery of its product). Process Engineering/Workflow Management selects smaller subprocesses of work tasks. The CMMI (and ISO and Malcolm Baldridge) select predetermined focus areas that have been shown historically to cause the most problems in specific types of businesses. The CMMI focuses on software engineering, systems engineering, hardware engineering, and integrated teams that must produce a product. The CMMI breaks down the focus areas into process areas that include such activities as quality assurance, project planning, configuration management, and requirements development. Model-based improvement is usually not quite as radical as BPR—although if needed in an organization, it can be. Also, while process (*what* is done) in the CMMI can be documented at the flow chart level, supporting procedures defining *how* to do the process are produced. And CMMI process areas can be tied to the larger, core business process, goals, and objectives in order to help solve problems in those areas. We show you how later.

Although all five types of approaches are different, there are many similarities. Each approach selects a process—not a product—to be improved. The result of the improvement may be an improved product, but it is the process that is the focus. Each approach uses a team, either formal or informally based. Planning and research are done prior to beginning the attempt. A definition of current processing is documented. A definition of the proposed change is produced. Results are communicated to those in the position of making the change. Piloting and training are recommended. And monitoring of the results occurs.

This book is about model-based improvement using the CMMI for Development as the model. More information about process and models continues below.

What Is a Process?

A process is a series of steps that help to solve a problem. The steps must be defined in such a way as to be unambiguous—that is, readily understood and capable of being followed in a consistent manner by anyone using the process. Why do we want to do things consistently? Are we promoting turning the workers into robots? No. What focusing on process does for your organization is the reduction of redundant work. Why re-create the wheel every time you begin a new project? If you are required to submit a project plan, why not have a procedure that tells you how to write one, plus an example of one that you can copy and paste from? Isn't that easier than just wringing your hands and worrying about it and sweating blood devising a new project plan for your new project? OK, you may not be a project manager, so you don't like the example about the project plan. Let's say you are a programmer. Does your manager ever ask you how difficult a particular program might be? Does he ever ask you how long it will take you to code each program? Or does he just give you a list of programs assigned to you and tell you when they are due? Do you ever have heartburn over his estimates? Do you ever say anything, or do you just work unpaid overtime because of his bizarre schedule? Having a process for estimating schedules that you have input to will create a more realistic schedule and help relieve some of the burden on you of having to adhere to something that just doesn't make sense. Does this scheduling process always work perfectly? Can you just say, "No, this schedule stinks, so my manager must change it?" Of course not. But it does give you some room for negotiation.

Processes are like recipes. A recipe tells you the ingredients, how to mix the ingredients, what temperature to use, and how long to cook something. But it doesn't teach you the techniques of slicing and dicing and mixing and beating and whipping and blanching and grilling and poaching and so on and so on. And recipes also leave room for some experimentation and modification. Some recipes even give you suggestions on how to make changes to the dish.

A process as used in process improvement usually is defined at a somewhat high level, with associated procedures supporting the process. The procedures are written in much more detail than the process. Examples follow.

Let's say that your organization is focusing on creating a risk management process. This risk process is being developed because the project managers in your organization have been unable to proactively predict troubling issues that end up affecting the delivery of their products to the customer. Perhaps they have delivered late because of high staff turnover and being unable to get enough people with the proper skills on their projects; or the people they get are pulled onto other projects when those projects run into trouble. Another risk may be that the budgets for the projects are usually overrun. So, all of the project managers get together and determine a risk management process that they feel will cover all (or at least most) of the risks they encounter. The risk management process they come up with is:

- Identify the risk
- Analyze the risk
- Categorize the seriousness and probability of the risk
- Mitigate the risk

Well, I'm sure these managers feel that they have done a brilliant job, but what is the problem with this process? It is too general. I'm sure that if I handed out this process for all of my managers to follow that each manager would interpret *how* to do this process differently. We are trying to find a way to document how we do work in the organization in a consistent way so that everyone will do things somewhat similarly, and so that people can benefit from the good work being done by others.

So, now we go back to the managers and say, "Great. You have a process. How do we do the steps in your process?" Well, that is a different problem. The managers are tasked with devising *procedures* for *how* to do *what* they have written as the steps in the process.

So, using our process example, the first item is "Identify the risk." The managers would need to come up with how they identify risks. One of the ways they might do this identification is to start tracking the problems they have in delivering products, and then find trends. From the list of trends, create a list of the ten most frequently occurring problems on the projects. The procedures would then discuss how to use the information in the list to estimate risks that might occur on another project. The third item in the list of steps in the risk management process is "Categorize the seriousness and probability of the risk." Maybe your organization defines risks as 1—most critical and most likely to occur; 2—critical but work may continue; and 3—not critical, work may continue, fix this problem during the next phase or release. The managers would need to come up with procedures for how to determine what would put a risk into category 1, 2, or 3.

These are just simplistic examples used to illustrate process versus procedures.

So why is focusing on process important? Why not focus on the product or the people or the technology used? Let us explain.

Writing standards for what a Requirements Specification should look like is a product focus. You are focusing on the template itself. For example, you might want your Requirements Spec to list all of the requirements for the system, categorize them as to whether they are system-level requirements, software requirements, hardware requirements, safety requirements, performance requirements, and so forth. Great, this is a good thing to do. But, how does anyone know which categories they fit in? This is where a requirements process comes in. It would tell you not only what the spec should look like, but *how* to write it—how to fill in the blanks for each paragraph in the spec. A requirements process would also tell you how to elicit requirements from your stakeholders (e.g., customers, end users, requirements analysts) and how to manage the changes to the requirements. The *product* focus would then continue on to what a Design Spec should look like, what coding standards should be followed, what test cases should consist of, and so forth. The *process* focus would then give guidelines to the people responsible for doing this work on *how* to do it.

Why not focus on the people? Puhleeeeez! Whenever anything goes wrong on a project, isn't it the first, visceral reaction to blame the people doing the work? Well, that's highly motivating (not!). I don't want you to think that people are not important—they are the most important part of any project or any work undertaken. But, not everyone can be as brilliant as everyone needs to be everyday. It's not like we wake up one day out of 365 days and say, "Yesterday I was just OK. Today I will be brilliant." Focusing on process puts the emphasis on having good processes to follow, not on hiring only brilliant people. Rather than having people work harder, have them work smarter. That's what process does for you.

Why not focus on technology? Have you ever heard the saying, garbage in garbage out? Well, that's what just plastering new technology onto an old problem does for you. We have been paid big bucks for converting existing systems from one language or database to another. There are even tools now that will do that for you (with a lot of work). What do you get? The same system you always had with both the old problems and the new ones. Technology does not provide a quick fix. But, it is the one answer that executives are most likely to choose because technology is easily quantifiable and easily budgeted. Look at the dot.com bust. Most of those companies sold quick-fix technologies without any underlying analysis of the problems organizations faced. Most of the dot.coms that operated without this sort of planning are out of business. Technology is our friend, but it is not the only answer to our problems.

Why focus on process? What personal benefit can you gain from all this work? What's in it for you? Well, the following examples are drawn from personal experience in some of the organizations we have helped along this path.

- Configuration Management—One individual had spent hours trying to find the correct version of source code to make a simple change. He was never sure before whether he had the latest copy of the source code. Now, after following procedures for change control, he is reasonably sure that the code he is using to make updates is actually the code used in production. No more searching for hours for the right program.
- Testing—Prior to this effort, developers handed the system to the testers and told them, "Here, write a test plan and test this. These are the changes I made." The test people were never quite sure how thorough their testing was. And they spent hours trying to figure out what the actual requirements were

for the system. (You test to ensure the requirements have been met.) Now, with process for the Requirements Traceability Matrix and the Requirements Specification, the testers spend less time figuring out what to do and more time actually testing. It has greatly simplified their jobs and greatly improved the testing of the resulting products.

■ Planning—Prior to this effort, the organization could not predict the number of projects that needed to be scheduled ahead of time. Now, with the use of the process for devising a Statement of Work, and the focus on the Project Planning process area, the organization is aware of the number of projects requested, what their initial requirements are, the approximate number of staff needed, the approximate size and complexity of the project, and how to prioritize the projects. Requests for support have actually been deferred based on these measures. Time is not wasted on developing systems that won't be used or fixing problems that go away by themselves.

■ Communication—There is more communication up and down the chain of command as well as across the organization. For example, the director of software engineering is talking to developers, and in some cases, the developers are talking back. This is good. Quality Assurance (QA) is reviewing products and processes across several projects. They are seeing the results of these processes and the problems, as well as the differences between the ways project teams perform. QA is also talking to the EPG (the process improvement team), and in some cases, swaying them to change some decisions made, based on how things are actually working (or not working).

So, is process the only answer? No. Process is part of the answer. Process, when supported by training, enough money, enough skilled people, proper tools, and management commitment, can help your organization.

Models

What is a model, and why do I have to use one? A model is considered a guideline of best practices found by studying other highly functioning and successful organizations. A model does not contain the steps needed or the sequence of steps needed to implement a process improvement program. The model used simply says, "This is a good thing to do, and this is a good thing to do." For example, the Project Planning process area suggests that you write a project plan. The Requirements Management process area recommends that you track changes to requirements.

There are many models to choose from, depending on the problems in your organization that you want to solve. Why use a model? Well, we have worked in many organizations that just decided to "improve." Without using a model as your basis of reference, you have nothing to plan your improvement around and nothing to measure your results against. Some organizations have decided that they didn't like the guidelines in the models used for process improvement in the industry, so they created their own. Most of these organizations failed. It is not easy to write a model. It takes a long time and it costs a lot of money. And remember, the models are summaries of the best practices of effective, successful organizations. So, it would behoove someone to follow most of the practices documented in these models. Most models allow an organization to substitute alternative practices for those practices in the chosen model that do not fit the organization. But beware—the more alternatives you select, the more you deviate from best practices in a model, the less likely you are of improving the problems in your organization.

A brief overview of some of the more frequently used models follows. Please do not consider this overview exhaustive, as we simply summarize the basic thrust of each model. We do not purport to be experts in all of these models. Those of you who are experts in any of the models may take exception to some of our statements. These statements are offered once again only as high-level summarizations.

"In the beginning," there were ISO and the CMM. ISO stands for International Standards Organization. The ISO 9000/9001 series generates a fundamental quality management framework. The ISO 9000 series is a set of documents that discuss quality systems to use when instituting quality assurance in an organization or enterprise. ISO 9000 itself is a guideline that directs the user as to which set of documents to use and the interrelationship of quality concepts. ISO 9001, 9002, and 9003 deal with external quality assurance pursuits, while ISO 9004 deals with internal quality assurance. ISO 9001 is used to ensure that quality systems are delivered by the supplier during several stages of creation (which may include design, development, production, installation, and servicing). This document is the most pertinent to software development and maintenance. ISO 9000-3 is used when applying ISO 9001 to the development, supply, and maintenance of software. ISO 9001 requires that a documented quality system be implemented, with procedures and instructions. ISO 9000-3 further specifies that this quality system be integrated throughout the entire life cycle.

CMM stands for the Capability Maturity Model. Most folks nowadays call it the CMM for Software. The reason for this appellation is that after the CMM was developed, several more CMMs relating to different areas were generated (e.g., Systems Engineering, Acquisition). The CMM was created to help manage organizations that develop software. The CMM was created by analyzing the activities of highly functioning software organizations; that is, those organizations that consistently delivered software systems to their customers on time, within the budget, and that actually worked. These activities became the 316 key practices in the CMM, and the practices themselves were grouped into categories called key process areas. There are 18 key process areas that focus on the best practices found among the organizations reviewed. The key process areas concentrate on such things as managing requirements, managing changes, creating project plans, tracking estimates against actuals, implementing quality assurance activities, instituting peer reviews, and training personnel in processes related to their job duties.

What's the difference between the CMM and ISO? Well, both were developed to improve the quality of systems. ISO was developed in Brussels, Belgium, and related originally to the manufacturing arena. The CMM was developed in the United States for managing the development of software systems. Over the years, the CMM made its journey across the ocean and is now used almost as much internationally as within the United States alone. ISO also crossed the pond making inroads into the United States in manufacturing businesses, concentrating most often in the Midwest.

ISO focuses mainly on broader issues of quality within an entire enterprise or company. Executives of these organizations are often interviewed. The main product of ISO is the creation of a quality manual that discusses quality initiatives to be implemented throughout the enterprise. The CMM takes a much more limited view. The CMM focuses on only software-intensive projects. It does not look at an entire enterprise or company. It describes an organization (admittedly, ambiguously) as several projects managed under one director (an example). Interviews may include an executive manager or two, but mostly focus on project managers and their team members.

If your organization is ISO certified, does that mean you are automatically CMM Level 3? No, it is like comparing apples and oranges. If you are CMM Level 3, does that mean you are ISO certified? No. Once again, although the two methods have similar goals, they are very different in implementation and scope. Chapter 4 in ISO 9001 is about 5 pages long, while sections 5, 6, and 7 of ISO 9000-3 are about 11 pages long. The CMMI is over 400 pages long. So, clearly, the two models are different.

The same comparison holds true for the CMMI.

The models we are the most familiar with are the CMM for Software and the CMMI. CMM and CMMI implement processes, which reflect best practices found in industry. The CMM focuses on the software domain of organizations. However, because the problems with software organizations were deemed to fall mostly in the management area, this book can be, and has been, used not only in software organizations but broadened to include most management situations.

The model that inspired this book is the CMMI. The CMMI officially expanded the scope of the CMM from software to the entire enterprise of organizations. That expansion includes systems engineering as well as software engineering, integrated product and process development (specialized teams that design and develop systems), and acquisition (procuring systems, and monitoring the procurement and management of contracts awarded).

Other models in use include the Federal Aviation Administration's (FAA's) CMM, which builds upon the original CMM and other model as they relate to FAA issues. However, parts of this model may also be extracted and used in other business endeavors (not just aviation).

Six Sigma is also being used more and more frequently. Six Sigma attempts to reduce the variation in processes to a very small number. Six Sigma focuses on improvements and measures that will lower the cost of doing business. Six Sigma consists of defining project goals and objectives; measuring narrow ranges of potential causes and establishing a baseline; analyzing data to identify trends and causes of the deviations; improving the processes at the identified cause level; and controlling the problem.

Some organizations are now merging Six Sigma and CMM/CMMI activities into one process improvement effort. Six Sigma focuses heavily on selecting a limited number of issues, measuring the problem (e.g., number of defects in a product line, excessive time to build a product), and then measuring the results (e.g., the effectiveness) of the fix. CMM/CMMI focuses on implementing best practices found in the industry and changing the infrastructure and culture of an organization. The two can complement each other. However, we feel that Six Sigma is better performed on only those organizations that have already been rated at a strong CMM/CMMI Maturity Level 3 or higher. Six Sigma requires a high degree of sophistication in aligning business objectives with Six Sigma techniques, as well as a high degree of sophistication in other areas of management (business, quality, process, and change).

Business Goals and Objectives

Much is made about aligning your process improvement effort to the business goals that the organization is trying to achieve. This alignment is easier said than done. Most organizations just beginning process improvement don't really have clearly defined business objectives. In fact, what we most often hear from executives when we ask them what they are trying to accomplish by doing process improvement is to reduce the number of people they need to staff projects and have the people who survive the cut become more productive—that is, have the people do more work in less time. Of course, that does not include the executive doing the talking. Well, process improvement will not allow you to significantly reduce your task force. In fact, especially over the short term, you may have to actually hire more people in order to structure process improvement efforts and staff them adequately. So this "goal" is simply wrong.

Another most often heard response to "what are your business goals as they relate to process improvement?" is to get Maturity Level 3 for contract awards. If these organizations could buy Level 3 (and there is some discussion as to the ability to buy a level rating), these organizations would be most willing to go that route.

The other problem we run into is when we ask, "What are your business objectives?" we repeatedly hear one answer: an incredulous, "Why, to make money of course!" The point of this discussion is that most organizations beginning process improvement are simply not sophisticated enough to have clear goals.

There is a technique that can be used to help define business goals and process improvement focus areas. It is called the Goal–Question–Metric technique. In this method, a workshop is held. It should actually be called the Problem–Goal–Question–Metric approach. During the workshop, a list of the most common problems found in the organization is presented. Questions are then asked relating to the problem, and the areas of the CMMI are used to help focus ensuing process improvement efforts. The approach starts with a business goal and works backward to identify improvement actions to achieve that goal. Here is a basic example:

Problem: We can't keep up with the number of requirements changes.
Goal: Improve our requirements change process.
Question: How can we improve our requirements change process?
Metric: Number of requirements changes submitted, approved, implemented, or canceled versus the number of original requirements documented. Time it takes to implement a change in requirements.
Associated Process Areas: Requirements Management (Level 2), Project Planning (Level 2), Product and Process Quality Assurance (Level 2), Requirements Development (Level 3).

The main difference between this approach and addressing the seven process areas in Level 2 of the CMMI staged representation simultaneously is that structuring your process improvement program to focus on key problems in your organization helps define the scope of initial efforts and their sequence. Some members of your process improvement team and of your organization will find this approach more relevant to their everyday work, and will therefore be more enthusiastic about the program.

Although we have discussed this Goal–Question–Metric approach, we do not strongly recommend it for low-maturity organizations. Why not? Because most beginning organizations do not have a clear understanding of business objectives and business goals. They also will not readily admit that there are problems in the organization. The example we used was pertinent to requirements problems in systems. However, most true business objectives are at a much higher level. For example, an organization that clearly understands business objectives would state that one of their business objectives would be to improve customer satisfaction by 10 percent by reducing the number of defects embedded in their systems and delivered to their customers by 15 percent. To truly be effective, this type of business objective, backed up by this metric, requires a sophisticated approach to identifying problems in organizations; fully defining the problem; relating the problem to existing, documented business goals; measuring the current process and its results; and measuring the expected versus realized outcome. This approach is way beyond most low-maturity organizations.

So, what to do? Since the approach above is used to structure your improvement efforts, why not use an officially approved appraisal method? We suggest that if you are using the CMMI, that a SCAMPI (Standard CMMI Appraisal Method for Process Improvement) be used. The SCAMPI is a method whereby a team is formed that examines any processes (both formal, and in low-maturity organizations, informal) that exist in an organization and rates their strengths and weaknesses as they relate to the CMMI. The organization will then decide which process areas to focus on first. Guidelines for beginning and assessing your process improvement trek are given in later chapters in this book.

Problems

The process focus is not without its challenges. That is a nice way of saying it ain't perfect. It you look at the last line of one of the preceding paragraphs, it states, "Process, when supported by training, enough money, enough skilled people, proper tools, and management commitment, can help your organization." Most people don't understand process until they've been struggling with it for at least a year. Training is considered a dirty word in some organizations—"if they don't have the skills, we don't hire them," or "we only hire skilled people." And as most of you know, if you are really good at something, your organization is going to place you on one project full time, and then pull you off that project and place you on one in trouble (full time), and then have you "help out" on another project in your "spare" time. And when you do a wonderful job on the project in crisis and bring it in on time, your reward is to get your butt kicked on the other two projects because you are late delivering to them. This example is an example of a dysfunctional, low maturity, yet commonly found organization.

The same problems occur in process improvement. You seldom get the "right" people. You get a lot of folks just waiting to retire, or out of rehab, or summer interns, or burnouts, or people who just can't code well. You staff up with five or six full-time process improvement team members, only to find them pulled off when their former projects run into trouble. Training for process improvement is absolutely mandatory, but once the people get the training and start to do the work, they become overwhelmed and decide to go back to their old jobs, or leave the company for greener pastures. Or, the organization decides to give a "condensed" version of the training because it is too expensive—both in dollars spent and in time spent not doing "real work." Or the organization buys a process improvement tool guaranteed to get you your level rating in one year, only to discover that you don't just plug it in—you have to actually write procedures and do work.

The answer? Well, just like anything else, there is no one answer except maybe the following—tell your boss (or whoever's idea this whole process improvement thing was) in a tactful way, to put his money where his mouth is. If he wants it, it will cost him—in dollars, people, and time, including his time. Do not commit to "Level 2 in 2 years" or any other such slogan. Commit to trying to improve your organization. And mention to the boss that most improvement models focus improvement activities on *management*—not worker bees and practitioners. See if he then wants to continue. Educating your boss, as well as the rest of the organization, is key to a smooth transition to the process improvement path.

Process improvement is really about *change*. No one really likes to change, unless the current way of doing things is so onerous and repulsive that they just can't stand it anymore. Most folks do not get to this state when working for an organization—they simply go elsewhere. So, no one in your organization will be really excited to adopt a program that makes them change the way they do their jobs. Most people have developed over the years their own system or process for doing their jobs. And if you are the process improvement specialist, you will be responsible for making them change. And guess what—you will also have to change the way you do your job. One way to get people to buy into this whole change/process thing is to have them write the procedures. If they can't or won't write, then get them to at least participate in meetings where they can voice their issues and contribute to creating the process for doing their work.

Summary

This chapter has attempted to introduce the novice process improvement individual to some terms and concepts commonly used, and why process improvement is important. This chapter should be considered a high-level overview. More information is contained in the following chapters of this book. The power of the CMMI lies in that it lets you define your job—how you do it and what gets produced from it. But with power comes responsibility. If you want to control how you do your jobs, you need to fully participate in the process improvement program.

Mistakes are a good thing. It shows you are trying. It shows you are improving after your mistakes go down. However, the predominant mantra in the industry is that mistakes are bad. If you make a mistake, you get hammered for it. There is no middle ground, no shades of gray. You are either 100 percent right or 100 percent wrong. With process improvement, if no mistakes are made, then the processes are probably not being used. Processes are generally not written "right" or perfectly the first time around; nor are they initially implemented and practiced correctly.

Also, please remember that although we say that process improvement involves skilled professionals with an objective, unbiased, professional attitude toward their work, everyone on the process improvement team has a large amount of personal investment in this effort. So things do tend to get personal. Try to see the big picture and try to be flexible.

Chapter 3

Structure of the CMMI

To explain the structure of the CMMI, we first use the staged representation of the model as our example; then we follow up with a brief discussion of the continuous representation. The reader is directed to read the next chapter concerning CMMI representations along with this chapter.

Terms and Definitions

Before we begin, there are two very important concepts that need to be discussed. They are:

- Implementation
- Institutionalization

Implementation is simply performing a task within the process area. (A process area is an area that the CMMI has selected that your organization needs to focus on, such as Project Planning or Configuration Management. It is a set of related tasks that address an area of concern.) The task is performed according to a process, but the action performed or the process followed may not be totally ingrained as part of the organization's culture.

Institutionalization is the result of implementing the process again and again. The process has become totally integrated into the organization. The process will continue after those who created it have left the organization. An infrastructure to support this way of doing business exists and provides support for the process and the individuals following it.

Other definitions that might prove helpful are:

- Development—The Construction phase of a life cycle, including Maintenance.
- Project—Activities and resources necessary to deliver a product to the customer. A project is not just a software project. A project can also consist of many projects. The term *program* is not used. A project is also expected to have a start and end date, with a formal project manager assigned. A task order may be a project or several task orders may make up a project. It all depends on size, structure of the organization, complexity, deliverable to be produced, and number of staff assigned to various roles.
- Product—A service or system or tangible output delivered to the customer.

Another term that is used frequently, is extremely important, yet is very difficult to define is *organization*. What is an organization? Well, normally an organization is a series of projects currently underway within a department. The term organization also implies people, structure of the people, and physical plant and equipment. So, if you are a developer you might be working on coding five programs to maintain an automobile insurance system, developing a small Web site to track customer complaints about medical reimbursement, and beginning to design a document management system to document work hours performed for payroll purposes. That sounds like three projects to me. However, depending on how your place of business is set up, you could be working in three different organizations—the auto insurance department, the medical insurance department, and the payroll department. Or, you could be working in just one organization—the technical information systems department. An organization can also consist of one individual! So, the definition of an organization depends.

Our advice is to develop improvement programs (and resultant appraisal) based on the three different organizations mentioned in the first scenario (automobile insurance, medical insurance, and payroll as three separate organizations). Why? Because each organization has different rules it must follow. For example, automobile insurance may have state department of transportation regulations to follow, medical insurance may have federal medical regulations to follow, and payroll may have federal IRS and state tax regulations to follow. Therefore, the processes will be different. For example, do you think a customer service department answering billing complaints from customers should be run the same way as a nuclear power plant? The nuclear power plant has environmental regulations, nuclear regulations, and other federal, state, and local policies it must implement in its processes. The customer service organization probably has much fewer. The margin of error allowed in the safety factor is also significantly different.

With CMMI, the definition of organization becomes even less clear. An organization can be one department headed by one director. Or it can be expanded to include the entire company or enterprise. Our advice? De-scope. Do not bite off more than you can chew when beginning process improvement efforts. They tend to mushroom anyway. Start small, like with the project in the earlier example doing Web-based medical insurance design and coding, and increase your efforts as necessary.

CMMI Model Structure

The CMMI is structured as follows:

- Maturity Levels (staged representation) or Capability Levels (continuous representation)
- Process Areas
- Goals—Generic and Specific
- Practices—Generic and Specific

Figure 3.1 shows the CMMI model components in the staged representation. Basically, maturity levels organize the process areas. Within the process areas are generic and specific goals, as well as generic and specific practices. One difference

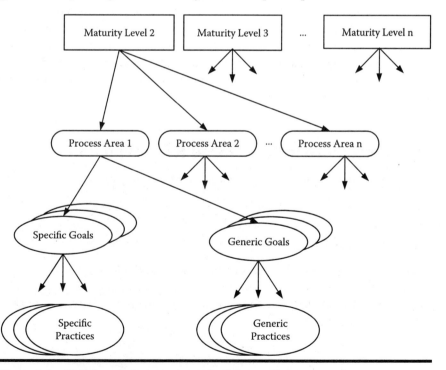

Figure 3.1   CMMI model components in the staged representation.

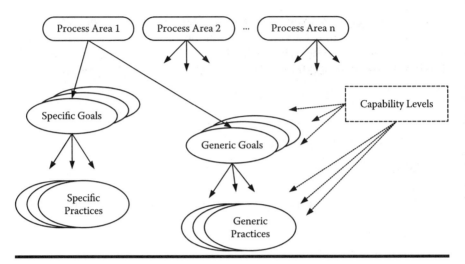

Figure 3.2   CMMI model components in the continuous representation.

between CMMI version 1.1 and version 1.2 (the current version) is that common features are no longer defined. *Common features* was a term used to categorize the generic practices. Chapter 4 discusses this idea in more detail. Removing the term *common feature* makes it easier for the user to understand the model structure.

Figure 3.2 shows the CMMI model components in the continuous representation. The continuous representation has specific goals that organize specific practices and generic goals that organize generic practices. Each specific and generic practice corresponds to a capability level. Specific goals and specific practices apply to individual process areas.

Model Structure for the Staged Representation

The staged representation is organized by assigning process areas to maturity levels.

Maturity Levels

A maturity level signifies the level of performance that can be expected from an organization. For example, Maturity Level 1 organizations have ad hoc processes. Maturity Level 2 organizations have a basic project management system in place. There are five maturity levels.

Process Areas (PAs)

Each maturity level consists of several process areas. A process area is a group of practices or activities performed collectively in order to achieve a specific objective. Examples include Requirements Management at Maturity Level 2; Requirements Development at Maturity Level 3; and Quantitative Project Management at Maturity Level 4.

Goals

Each PA has several goals that need to be satisfied in order to satisfy the objectives of the PA. There are two types of goals:

1. Specific goals (SG): goals that relate only to the specific PA under study
2. Generic goals (GG): goals that are common to multiple PAs throughout the model. These goals help determine whether the PA has been institutionalized.

Practices

Practices are activities that must be performed to satisfy the goals for each PA. Each practice relates to only one goal. There are two types of practices:

1. Specific practices (SP): practices that relate to specific goals
2. Generic practices (GP): practices associated with the generic goals for institutionalization

For example, in the Project Planning PA, one of the specific practices is to write a Project Plan. Another is to estimate the number of people needed and to derive a schedule. Subpractices and examples are provided to help explain the practices in more detail.

Relationship between Goals and Practices

Every PA has several goals that must be satisfied. Because goals are at a high level, each goal has practices associated with it. Practices are specific tasks that should be performed within the PA to achieve the goal. There are both generic and specific goals. There are both generic and specific practices.

Model Structure for the Continuous Representation

The continuous representation uses the same basic structure as the staged representation. However, each PA belongs to a Process Area Category. A Process Area Category is just a simple way of arranging PAs by their related, primary functions. The Process Area Categories with their associated PAs follow.

Process Management

These PAs consist of common functions related to defining, planning, implementing, and monitoring a process. Notice that they all reside at the organizational level, not the project level, and are listed in increasing order of sophistication and complexity. There are five Process Management PAs:

■ Organizational Process Focus
■ Organizational Process Definition (with Integrated Product and Process Development—IPPD)
■ Organizational Training
■ Organizational Process Performance
■ Organizational Innovation and Deployment

Project Management

These PAs consist of functions related to planning, tracking, and controlling projects, and are listed in increasing order of sophistication and complexity. There are six Project Management PAs:

■ Project Planning
■ Project Monitoring and Control
■ Supplier Agreement Management
■ Integrated Project Management (with Integrated Product and Process Development—IPPD)
■ Risk Management
■ Quantitative Project Management

Engineering

These PAs consist of technical functions related to building and delivering a product, and are listed in increasing order of sophistication and complexity. There are six Engineering PAs:

- Requirements Development
- Requirements Management
- Technical Solution
- Product Integration
- Verification
- Validation

Support

These PAs consist of related support functions related to managing changes, ensuring quality, measuring results and activities, and structured decision making. They are listed in increasing order of sophistication and complexity. There are five Support PAs:

- Configuration Management
- Process and Product Quality Assurance
- Measurement and Analysis
- Decision Analysis and Resolution
- Causal Analysis and Resolution

In the previous version of the CMMI, there were both base practices and advanced practices. Base practices were those practices that resided at Capability Level 1. Base practices essentially involved identifying the scope of work and performing the process informally without following a documented process description or plan. Advanced practices were those practices that showed more sophistication and rigor in a process area. Advanced practices could build on base practices. Now, in version 1.2, there are only the specific practices. They match the practices in the staged representation.

The degree to which the practices are performed may vary from individual effort to individual effort. A capability level is not a maturity level. Capability Level 1 simply means that the specific practices are performed in some way in your organization. So, these practices are very simple building blocks in the stratification of attaining capability levels.

Goals and Practices

Specific goals and practices relate to specific process areas and relate to tasks that make sense for that process area only. For example, Project Planning requires a project plan. Quantitative Project Management requires a process performance baseline. Generic goals and practices relate to multiple process areas. So, Requirements Management, if desiring a Capability Level 2, would have to establish an organizational policy, plan the process, and train people. To attain Capability Level 3, Requirements

Management must do the aforementioned actions, as well as define the process and collect improvement information relating to the process. Project Planning and Organizational Process Focus would have to do the same as well. So the generic goals and practices can be applied to all process areas. Both specific goals and practices and generic goals and practices must be satisfied to achieve the capability level. Alternatives that clearly and unequivocally accomplish a result that meets the goal may be substituted. Again—required, expected, and informative components.

Generic Goals and Practices

Basically, each capability level has one generic goal associated with it. Each generic practice maps to only one generic goal. The generic goals and generic practices map directly to one or more PAs, and basically summarize the concepts of each PA. The generic goals and generic practices are displayed in Table 3.1.

Table 3.1   Generic Goals, Generic Practices, and Related Process Areas

Generic Goal and Generic Practice	Related Process Area
Generic Goal 1: Achieve Specific Goals of Each Process Area	
GP 1.1: Perform Specific Practices of the Process Area	Specific practices of one or more Process Areas, depending on the extent of the model to be achieved
Generic Goal 2: Institutionalize a Managed Process	
GP 2.1: Establish an Organizational Policy	Project Planning
GP 2.2: Plan the Process	Project Planning
GP 2.3: Provide Resources	Project Planning
GP 2.4: Assign Responsibility	Project Planning
GP 2.5: Train People	Organizational Training Project Planning
GP 2.6: Manage Configurations	Configuration Management
GP 2.7: Identify and Involve Relevant Stakeholders	Project Planning Project Monitoring and Control Integrated Project Management (with IPPD)
GP 2.8: Monitor and Control the Process	Project Monitoring and Control Measurement and Analysis
GP 2.9: Objectively Evaluate Adherence	Process and Product Quality Assurance
GP 2.10: Review Status with Higher Level Management	Project Monitoring and Control
Generic Goal 3: Institutionalize a Defined Process	
GP 3.1: Establish a Defined Process	Integrated Project Management Organizational Process Definition
GP 3.2: Collect Improvement Information	Integrated Project Management Organizational Process Focus Organizational Process Definition
Generic Goal 4: Institutionalize a Quantitatively Managed Process	
GP 4.1: Establish Quantitative Objectives for the Process	Quantitative Project Management Organizational Process Performance
GP 4.2: Stabilize Subprocess Performance	Quantitative Project Management Organizational Process Performance
Generic Goal 5: Institutionalize an Optimizing Process	
GP 5.1: Ensure Continuous Process Improvement	Organizational Innovation and Deployment
GP 5.2: Correct Root Causes of Problems	Causal Analysis and Resolution

For more information concerning how to interpret and apply the generic practices, please refer to later Chapters 5 through 8 titled "Understanding Maturity Level" 2, 3, 4, or 5, respectively. These chapters summarize the concepts expressed in the PA and generic practices and are arranged by maturity level. Later chapters give more information pertaining to implementation.

Target Profile

A target profile is a list of process areas and their corresponding capability levels. One example is when comparing maturity levels to capability levels. Capability Level 3 can only be determined as equivalent to Maturity Level 3 in the staged representation when all of the goals for all of the process areas at Maturity Levels 2 and 3 in the staged representation have been met. So the target profile 3 would include satisfying seven process areas at Maturity Level 2 plus eleven process areas at Maturity Level 3. An organization may decide on its own unique target profile. For example, a contracting company specializing in providing third-party Independent Verification and Validation services may select a target profile of Capability Level 2 for Project Planning and Project Monitoring and Control, and Capability Level 3 for Verification and Validation.

Target Staging

Target staging is a sequence of target profiles that describe the path of process improvement the organization will take. Care should be taken to ensure that dependencies between the generic practices and process areas are implemented. This is where the organization documents the PAs it will focus on, justifies this approach, and tracks the PAs back to business objectives.

Achievement Profile

Used in the continuous representation, this profile is basically a bar chart of each process area that shows how much of the PA has been achieved and how much has not been achieved. When the reader views it to determine how much of the process area has been achieved, it is called an *achievement profile*. When the reader views it to determine what is left to be achieved, it can be called a *target profile*.

Capability Level Profile

This profile (or chart) is a list of process areas and their corresponding capability level. This profile can be constructed by using the target profile to show what is left to be done or the achievement profile showing what has been successfully

Table 3.2   Process Areas with Maturity Level and Category

Process Area	Maturity Level (staged representation)	Process Area Category (continuous representation)
Requirements Management	2	Engineering
Project Planning	2	Project Management
Project Monitoring and Control	2	Project Management
Supplier Agreement Management	2	Project Management
Measurement and Analysis	2	Support
Process and Product Quality Assurance	2	Support
Configuration Management	2	Support
Requirements Development	3	Engineering
Technical Solution	3	Engineering
Product Integration	3	Engineering
Verification	3	Engineering
Validation	3	Engineering
Organizational Process Focus	3	Process Management
Organizational Process Definition (with IPPD)	3	Process Management
Organizational Training	3	Process Management
Integrated Project Management (with IPPD)	3	Project Management
Risk Management	3	Project Management
Decision Analysis and Resolution	3	Support
Organizational Process Performance	4	Process Management
Quantitative Project Management	4	Project Management
Organizational Innovation and Deployment	5	Process Management
Causal Analysis and Resolution	5	Support

performed, or both profiles to show both sets of information. It's easy: use a bar chart that is shaded to show what has been accomplished. What is not shaded shows what is left to be done.

CMMI focuses on institutionalization. Goals cannot be achieved without proving institutionalization of the process. Generic goals and generic practices support institutionalization and increasing sophistication of the process. Specific goals and specific practices support implementation of the process area. Process maturity and capability evolve. Process improvement and increased capability are built in stages because some processes are ineffective when others are not stable.

Table 3.2 shows the process areas contained in each maturity level in the staged representation and the corresponding Process Areas Category in the continuous representation.

Other Components

There are other terms and components that relate to both representations. They are:

- ■ Typical Work Products—Each process area gives examples of typical documents, deliverables, or other outputs produced within the process area.
- ■ Subpractices—Lower-level practices that provide more information about the practice. For example, the practice may be to write a project plan. The

subpractice would offer information as to what should go into the project plan itself.

- Discipline Amplifications—Simple guidance offered to direct the user as to which discipline is more relevant for specific practices, or to offer some guidance in applying the PA to the discipline. The disciplines are Systems Engineering, Software Engineering, and Hardware Engineering. Supplier Sourcing as a separate discipline has been eliminated from this CMMI version. Its concepts have been incorporated into two specific process areas, and into notes, tips, and hints. Integrated Product and Process Development (IPPD) has been renamed as an *addition*.
- Addition—Any information or material that adds to the scope of the model or how it should be used. This information is targeted for a particular user community. Currently, the only addition to the CMMI version 1.2 is Integrated Product and Process Development (IPPD).
- Constellations—Different types of CMMIs focusing on different topics. Currently, there are three constellations under development: the CMMI for Development (version 1.2, the current version), CMMI for Services (focusing on labor services provided, not necessarily product development), and CMMI for Acquisition (focusing on procurement and acquisition topics). Constellations also include the associated products, such as training materials and appraisal methods.
- Elaborations—More information and examples concerning generic practices.
- Hints, tips, and X-Refs—Brief notes in the margins that contain bits of information on how a practice relates to another practice or process area, why the practice is important, why it is included here, more guidance on what the practice actually means, or how the practice might be used or implemented in an organization.
- Labels—Each practice has a full name but is often documented and referred to by its shortened name or label. An example is in the continuous representation, Generic Practice 4.2. The label of this practice is Stabilize Subprocess Performance. The entire name of the practice is "Stabilize the performance of one or more subprocesses to determine the ability to achieve the established quantitative quality and process–performance objectives."
- Resources—In the previous CMM for Software, resources generally referred to only people, for example, staff, individuals, personnel. In the CMMI, resources can mean not only people, but also equipment, funds, facilities, and technology.

So, what do you really have to do? Are all of these elements as important as the next? No. The CMMI gives us some guidance as to what is a required component, an expected component, and simply informative.

Required, Expected, and Informative Components

■ *Goals* are *required* to be achieved.

■ *Practices* are *expected* to be followed. Alternative practices that achieve the same concept may be substituted when the practice listed does not meet business objectives or fit the organization. Alternatives must be justified, documented, planned, implemented, and measured. The alternative substituted must be equal to the intent of the original practice. Don't try to substitute another practice because your organization is having trouble instituting the original practice.

■ *Subpractices, elaborations, typical work products,* and *notes* are *informative* and are used to help the reader understand the intent of the goals and practices, as well as how they may be achieved. **Do not discount the subpractices!** Sometimes, they are much more helpful and specific in understanding the activity than their associated practice.

Summary

No matter which representation of the CMMI is used, each has levels. Within each level are generic goals pertaining to all of the process areas in that level and specific goals pertaining only to a specific process area. Goals have practices associated with them. Practices are associated with only one goal.

So, let's stop all the nonsense right now—there is really only one representation of the CMMI model. There are two approaches to using the model—the staged approach and the continuous approach. These approaches are discussed in the next chapter.

Chapter 4

CMMI Representations

There are two different representations of the CMMI. They are the staged representation and the continuous representation.

The following discussion contains a lot of "CMMI-ese." There is just no way around it. When using the CMMI, you must use the terminology associated with it. However, the words are sometimes confusing. A trick we use is to look at the words as separate entities and then just turn them around. For example, the next paragraph contains the words *process capability*. Well, what is that? Look at the words. *Process capability* is how *capable* is our *process* of actually providing us with the results we are looking for. And so on. Good luck.

The Staged Representation

The staged representation focuses improvement on the process capability an organization can expect to attain; however, this expected capability (or ability to function in a mature manner) is contained within maturity levels, or stages. There are five maturity levels, with each level providing the foundation for further improvements. This structure mirrors that of the previous CMM for Software.

Maturity Level 1—Initial

Organizations have no structured process in place. Development is chaotic and ad hoc. Budgets and schedules are often exceeded. Product quality cannot be predicted. Maturity Level 1 is considered ad hoc—meaning you make it up as you go along, which is something we want to avoid—so this level has no real structure associated with it. That is, this level represents a chaotic approach toward developing products. If chaos were structured, it would not be chaotic. So, there is nothing structured in Level 1, and being Level 1 is a bad thing.

Maturity Level 2—Managed

Basic project management processes are in place and are followed. Institutionalization is achieved by satisfying the generic goals and generic practices for Level 2 that include:

- Adhering to organizational policies
- Following a documented plan and process description
- Applying adequate funding and resources
- Maintaining appropriate assignment of responsibility and authority
- Training people in their appropriate processes
- Placing work products under appropriate configuration management
- Monitoring and controlling process performance, and taking corrective action
- Objectively reviewing the process, work products, and services, and addressing noncompliance
- Reviewing the activities, status, and results of the process with appropriate levels of management, and taking corrective action
- Identifying and interacting with relevant stakeholders

Level 2 begins with basic management practices and continues with increasingly sophisticated focus areas that belong within a specific level.

Maturity Level 3—Defined

The organization has achieved all of the goals of Level 2. There is an organizational way of doing business, with tailoring of this organizational method allowed under predefined conditions. The organization has an organization's set of standard processes (OSSP). The following characteristics of the process are clearly stated:

- Purpose
- Inputs
- Entry criteria
- Activities
- Roles
- Measures
- Verification steps
- Outputs
- Exit criteria

Level 3 continues with defining a strong, meaningful, organizationwide approach to developing products. An important distinction between Level 2 and Level 3 is that at Level 3, processes are described in more detail and more rigorously than at Level 2. Processes are managed more proactively, based on a more sophisticated understanding of the interrelationships and measurements of the processes and parts of the processes. Level 3 is more sophisticated, more organized, and establishes an organizational identity—a way of doing business particular to this organization.

Maturity Level 4—Quantitatively Managed

For Maturity Level 4, the organization has achieved all of the goals of Levels 2 and 3. The organization controls its processes by statistical and other quantitative techniques. Product quality, process performance, and service quality are understood in statistical terms and are managed throughout the life of the processes.

Level 4 focuses on using metrics to make decisions and to truly measure whether progress is occurring and your product is improving. Distinctions between Level 3 and Level 4 are that at Level 3, processes are *qualitatively* predictable. At Level 4, processes are *quantitatively* predictable. Level 4 addresses *special causes* of process variation and takes corrective action.

Maturity Level 5—Optimizing

The organization has achieved all of the goals of Levels 2, 3, and 4. Processes are continually improved based on an understanding of *common* causes of variation within the processes.

Level 5 is nirvana. Everyone is a productive member of the team, defects are reduced, and your product is delivered on time and within the estimated budget.

Table 4.1 displays each maturity level and its associated process areas.

In the staged representation, the maturity levels serve as process boundaries—meaning that the efforts documented in that maturity level relate *only* to that maturity level. For example, Requirements Management is a Level 2 process area. The next process area in Level 2 is Project Planning. Then there is Project Monitoring and Control, Supplier Agreement Management, Measurement and Analysis, Process and Product Quality Assurance, and Configuration Management. So, to be considered a Maturity Level 2 organization, the projects undergoing process improvement need to satisfy the goals for all of the process areas for Maturity Level 2.

In Maturity Level 3, there are the following process areas:

■ Requirements Development
■ Technical Solution
■ Product Integration

Table 4.1   Process Areas By Maturity Level

Process Area	Maturity Level (staged representation)
Requirements Management	2
Project Planning	2
Project Monitoring and Control	2
Supplier Agreement Management	2
Measurement and Analysis	2
Process and Product Quality Assurance	2
Configuration Management	2
Requirements Development	3
Technical Solution	3
Product Integration	3
Verification	3
Validation	3
Organizational Process Focus	3
Organizational Process Definition (with IPPD)	3
Organizational Training	3
Integrated Project Management (with IPPD)	3
Risk Management	3
Decision Analysis and Resolution	3
Organizational Process Performance	4
Quantitative Project Management	4
Organizational Innovation and Deployment	5
Causal Analysis and Resolution	5

- Verification
- Validation
- Organizational Process Focus
- Organizational Process Definition + Integrated Product and Process Development (IPPD)
- Organizational Training
- Integrated Project Management + Integrated Product and Process Development (IPPD)
- Risk Management
- Decision Analysis and Resolution

So, an organization seeking to be Maturity Level 3 would need to structure their process improvement program to satisfy the goals for *both* Level 2 and Level 3. The point to note is that the process areas listed in Level 2 are not listed in Level 3, and vice versa. The same holds true for Maturity Level 4 and Maturity Level 5. You must satisfy all of the goals in the previous levels plus the goals for the current level in order to attain the maturity level rating. Each maturity level consists of process areas. Each process area contains goals that must be satisfied. Each goal has certain practices or actions associated with it.

The Continuous Representation

The continuous representation has the same basic information as the staged representation, just arranged differently; that is, in capability levels not maturity levels, and process area categories. The continuous representation focuses process improvement on actions to be completed within process areas, yet the processes and their actions may span different levels. More sophistication in implementing the practices is expected at the different levels. These levels are called capability levels. There are six capability levels:

Level 0: Incomplete
Level 1: Performed
Level 2: Managed
Level 3: Defined
Level 4: Quantitatively Managed
Level 5: Optimizing

What's a capability level? Capability levels focus on maturing the organization's ability to perform, control, and improve its performance in a process area. This ability allows the organization to focus on specific areas to improve performance of that area. A brief explanation of each capability level follows.

Capability Level 0: Incomplete

An incomplete process does not implement all of the Capability Level 1 specific practices in the process area that has been selected. This is tantamount to Maturity Level 1 in the staged representation.

Capability Level 1: Performed

A Capability Level 1 process is a process that is expected to perform all of the Capability Level 1 specific practices. Performance may not be stable and may not meet specific objectives such as quality, cost, and schedule, but useful work can be done. This is only a start, or baby step, in process improvement. It means you are doing something, but you cannot prove that it is really working for you.

Capability Level 2: Managed

A managed process is planned, performed, monitored, and controlled for individual projects, groups, or stand-alone processes to achieve a given purpose. Managing the process achieves both the model objectives for the process as well as other objectives, such as cost, schedule, and quality. As the title of this level states, you are actively managing the way things are done in your organization. You have some metrics that are consistently collected and applied to your management approach.

Remember, metrics are collected *and used* at all levels of CMMI, in both the staged and continuous representations. It is a bitter fallacy to think that an organization can wait until Level 4 to use the metrics.

Capability Level 3: Defined

A defined process is a managed process that is tailored from the organization's set of standard processes. Deviations beyond those allowed by the tailoring guidelines are documented, justified, reviewed, and approved. The organization's set of standard processes is just a fancy way of saying that your organization has an identity. That is, there is an organizational way of doing work that differs from the way another organization within your company may do it. So, let's say there are two companies developing anvils. Those two companies are Road Runner Industries and Wily Coyote Industries. The people at Road Runner Industries consistently beat the pants off Wily Coyote Industries when developing anvils. Why? Because Road Runner Industries has a special way, specific to them, of developing anvils. It is documented, measured, people are trained in it, and the results are tracked.

Capability Level 4: Quantitatively Managed

A quantitatively managed process is a defined process that is controlled using statistical and other quantitative techniques. Product quality, service quality, process performance, and other business objectives are understood in statistical terms and are controlled throughout the life cycle. Yep, this is where such ideals as statistical process control come into being. However, the point we would like to make is *keep it simple*. Metrics do not have to be difficult to be useful. In fact, the opposite holds true. We don't want to have to grit our teeth and get a tension headache every time we think about collecting and analyzing the metrics collected in our organization. Make them meaningful and associate them with some problem you would like to conquer. For example: Let's say your company makes personal computers and ships them to customers. One day you are sitting at your desk and receive a call from an irate customer. How did it get to you? Who knows, but it did. (This could be an opportunity in disguise.) The customer describes his tale of woe and ends up with stating that the PC arrived at his house with the box intact and unopened, but the monitor was smashed to bits. Well, if this is your first phone call about it, and you are busy, and this is not your job, you might ignore it. But, if you start receiving five such calls every day, you might want to start counting the number of calls, analyzing where the problem was injected into the shipping process, institute a new process for fixing this defect, and track the effectiveness of your process. Then, by analyzing the number of defects expected in prior months versus the actual number of defects this month, you can come up with a standard number of expected defects. When this number is exceeded, the process is broken and must be fixed. Also, you can work on reducing this number. That's quantitatively managing.

Capability Level 5: Optimizing

An optimizing process is a quantitatively managed process that is improved based on an understanding of the common causes of process variation inherent in the process. It focuses on continually improving process performance through both incremental and innovative improvements. Both the defined processes and the organization's set of standard processes are targets of improvement activities. Level 4 focuses on establishing baselines, models, and measurements for process performance. Level 5 focuses on studying performance results across the organization or entire enterprise, finding common causes of problems in how the work is done (the process(es) used), and fixing the problems in the process. The fix would include updating the process documentation and training involved where the errors were injected. So the process may only be broken at the project level; or, it could be entirely broken, and the process at the organizational level and all resultant levels may need to be repaired.

The continuous representation contains the same basic information as the staged model; the information is just arranged differently. The information (process areas, goals, practices) is arranged in what we call functional categories; that is, each process area is grouped by the functionality it performs. There are four types of process categories:

- Process Management Processes
- Project Management Processes
- Engineering Processes
- Support Processes

So, for example, in the continuous representation, the Project Management Processes category contains the following process areas in the following order:

- Project Planning
- Project Monitoring and Control
- Supplier Agreement Management
- Integrated Project Management (with IPPD)
- Risk Management
- Quantitative Project Management

These process areas are all related in some way. They are categorized as Project Management Processes. Although an organization may select which processes to focus improvement efforts on when using the continuous representation, this representation seems to suggest that if your organization needs help in improving its project management approach to product development, start with these process areas in this order.

The continuous representation does not overtly suggest a sequence to use for process improvement; however, a sequence is implied. In the list of Project Management Processes, it would be ludicrous for an organization to attempt to institute Quantitative Project Management before successfully achieving the goals of the Project Planning process area (as Quantitative Project Management is more sophisticated and more complex than Project Planning). If you review the order of the process areas in the list, you will surmise that the less sophisticated process areas are listed first, with the more sophisticated process areas following. For example, before you can focus on Project Monitoring and Control, Project Planning should be in place. It seems that the continuous representation is saying that Project Planning should be attempted first, followed much later by Risk Management because Risk Management is more sophisticated (and probably more complicated to institute) than Project Planning. Also, without the basis of Project Planning, Risk Management could not be performed effectively.

A subtler, less obvious subject that bears discussing is that of generic practices and how they relate to process areas, maturity levels, and capability levels. Process areas at Maturity Level 2 in the staged representation include entire process areas for planning, managing changes, ensuring quality, and tracking progress. The generic practices for Capability Level 2 in the continuous representation also include statements for the same things—planning, managing changes, ensuring quality, and tracking progress. Generic practices are used to determine whether generic goals have been satisfied. Generic goals must be satisfied to achieve a level—either a capability level or a maturity level. What this means is that because an organization is expected to implement the generic practices, an organization using the continuous representation and selecting separate process areas to focus on must in reality also satisfy the basic concepts of Maturity Level 2 in the staged representation. An example follows.

An organization may decide to use the continuous representation. This organization selects the process area of Technical Solution and is seeking a Capability Level 2 for it. To achieve this capability level, all of the specific practices for Technical Solution are expected to be implemented, and all of the generic practices for this level are expected to be instituted. That means that activities surrounding planning, managing changes, ensuring quality, and tracking progress for Technical Solution must be addressed. To address these issues and institute the generic practices, the organization discovers that it must actually backup a bit and also focus on the process areas of Project Planning, Project Monitoring and Control, and Configuration Management. So, although it may appear that an organization can

Table 4.2   Process Areas By Category

Process Area	Process Area Category (continuous representation)
Organizational Process Focus	Process Management
Organizational Process Definition (with IPPD)	Process Management
Organizational Training	Process Management
Organizational Process Performance	Process Management
Organizational Innovation and Deployment	Process Management
Project Planning	Project Management
Project Monitoring and Control	Project Management
Supplier Agreement Management	Project Management
Integrated Project Management (with IPPD)	Project Management
Risk Management	Project Management
Quantitative Project Management	Project Management
Requirements Management	Engineering
Requirements Development	Engineering
Technical Solution	Engineering
Product Integration	Engineering
Verification	Engineering
Validation	Engineering
Measurement and Analysis	Support
Process and Product Quality Assurance	Support
Configuration Management	Support
Decision Analysis and Resolution	Support
Causal Analysis and Resolution	Support

skip process areas when using the continuous representation, the actions of those process areas must be met.

Table 4.2 displays the process areas by process category from the continuous representation.

Which One Should I Use?

It Depends …

The staged representation is most like the most currently accepted models, such as the CMM for Software. It is very useful for appraisals; most recent procurements have mandated contract awards based on maturity level ratings. Following the staged representation produces a maturity level rating.

The continuous representation was designed to tailor the model and process improvement approaches focusing on specific categories that may match those areas in your organizations where problems exist. For example, let's say your organization does only Independent Verification and Validation. You do not write software. You produce no product. As an independent third party, you simply review those products produced by some other party, and you write your report. This type of organization might want to focus on the Verification, Validation, and Product

Integration process areas. The continuous representation allows this approach to take place.

One approach to take in selecting which representation to use is to consider two questions:

- How much experience does your organization have with process improvement? Why? Because we believe that the continuous representation requires a higher level of process improvement understanding than the staged representation. The staged representation embeds process area decisions that an inexperienced organization may not be prepared to make. For example, an organization just beginning process improvement usually has little idea as to where to start. The staged representation tells you to begin at the beginning—Maturity Level 2—and after attaining that level, continue to the next—Maturity Level 3. And so on. Within those levels are the process areas to include in your process improvement strategy. So, when just beginning, an organization may state, "We will begin with Maturity Level 2 which means satisfying the goals for all of the process areas in Maturity Level 2." The organization would then prioritize which process areas to focus their efforts on first (see subsequent chapters of this book for how to set up and structure your process improvement initiative). Our experience has also shown that organizations inexperienced in process improvement often put too much focus on technological solutions and not enough on management issues. Therefore, an inexperienced organization using the continuous representation might focus its efforts on the Engineering Processes, as opposed to those emphasizing project and process management. While improving engineering is, of course, important, without the foundation of strong project and process management, it is likely that engineering improvements would not be sustained, if accomplished at all. Those organizations that are more experienced with process improvement, and more experienced with identifying and mapping their organizational weaknesses to areas where the CMMI can offer help, would probably be able to use the continuous representation more successfully. Remember, the continuous representation allows an organization to select (that means pick and choose) which process areas to focus on by determining which of the process areas match the organization's business needs and objectives.
- What model(s) is your current process program based on? Our experience shows that an organization should build on the positive experiences it has had with other models used in that organization. CMMI requires enough changes without introducing unnecessary confusion. So, if you have been happy with the staged structure, continue to use it. If you have been happy with the continuous structure, continue to use it. If you want to try something new, then be our guest. Just remember, whenever you introduce something new,

Table 4.3   Representation Selection Matrix

Approaches	Based on CMM for Software	Based on SECM or Related Model	High Process Improvement Experience	Low Process Improvement Experience
		Current Process Improvement Program		
Staged Representation	+ Builds on current experience − May overlook interpretation issues	− Learning curve for new paradigm + Defined sequence of improvements		+ Easier to understand + Helps maintain focus
Continuous Representation	− Learning curve for new paradigm + Allows focus on significant area	+ Builds on current experience + Can continue with current plans	+ Supports informed decisions	− Bad focus decisions likely
Start with Continuous Move to Staged	− Major short-term impact + Allows focus on significant area	− Minor short-term impact + Longer-term easier comparison	+ Able to make informed focus decision	+ Harder to build experience
Start with Staged Move to Continuous	− Minor short-term impact + Longer-term focus on significant areas	− Major short-term impact		+ Easier to build experience

you introduce new problems and new headaches. But you also may stimulate and revive your organization's process improvement effort.

Table 4.3 shows the impact of process improvement experience and current model experience on the representation decision. Four approaches are shown in the left column. The four right columns represent model experience and process improvement experience. An entry with a + sign indicates a positive impact and a − sign a negative impact.

The two representations are not mutually exclusive! Each representation contains the same basic information—it is just structured differently. Each representation promotes process improvement and can be used in appraisals. The continuous representation allows the organization to choose which process areas to focus on, as well as which discipline to focus on (software engineering, systems engineering, hardware engineering). The CMMI also suggests that tailoring of the model may be done but …

Caveat: The more tailoring of the model done, the less likely an organization is to achieve its improvement goals. The CMMI contains best practices of organizations. If you deviate from a best practice, you must strongly justify why, and substitute another practice that satisfies the intent of the CMMI practice originally listed. Intent is like beauty—different in the eye of every beholder. It is also difficult to define intent. Most organizations try to justify their not doing something in the model. What they really would like to write, but can't for obvious reasons is, "It

Table 4.4 Equivalent Staging

Name	ML	CL1	CL2	CL3	CL4	CL5
Requirements Management	2					
Measurement and Analysis	2					
Project Monitoring and Control	2		**Target**			
Project Planning	2		**Profile 2**			
Process and Product Quality Assurance	2					
Supplier Agreement Management	2					
Configuration Management	2					
Decision Analysis and Resolution	3					
Product Integration	3					
Requirements Development	3					
Technical Solution	3					
Validation	3		**Target**		**N/A**	**N/A**
Verification	3		**Profile 3**			
Organizational Process Definition	3					
Organizational Process Focus	3					
Integrated Project Management	3					
Risk Management	3					
Organizational Training	3					
Organizational Process Performance	4		**Target**			
Quantitative Project Management	4		**Profile 4**			
Organizational Innovation and Deployment	5		**Target**			
Causal Analysis and Resolution	5		**Profile 5**			

was too hard for us to do. We didn't have the money. We didn't have the people. We didn't have the time before the appraisal team came in. It is inconvenient for us to do what the CMMI says." These are not good justifications for not doing something described in the model.

There is also the concept of Equivalent Staging. What is Equivalent Staging? It is an attempt to match maturity levels in the staged representation to capability levels in the continuous representation. The levels compared are called *Target Staging*. Target Staging is a sequence of targeted process areas that describe the path of process improvement the organization will take. Care should be taken to ensure that dependencies between the generic practices and process areas are implemented. This is where the organization documents the process areas it will focus on, justifies this approach, and tracks the process areas back to business objectives. Table 4.4 shows the Equivalent Staging between maturity levels (as indicated in column ML) and capability levels (as indicated in columns CL1 through CL5).

Here's where it gets confusing. The continuous approach using capability levels has two generic goals (and associated generic practices) for Level 4, and two generic goals (and associated generic practices) for Level 5. The staged approach using maturity levels does not have those two generic goals and generic practices. The staged approach uses entire process areas that reside at Maturity Levels 4 and 5. That means that instead, you need to satisfy the *specific goals and practices* for the corresponding process areas (Organizational Process Performance [OPP] and Quantitative Project Management [QPM] for Target Profile 4, and Organizational

Innovation and Deployment [OID] and Causal Analysis and Resolution [CAR] for Target Profile 5); plus, you need to satisfy the *generic goals and practices* for Capability Levels 1, 2, and 3 (not 4 or 5). Careful reading of the table should lead you to conclude that to achieve Target Profile 3, an organization needs to satisfy the goals for all of the process areas in Maturity Levels 2 and 3—even if using the continuous representation. Remember, not all of the process areas contained within Maturity Level 3 in the staged representation are also contained within the process categories for Capability Level 3 in the continuous representation. Proceed along this path with caution.

At this time, the authors of this book have read of procurements that allow either a maturity level or a capability level to be used for contract awards. However, we have no firsthand knowledge of contracts having been awarded using capability levels. Most procurements and contract awards are based on achieving maturity level ratings.

The interesting point to make here is that the staged representation is really continuous; and the continuous representation is really staged. In other words, because of all the interdependencies among the process areas and relationships that must be met among the generic goals and practices, everything is related to everything else. For example, in the staged representation, you cannot really plan your project in Project Planning (Level 2) if you haven't already begun to manage your requirements in Requirements Management (Level 2). So Requirements Management feeds into Project Planning. How can you manage requirements (Requirements Management Level 2) if you haven't defined them in some way, shape, or form yet (Requirements Development Level 3)? How can you effectively start a process improvement program if you don't set up a group of people and follow the guidelines in Organizational Process Focus (Maturity Level 3)? Yet, that is Level 3, and the organization is just starting its process improvement program, so the organization is at Level 1. How can you have Verification, Validation, and Product Integration as separate entities? Generally, in most organizations, if you do one, you must do the others. The CMMI states that using the continuous representation, and focusing on capability levels, allows an organization to select process areas within process categories to focus their process improvement efforts. In the continuous representation, how can you attempt Validation, or Verification, or practically any other process area without also tackling to some extent Project Planning, Project Monitoring and Control, and Product and Process Quality Assurance? The generic practices correspond to their associated process areas, but more information and guidance are contained in the process areas than in the generic practices. So, those of you thinking of selecting the continuous representation so that you can select only a few process areas for improvement will find that you are sadly mistaken. Everything is related. The different representations used are simply to help the reader understand the basic tenets of the model.

Our Mandate

We are tired of discussing which representation is better than the other. They are really both the same. What is different is the approach taken to structure and implement improvements. The staged approach follows a defined path of selected process areas. The continuous approach allows the selection of an individual process area or process areas.

In the staged approach, beginning with Maturity Level 2, there are seven process areas. You would probably not tackle all seven areas simultaneously. You might select Requirements Management and Project Planning. You would implement all of the specific practices for those two areas and the generic practices at Level 2. You would then continue with the remaining five process areas defined for Maturity Level 2. After implementing all generic practices and specific practices *for all of the process areas listed in Maturity Level 2*, you would be considered Maturity Level 2.

Using the continuous approach, you might feel that your organization really needs the most help with Project Planning. So you implement the specific practices of that area, and then continue with the generic practices. Guess what? You are now at Capability Level 2. If you continue with all of the process areas listed in the staged approach (the remaining six), implementing the process areas, and the specific and generic practices for those process areas, you have now switched to the staged approach. However, maybe you feel that you would like to continue focusing on Project Planning. You could now institute the generic practices for Level 3. If you did that, you would be at Capability Level 3 for Project Planning. Maybe you decide you like doing process improvement because the organization has seen the benefits of it. So you continue focusing on Project Planning, but also decide to try implementing Requirements Management. You institute just the specific practices for Requirements Management while also instituting the Level 3 generic practices for Project Planning. If you accomplish both areas successfully, you are now at Capability Level 1 for Requirements Management and Capability Level 3 for Project Planning. You are back using the continuous approach.

The point is, you have followed the same book and the same information. You have just selected a subset of all possible process areas listed in the staged approach at Maturity Level 2. But you performed the same work and used the same book. Only your selection of process areas and practices differed. That is the difference between representations—the extent of practices and the number of process areas implemented in your organization. Although the wording was slightly different in the previous version of the CMMI, the information contained in both representations is now the same.

Because it is really the same book, we prefer to refer to them as *approaches*, and not *representations*.

Summary

Although the CMMI is promoted as having two very different representations, the representations are really more similar than dissimilar. Instituting the practices and subpractices is where the real benefits may be found. There are no new generic goals for Maturity Levels 4 and 5 in the staged representation because the process areas included in Maturity Level 4 and Level 5 include the basic tenets of those goals. The continuous representation *does* have generic goals because the continuous representation allows the selection of various process areas. So, your organization may decide not to select the process areas in Maturity Level 4. If you do that, yet want to implement quantitative measures for selected areas, then the generic goals of the continuous representation have been added to ensure that the basic concepts of statistical control and its application will be met.

CMMI PROCESS
AREAS

Chapter 5

Understanding Maturity Level 2: Managed

This chapter is designed to help the reader understand the basic tenets of Maturity Level 2 in the staged representation of the CMMI. However, because this chapter consists of summaries of the process areas, anyone wishing to get a better idea of the model, no matter which representation is to be used, can benefit from this chapter. Once again, we are not attempting to teach the CMMI. We simply offer a condensed version of the various areas and key points to consider.

Two new concepts are introduced in Level 2 in CMMI. They are:

- Supplier Agreement Management
- Integrated Product and Process Development (IPPD)

The process area Supplier Agreement Management (SAM) has been changed to include the concepts of Integrated Supplier Management (ISM) from the previous version of the CMMI (version 1.1). ISM previously resided at Level 3 in the previous version of the CMMI. The basic tenets of Integrated Supplier Management have been incorporated into SAM here at Level 2.

SAM has to do with ensuring that any organization or business external to the actual project is selected and monitored appropriately. This external source (supplier) may be responsible for delivering either a product or a service and may be involved in the design, development, maintenance, manufacture, modification, upgrade, or supply of any of the items required to produce the product. This supplier generates an agreement (contract) with the acquiring body, and it is this agreement that is used to effectively manage the effort provided by the supplier. This agreement must be properly defined, documented, used, monitored, and measured. SAM replaced Software Subcontract Management (SSM) in the CMM for Software. SSM was the key process area most often tailored out of assessments and software process improvement activities because if there were no subcontractors used, then this area did not apply. Although SAM has been broadened somewhat, it is still the most tailored-out process area. In fact, it is the only process area that is allowed to be tailored out—that means, SAM may be declared "not applicable" to the organization's business. Including SAM in the CMMI also makes a correlation to the Software Acquisition Capability Maturity Model (SA-CMM) more plausible. Although both SAM and the Software Acquisition Model discuss suppliers, vendors, procurements, and acquisition roles, more information from a different perspective (i.e., that of an acquisition or procurement office) may be found in the Acquisition Model.

IPPD is about forming teams that include subject matter experts from all areas needed to produce the product for the customer. Suffice it to say that IPPD is about establishing and conducting integrated teams in a formal manner. An example might be when building a new jet fighter. This effort would require hundreds or thousands of individuals to work on developing all parts of the plane, including the sophisticated software systems for navigation, landing, communications, and attack; the actual construction of the hardware and fuselage of the plane; safety engineers to test safety-critical parts and functioning; mechanics to ensure that the plane would be easy and quick to repair under emergency and nonemergency conditions; pilots to ensure that the plane could actually be flown; documentation experts to ensure that all necessary documentation and manuals were written correctly; and others. In cases such as this one, rather than try to include comments and ideas from everyone working on the project (that is, to design and deliver a working jet fighter plane), representatives from each area would be assigned to an Integrated Product Team (IPT). This team would develop a shared vision of what the final product should look like and what its final functionality should include. They would also be responsible for ensuring that input from all areas was included in the requirements gathering, design, development, testing, and final delivery of the product.

The information contained in Maturity Level 2 concerning IPPD is mostly just that—for information purposes only. The information provided consists of hints, tips, and examples. IPPD has been incorporated at all levels throughout the CMMI by adding elaborations (more information and examples) within certain specific practices. IPPD applies specifically to the Integrated Teaming concept that is often used within the United States Department of Defense. If your organization does not use integrated teams, do not worry about it. If you feel they would benefit your organization, then fine. Go ahead and try them. But do not feel you must reorganize and restructure your development and maintenance activities in this way just because it is documented in the CMMI. More information about this addition can be found in the next chapter discussing Maturity Level 3.

When comparing the CMMI version 1.1 to the current CMMI version 1.2, and to the previous CMM for Software, what's been left out? The categorization of generic practices into common features (Commitment to Perform, Ability to Perform, Directing Implementation, and Verifying Implementation) has been removed. That is, the term *common feature* is gone, but the concept remains the same—we are just using the term *generic practice* instead of *common feature*. There are no longer explicit, specific project manager reviews or specific senior management reviews. It is left up to the organization to determine where in the bureaucratic reporting structure *higher-level management* resides. The glossary defines higher level management as someone who does not have authority for day-to-day functions and has more of a strategic focus. However, we have seen organizations simply define senior management as the next higher level of management. For example, if you are a programmer, then your team leader may be the higher-level management that you report your status to. If you are a project manager, the director of software engineering may be your higher-level manager. So, information is still being reported to the project manager and to senior management—the hierarchy is simply not defined explicitly. In fact, few groups or bureaucratic structures are directly specified (for example, no mention of the Software Quality Assurance group). Also, there are no specific references or requirements for a Quality Assurance review.

Moving from Level 1 to Level 2

The biggest hurdle that most organizations face when embarking on the journey from an immature organization to a more mature one is the jump from Level 1 to Level 2. Level 1 is characterized by ad hoc processes; that is, processes that the people doing the work have created themselves to accomplish their tasks. The problem with this method is that redundant work is often done, people do not share their methods across the organization, and some approaches are in opposition to actually making the organization run more effectively. While some individual approaches may work for a particular individual, that person's approach may actually conflict with work being done downstream. The results are more rework, delays, and frustration. Turf wars are common, and the organization functions due to the heroics of its people. When these people move on (or burn out), the organization suffers.

Level 2 is characterized by individuals sharing their lessons learned and best practices, and devising preliminary processes that will function at the project level, and in some cases, across the organization as a whole. Level 2 focuses on management issues that affect normal, day-to-day work routines. Level 2 consists of seven process areas that contribute to project management efficiencies.

There are seven process areas (PAs) that make up Level 2. They are:

- Requirements Management
- Project Planning

- Project Monitoring and Control
- Supplier Agreement Management
- Measurement and Analysis
- Process and Product Quality Assurance
- Configuration Management

Each process area has specific goals (specific to that process area) and generic goals that are applied to every process area in that maturity level. Generic goals for Maturity Level 2 are listed below. These goals lead to institutionalizing the process area; that is, when an organization ensures that these goals are practiced consistently across the organization, the process area associated with these goals will continue to be applied appropriately in the organization even after those who created the procedures for this area have left. The generic goals and their corresponding generic practices for Maturity Level 2 are:

Generic Goal 2:   Institutionalize a Managed Process
    Generic Practice 2.1   Establish an Organizational Policy
    Generic Practice 2.2   Plan the Process
    Generic Practice 2.3   Provide Resources
    Generic Practice 2.4   Assign Responsibility
    Generic Practice 2.5   Train People
    Generic Practice 2.6   Manage Configurations
    Generic Practice 2.7   Identify and Involve Relevant Stakeholders
    Generic Practice 2.8   Monitor and Control the Process
    Generic Practice 2.9   Objectively Evaluate Adherence
    Generic Practice 2.10 Review Status with Higher Level Management

Each process area has specific and generic goals. Both types of goals must be satisfied to successfully achieve the benefits of process improvement for that process area.

For the continuous approach, the generic goals (GG) and generic practices (GP) for each capability level that must be satisfied for each selected process area are:

Capability Level 1:
    GG1   Achieve Specific Goals
        GP 1.1   Perform Specific Practices
Capability Level 2:
    GG2   Institutionalize a Managed Process
        GP 2.1   Establish an Organizational Policy
        GP 2.2   Plan the Process
        GP 2.3   Provide Resources
        GP 2.4   Assign Responsibility
        GP 2.5   Train People
        GP 2.6   Manage Configurations

GP 2.7   Identify and Involve Relevant Stakeholders
GP 2.8   Monitor and Control the Process
GP 2.9   Objectively Evaluate Adherence
GP 2.10   Review Status with Higher Level Management
Capability Level 3:
GG3   Institutionalize a Defined Process
GP 3.1   Establish a Defined Process
GP 3.2   Collect Improvement Information
Capability Level 4:
GG4   Institutionalize a Quantitatively Managed Process
GP 4.1   Establish Quantitative Objectives for the Process
GP 4.2   Stabilize Subprocess Performance
Capability Level 5:
GG5   Institutionalize an Optimizing Process
GP 5.1   Ensure Continuous Process Improvement
GP 5.2   Correct Root Causes of Problems

Each capability level builds on the previous level. So, to be Capability Level 5, the organization must satisfy the specific practices for the selected process area (Capability Level 1), plus the generic practices for Capability Levels 2, 3, 4, and 5.

Each process area is described below. We begin by describing the purpose of the process area (directly from the CMMI), listing specific goals for the process area by goal label, discussing anything interesting or unusual about the process area, and then summarizing the process area. The abbreviations used are SG for specific goal and SP for corresponding specific practices.

The Process Areas for Maturity Level 2: Managed

Requirements Management

The purpose of Requirements Management (REQM) is to manage the requirements of the project's products and product components and to identify inconsistencies between those requirements and the project's plans and work products.

Specific Goals and Practices for This Process Area:
SG1 Manage Requirements
SP 1.1   Obtain an Understanding of Requirements
SP 1.2   Obtain Commitment to Requirements
SP 1.3   Manage Requirements Changes
SP 1.4   Maintain Bidirectional Traceability of Requirements
SP 1.5   Identify Inconsistencies between Project Work and Requirements

Why is Requirements Management at Level 2? Why is there another process area called Requirements Development at Level 3? What's the difference? Requirements Management for Level 2 is all about managing already existing requirements; that is, those requirements that have been elicited from the customer, are documented, and are ready to be worked or are in the process of being worked. This PA refers to capturing and managing the requirements that set the scope of the project. It is at this level because if you don't set the scope you cannot control how much work will need to be done by the project. So, at this level, requirements already exist, and we are basically just managing the changes to them. Requirements Development at Level 3 is all about identifying requirements at a high level and decomposing them down to more detailed, testable levels. Because you need to have requirements in existence before you can manage changes to them, why isn't Requirements Development at Level 2? Because eliciting requirements, developing them, and ensuring that they are "good" requirements is much more difficult and sophisticated a concept. Since Level 2 is the first level in the CMMI with process areas, and Level 2 is about building a foundation for further process improvement, it sort of makes sense that managing requirements resides at this level, and creating requirements is at the next level. Another way of looking at it is to consider that the CMMI is not really a model for *improvement* (although it does lead to improvement); but is really a model for *appraising* or evaluating an organization's improvement effort. If you look at the model as an appraisal model, then the first level appraised should be easier than the next and the next and the next.

The counterpoint is that we really do have an improvement model. The reason Requirements Development is at Level 3 is that technical organizations have to do something to define and refine requirements first, before they can begin to manage them. Sometimes this same technical organization will then forget that they have to manage the requirements they have defined, in addition to just defining requirements. Also, some organizations (especially outsourcing organizations) receive the requirements from their customer and are not allowed to make major refinements to them. In that case, this type of organization does a little bit of refinement to the base requirements, and then begins managing the changes to them that must be made in order to fulfill their contract.

Another point to remember is that most organizations develop requirements first, so if it makes sense in your organization to form one team to improve processes for both gathering requirements and managing changes to them, fine, do it. Most organizations handle process improvement this way. But appraisal teams must remember that they cannot dun an organization during an appraisal for failing to attack requirements development at Level 2 when the concept is not concentrated on until Level 3.

Items to note in this process area are that bidirectional traceability is listed as a practice, which means that it is an expected component. In the CMM for Software, requirements traceability was not mentioned until Level 3 in the Software Product Engineering Key Process Area. However, most organizations realized that they could not adequately manage changes to requirements without tracing those requirements in some way. Traceability tools are mentioned as part of the elaboration for GP 2.3 Provide Resources, and are examples of work products reviewed (Requirements Traceability Matrix—RTM) for GP 2.9 Objectively Evaluate Adherence. Most organizations had actually constructed RTMs in order to manage their requirements, but now it is an *expected* practice in the CMMI. Constructing and using an RTM is not a trivial exercise. So this practice in this process area is an example of considerable growth.

Organizations have asked how far forward and backward must they trace requirements. Our answer is as far forward and backward as you can. It is not enough to trace one high-level requirement from the Requirements phase straight to the Test phase. Why? Because when problems occur in test (and they will), the fix for the problem may be found back in the Requirements phase, or the Design phase, or the Development phase. That's the purpose of tracing requirements—to assist in finding where the problem occurred so it can be fixed more quickly. So, the CMMI is recommending that you trace each of your high-level requirements to their ("spawned" or) lower-level requirements derived from one or more higher-level requirements; then trace each lower-level requirement to its "point of development," that is, to the design specification that satisfies that one requirement; then to the test case and scenario and test result that satisfies that requirement and design specification; then the implementation step that ensures that that requirement has been installed in the customer's environment. In addition, any part of the project plan or other documentation that is used to support the development of the requirement should also be tracked in as much detail as possible (which can mean citing the chapter number and paragraph that supports the requirement, and any interfaces with other systems, files, or data as well). So, traceability can become very complicated, but speaking from experience, it is very much worth the trouble.

Another example of growth of this model is GP 2.8 Monitor and Control the Process. In the previous version of the CMMI (version 1.1), we actively proposed that our clients focus on measurements for this generic practice. Even though the label for the generic practice says "monitor and control," it is not possible to do a good job of monitoring and controlling a process without also measuring the process and tracking against the measurements. We still believe this concept to be true. However, the examples for GP 2.8 for REQM clearly state both ideas—yes, please measure this process area (via measuring requirements volatility for example), but also please monitor and control this area by producing and following a schedule that clearly states when you intend to review and analyze any proposed requirements changes.

The IPPD information simply states that each member of the Integrated Team must realize that he must make a commitment to working effectively with his team members, not only to producing his assigned product.

Things that most organizations tend to forget about this process area:

■ You must devise a method for deciding who is an appropriate requirements provider.
■ This is where acceptance criteria are generated.
■ Bidirectional traceability is both horizontal and vertical; that is, you must trace your high-level requirements down to their decomposed, lower-level requirements, and back up; and you must trace the requirements to their corresponding work products or usage—which means that you must trace the requirement (i.e., each requirement) through to its design, code, test case, test results, changes, plans, updated plans, resources, assigned personnel, and so forth, and back. This is not an easy task.

There are no generic practices that directly map to this PA.

Requirements Management includes understanding the requirements for all parts and components of the system (not just software); obtaining customer, management, and developer commitment to the requirements; managing changes to the requirements; maintaining traceability from the requirements forward in the development cycle, as well as backward to discover where changes may have introduced problems; and identifying inconsistencies between the requirements, ensuing work products, and ensuing activities. Requirements Management feeds into Project Planning, Project Monitoring and Control, Technical Solution (Level 3), and so forth. This process area forms the basis of project development, so it touches just about every process area in the model. Remember, the scope of the model has greatly expanded. Not only are you devising and managing requirements for software, but for all parts of the product.

Project Planning

The purpose of Project Planning (PP) is to establish and maintain plans that define project activities.

Specific Goals and Practices for This Process Area:
    SG1   Establish Estimates
        SP 1.1   Estimate the Scope of the Project
        SP 1.2   Establish Estimates of Work Product and Task Attributes
        SP 1.3   Define Project Life Cycle
        SP 1.4   Determine Estimates of Effort and Cost
    SG2   Develop a Project Plan
        SP 2.1   Establish the Budget and Schedule
        SP 2.2   Identify Project Risks
        SP 2.3   Plan for Data Management

      SP 2.4   Plan for Project Resources
      SP 2.5   Plan for Needed Knowledge and Skills
      SP 2.6   Plan Stakeholder Involvement
      SP 2.7   Establish the Project Plan
    SG3   Obtain Commitment to the Plan
      SP 3.1   Review Plans That Affect the Project
      SP 3.2   Reconcile Work and Resource Levels
      SP 3.3   Obtain Plan Commitment

Although we have used the labels of the practices (the shortened names of the practices), the actual practice itself uses "establish and maintain," not just "establish." Let's talk about that phrase "establish and maintain." Sometimes in the CMMI, a word is just a word. Other times, the words have special meanings. That's the case here. "Establish and maintain" does not just mean to create and control. It means that you must *define* the plans, *document* the plans, use the plans, *monitor* what happens when using the plans, and measure the results of the plans. This phrase should be applied to all documentation created for process improvement. We say, "Just because you have crates of documentation, if you don't use it, you ain't got it." So use the plan; don't just stick it up on your shelf and show it to the auditors when they come to town.

SP 1.1 discusses Estimating the Scope of the Project, but in actuality is expecting a work breakdown structure (WBS). The CMM for Software did not expect a WBS, although this instance is probably an inclusion of a best practice from other organizations.

SP 1.2 discusses size. There are individuals who disagree with using size as a data point when estimating work products and tasks, but size is a relevant point of focus. For example, a large project is usually more complicated and requires more people and perhaps more specialized skills than a small project. However, there are no hard and fast rules for what constitutes a small or large project. It depends on the organization and on the experience and types of projects usually produced by your organization.

A Data Management Plan is now expected (SP 2.3). That plan covers how to manage all of the data and documentation your project will create, acquire, or require. Listed as work products are privacy and security requirements, security procedures, schedule for collection of project data, format descriptions, and mechanisms for reproduction and distribution. You should discuss how you will identify, collect, and make changes to the data that are necessary for your project, and why that data are necessary in the first place. The purpose of this practice is to make you think about why you are collecting this information, how it will be used, and how you will make changes and protect the data from being used in an abusive manner. Sounds like a lot of work.

Although in this book we use the label of the specific practice, there are three instances where we would like to call your attention to the actual name of the practice itself because the elongated name gives more meaning than the label:

- SP 1.1 Estimate the Scope of the Project. The actual practice wording is "Establish a top-level work breakdown structure (WBS) to estimate the scope of the project." Notice that the WBS is specifically referenced here.
- SP 1.4 Determine Estimates of Effort and Cost. The actual practice is "Estimate the project effort and cost for the work products and tasks based on estimation rationale." Notice that the use of the estimation rationale is called for, and that both work products and tasks are to be estimated using that rationale. So, document how you came up with your estimates, and why you chose the numbers you chose.
- SP 2.2 Identify Project Risks becomes "Identify and Analyze Project Risks." So, here is a reminder that not only must you identify the risks, but you must also analyze them. We have had clients say that as long as they simply list the risks in the project plan, they have fulfilled their risk requirement in project planning. This practice seems to require more than just a list. It seems to advocate that something must be done to determine their impact, probability, and priority.

Things that most organizations tend to forget about this process area:

- You must document the rationale for your estimates in enough detail so that the estimates could be reconstructed by someone unfamiliar with the project, if necessary. So just sitting around and coming up with estimates off the top of your head and not documenting that approach is wrong. Also, historical data or models or even industry benchmarks are listed as examples as starting points for your estimates. The cry goes up, "But this is a new project! We don't have any historical data!" Then we guess you can't use historical data then, now can you? Use your brain. If the model suggests you do something that does not pertain to your situation, then don't do it! Some organizations when faced with this dilemma just decide to throw out the model and say, "CMMI is not right for us. We are unique." We suggest that you read and analyze the CMMI and decide what you can use and what you can't use. Take what you need and leave the rest.
- Interdependencies and risk analysis are introduced here. They are just introduced. They are more detailed in later process areas.
- Interfaces are introduced in SP 3.3 Obtain Plan Commitment.
- There can be many, many plans that make up the "overall project plan."
- Plans should be updated as things change, and copies of the original and any ensuing plans with their changes must be kept. Don't overwrite the original plan. Updating your plan is an example of *replanning*.

The generic practice that most closely matches this PA is GP 2.2 Plan the Process. Other GPs that can trace guidance back to this PA include GP 2.3 Provide Resources, GP 2.4 Assign Responsibility, GP 2.5 Train People, and GP 2.7 Identify and Involve Relevant Stakeholders.

Project Planning includes identifying and documenting the scope of the project in order to define and maintain work boundaries; estimating size and complexity of work products; estimating tasks, effort, and cost; defining the project life cycle or selecting a preexisting life cycle that matches the project; determining preliminary and follow-on budgets and schedules; identifying and documenting project risks; planning the extent to which stakeholders should become involved to ensure success; planning for managing information, staff, computer resources, and hardware; and planning for the training needs of project team members. The scope of work here has greatly expanded from just planning the software portion of a project to planning the design, development, and delivery of the entire product. This work will include systems engineering.

Project Monitoring and Control

The purpose of Project Monitoring and Control (PMC) is to provide an understanding of the project's progress so that appropriate corrective actions can be taken when the project's performance deviates significantly from the plan.

Specific Goals and Practices for This Process Area:
SG1   Monitor Project against Plan
  SP 1.1   Monitor Project Planning Parameters
  SP 1.2   Monitor Commitments
  SP 1.3   Monitor Project Risks
  SP 1.4   Monitor Data Management
  SP 1.5   Monitor Stakeholder Involvement
  SP 1.6   Conduct Progress Reviews
  SP 1.7   Conduct Milestone Reviews
SG2   Manage Corrective Action to Closure
  SP 2.1   Analyze Issues
  SP 2.2   Take Corrective Action
  SP 2.3   Manage Corrective Action

SP 1.1 talks about Monitoring Project Planning Parameters. In this case, *parameters* is just a big word for project planning "stuff." Things like cost, size, effort, actuals, and estimates. Some of the subpractices for this practice suggest that this monitoring effort may be done simultaneously with Project Planning, not after. For example, most of the subpractices discuss reviewing the project plan (which comes out of the previous Project Planning Process Area). Subpractices 1.5 and

1.6 specifically describe monitoring project personnel skill levels and documenting "significant" deviations in project planning parameters. So this process area has some linkage back to what is occurring in the Planning area.

Reviews are held "regularly" versus event-driven. While we encourage regular reviews of project activities, we also encourage event-driven reviews. Event-driven reviews may be held when an "event" occurs, which usually means when something bad has happened or might happen—like missing a due date or funding being temporarily suspended. One simple method to determine whether you are holding your meetings regularly enough is to measure the number of issues or action items coming out of each review meeting. If the number of issues increases, you may need to hold your meetings a bit more regularly—that means more meetings. Also make sure that any steering committees that exist are actively playing a role, and that the role they play is appropriate. While some steering committees take a too hands-on an approach, most just want to know "how's it going?" And of course the answer they expect to hear and want to hear is "fine." Keep your steering committee informed. Also, are your process improvement leaders getting feedback and comments back from the project members? No news is *not* good news.

How many reviews should be held? Who knows—it depends on your organization, the size of the project, the complexity, the visibility, and so forth. If your project is a six-month project with only three or four people, you probably hold informal meetings every day. The project manager is probably another programmer, and everyone basically knows what everyone else is doing, what is working, and what isn't. You probably share the same cubicle. In larger projects that take up to six years with 600 people, this is not the case. In this case, formal meetings must be coordinated and held on a regular basis, with minutes taken, and issues formally entered into an action item database for tracking. In this case, we would normally expect to see a weekly meeting held within every organizational unit (software, systems engineering, hardware, etc.) between the manager of the unit and his supervisors and workers, and then another meeting held weekly that includes the managers of the units and senior-level management. Meetings held twice a week or once a month with the customer would probably work, unless the project is in the early stages of requirements gathering or in the test phase or in trouble. In those cases, we would expect meetings to be held either once a week or even every day.

Reviews should be scheduled in the project plan. If the reviews are documented in the schedule, then they will probably occur. Meetings should produce meeting minutes, action items should be tracked, and people who attend should also be monitored. Informal meetings may occur, but don't substitute informal meetings when formal ones are needed.

Things that most organizations tend to forget about this process area:

■ This process area is tied to the Project Planning PA. Without having a credible project plan, this process area cannot be satisfied. The project plan coming out of Project Planning is the basis for activities in the Project Monitoring and Control PA.

■ Document your reviews with management, and any other reviews and status meetings that you feel may be necessary. Informal meetings do not need to be documented; however, the *results* of those meetings may need to be documented, especially if the results will impact schedules, planning, staffing, or strategies.

The generic practice that most closely matches this PA is GP 2.8 Monitor and Control the Process. This is where the reader is referred to consider taking corrective actions when deviations from a process are found. However, the other portion of GP 2.8 that needs to be satisfied is measurement, covered by the Measurement and Analysis PA. Other GPs that relate to this PA are GP 2.7 Identify and Involve Relevant Stakeholders, and GP 2.10 Review Status with Higher Level Management. Guidance given includes that reviews should be both periodic (that is, routinely scheduled and held as scheduled) and event-driven (when something unexpected happens or when an "event"—such as reaching a milestone—has occurred).

Project Monitoring and Control includes monitoring the attributes of the project specified in the project plan; monitoring the staff availability and stakeholder involvement; monitoring and revising project risks; monitoring information handling; conducting reviews to ensure progress is being made (usually conducted at least at major milestone completion); bringing to light potential problems and issues, and analyzing those issues; and taking corrective action to ameliorate project issues.

Supplier Agreement Management

The purpose of Supplier Agreement Management (SAM) is to manage the acquisition of products from suppliers.

Specific Goals and Practices for This Process Area:
SG1 Establish Supplier Agreements
 SP 1.1 Determine Acquisition Type
 SP 1.2 Select Suppliers
 SP 1.3 Establish Supplier Agreements
SG2 Satisfy Supplier Agreements
 SP 2.1 Execute the Supplier Agreement
 SP 2.2 Monitor Selected Supplier Processes
 SP 2.3 Evaluate Selected Supplier Work Products
 SP 2.4 Accept the Acquired Product
 SP 2.5 Transition Products

First things first: This process area does not apply to projects where the supplier or his employee is integrated into the project team, uses the same processes, and reports to the same management as the product developers/project members. If the supplier or his employees are directly incorporated into the project team, and the employee is treated just like any other member of the team (except that his paycheck is signed by the supplier organization), then this PA does not apply to you.

This process area has undergone the most significant changes from the previous version of the CMMI. Two specific practices were added to Goal 2: SP 2.2 Monitor Selected Supplier Processes and SP 2.3 Evaluate Supplier Work Products. Basically, the concept of developing and reviewing a formal agreement (such as a contract or license) with a supplier or vendor external to your organization was incorporated with selecting the supplier. As discussed previously, this book uses the practice labels, and not the entire practice. However, please review SP 1.2 Select Suppliers. The entire practice is much different from the label. The entire practice reads, "Select suppliers based on an evaluation of their ability to meet the specified requirements and established criteria." SP 1.3 Establish Supplier Agreements is really about that phrase "establish and maintain" formal agreements with the supplier. The previous version of the CMMI had a specific practice devoted to commercial-off-the-shelf (COTS) products. This specific practice has been removed from the current version; however, guidance for COTS products is now sprinkled in among the subpractices and examples.

If your organization does not have external suppliers (including contractors providing services) this process area may be not applicable for your organization. However, considering the expanded nature of the model, this N/A seems less and less likely. Your organization probably will have formal agreements for delivery or development or installation of hardware, tools, COTS products, simulators, and so forth. This area is not just about subcontracting, as in the CMM for Software.

While Release Management is not covered extensively in the CMMI, some guidance for releasing the product built by suppliers is described here. Evaluating project risks that might occur, and Acceptance Testing, are also discussed in this process area.

Things that most organizations tend to forget about this process area:

■ Even though the wording specifies "products and product components," the practices also include services provided.
■ Your products being developed need to be managed by the practices in the Supplier Agreement Management process area or the practices in the Project Planning and Project Monitoring and Control process areas.

This PA is the only PA that may be tailored out—that means that you do not have to implement this PA if it does not pertain to your organization.

This PA does not map to any generic practice.

Supplier Agreement Management includes determining the type of acquisition the project requires; determining the type of products or product components to be acquired; selecting appropriate suppliers; defining, executing, and monitoring agreements with and activities of the chosen suppliers; and accepting and deploying products developed by suppliers into the project.

Measurement and Analysis

The purpose of Measurement and Analysis (M&A) is to develop and sustain a measurement capability that is used to support management information needs.

Specific Goals and Practices for This Process Area:
SG1   Align Measurement and Analysis Activities
    SP 1.1   Establish Measurement Objectives
    SP 1.2   Specify Measures
    SP 1.3   Specify Data Collection and Storage Procedures
    SP 1.4   Specify Analysis Procedures
SG2   Provide Measurement Results
    SP 2.1   Collect Measurement Data
    SP 2.2   Analyze Measurement Data
    SP 2.3   Store Data and Results
    SP 2.4   Communicate Results

This process area describes what to do when instituting a measurement process in your organization, not just which measurements to collect. This process area should be considered global because all processes should be measured, and most work products also produce meaningful metrics.

M&A appeared in the CMM for Software as a common feature throughout all of the CMM. M&A is now its own process area at Level 2. Why? Because high-maturity organizations stated quite clearly that the key to success in process improvement is measurement and actually using those measures to make decisions and monitor the process improvement effort. The authors of this book agree that measurement is key. When the previous version of the CMMI was released, we felt that this process area, while certainly relevant and necessary, was too complicated to reside at Level 2. We have now changed our view. While instituting a measurement approach and repository is not an easy task, it is so necessary for success of any process improvement initiative that we agree that this task should be initiated early in the process improvement effort. We were also surprised that most organizations did not have as much trouble beginning this effort. Now, there is a difference between *beginning* and *successfully implementing*. But Level 2 is all about beginning the journey and not necessarily about refining your effort into something with no errors, no mistakes.

The M&A process area expects that measurements are aligned to business goals. One problem that we continue to see in low-maturity organizations (that is, those organizations just beginning to follow the CMMI path) is that of defining business objectives and goals. In these organizations, we have repeatedly been told that the business goal or the business objective (no distinction is made between the two terms) is to make money. That goal is a bit too broad to appropriately tie to M&A practices and to track against. This expectation may be too much for a low-maturity organization. With little or no experience in measurement, it is easy for an organization to go either too far and measure everything or not far enough and only measure things that they "already know" are important.

One improvement that we noticed in this process area is the addition of a few more examples of work products, measures, measurement results, and improvement information.

The other reason for breaking out measurement into its own process area was that organizations were good at collecting measurements but not in actually using the measurements. While creating this process area as a separate entity has not really ended that problem, it has made organizations more aware of the importance of measurements and tracking against those measurements.

Things that most organizations tend to forget about this process area:

■ You have to tie your measurements back to meaningful business goals—not just collect something because it has always been collected or not just collect something because the book tells you to in the examples. So don't measure everything listed as an example—but, also, don't just pay lip service to this area. Prove that you are collecting the right measurements that will truly help track progress and failure of your process improvement effort and of your business activities. Our chapters on measurement give you some examples of what measures to collect and how to determine their suitability for you organization and project.

■ This process area is about defining a measurement effort in your organization. Don't forget to measure your measures. That is, you also must track the time and effort and effectiveness of your measurement effort itself.

The generic practice that most closely matches this PA is GP 2.8 Monitor and Control the Process. The M&A process area, plus the Project Monitoring and Control PA must both be implemented to satisfy GP 2.8. Measurements should focus on the process, its products, and its services.

Measurement and Analysis includes defining measurement objectives; defining measures and procedures for collecting, storing, and analyzing metrics; executing the procedures to collect and analyze measurement data; storing the data and results in a manner fostering their usage by appropriate parties; and reporting measurement information to individuals and groups requiring the information.

A basic step-by-step approach to measurement is:

■ Select the process to measure
■ Select the measures

- Determine when to collect data
- Determine how to collect data
- Record and store the information
- Analyze data for consistency and accuracy
- Chart the results
- Review the chart
- Do something (corrective actions)

Process and Product Quality Assurance

The purpose of Process and Product Quality Assurance (PPQA) is to provide staff and management with objective insight into processes and associated work products.

Specific Goals and Practices for This Process Area:
SG1 Objectively Evaluate Processes and Work Products
    SP 1.1 Objectively Evaluate Processes
    SP 1.2 Objectively Evaluate Work Products and Services
SG2 Provide Objective Insight
    SP 2.1 Communicate and Ensure Resolution of Noncompliance Issues
    SP 2.2 Establish Records

The term used is to *objectively evaluate adherence*. This term is defined in the glossary as reviewing activities and work products against criteria that minimize subjectivity and bias by the reviewer. The reference to the term *audit* is further defined in the glossary as "an independent examination of a work product or set of work products against specific criteria (such as requirements)." The concept of independence is addressed by the GP 2.4 Assign Responsibility and states that those people assigned to perform this role should have "sufficient" independence and objectivity. In the verbiage following the purpose statement (Introductory Notes) at the beginning of the process area itself, some discussion of objectivity and independence may be found. These paragraphs discuss embedded quality assurance and independent QA groups. It is stated that "Those performing quality assurance activities for a work product should be separate from those directly involved in developing or maintaining the work product. An independent reporting channel to the appropriate level of organizational management must be available so that noncompliance issues may be escalated as necessary." In our previous book, we reminded the authors of the CMMI that *processes* are not *products*; and that notes are simply informative and not normative—that is, that these dicta may prove useful for understanding the intent of the area, but are not mandatory for process improvement implementation or appraisal. We also found that by burying the definition of objectivity and independence in these paragraphs, a less-than-stellar implementation of this process area could be promoted.

While we still have the same concern, we now feel that the authors of the CMMI have tried to do a better job of clearly defining what *objective* truly means. However, we are concerned about the discussion that seems to imply that peer reviews can be substituted for independent QA. Close reading of the information contained in the paragraphs following the purpose statement states that while peers can perform QA tasks, they must receive QA training, must not be involved in the production of the material reviewed, and must have an independent reporting chain. QA checklists should also be used. Please remember that peer reviews (as defined in the Verification process area) cannot be substituted for independent QA.

Notice that the CMMI specifically calls out quality assurance reviews and activities for both product and process. Under the CMM for Software, Verifying Implementation 3 involved Software Quality Assurance. SQA groups were directed to review both products and processes. However, organizations tended to either focus on SQA reviews for products (reviewing documentation against formatting standards) or reviewing process adherence (whether SQA reviews were held as documented in the process descriptions and the procedures). Few organizations realized that both types of reviews were necessary. So now the CMMI emphasizes that both must occur by including both in the name of the process area and in the specific practices.

To audit processes, simply review whether they were followed as documented, why or why not, where the problems are, and where improvements are needed. To audit products, use product standards and checklists to ensure compliance. Reviewing for content (as opposed to form or image) may best be left up to the peer review process and the technical review process. It is often simply too difficult to get Quality Assurance personnel to review for "good" content, as this requires vast technical knowledge. Most techies prefer to stay techies, and getting superior technical experts into a QA role is difficult—not impossible, but difficult. If your organization would like to attempt this feat, we suggest rotating developers into QA, and QA personnel into the Development arena. In some organizations, before someone can become a project manager, he must have served duty in both QA and Technical development areas. Another way of trying to incorporate technical expertise into QA reviews is to perform audits with both technicians and QA individuals participating side by side. This approach is similar to the introductory notes that discuss allowing peers to perform QA tasks.

SP 2.1 Communicate and Ensure Resolution of Noncompliance Issues at first seems to indicate that all the Quality Assurance people must do is report the problem and move on. But the full practice reads, "Communicate quality issues and ensure resolution of noncompliance issues with the staff and managers," with subpractice 7 describing tracking issues to resolution.

Things that most organizations tend to forget about this process area:

■ You also need someone to independently review your QA activities and results. This review can be done by another organization in your company, outside your own organization, or by companies that specialize in performing Independent Verification and Validation or other formal external audits. Some organizations also use the SCAMPI appraisal itself as part of this external review.

■ PPQA is the most often abused process area that we see when performing appraisals. Do not abuse or misuse this PA! If you decide that it is too much trouble to properly implement PPQA in your organization (that is, as defined in the CMMI), then don't bother to introduce the CMMI into your organization. Period.

The generic practice that most closely matches this PA is GP 2.9 Objectively Evaluate Adherence. Another attempt at emphasizing and defining *objectivity* is found in the paragraphs describing this GP. The guidance offered reads, "People not directly responsible for managing or performing the activities of the process typically evaluate adherence. In many cases, adherence is evaluated by people within the organization, but external to the process or project, or by people external to the organization."

Process and Product Quality Assurance includes providing a strategy and procedures for objectively evaluating processes and products; identifying personnel to fulfill this role objectively; reporting quality issues and noncompliance; and producing reports that provide verification that quality reviews were conducted and their results.

Configuration Management

The purpose of Configuration Management (CM) is to establish and maintain the integrity of work products using configuration identification, configuration control, configuration status accounting, and configuration audits.

Specific Goals and Practices for This Process Area:
  SG1   Establish Baselines
      SP 1.1   Identify Configuration Items
      SP 1.2   Establish a Configuration Management System
      SP 1.3   Create or Release Baselines
  SG2   Track and Control Changes
      SP 2.1   Track Change Requests
      SP 2.2   Control Configuration Items
  SG3   Establish Integrity
      SP 3.1   Establish Configuration Management Records
      SP 3.2   Perform Configuration Audits

CMMI version 1.2 has included more information about the different types and levels of baselines and the different types of configuration audits that should be applied.

Configuration Management is not just setting up libraries for files and then migrating files back and forth. It is also not about buying tools that will migrate files and tell you when they were moved or that a change has been made. Configuration Management is about defining configuration items. *Configuration items* is a well-known term for DOD clients but is not so well known outside of that arena. We use the following example. When a software system is being designed, it can be broken up into several pieces. Those pieces may be the files, the data elements within those files, programs, reports, and integrated or called modules. Those pieces can be termed *configuration items*. An organization can have both high-level configuration items and then lower-level configuration items that result from decomposing the high-level items into lower-level, more detailed, smaller pieces. Each piece (or configuration item) is assigned a label and a number to aid in tracking that all pieces of the desired system are included as part of the delivered product. It also helps in tracking changes, planning the effort, and auditing functionality satisfied.

Configuration Management is also about establishing baselines. Baselines are basically where you draw a line in the sand and say, "OK, anything developed past this point, or any changes made past this point, must go through some sort of official review before being incorporated into the rest of the system." Factors such as impacts to already existing modules, costs, skill sets required, schedules and due dates, and technical feasibility are all analyzed before the modification or addition is made. The CMMI does not tell you when to establish a baseline. It just encourages you to do so. So when should baselines be established? Well, once again, we don't know your organization, but usually baselines are set after requirements have been approved and signed off, the design has been signed off, testing has finished, and the product has been delivered and is ready to enter the maintenance phase.

Configuration Management duties include *verifying* the contents of libraries and files. A tool may be used to track that changes were made, but a tool is usually not sophisticated enough to tell you what the change was and how this change affects the rest of the system. So a human being must be involved in reviewing and analyzing the effects of any changes. This type of review is a Configuration Audit. Both the CMMI and the CMM for Software discuss ensuring the "completeness and correctness" of the material in the libraries. However, the CMM for Software did not define what "completeness and correctness" meant. Because of that, some organizations included physical configuration audits (where the physical structure of the system is reviewed against changes) and not functional configuration audits (where requirements are traced to confirm that they have been satisfied within elements of the system). SP 3.2 Perform Configuration Audits seems to imply that to ensure "completeness and correctness," both functional and physical configuration audits of the products/work products/components, as well as an audit of configuration management records and configuration items, should also occur.

Although throughout the CMMI specific groups are generally not mentioned, in Configuration Management subpractice 1 of SP 1.3 Create or Release Baselines does specifically mention the Configuration Control Board (CCB). A *release* is the product that is released to the customer for use. A *build* is the work product that is passed on to other internal departments for further usage or work. Formal procedures for Release Management are not covered. This area also focuses on having a formal change request process in place.

Things that most organizations tend to forget about this process area:

- There are several different types of baselines. There can be *formal baselines* that have been formally agreed to by a formal group, as well as *informal baselines*. Informal baselines are what the original CMM for Software referred to as *Developmental* baselines. Basically, in Developmental baselines, two programmers are assigned to update the same program or piece of code. In this case, one programmer agrees with the other programmer to wait to make his fix until the other guy has completed his fix, tested it, and uploaded it into Production. That way, both fixes get loaded correctly. Without this informal agreement, only the last fix would get loaded into Production. The first fix made the first programmer would have been overwritten by the fix completed by the second programmer. The organization needs to define when each type of baseline (formal or developmental) should be used.

The generic practice that most closely matches this PA is GP 2.6 Manage Configurations. The term configuration *control* is used instead of the previous term from CMMI version 1.1, configuration *management*, when describing appropriate levels of configuration activities. We believe this change in wording is to emphasize version control as well as formal baseline configuration management.

Configuration Management includes defining configuration items; developing or implementing support tools, techniques, procedures, and storage media; generating and maintaining baselines; tracking change requests and controlling changes; documenting the results of the configuration management effort; and performing configuration audits.

Summary

Although at first glance it appears that Level 2 of the CMMI has not changed significantly from Level 2 of the CMM for Software, reality must set in. While the words in the CMMI and the layout of the process areas appear to be very similar, they are not. Remember, the CMMI includes Systems Engineering, Software Engineering, Integrated Product and Process Teams, and some supplier interactions. So when planning and implementing these process areas, all levels and departments that will be necessary to create the final product (and any interim products) must be included.

There is also redundancy across the model. This redundancy is supplied to allow the user to properly implement the model, despite whether he chooses the staged or continuous approach. Examples at Level 2 are that the Measurement and Analysis process area, Configuration Management, and Product and Process Quality Assurance area must be performed at all levels and within all process areas, not just Level 2. Further redundancy is shown within the generic practices. For example, GP 2.2 Plan the Process can be traced back to the Project Planning process area. GP 2.4 Train People is related to Organizational Training at Level 3. GP 2.8 Monitor and Control the Process is a reflection of the Project Monitoring and Control process area. GP 2.6 Manage Configurations reflects the Configuration Management process area. GP 2.9 Objectively Evaluate Adherence is directly related to Product and Process Quality Assurance. The argument has been made that these redundancies are included to aid the reader in how to implement the Generic Practices.

While this redundancy may be a problem during various appraisals (for example, when appraised, if GP 2.6 is not followed in the Project Planning process area, does that mean that the organization is dunned in both Project Planning and in Configuration Management? Is this double jeopardy? To what degree is the organization in violation? Are these "showstoppers"?), we have come to realize that this redundancy is a good thing. It ensures that the generic practices (which represent institutionalization) have been instituted, despite which representation of the model has been chosen. Please see our previous chapter discussing the structure and representations of the model for further examples and discussion.

Chapter 6

Understanding Maturity Level 3: Defined

This chapter is designed to help the reader understand the basic tenets of Maturity Level 3 in the staged representation of the CMMI. However, because this chapter consists of summaries of the process areas, anyone wishing to get a better idea of the model, no matter which representation is to be used, can benefit from this chapter. Once again, we are not attempting to teach the CMMI. We simply offer a condensed version of the various areas and key points to consider.

Moving from Level 2 to Level 3

Maturity Level 3 differs from Level 2 in that now an organizational way of doing business has been developed. What that means is that the best practices and lessons learned from the projects have bubbled up to the organizational level to create an organizational identity. There are common, shared approaches for performing daily tasks on each project. For example, estimating the size of a project may be done using the Delphi Technique (basically subject matter experts discussing best-case and worst-case estimates), a standard metric may have been institutionalized (such as using function points instead of lines of code), and a standard tool may be in use to actually calculate the size.

This organizational way of doing business is documented in the Organization's Set of Standard Processes (OSSP). However, should a project need to tailor this OSSP to more adequately fit its needs, then that tailoring request is bought to a decision-making body (usually the Engineering Process Group [EPG]), and if appropriate, the request is granted. An example may be a legacy system that calculates size by lines of code instead of by function point. Rather than reengineer the millions of lines of code in the system in order to use a tool to count function points, and rather than do it manually, the project is simply allowed to continue calculating size by lines of code. The Delphi Technique is still used, but lines of code is the measurement.

To perform at Level 3, an organization must have satisfied all of the goals for all of the process areas (PAs) in both Level 2 and Level 3. Sometimes exceptions may be made. Caution should be exercised however. Entire *process areas* are generally not allowed to be tailored out of consideration. *Practices* may be tailored out if replaced by sufficient alternative practices. Remember: the more tailoring done, the less likely an organization is to achieve improvement, and the less likely the organization is to achieve a maturity level through an appraisal.

The CMMI makes a point of stating that at Level 3, the organization has more distinctly defined its processes. We feel that this statement leads the reader to many wrong conclusions. This statement does not mean to wait until Level 3 to define your processes. When defining processes, an organization should always try to define them so that they can be followed—even at Level 2. Processes are at a high level—it is their associated procedures that detail how to perform the processes. Please review Chapter 15 of this book for more information.

The CMMI suggests the following attributes of a process. We suggest that you follow this guideline. However, we also suggest that you add what needs to be added. Some organizations have added interface requirements and process performance metrics. Some organizations have also combined the inputs and entry criteria into one attribute, and the outputs and exit criteria into one attribute. While purists will object to that, we have seen it work in organizations. And after all—the beef is in the procedures, not the processes.

The following items are to be included in a process definition:

Purpose—Purpose of the process.

Inputs—Work products, plans, approval memoranda (usually nouns).

Entry criteria—What must be triggered before this process can start? (Usually the exit criteria of the previous step or process. Usually stated as a verb.)

Activities—Tasks that must be performed. These tasks are usually later broken down into the detailed procedures for *how* to perform the tasks.

Roles—Who does what? (Usually by position.)

Measures—What measures does this process produce?

Verification steps—What reviews are performed to determine that this process is followed and is producing the correct results? (Usually management and quality assurance reviews, but sometimes can include customer, peer, and project team reviews.)

Outputs—Work products, plans, approved products (can be the completed inputs).

Exit criteria—How do we know when it is time to stop this process? (Usually expressed in verbs, and usually becomes the entry criteria for the next process step or next process.)

Another distinction is made concerning processes. A *managed* process is a process that tackles project management efforts, is planned and executed according to a policy, is monitored, and reviewed to ensure adherence to its process description. This is the type of process expected at Maturity Level 2. A *defined* process builds upon a managed process by creating an organizational process that is then tailored to fit the needs of a particular project and involves gathering information related to improvement efforts undertaken by the organization in order to improve both the organization-level process and the project-level process. This is the type of process expected at Maturity Level 3.

There are 11 process areas for Level 3. They are:

■ Requirements Development
■ Technical Solution
■ Product Integration
■ Verification
■ Validation
■ Organizational Process Focus
■ Organizational Process Definition (with IPPD)
■ Organizational Training
■ Integrated Project Management (with IPPD)
■ Risk Management
■ Decision Analysis and Resolution

You will notice that Level 3 has expanded to include engineering process areas and Integrated Product and Process Development (IPPD; explained in Chapter 5).

The generic goals for Level 3 are somewhat different from Level 2. The generic goals for Levels 2 and 3 are listed below. We use the abbreviations GG for generic goal and GP for generic practice.

GG2 Institutionalize a Managed Process
    GP 2.1   Establish an Organizational Policy
    GP 2.2   Plan the Process
    GP 2.3   Provide Resources
    GP 2.4   Assign Responsibility
    GP 2.5   Train People
    GP 2.6   Manage Configurations
    GP 2.7   Identify and Involve Relevant Stakeholders
    GP 2.8   Monitor and Control the Process
    GP 2.9   Objectively Evaluate Adherence

GP 2.10   Review Status with Higher Level Management
GG3:   Institutionalize a Defined Process
GP 3.1   Establish a Defined Process
GP 3.2   Collect Improvement Information

To satisfy the goals for Level 3, the goals for Level 2 must be satisfied as well. This mandate holds true for both the specific goals (listed in each process area below) and the generic goals listed above. So, reviewing the list of generic goals above reveals that the generic goals for Level 2 are still there, plus the addition of one more goal for Level 3 (GG3) and two more corresponding generic practices (GP 3.1 and GP 3.2). The Level 3 generic goal is Institutionalize a Defined Process; and the two generic practices that make that goal possible are Establish a Defined Process and Collect Improvement Information. So the CMMI is asking us to implement these practices for each individual process area.

For the continuous approach, the generic goals and generic practices for each capability level that must be satisfied for each selected process area are:

Capability Level 1:
    GG1   Achieve Specific Goals
        GP 1.1   Perform Specific Practices
Capability Level 2:
    GG2   Institutionalize a Managed Process
        GP 2.1   Establish an Organizational Policy
        GP 2.2   Plan the Process
        GP 2.3   Provide Resources
        GP 2.4   Assign Responsibility
        GP 2.5   Train People
        GP 2.6   Manage Configurations
        GP 2.7   Identify and Involve Relevant Stakeholders
        GP 2.8   Monitor and Control the Process
        GP 2.9   Objectively Evaluate Adherence
        GP 2.10   Review Status with Higher Level Management
Capability Level 3:
    GG3   Institutionalize a Defined Process
        GP 3.1   Establish a Defined Process
        GP 3.2   Collect Improvement Information
Capability Level 4:
    GG4   Institutionalize a Quantitatively Managed Process
        GP 4.1   Establish Quantitative Objectives for the Process
        GP 4.2   Stabilize Subprocess Performance
Capability Level 5:
    GG5   Institutionalize an Optimizing Process

GP 5.1   Ensure Continuous Process Improvement
GP 5.2   Correct Root Causes of Problems

Each capability level builds on the previous level. So, in order to be Capability Level 5, the organization must satisfy the specific practices for the selected process area (Capability Level 1), plus the generic practices for Capability Levels 2, 3, 4, and 5.

The following sections discuss each process area for Level 3. We use the abbreviations SG for specific goal and SP for corresponding specific practices.

Process Areas for the Maturity Level 3: Defined

Requirements Development

The purpose of Requirements Development (RD) is to produce and analyze customer, product, and product component requirements.

Specific Goals and Practices for This Process Area:
SG1   Develop Customer Requirements
  SP 1.1   Elicit Needs
  SP 1.2   Develop the Customer Requirements
SG 2   Develop Product Requirements
  SP 2.1   Establish Product and Product Component Requirements
  SP 2.2   Allocate Product Component Requirements
  SP 2.3   Identify Interface Requirements
SG3   Analyze and Validate Requirements
  SP 3.1   Establish Operational Concepts and Scenarios
  SP 3.2   Establish a Definition of Required Functionality
  SP 3.3   Analyze Requirements
  SP 3.4   Analyze Requirements to Achieve Balance
  SP 3.5   Validate Requirements

SP 1.1 Elicit Needs, when expanded to its full name reads, "Elicit stakeholders needs, expectations, constraints, and interfaces for all phases of the product lifecycle," and in the explanatory notes underneath it, states that this practice also includes identifying needs not explicitly stated by the customer. There are examples of requirements that might not be relayed to you by your customer, such as business policies and environmental standards that must be followed, reuse commitments, and so forth. This practice is the result of incorporating the wording from a practice in the continuous representation in the previous CMMI.

SP 3.4 Analyze Requirements to Achieve Balance means to review what the stakeholder needs with what you can really deliver in the allotted time and with your allotted budget. The "stakeholder" mentioned here seems to relate most closely to the customer. The customer needs tend to focus on cost, schedule, risk, and high-level functionality (i.e., will this thing work when you deliver it to me?). If you are the project manager, you also need to review (and balance) what the customer needs with what your project team can deliver. You also need to reconcile conflicting requirements from various other stakeholders.

SP 3.5 Validate Requirements has been shortened. It used to say, "Validate requirements using comprehensive methods" and advocated using multiple validation techniques as necessary. The idea of using multiple techniques is now embedded in the wording below the practice itself and advises us that multiple techniques are a sign of a more mature organization. This practice is the result of incorporating the wording from a practice in the continuous representation in the previous CMMI. This practice also reinforces the importance of ensuring that you have the "right" requirements (i.e., the requirements that will produce a viable, accurate, fully functioning product) early in the development process. It also somewhat overlaps with the Validation Process Area.

In the previous CMMI, SP 1.2 from Technical Solution (Evolve Operational Concepts and Scenarios) has been incorporated into RD SP 3.1 Establish Operational Concepts. SP 3.5 has now combined validating requirements with validating them with comprehensive methods from the previous CMMI.

Requirements Development is where requirements are initially defined and documented. Requirements Management at Level 2 is where changes are administered. Requirements Development gathers requirements and then must usually refine these requirements in some way—by stating them more clearly, determining whether they are redundant or inconsistent with other requirements, and breaking them down into more detailed and traceable requirements.

Some readers may think that they can skip this process area because they are not doing "development," that is, "new" development, because they are a Maintenance shop. The CMMI makes it very clear that no matter whether you are in new development or in maintenance mode, there are always new requirements or changes to existing requirements that require definition, refinement, user interaction, and so forth. That is, all of the behaviors necessary to produce complete and accurate requirements, and discussed in this process area.

The CMMI uses the terms *product, product component,* and *component.* Examples of these terms might be that a product is the final deliverable, such as a jet fighter plane capable of flying and firing missiles. The product components might be the navigation system, the fire control system, the fuselage, the landing equipment, the communication system. The components might be software to determine the distance from the ground, the software to aim a missile, the control panel, the tires, and the headphones. The manufacture of a communication system may have a different mapping, starting with the communication systems product, radios and antennas as product components, and the receiver, transmitter and tuner software as components. The concept of *services* has also been explicitly added to this process area, so that the reader is reminded that requirements to provide a service must also be defined and satisfied.

This process area introduces the *Concept of Operations* or, using the CMMI term, *operations concept*. This document is usually the first document written when determining whether to pursue development of a product. It is usually a high-level statement of the desired functionality, and a preliminary plan and schedule for development, to justify initiating this new project to higher-level management. This document is then passed on to higher-level management to make a go/no go decision to approve and fund the new project. The Concept of Operations document is then used as the basis for further requirements identification and refinement, as well as project planning. This concept works well in a Department of Defense (DOD) environment or when attempting to build a highly complex product with many people. However, in the commercial, non-DOD world, these documents are generally not used. This can be a problem when following the CMMI because this document is expected in several practices throughout the model. Organizations that are not DOD-like generally rely on object-oriented techniques, use cases, or man–machine interface documentation to satisfy this concept.

Beta testing of requirements is mentioned here.

Things that most organizations tend to forget about this process area:

- Maintenance shops also do development.
- Even if you get your requirements directly from the customer, some refinement and analysis of them is always necessary.
- Developing and analyzing requirements never stops until the entire application is either delivered to the customer for final handoff, or is dead and buried.

There are no generic practices that directly map to this process area.

Requirements Development includes collecting and eliciting customer requirements from all involved parties at all levels; breaking down those high-level requirements into lower-level, more detailed requirements, and assigning them to categories for further development; defining interfaces among the requirements and any other areas necessary to fulfill the requirements; more adequately defining and documenting the operational need, concept, scenario, and functionality desired; ensuring that the requirements are complete, required, and consistent; negotiating needs versus wants versus constraints; and validating the requirements against risk in the early phases of the project.

Technical Solution

The purpose of Technical Solution (TS) is to design, develop, and implement solutions to requirements. Solutions, designs, and implementations encompass products, product components, and product-related life-cycle processes either singly or in combination as appropriate.

Specific Goals and Practices for This Process Area:
SG1   Select Product Component Solutions
    SP 1.1   Develop Alternative Solutions and Selection Criteria
    SP 1.2   Select Product Component Solutions
SG2   Develop the Design
    SP 2.1   Design the Product or Product Component
    SP 2.2   Establish a Technical Data Package
    SP 2.3   Design Interfaces Using Criteria
    SP 2.4   Perform Make, Buy, or Reuse Analyses
SG3   Implement the Product Design
    SP 3.1   Implement the Design
    SP 3.2   Develop Product Support Documentation

We have some wording changes in the practices sprinkled throughout this process area, but the concepts remain the same. For example, there is no longer a reference in a specific practice to "detailed" alternative solutions and criteria, and the entire practice describing evolving operational concepts is gone. SP 2.3 Design Interfaces has been combined with Establish Interface Descriptions from the continuous representation from the previous CMMI.

Technical Solution implies a complex product requiring a complicated approach. New items included tend to relate to the Systems Engineering and Hardware sides of the organization. A complex system requires more groups and more people. The Technical Data Package is used to coordinate these group efforts, as well as to satisfy procurement interests. The package includes such items as product architecture description, allocated requirements, process descriptions as they relate to products, interface requirements, materials requirements, fabrication and manufacturing requirements, verification requirements, conditions of use, operating and usage scenarios, and decision rationale. That's a lot more than what was recommended by the CMM for Software. In our experience, some of this information can be found directly in the Request for Proposal and the Statement of Work from the customer. Some of it can be found in process documentation within the organization, some of it can be found in the contract between the suppliers/servicers, some in the Requirements documentation, and some of it in the Design documentation. Maybe this package is just recommended as sort of a checklist to ensure that the supplier is delivering everything necessary to complete the product. However, if this documentation can be found elsewhere, is the CMMI requiring the project to collect this information and store it in one place? Is this redundant? Would it be better to include this practice in perhaps Product Integration?

Technical Solution also expects a formal approach to providing solutions—that is, to suggest alternatives and then study them. This approach is beneficial for large systems but probably overbearing for smaller ones. If an organization plans to undertake a new approach to an old problem, to use new technology, or to develop a totally new product, then this approach seems worthwhile. For example, we were once asked to do a feasibility study and alternatives analysis to determine whether using a specific programming language and database should be used to develop a warehouse system for a client. Because the client had already determined that this language would be used, as all of their software systems used this language and converting to something new would require a complete and costly overhaul of all of their code, the expected outcome was a resounding yes. This process area may promote a more balanced approach to deriving and evaluating alternatives, although there are always ways to get around the rules.

In this process area, when the model refers to processes, the model generally does not mean *process improvement*–type processes, but *design* processes. That is, the processes they are talking about in this PA focus on the technical steps necessary to produce the product. They do not focus on processes used to manage the project or manage the process for Technical Solution or the process used to improve processes in an organization. They are totally focused on engineering the product.

Peer reviews are mentioned in this process area. Technical Solution gives the reader some guidance on which products should be peer reviewed (SP 3.1 and SP 3.2 specifically discuss design and support documentation). The Organizational Process Definition process area also includes items and artifacts to be peer reviewed, including the Organization's Set of Standard Processes, life-cycle models, tailoring guidelines, measures, and the project's defined processes (also discussed in Integrated Project Management). We recommend that each PA be read for guidance on which products from each PA should be peer reviewed. For guidance on the steps to follow when planning and conducting a peer review, see the Verification process area.

Maintenance considerations for compatibility issues related to the future release of commercial off-the-shelf (COTS) products are broached here. Identify Candidate COT Products is a new subpractice used in developing alternative solutions (SP 1.1). Evolving operational scenarios previously found here has been moved to the Requirements Development PA. Unit testing is mentioned here. The operations concept is also used in this PA.

Things that most organizations tend to forget about this process area:

■ What is a Technical Data Package? Basically, it is everything you ever documented or even thought of documenting. At first, we thought devoting a specific practice to this idea was overkill. However, we do believe that it is a good practice to keep beneficial, important documentation readily available and readily accessible. Make sure, however, that members of your organization know what this term means. Also make sure that if the documentation is supposed to be useful, then it should actually be used.

■ Yes, you do need to investigate alternative solutions to satisfying the requirements. Yes, we know that your customer may have told you that you *must* do it his way or that you are contractually obligated to do it his way; but, you owe it to your customer to at least consider alternatives. The customer may not agree with them, in which case, you don't do them. But most customers do not know how to develop solutions and produce viable systems—that's why they hired you. And please document the alternatives you came up with, how they were derived, and why they were accepted or not accepted by your customer.

There are no generic practices that directly map to this process area.

Technical Solution includes determining how to satisfy the requirements via analysis of different alternatives and methods; creating operational scenarios; selecting solutions and follow-on designs; generating a technical data package that may include development methodologies, bills of material, life-cycle processes, product descriptions, requirements, conditions of use, rationale for decisions made, and verification criteria; defining and documenting detailed interface information; determining whether to make, buy, or reuse; and implementing the design and generating supporting documentation.

Product Integration

The purpose of Product Integration (PI) is to assemble the product from the product components, ensure that the product, as integrated, functions properly, and deliver the product.

Specific Goals and Practices for This Process Area:
SG1   Prepare for Product Integration
     SP 1.1   Determine Integration Sequence
     SP 1.2   Establish the Product Integration Environment
     SP 1.3   Establish Product Integration Procedures and Criteria
SG2   Ensure Interface Compatibility
     SP 2.1   Review Interface Descriptions for Completeness
     SP 2.2   Manage Interfaces
SG3   Assemble Product Components and Deliver the Product
     SP 3.1   Confirm Readiness of Product Components for Integration
     SP 3.2   Assemble Product Components
     SP 3.3   Evaluate Assembled Product Components
     SP 3.4   Package and Deliver the Product or Product Component

SP 3.1 Confirm Readiness of Product Components for Integration is expanded to "Confirm, prior to assembly, that each product component required to assemble the product has been properly identified, functions according to its description, and that the product component interfaces comply with the interface descriptions." The entire practice gives a little more information as to what is expected than the practice label gives to the reader.

This process area is the favorite of one of the authors of this book. Why? Because this is where the product comes together and you get to see the results of your work. It is also where you deliver the product, and that means you get paid.

This process area expects the project to demonstrate each step to the user. This activity should probably be done by demonstrating one or a few modules at a time, rather than the entire system. If a phased approach for development has been used, then this process area would expect to build a little, test a little, demonstrate a little, and deliver a little, module by module. Integration testing (as defined by and used by software engineers) is almost discussed here. The PA talks about testing integrated modules as an example, but it seems to mean tangible products that are being tested, not just software modules. This process area also overlaps with the Verification and Validation process areas, which may occur in parallel.

This process area is not release management. Releasing products is covered somewhat in Configuration Management, Supplier Agreement Management, and Technical Solution.

Things that most organizations tend to forget about this process area:

- The nightly build does not satisfy all of the Product Integration process area practices. Just running the automated build nightly does not constitute planning an integration sequence. You must analyze the problems that occur and see if any of the integrated components conflict with remaining components or modules or requirements. Also, the emphasis is on being proactive and identifying problems early, rather than being *reactive* to problems that pop up during the nightly run.

There are no generic practices that directly map to this process area.

Product Integration includes determining how to assemble the product and what the sequence of assembly should be; creating an operational environment in which to satisfactorily deploy the product; documenting procedures and criteria for integrating the product; ensuring adequate integration of interfaces; and delivering the product.

Verification

The purpose of Verification (VER) is to ensure that selected work products meet their specified requirements.

Specific Goals and Practices for This Process Area:

SG1 Prepare for Verification

SP 1.1 Select Work Products for Verification

SP 1.2 Establish the Verification Environment

SP 1.3 Establish Verification Procedures and Criteria

SG2 Perform Peer Reviews

SP 2.1 Prepare for Peer Reviews

SP 2.2 Conduct Peer Reviews

SP 2.3 Analyze Peer Review Data

SG3 Verify Selected Work Products

SP 3.1 Perform Verification

SP 3.2 Analyze Verification Results

"Identify corrective actions" has been removed from SP 3.2 to emphasize that corrective actions are now handled as part of the Project Monitoring and Control (PMC) PA. Verification ensures that the requirements have been met (you built it right). Validation ensures that the product meets its intended use (you built the right thing). For more information on Validation, please read the process area in the next section.

Peer reviews are included in this part of the text.

The Verification PA allows the usage of test setups and test simulators. Sometimes, the same test setups and simulators may be used for Validation as well—you just use them for different purposes, looking for different things. Acceptance testing is mentioned here. The overall term *testing* is used in this process area, but never truly spelled out. Some examples of testing are testing types—path coverage, stress, test case reuse, and so forth—but testing by software life-cycle phase, that is, unit–integration–system–acceptance–regression, is not covered.

Things that most organizations tend to forget about this process area:

- You don't need to test everything.
- You do need to test almost everything.
- You cannot test in quality.
- You must do both peer reviews and testing. You can peer review and test the same products or different products. Try to ensure total coverage of the product, by one means or the other, if possible.
- What is a peer? If you are peer reviewing code, a peer is a coder. If you are peer reviewing a project plan, a peer is another project manager. Do not mix people of different job status—for example, do not mix project managers in with coders. They are not peers. Likewise, the vice president of software engineering is also not a peer. The customer is not a peer. If someone wants to know what is going on during the project, have him attend a status meeting or a technical review or some other sort of demonstration.

- A peer review board is not one person. The strength of peer reviews is in getting several people together who know something about the product or work product being developed and having them discuss it. Synergy then develops during the review itself.
- Peer reviews are not the place to wax philosophic. Keep them short and sweet and focused on finding errors in the product, not on how to fix them, or how you would do it better.
- You must ensure that the errors found during a peer review are resolved. Another peer review may be necessary. Quality Assurance should also check to see that these problems have been resolved.

There are no generic practices that directly map to this process area.

Verification includes selecting which work products are to be verified; creating the environment necessary for verification of those products; documenting procedures and criteria for verification and then following those procedures; conducting peer reviews; and verifying the product and taking any corrective actions needed.

Validation

The purpose of Validation (VAL) is to demonstrate that a product or product component fulfills its intended use when placed in its intended environment.

Specific Goals and Practices for This Process Area:
SG1   Prepare for Validation
    SP 1.1   Select Products for Validation
    SP 1.2   Establish the Validation Environment
    SP 1.3   Establish Validation Procedures and Criteria
SG2   Validate Product or Product Components
    SP 2.1   Perform Validation
    SP 2.2   Analyze Validation Results

SP 2.2 no longer contains the words "identify issues." Notes were added to emphasize that these activities are performed incrementally and involved relevant stakeholders. Validation includes the same strategies as for Verification, except this time we create what is necessary to *validate* the product, not verify the requirements were satisfied. Validation involves creating an environment as close as possible to the environment in which the product will be used in order to perform final testing of the product. However, this is not always a logical, practical thing to do. An example follows. When one of the authors of this book was working as a subcontractor on a defense contract, we were required, as part of the contract, to build the product and test the product in the same environment as it would be used. Well, the system under development was only going to be used by six people at any given time, although it could be used by up to two hundred simultaneous users during peak loads. So the powers-that-be overseeing the contract decided that, if only six people were going to use the system at any given time, then only six personal computers would be necessary. The project managers had determined that to meet the time constraints for the project (a large, database-driven claims processing system), fifteen programmers, three database administrators, five test personnel, and one database manager were needed. That adds up to needing at least twenty-four personal computers. We were allowed six. The solution was to work shift-work and share the computers. This contract was canceled after three years and no usable code was produced.

Are we saying it is a bad practice to create similar environments? No, not at all. It is very worthwhile to test products in their ultimate environment and to design products for their ultimate use. We are in favor of this. Just remember that it can get expensive and complicated. Plan ahead and plan wisely.

Because this PA can also require simulators to be built, one might want to consider the unique training requirements necessary to build the intended-use environment.

Things that most organizations tend to forget about this process area:

- Most of the issues discussed in Verification apply here. You don't need to test everything. You do need to test almost everything. You cannot test in quality.
- Validation is not performed at the end of the project. It can be performed throughout the development life cycle, depending on the product being produced.
- Make sure you plan in detail any tests to be performed by the users or in the user environment.
- If you are simulating the user environment, make sure it truly replicates the actual environment. This will require planning and testing of the environment itself.
- If you are developing a Web-based system using the Web that your users will use, then you may have satisfied Validation without knowing about it. Basically, if you are developing and testing the system using the same resources and procedures that the users will use (or are using), you may have this PA covered.

There are no general practices that directly map to this process area.

Validation asks: are you building the right product? It includes selecting products and approaches for validating products, generating the validation environment, documenting validation criteria and procedures; conducting the validation activities; and analyzing the results and any issues that arise from conducting the validation process.

Organizational Process Focus

The purpose of Organizational Process Focus (OPF) is to plan, implement, and deploy organizational process improvements based on a thorough understanding of the current strengths and weaknesses of the organization's processes and process assets.

Specific Goals and Practices for This Process Area:

SG1   Determine Process Improvement Opportunities
    SP 1.1   Establish Organizational Process Needs
    SP 1.2   Appraise the Organization's Processes
    SP 1.3   Identify the Organization's Process Improvements
SG2   Plan and Implement Process Improvements
    SP 2.1   Establish Process Action Plans
    SP 2.2   Implement Process Action Plans
SG3   Deploy Organizational Process Assets and Incorporate Lessons Learned
    SP 3.1   Deploy Organizational Process Assets
    SP 3.2   Deploy Standard Processes
    SP 3.3   Monitor Implementation
    SP 3.4   Incorporate Process-Related Experiences into the Organizational Process Assets

The wording of the Purpose statement has changed slightly. The new wording emphasizes that improvements to processes will be planned and incorporated into the organization based on an understanding of the strengths and weaknesses of organizational assets, discovered through a structured appraisal process. This wording basically tells the reader how to perform this process area; that is, that you must plan the activities and must understand what your strengths and weaknesses are. While this might sound facile or obvious, it is not. It is a common mistake for most organizations just starting process improvement to just jump into the effort. There is no understanding of where the organization currently is, what they have that is useful and not useful, what really constitutes a strength or weakness in their organization, and how to discover the answers. In ensuing chapters, we explain how to structure your process improvement initiative, beginning with a detailed evaluation of how your organization really works. All of these expected activities are neatly summed up in the Purpose statement of this PA.

Incorporating improvements that were made to organizational processes into project processes at the start of the project is a new focus. Piloting processes is mentioned here. Candidate process improvements and process improvement proposals are mentioned here in the subpractices. Specific Goal 3 has been added to emphasize actual implementation and tracking of processes and incorporating Lessons Learned.

OPF introduces who should be doing process improvement and what process improvement is. The Engineering Process Group (EPG) is mentioned here—one of the few groups still retained in the model. The EPG is the group responsible for planning process improvement and implementing the plans. Members may or may not be involved in any initial appraisals comparing their organization to what is included in the CMMI. The process area essentially describes how to initiate, diagnose, evaluate, act, and learn from process improvement in an organization. Those of you familiar with the IDEAL model will recognize the use of this acronym for the layout of the process area.

One recommendation we have in this area concerns the formation of the EPG. Some organizations have decided to form a separate EPG for each discipline—that is, one EPG for Systems Engineering, one for Software Engineering, and one for IPPD. Those organizations have quickly found that this separation of duties based on job defeats the purpose of the EPG. The purpose of the EPG is to define an integrated process for process improvement and to implement this process seamlessly throughout the entire organization. By forming separate groups, feedback and communication are not really there. We recommend that you form one EPG that has representatives from the various areas and disciplines. How big should it be? We have found that the optimum number of full-time, fully engaged people on this type of team should be about ten. Any more and decision making becomes too lengthy and obfuscated. Too few and there are not enough people to do the work.

Yes, you can have levels of EPGs, just like there could be levels of Software EPGs when using the Software CMM. Just don't get too hierarchical, and too bureaucratic. This group must do real work in the process improvement area.

For more information, please see Chapter 12, "People, Roles, and Responsibilities."

Things that most organizations tend to forget about this process area:

■ This PA probably has the most "churn" in the beginning of any process improvement effort. That is because the people who staff it (the EPG) are as unfamiliar with process improvement as everyone else in the organization. If you decide to staff this group with personnel who have supposedly already "done" process improvement somewhere else, make sure they are flexible. Just because they did it one way at another organization, does not mean that way will work for you. Please read our Chapter 12 concerning people, roles, and responsibilities for more hints on how to set up an effective EPG.

■ Don't try to change everything at once. Do a little at a time.

■ After one or two years on the EPG, rotate some of the members out! You need new blood, new ways of thinking, new ways of meeting new challenges. Plus, the members of the EPG are more likely to create and implement usable processes if they must return to their previous jobs and follow those processes. Also, we have noticed that once an EPG struggles with creating and implementing processes, they are reluctant to make changes to them.

The generic practice that most closely maps to this process area is GP 3.2 Collect Improvement Information (most directly mapping to SP 3.4 Incorporate Process-Related Experiences into the Organizational Process Assets).

Organizational Process Focus includes establishing a fundamental understanding of what process is and why it is important to an organization; assessing current processes in the organization and identifying areas in need of improvement; creating and following action plans for improvement; determining how to institute process improvement in the organization and what plans and documentation will be needed; and reviewing the process improvement effort itself and instituting improvements in this area.

Organizational Process Definition + IPPD

The purpose of Organizational Process Definition (OPD) is to establish and maintain a usable set of organizational process assets and work environment standards.

For IPPD: Organizational Process Definition + IPPD also covers the establishment of organizational rules and guidelines that enable conducting work using integrated teams.

Specific Goals and Practices for This Process Area:
SG1 Establish Organizational Process Assets
    SP 1.1 Establish Standard Processes
    SP 1.2 Establish Life Cycle Model Descriptions
    SP 1.3 Establish Tailoring Criteria and Guidelines
    SP 1.4 Establish the Organization's Measurement Repository
    SP 1.5 Establish the Organization's Process Asset Library
    SP 1.6 Establish Work Environment Standards
IPPD Addition:
SG2 Enable IPPD Management
    SP 2.1 Establish Empowerment Mechanisms
    SP 2.2 Establish Rules and Guidelines for Integrated Teams
    SP 2.3 Balance Team and Home Organization Responsibilities

There were significant changes made to this PA. The most noticeable is the addition of IPPD concepts. IPPD stands for Integrated Product and Process Development. IPPD builds systems by including teams and input from as many relevant stakeholders as possible in order to get as much relevant information as possible to develop a product that works for everyone who will use it. This is a very formal, systematic approach toward development by teams of subject matter experts in various subjects, and includes group vision statements, charters, etc. This approach is commonly used in DOD endeavors. So, if you are not using this approach, *you don't have to*. It is optional. If you would like to try this approach, remember that it is formal and structured—not just getting everyone sitting around a table (when convenient to their other work tasks and schedules) and philosophizing about how to develop a system.

SP 1.6 was added to concentrate on work environment standards, which matches the additional phrase at the end of the Purpose statement. Specific Goal 2 is an optional goal that was added as the inclusion of IPPD to this area. The practices under Specific Goal 1 include the previous practices from the previous version of the CMMI for this PA.

So, what are work environment standards? Examples provided include procedures for work environment safety and security, procedures for how to operate in the work environment, standards for common tool usage, standardization of hardware and software for workstations. While this is a new practice, it is something that most organizations either already have (but may not be documented) or struggle with. So, organizations using the previous CMMI will need to do a little work here.

The PA is Organizational Process Definition because this is where you define and document your organizational processes. No big surprises there. The process asset library is commonly referred to as the PAL.

The measurement repository discussed here is different from what is mentioned in Measurement and Analysis at Level 2. The measurement repository at Level 2 is primarily concerned with project-level data stored in project-level repositories. At Level 3, the information from the projects is now collected and stored at an organizational level, and combined and integrated into organizational metrics that are meaningful to the organization as a whole. For example, at Level 2, the repository may contain when the Requirements phase began and when it ended; when the Design phase began and when it ended; when Construction began and when it ended; when Testing began and when it ended; and when Implementation began. The repository may also contain defects found in testing. Each project has a repository, and each project collects these data to run their own projects. At Level 3, these metrics are bubbled up from the projects and studied cumulatively to try to predict trends across the projects. For example, if one project was late getting out of the Testing phase because many errors were found, did that project skimp on the Requirements phase? Is there a correlation? If all of the project data are studied from all of the projects, and all of the projects except one had the same problem, what is it about that one project that made it different? Was it better? Can we devise a "standard" length of time to be set for requirements to improve functioning downstream (like in the Test phase)?

Once an organizational-level repository has been built (based on historical, project-level data from the past) any project-level repository can also use the organizational-level repository as its foundation for building or updating its own (project) repository. This gives the project manager an idea of how to plan his project, where the bottlenecks commonly occur (or occurred in the past), and how long to schedule activities.

Tailoring is also discussed here. The organization must document its criteria for when tailoring of the organization's processes can be done by a project and what those tailoring guidelines and rules are. However, if you find that you are tailoring often, and tailoring more information from the OSSP, can you really state that you have a standard organizational process? We don't think so. Doesn't sound very standard to us.

Things that most organizations tend to forget about this process area:

■ How to document processes that can be used. Individuals create processes that are either too complex to properly implement or too high-level to properly implement. You will need to rewrite, replan, and repilot your processes and procedures.

■ There are differences between the types of documentation you will need to produce (see our chapters on process documentation—Chapters 13, 14, and 15).

■ IPPD is optional. If you are just starting out in process improvement and don't currently use formally integrated teams (as defined by the CMMI), we suggest that you not try to institute this concept. You will already have your hands full just trying to set up a basic process improvement team focusing on one process area.

Although IPPD is optional, and requires a significant investment in time and resources and culture change for some organizations, reading the IPPD information can benefit anyone who must perform on or manage any type of team. It is about "people" issues—decision making, commitment, prioritizing (and getting credit for) work assignments, and so forth. Because most of us work on some type of team nowadays, the guidelines documented here can prove useful.

The generic practice that most closely matches this process area is GP 3.1 Establish a Defined Process. Other generic practices that can trace guidance back to this process area include GP 3.2 Collect Improvement Information.

Organizational Process Definition includes generating the Organization's Set of Standard Processes (OSSP); describing various life cycles approved for use; documenting tailoring criteria and guidelines; and creating and maintaining the measurement repository and process asset library.

Organizational Training

The purpose of Organizational Training (OT) is to develop the skills and knowledge of people so they can perform their roles effectively and efficiently.

Specific Goals and Practices for This Process Area:

SG1 Establish an Organizational Training Capability
   SP 1.1 Establish the Strategic Training Needs
   SP 1.2 Determine Which Training Needs Are the Responsibility of the Organization
   SP 1.3 Establish an Organizational Training Tactical Plan
   SP 1.4 Establish Training Capability
SG2 Provide Necessary Training
   SP 2.1 Deliver Training
   SP 2.2 Establish Training Records
   SP 2.3 Assess Training Effectiveness

Not much new here. There are additional subpractices that emphasize safety and security training, and training for IPPD efforts.

This PA expects a Strategic Training Plan coming from the OSSP, as well as business plans, process improvement plans, defined skill sets of existing groups, missing skill sets of existing groups, skill sets needed for any nonexistent groups necessary to be formed, mission statements, and vision statements. And all of these things are tied into training plans. That's a lot of documentation that many smaller organizations do not have and do not need. Small organizations tend to operate at the tactical planning level and not at the strategic level. This PA expects a Strategic Plan that leads to a Tactical Plan.

Organizational-level training plans bubble up from project-level training plans and needs. Organizations also need to evaluate the effectiveness of the training received. That does not necessarily mean that the class fills out an evaluation after the class has been received. It means that the organization must track the value of the training it has received. Is what you learned what you needed to learn to do the job?

This process area is not about knowledge management. While you may define core competencies and certifications necessary, the concepts are not that similar. For a clearer discussion of knowledge management, please review the People CMM, which gives much more guidance.

Things that most organizations tend to forget about this process area:

■ A strategic vision is usually more than one year. So, strategic plans should include at least a *vision* of what the Training Organization or training vision should be in the future, with schedules and budgets for the coming year.

■ Tactical Plans may be included as part of Project Planning in the Project Plan. That is, if the project needs to plan for training, it will include the schedules and budget for that training in the Project Plan.

■ Some organizations have a two- to five-year strategic plan, which is more of a vision than a plan; then, a tactical plan for the coming year, which focuses on specific classes to be held, when, and how much they will cost; and then,

the Project Plan (or Project Training Plan) that uses the strategic and tactical plans as input to create their training plan based on the needs of the project.
■ It doesn't matter what you call these plans, as long as this information is contained clearly and completely somewhere. We would hope that you would document this stuff in a straightforward, easily accessible manner.

The generic practice that most closely matches this process area from an organizational point of view is GP 2.5 Train People. GP 2.2 Plan the Process matches this process area from a project perspective.

Organizational Training includes determining the strategic training needs of the organization and how to achieve them; procuring or delivering the training; and tracking its effectiveness.

Integrated Project Management + IPPD

The purpose of Integrated Project Management (IPM) is to establish and manage the project and the involvement of the relevant stakeholders according to an integrated and defined process that is tailored from the organization's set of standard processes.

For IPPD: Integrated Project Management + IPPD also covers the establishment of a shared vision for the project and the establishment of integrated teams that will carry out the objectives of the project.

Specific Goals and Practices for This Process Area:
SG1   Use the Project's Defined Process
   SP 1.1   Establish the Project's Defined Process
   SP 1.2   Use Organizational Process Assets for Planning Project Activities
   SP 1.3   Establish the Project's Work Environment
   SP 1.4   Integrate Plans
   SP 1.5   Manage the Project Using the Integrated Plans
   SP 1.6   Contribute to the Organizational Process Assets
SG2   Coordinate and Collaborate with Relevant Stakeholders
   SP 2.1   Manage Stakeholder Involvement
   SP 2.2   Manage Dependencies
   SP 2.3   Resolve Coordination Issues
IPPD Addition:
SG3   Apply IPPD Principles
   SP 3.1   Establish the Project's Shared Vision
   SP 3.2   Establish the Integrated Team Structure
   SP 3.3   Allocate Requirements to Integrated Teams
   SP 3.4   Establish Integrated Teams
   SP 3.5   Ensure Collaboration among Interfacing Teams

This process area has changed mainly by rewording and combining practices. The concepts remain the same. IPPD is optional and is reflected in the third goal (reduced from two goals in the previous CMMI). SP 1.3 includes the addition of work environment standards (discussed earlier in Organizational Process Definition + IPPD). There is also an emphasis on developing a project-level defined process for any new project at the start of the project and throughout its life.

The policies written for this process area should include when to include IPPD activities and when not.

This PA is supposed to be the evolution of Project Planning, and Project Monitoring and Control from Level 2, plus more sophistication for Level 3. That means that this PA involves more rigorous techniques for planning and monitoring projects within the organization. In this PA, each project reviews the OSSP and tailors the OSSP to fit a project's specific needs. The result is called the project's defined process, and yes, it must be documented. This process is then used to help build the project plan.

The difference between the standard processes, tailoring guidelines, and procedures mentioned in Organizational Process Definition (OPD) and here in Integrated Project Management (IPM) is that the documentation is created and stored in OPD and used in IPM on the projects.

The difference between management at Level 2 and at Level 3 is that Level 3 uses a set of organizational plans, processes, and assets (templates, checklists) based on best practices and lessons learned. The measurement repository is used for generating achievable estimates, based on past performance. The repository of project and organizational information discussed in this PA becomes the basis of the performance baselines at Level 4.

Risk is not really discussed much here, at least not as much as in the CMM for Software. This PA offers guidance as to when incorporate risk strategies and planning into project management, but the real details are included in the Risk Management process area.

SG1 Use the Project's Defined Process makes this process a required element. Previous definitions of process in the CMMI were simply informative or expected as part of the OSSP.

IPPD focuses on establishing and using a shared vision of what the project is to accomplish by way of using the IPPD team structure (Integrated Product Teams [IPTs]). The tips contained in the margins contain information on team interactions and why the practice was included in the PA.

Things that most organizations tend to forget about this process area:

■ The Project's Defined Process (PDP). This process is actually one or more documents that describe how the project functions in a step-by-step manner (usually either by process area or by life-cycle phase). It uses the OSSP as input and tailors the OSSP to fit the project. In some cases, especially when the organization is small and nondiverse, the OSSP can be used as the PDP, as appropriate.

The generic practice that most closely matches this process area is GP 3.1 Establish a Defined Process. Other generic practices that can trace guidance back to this process area include GP 2.7 Identify and Involve Relevant Stakeholders and GP 3.2 Collect Improvement Information.

Integrated Project Management includes defining a process or processes at the project-level when necessary that are tailored from the organizational process(es); using the processes and documentation developed from the organization; integrating all plans (including plans for each process area as well as project management plans) with the project's defined process; managing the project according to the plan; incorporating measurements, documentation, and improvements into the project or organizational-level repositories and processes; ensuring stakeholder involvement; tracking critical dependencies; and resolving issues. For Integrated Project Management + IPPD, defining a shared vision of the project among all involved parties; determining the structure of the integrated team; establishing the team; and ensuring that the team has all relevant documentation and information needed to guide it in understanding the project and developing the product are necessary.

Risk Management

The purpose of Risk Management (RSKM) is to identify potential problems before they occur so that risk-handling activities can be planned and invoked as needed across the life of the product or project to mitigate adverse impacts on achieving objectives.

Specific Goals and Practices for This Process Area:
SG1   Prepare for Risk Management
    SP 1.1   Determine Risk Sources and Categories
    SP 1.2   Define Risk Parameters
    SP 1.3   Establish a Risk Management Strategy
SG2   Identify and Analyze Risks
    SP 2.1   Identify Risks
    SP 2.2   Evaluate, Categorize, and Prioritize Risks
SG3   Mitigate Risks
    SP 3.1   Develop Risk Mitigation Plans
    SP 3.2   Implement Risk Mitigation Plans

Some sort of risk identification and control is touched upon in almost all of the process areas. In Project Planning and Project Monitoring and Control, risks are identified and strategies for handling the risks are introduced. Evaluating project risks and the impacts of probable risks are addressed. The Risk Management process area is much more proactive, involving identification of risk parameters, formal strategies for handling risks, preparing risk mitigation plans, and structured risk assessments. Technical Solution discussed risk in terms of risks involved in selecting alternative solutions and reducing risks in make–buy–reuse decisions. The Decision Analysis and Resolution process area discusses evaluation processes used to reduce risks made in making decisions and analyzing alternatives. Although preparing for risks can be considered an organizational-level task, mitigating risks is usually the responsibility of the project.

Periodic and event-driven reviews should occur on the project to summarize the most critical risks that may occur. Make sure you review risks during periodic reviews. Why? Because discussing risks only during an "event" (usually a bad thing like the risk has already happened and now what do we do about it) only gives exposure to your project when problems are about to occur. Plus, risk probability changes over time and over the course of the project. The risk culture of senior management in a Level 1 organization is simply, "Don't tell me. I don't want to know. Only tell me that things are fine." The risk culture in a Level 3 and above organization is more proactive. They want to hear what might happen and what to do about it.

Disaster Recovery may be included as part of an organization's risk management culture and is included in a subpractice. Considering the risks associated with Continuity of Operations has also been added. A risk repository can be built at the organization level that contains the risks that most frequently were realized on projects and their solutions. This repository can help project managers avoid these known risks on their projects.

Things that most organizations tend to forget about this process area:

■ This PA is the big time of risk management. This PA is not just about listing risks and reviewing them at project meetings. It is about studying the risks and measuring their impact and probability on project activities. For example, an illustration of increased maturity and sophistication required for your organization between Level 2 risk management and Level 3 risk management is taken from the old CMM for Software. In the old CMM, the measures taken for each identified software risk included "the realized adverse impact compared to the estimated loss; and the number and magnitude of unanticipated major adverse impacts to the software project, tracked over time." Sounds like more than just sitting around in a project meeting reviewing a risk list.
■ The main focus of this PA is on project risks. However, the same concepts can be applied to organizational risks.

There are no generic practices that directly map to this process area.

Risk Management includes identifying and categorizing risks; generating a risk management strategy; analyzing risks; documenting risk mitigation plans; mitigating risks; and monitoring the risk effort.

Decision Analysis and Resolution

The purpose of Decision Analysis and Resolution (DAR) is to analyze possible decisions using a formal evaluation process that evaluates identified alternatives against established criteria.

Specific Goals and Practices for This Process Area:
SG1 Evaluate Alternatives
    SP 1.1   Establish Guidelines for Decision Analysis
    SP 1.2   Establish Evaluation Criteria
    SP 1.3   Identify Alternative Solutions
    SP 1.4   Select Evaluation Methods
    SP 1.5   Evaluate Alternatives
    SP 1.6   Select Solutions

The Purpose statement has changed by replacing the words "using a structured approach" with "using a formal evaluation process." This evaluation process is further explained by the Introductory Notes under the Purpose statement and lists the steps necessary to follow as part of the approach. Some organizations, in response to this PA, have stated that they do not need a formal mechanism to make decisions; nor do they need formal guidelines for choosing alternatives. Appraisal teams must ensure that these mechanisms are used, which can also prove difficult. This area could prove useful in the vendor selection process. The choice of which alternative or platform or architecture or language or new technology overlaps somewhat with Technical Solution. The type of testing mentioned here concerns testing the possible solution approaches.

Why is this process area needed? The rationale is to provide managers and analysts with a mechanism to make decisions. This mechanism requires a formal approach to determine which issues need the formal approach of DAR and what that mechanism should be. However, if you are having trouble making a decision, it seems this PA simply gives you more things to consider when making a decision, which increases the difficulty of making that decision, so that no decision ends up being made or the decision may be delayed. It's like saying, "You need to make a decision about which decision to make. Now, decide how to make the decision for the decision, and then make the decision." Well, if you could make a decision in the first place, don't you think you would have? And does this area really help you do that? We think not. Another way to look at this PA is as follows: You ask your boss for a new server. If he agrees, he just says yes, go get one. If not, he makes you follow the guidelines in this PA, hoping you will just give up and go away.

Well, that was our cynical response to the inclusion of this PA in the previous CMMI version. We have been quite happily surprised at the acceptance among our clients of this PA. They really like it and appreciate the guidance given. They also tend to use it more frequently as part of choosing alternatives in Technical Solution. There is still some resistance to this PA when we have tried to introduce the basic concepts into lower-maturity organizations that are just beginning the process improvement journey.

Things that most organizations tend to forget about this process area:

■ You must define when this PA should be used. Otherwise, some projects will use it for every decision, and some projects will not use it at all.
■ You must create and document "established criteria." These criteria are used to judge proposed alternatives. Your criteria may already have been established as part of a technical or contractual requirement. However, the criteria for allowing or disallowing an alternative may change, depending on changes to the project involved with budget, personnel, schedule, safety, and other unanticipated factors. Document all changes to the criteria, why the change was made, who initiated the change, and the impact and results of the change.

There are no generic practices that directly map to this process area.

Decision Analysis and Resolution includes determining which decisions will be part of a formal decision-making evaluation process; creating evaluation criteria; determining the types of evaluation methods to use; and determining alternative solutions.

Summary

Level 3 takes the best practices and lessons learned from Level 2 and integrates them at the organizational level. Level 3 requires more sophistication than Level 2. This sophistication is not achieved overnight—it is the result of maturing in your understanding of what the organization does, what it should do, what it can become capable of doing, and why it should do these things. Integrated Project Management may be considered the evolution of Project Planning and Project Monitoring and Control from Level 2. Risk Management can be considered the evolution of risk considerations in Project Planning and Project Monitoring and Control from Level 2 to Level 3.

Level 3 has 11 PAs—that is down from the 14 PAs in the previous version of the CMMI (thank you very much!); but it is still a lot of areas to implement in one level.

Level 3 is divided into four basic process categories:

- Engineering PAs: Requirements Development, Technical Solution, Product Integration, Verification, and Validation
- Process Management PAs: Organization Process Focus, Organization Process Definition, and Organizational Training
- Project Management PAs: Integrated Project Management and Risk Management
- Support PAs: Decision Analysis and Resolution

Redundancies? Of course. Two that come to mind are Generic Practice 3.1 Establish a Defined Process that overlaps with Organizational Process Definition, and Generic Practice 3.2 Collect Improvement Information that overlaps with Organizational Process Focus.

One important concept must be discussed. The overview of Maturity Level 3 in the staged representation of the CMMI states, "Another critical distinction is that at maturity level 3, processes are typically described in more detail and more rigorously than at maturity level 2." We feel this sentence can lead to great misunderstandings and ultimate failure of your process improvement effort if interpreted incorrectly. Processes should always be defined at the level of detail necessary to be followed consistently. Procedures written can document how to perform the processes in more detail. But some organizations have decided, based on this sentence in the CMMI, that processes do not have to be written until Level 3. That is not correct! We believe that what the authors of the CMMI are trying to say is that it is just natural that, as your organization matures and you become more adept at writing, you will get better at writing better process documentation. The generic practices support the view that processes are required at Level 2. Generic Practice 2.2 Plan the Process specifically states that "establishing a plan includes documenting the plan and providing a process description … The plan for performing the process typically includes the following … Process Description …" Generic Practice 2.3 Provide Resources describes ensuring that resources necessary to perform the process as described by the plan are available. The remaining generic practices at Level 2 also support performing the process. In order to perform the process, it must have been written. Generic Practice 3.1 Establish a Defined Process (a Level 3 generic practice) relates to tailoring a project-specific process from an organizational-level standard process; not that this is the level where process documentation is written.

Chapter 7

Understanding Maturity Level 4: Quantitatively Managed

This chapter is designed to help the reader understand the basic tenets of Maturity Level 4 in the staged representation of the CMMI. However, because this chapter consists of summaries of the process areas, anyone wishing to get a better idea of the model, no matter which representation is to be used, can benefit from this chapter. Once again, we are not attempting to teach the CMMI. We simply offer a condensed version of the various areas and key points to consider.

Moving from Level 3 to Level 4

Level 4 is all about numbers. The projects are managed "by the numbers." Organizational decisions are made "by the numbers." Processes, services, product quality are all measured "by the numbers." At Level 4, the organization has achieved all of the goals of Levels 2 and 3. Processes, although *qualitatively* stable and predictable at Level 3, can be proved to be *quantitatively* stable and predictable at Level 4. The major difference between Level 4 and the next level, Level 5, is that Level 4 analyzes the data collected, determines *special* causes of variation from the norm, and supports quantitative management and control. You do this to make your processes predictable. Level 5 addresses *common* causes of variation. So, for Level 4, an organization needs data that are stable and consistent. The major preoccupation of assessors when reviewing Level 4 is, "Did this organization mix apples and oranges? Are the data really accurate? Did this organization collect the right data and did they collect the data right?" To get "good" data, an organization usually has to collect data for several years, or at least through several projects and several life cycles of the projects. And when you first begin collecting data, they will not be consistent data.

Measurement data are collected beginning with Level 2 in the staged representation, and in most organizations, actually begin being collected at Level 1. The problem is the data are not clean and consistent because the processes used on the projects (where the data are collected and used) are not yet stable and consistent. Data in and of themselves are not magical. They simply reflect what is going on in the projects. The point is, an organization cannot go to Level 4 overnight, and the focus is on the data.

What problems do we see in organizations when they decide to move from Level 3 to Level 4? At Level 3, measures are collected and preliminary thresholds are established, usually relating to size and effort. If the thresholds are exceeded, some sort of corrective action is undertaken. At Level 4, the control limits are based on years of historical data and trends analyses done on those data. More data are collected, and, therefore, more limits are established, monitored, and refined as necessary. At Level 3, the data may be somewhat inconsistent and "dirty." Although in a perfect world we would like to see "clean" data at Level 3, the focus on Level 3 is on organizational process, not necessarily on stabilized, normalized, statistically accurate data—which is exactly what Level 4 expects. One problem that we see in some organizations that have barely met the criteria for Level 3 is that the processes are not always followed consistently across the organization. Now, one writer of this book has stated that in that case, this organization is not Level 3 and should never have been awarded Level 3. The other writer of this book, after many arguments and nights spent sleeping on the couch which he definitely deserved for having such a stupid opinion, finally agreed, with the following caveat: it all depends on what the organization does to enforce consistency, how important the consistency issue was to the appraisal team, what type of appraisal was done to award the level, and who was on the team. So those of you new to process improvement, expecting black-and-white answers, and no wiggle room in interpreting, implementing, and assessing this effort, are in for a letdown. Please review the Appendix B, "Myths and Legends of the CMMI," and Chapter 20, "Appraisals Using the CMMI," for more information.

At Level 3, we have also seen that tailoring the organizational process can get out of hand. That is, there is so much tailoring of the process, that it cannot be judged to be a "standard" process. The measurement culture at Level 3 also is not often well understood. People may not really understand why they are collecting the metrics they collect—only that they are "required" by the model, so that's why they are collected. The metrics may not be studied for consistency and clarity, or may not be closely analyzed to determine *why* the numbers are inconsistent, and whether that represents a potential problem or not. Because the numbers can be "wild," management decisions made using the numbers can be pretty much off base. And with inconsistent data, you really can't compare the performance of several projects against one another to truly analyze trends.

At Level 4, managers and analysts must use the data, and apply statistical and quantitative techniques to help monitor activities, identify potential problems, and note areas that need attention. The instructions for the CMM for Software at Level 4 said basically keep it simple. The measurements here in the CMMI, and suggested techniques, are very sophisticated and are more difficult to implement.

Level 4 is about making processes stable and predictable. Level 5 is about making improvements to stable processes to improve the functioning of your organization.

Why do all this measurement stuff? Because it supports a proactive approach toward managing projects.

There are two process areas (PAs) for Level 4. They are:

■ Organizational Process Performance
■ Quantitative Project Management

Note that there are no additions to the list of generic goals at Level 4 from Level 3. What makes this maturity level different are the two process areas. The generic goals are listed below. We use the abbreviations GG for generic goal and GP for generic practice.

GG2   Institutionalize a Managed Process
    GP 2.1   Establish an Organizational Policy
    GP 2.2   Plan the Process
    GP 2.3   Provide Resources
    GP 2.4   Assign Responsibility
    GP 2.5   Train People
    GP 2.6   Manage Configurations
    GP 2.7   Identify and Involve Relevant Stakeholders
    GP 2.8   Monitor and Control the Process
    GP 2.9   Objectively Evaluate Adherence
    GP 2.10   Review Status with Higher-Level Management
GG3   Institutionalize a Defined Process
    GP 3.1   Establish a Defined Process
    GP 3.2   Collect Improvement Information

To satisfy the goals for Level 4, the goals for Levels 2 and 3 must be satisfied as well. This mandate holds true for both the specific goals (listed in each process area below) and the generic goals listed above.

For the continuous approach, the generic goals and generic practices for each capability level that must be satisfied for each selected process area are:

Capability Level 1:
    GG1   Achieve Specific Goals
        GP 1.1   Perform Specific Practices
Capability Level 2:
    GG2   Institutionalize a Managed Process
        GP 2.1   Establish an Organizational Policy
        GP 2.2   Plan the Process
        GP 2.3   Provide Resources
        GP 2.4   Assign Responsibility
        GP 2.5   Train People
        GP 2.6   Manage Configurations
        GP 2.7   Identify and Involve Relevant Stakeholders
        GP 2.8   Monitor and Control the Process
        GP 2.9   Objectively Evaluate Adherence
        GP 2.10 Review Status with Higher-Level Management
Capability Level 3:
    GG3   Institutionalize a Defined Process
        GP 3.1   Establish a Defined Process
        GP 3.2   Collect Improvement Information
Capability Level 4:
    GG4   Institutionalize a Quantitatively Managed Process
        GP 4.1   Establish Quantitative Objectives for the Process
        GP 4.2   Stabilize Subprocess Performance
Capability Level 5:
    GG5   Institutionalize an Optimizing Process
        GP 5.1   Ensure Continuous Process Improvement
        GP 5.2   Correct Root Causes of Problems

Each capability level builds on the previous level. So, in order to be Capability Level 5, the organization must satisfy the specific practices for the selected process area (Capability Level 1), plus the generic practices for Capability Levels 2, 3, 4, and 5.

The following pages discuss each process area for Level 4. We use the abbreviations SG for specific goal and SP for corresponding specific practices.

The Process Areas for Maturity Level 4: Quantitatively Managed

Organizational Process Performance

The purpose of Organizational Process Performance (OPP) is to establish and maintain a quantitative understanding of the performance of the Organization's Set of Standard Processes (OSSP) in support of quality and process–performance objectives, and to provide the process–performance data, baselines, and models to quantitatively manage the organization's projects.

> Specific Goals and Practices for This Process Area:
> SG1 Establish Performance Baselines and Models
> > SP 1.1 Select Processes
> > SP 1.2 Establish Process–performance Measures
> > SP 1.3 Establish Quality and Process–performance Objectives
> > SP 1.4 Establish Process–performance Baselines
> > SP 1.5 Establish Process–performance Models

SP 1.1 has changed wording. The complete practice now reads, "Select the processes or subprocesses (not process elements) in the organization's set of standard processes that are to be included in the organization's process performance analysis." This process area includes measurements for both process and product. Additionally, service has also been specifically presented as an area appropriate for measurement (remember, the CMMI believes that "service" can be part of the "product"). This process area combines these measures to determine both the quality of the process and the product in quantitative terms.

Process performance baselines and process performance models are now included in goals for this process area and not just as suggested best practices. A *process performance baseline* (PPB) documents the historical results achieved by following a process. A PPB is used as a benchmark for comparing actual process performance against expected process performance. A *process performance model* (PPM) describes the relationships among attributes (for example, defects) of a process and its work products. A PPM is used to estimate or predict a critical value that cannot be measured until later in the project's life—for example, predicting the number of delivered defects throughout the life cycle. More information on PPBs and PPMs can be found in Chapter 19, "A High Maturity Perspective."

Remember, don't wait until Level 4 to focus on measurements and to start collecting measures—that's way too late. The Measurement and Analysis process area resides at Level 2, so if you are attempting to achieve a Level 2 maturity level rating, this is probably not a process area to tailor out. And if you are using the continuous representation, which supposedly allows you to select which process areas to use, Measurement and Analysis should also be selected.

At Level 2, measures are collected, stored in a database per project, bubble up to an organizational database in Level 3, are reviewed for consistency and accuracy at Level 3, and then, at Level 4, have statistically-based controls applied to them. What to put under statistical control depends on where the problems are in your organization, and which processes and measures will add value to your management techniques. This statement implies that not all processes must be put under statistical control. But, we suggest that for Level 4, and for this process area in particular, the OSSP must be understood from a statistical point of view.

The most common measurements we see in use for this process area are size, effort, cost, schedule, and product defect density. The measurements for these data points are usually displayed in ranges and not by absolute points. Subsets of measures can be generated to be applied based on domains, new development versus maintenance, and type of customer. The CMMI has added some examples of candidate subprocesses to select for performance measurement and modeling.

Performance-related measurements can include schedule variance (lateness), effort variance, and unplanned tasks. Quality-related measurements may include rework and defects. These defects can be collected during all life-cycle phases, including requirements inspections, design inspections, code inspections, unit testing, integration testing, and system testing. Process-related measures that we commonly see can be found by reviewing Productivity at the different phases of life cycles. For example, in Testing, how many hours were spent deriving test cases versus how many tests were actually completed?

To be even more confusing, this PA refers to *process* performance as including both *process* measures and *product* measures. Then later, it refers to "*quality* and *process*–performance objectives" to emphasize the importance of *product* quality. The confusion comes in because product measures are primarily used in organizations to demonstrate quality. This PA refers to process measures as including effort, cycle time, and defect removal effectiveness. Product measures include reliability and defect density. However, the same source data (for example, defects) can be used for both product and process measures. A process measure would be defect removal effectiveness (the percentage of existing defects removed by a process), such as the inspection process or the testing process. A product measure would be defect density (the number of defects per unit or product size), such as number of defects per thousand lines of code that reflects the quality of the product. Basically, it might help to translate in this PA that Quality measure = Product measure.

Training is critical in this PA, in both modeling techniques and in quantitative methods.

There are no new generic goals for Levels 4 and 5 in the staged representation because the process areas include the basic tenets. The continuous representation *does* have generic goals because the continuous representation allows the selection of various process areas. So, you may decide not to select the process areas in Maturity Level 4. If you do that, then the generic goals of the continuous representation have been added to ensure that the basic concepts of statistical control and application will be met.

This process area covers both project-level and organization-level activities. Selecting processes to measure and selecting appropriate measures themselves can be iterative to meet changing business needs. Establishing quality and process objectives can be iterative as well, based on fixing special causes of variation.

An example of the importance of not mixing "apples and oranges" in this process area follows. Suppose you are collecting peer review data. You collect defect data resulting from peer reviews. You may collect the number of defects found and the type of defect (code, requirement, design, etc.). Be sure to analyze that data appropriately. For example, if one review of code produces 17 defects that may not sound like much, while another review of another program results in 25 defects, which is obviously more than from the first product reviewed. But, by reviewing the number of lines of code for each product you discover that review number one resulting in 17 defects occurred in a program with only 11 lines of code, while the second review that resulted in 25 defects was conducted on a program of 1,500 lines of code. The 17 defects were so severe that the program needed a total rewrite, while the 25 defects were mostly cosmetic, with only one or two potential problem areas. So, you must study the data produced in terms of the number of defects, type, severity, number of pages or lines of code reviewed, complexity, domain, and type of technology used.

Measures can usually be traced back to life-cycle activities and products. For example, percent of changes to the Requirements Document, while reviewing the product itself, can demonstrate problems with the process used for collecting requirements and physically writing the document. These numbers can then be used to include more rigorous training in this area of weakness. You might also consider reviewing the number of defects that come out of the Requirements phase versus the number of defects out of the Test phase. One study has determined that 85 percent of defects found in the Test phase were introduced in the Requirements phase.

We admit, measurement programs can become onerous. The CMMI's response to this criticism is that measurements should be tied to business objectives of the organization. So, if you are highly driven by time-to-market, you would focus on product defects and the scheduling effort. Decisions to release the product with an "appropriate" limit of defects would be made by senior management in order to make the schedule date. That "appropriate" part should be determined based on historical data (and analysis of that data and your measurement repository) for the *number* of defects that can be released into the marketplace, and the *types* of defects that can be released into the marketplace and still satisfy the customer and make the product work.

Things that most organizations tend to forget or get wrong about this process area:

- The organization either builds too many models or not enough. This approach is the same approach we see when trying to select appropriate measures to collect at Level 2 and in trying to write effective process documentation when beginning the process improvement effort.
- Nobody really understands the models that are built (except *maybe* the guy who built them).
- The models aren't really used to make decisions.

The generic practices that map directly to this process area are GP 4.1 Establish Quantitative Objectives for the Process and GP 4.2 Stabilize Subprocess Performance.

Organizational Process Performance includes deciding which processes to include as part of statistical performance analyses; defining metrics to use as part of the process performance analyses; defining quantitative objectives for quality and process performance (quality and process "by the numbers"); and generating process performance baselines and models.

Quantitative Project Management

The purpose of Quantitative Project Management (QPM) is to quantitatively manage the project's defined process to achieve the project's established quality and process–performance objectives.

Specific Goals and Practices for This Process Area:
SG1   Quantitatively Manage the Project
    SP 1.1   Establish the Project's Objectives
    SP 1.2   Compose the Defined Process
    SP 1.3   Select the Subprocesses That Will Be Statistically Managed
    SP 1.4   Manage Project Performance
SG2   Statistically Manage Subprocess Performance
    SP 2.1   Select Measures and Analytic Techniques
    SP 2.2   Apply Statistical Methods to Understand Variation
    SP 2.3   Monitor Performance of the Selected Subprocesses
    SP 2.4   Record Statistical Management Data

In this process area, usage of the organizational level measurement repository is refined. This PA describes what projects need to do to manage quantitatively. Generally speaking, we have seen that with the distribution of labor experienced managers and measurement personnel identify measures, senior level project personnel collect the measures, and projects use the measures. Training for each role needs to be addressed.

SP 1.2 Compose the Defined Process and SP 1.3 Select the Subprocesses That Will Be Statistically Managed are closely related. For example, you compose the (project's) defined process based on the quantitative understanding you have gained from process performance baselines and models, and select the subprocesses that most contribute to process performance. This paragraph gives a very brief approach on how to understand and implement these two practices. OPP (the previously discussed process area) focuses on an organizational view of your processes. QPM focuses on looking at the processes used on a particular project. So, look at your organization's processes (your OSSP discussed in Maturity Level 3) and, using the quantitative data and the results of your organizational process performance baselines and models from OPP, determine where your organization needs to improve. Then look at your project's defined process (or processes, also discussed in Maturity Level 3). Determine which project process can contribute to improving the aforementioned organizational process. Your project's defined process can be decomposed to discrete subprocesses, and then to the most relevant subprocess that is contributing to poor performance. Model that one, and see what results you obtain. Incorporate any needed improvements into your project processes and your organizational processes, where appropriate. This explanation is a very short overview of quantitatively managing project and organizational processes. Please, please see our Chapters 18 and 19 on statistical process control and high maturity concepts, respectively.

Project managers should do at least a weekly review of the project measures and how they are being used. This information is usually communicated to senior management. A measurement group is usually needed to support measurement activities. Collection of data is easier if automated tools are used. Manual collection of data can be burdensome and can lead to abandonment of this effort. Automated tools are very helpful, but do not go out and buy a tool willy-nilly. Most tools cannot support the very project-specific and organization-specific measures that need to be taken. And remember the Level 3 process area, Requirements Development? Well, before you buy a tool, you are supposed to define the requirements of that tool—not buy a tool and then define the requirements that it happens to meet. We have found that the best tools for collecting and storing metrics have been developed by the organization itself. So, you've got programmers—use them. Get them to develop a tool or tools. This approach also gets buy-in from them for some of the process improvement activities. What's the best tool? Your brain. God gave you a brain—use it. Remember, not only do you need to *collect* the data—you need to *analyze* it as well. Your brain will certainly come in handy for that part.

There can be several organizational measurement repositories, or layers within one overall repository, so as to not mix data that may lead to misleading numbers and bad decisions. Repositories require years of historical data using the same, normalized data, and reviews and analyses of these data. Training and practice in this effort need to occur. Running projects quantitatively is not an overnight transition.

A bad example of collecting data and using them follows. Most organizations simply ask, "How many years must we go to prove that we have met the criteria for historically accurate data?" Wrong question. One organization collected data for 15 years about their projects. The data collected for 14 years were simply when the project started and when it ended. Each project took about seven years to complete. We find it difficult to imagine any real value that was added to these projects by simply collecting start and end dates. The fifteenth year of data collection included the start of each phase of software development and the end—Requirements start and end, Design start and end, Code start and end, Test start and end, and Installation start and end. Although we can find much more value in these types of data and their collection, we believe that having only one year of the data was not enough, especially since each project ran almost seven years, and most of the projects were only in the Requirements phase. So comparisons for bottlenecks and other trends were almost impossible, and would be inaccurate. However, the organization tried to advise us that these data met the criteria for stable, consistent data because they had data for as far back as 15 years. Sorry, no cigar. By the way, this example occurred during an external evaluation of an organization seeking a Maturity Level 4 rating.

Things that most organizations tend to forget about this process area:

■ Make sure the project manager (or whoever will actually use these data to manage the project) is involved in determining which measures he will need.
■ Train the people collecting the data and the people who will use the data.
■ Make sure that decisions are made that show that these data and models were used. If they are not used, they do not really exist. Show how the project's defined process was changed, reviewed, or influenced by these data.
■ Make sure you have examples of using process, product, and quality measures and models.

The generic practices that map directly to this process area are GP 4.1 Establish Quantitative Objectives for the Process and GP 4.2 Stabilize Subprocess Performance.

Quantitative Project Management includes quantitatively defining project objectives; using stable and consistent historical data to construct the project's defined process; selecting subprocesses of the project's defined process that will be statistically managed; monitoring the project against the quantitative measures and objectives; using analytical techniques to derive and understand variation; and monitoring performance and recording measurement data in the organization's measurement repository.

Summary

The previous version of the CMM for Software said of Level 4, keep it simple. Organizations involved in piloting CMMI have admitted that the bar has been raised significantly. Do we believe that measurement is necessary? Absolutely! However, Level 4 is where senior management commitment and participation really come to the fore. Business decisions are supposed to be made based on the numbers. Have you ever sat in any senior- and executive-level meetings? You are lucky if you get ten minutes with these people. And they are not overly fond of viewing slide after slide of esoteric charts and graphs. They want to know the bottom line—are we making money? And the one chart that they all love, which is not particularly popular in the world of statistics is the pie chart.

Our recommendation is still to start simple. If you can then refine your approaches and include more complicated approaches as needed, then fine—go for it. But most small organizations will find this level very difficult to implement as written, based on the number of people needed to make this run smoothly and based on the type of expertise needed. And this level may not prove all that beneficial (using cost-benefit analyses) to these organizations anyway.

Chapter 8

Understanding Maturity Level 5: Optimizing

This chapter is designed to help the reader understand the basic tenets of Maturity Level 5 in the staged representation of the CMMI. However, because this chapter consists of summaries of the process areas, anyone wishing to get a better idea of the model, no matter which representation is to be used, can benefit from this chapter. Once again, we are not attempting to teach the CMMI. We simply offer a condensed version of the various areas and key points to consider.

Moving from Level 4 to Level 5

At Level 5, an organization has achieved all of the goals of Levels 2, 3, and 4. Level 5 concentrates on improving the overall quality of the organization's processes by identifying common causes of variation (as opposed to special causes of variation at Level 4), determining root causes of the conditions identified, piloting process improvements, and incorporating the improvements and corrective actions into the Organization's Set of Standard Processes (OSSP) or, as appropriate, just the project's defined process. Although innovative, radical approaches to introduce change into an organization are often undertaken, most organizations have found that an incremental approach works better and has longer-lasting results.

There are two process areas (PAs) for Level 5. They are:

- Organizational Innovation and Deployment
- Causal Analysis and Resolution

Note that there are no additions to the list of generic goals at Level 5 from Level 3. What makes this maturity level different is the two process areas. The generic goals are listed below. We use the abbreviations GG for generic goal and GP for generic practice.

GG2　Institutionalize a Managed Process
　　GP 2.1　Establish an Organizational Policy
　　GP 2.2　Plan the Process
　　GP 2.3　Provide Resources
　　GP 2.4　Assign Responsibility
　　GP 2.5　Train People
　　GP 2.6　Manage Configurations
　　GP 2.7　Identify and Involve Relevant Stakeholders
　　GP 2.8　Monitor and Control the Process
　　GP 2.9　Objectively Evaluate Adherence
　　GP 2.10　Review Status with Higher-Level Management
GG3　Institutionalize a Defined Process
　　GP 3.1　Establish a Defined Process
　　GP 3.2　Collect Improvement Information

To satisfy the goals for Level 5, the goals for Levels 2, 3, and 4 must be satisfied as well. This rule holds true for both the specific goals (listed in each process area in the following section) and the generic goals listed above.

For the continuous approach, the generic goals and generic practices for each capability level that must be satisfied for each selected process area are:

Capability Level 1:
　GG1　Achieve Specific Goals
　　　GP 1.1　Perform Specific Practices
Capability Level 2:
　GG2　Institutionalize a Managed Process
　　　GP 2.1　Establish an Organizational Policy
　　　GP 2.2　Plan the Process
　　　GP 2.3　Provide Resources
　　　GP 2.4　Assign Responsibility
　　　GP 2.5　Train People
　　　GP 2.6　Manage Configurations
　　　GP 2.7　Identify and Involve Relevant Stakeholders
　　　GP 2.8　Monitor and Control the Process
　　　GP 2.9　Objectively Evaluate Adherence
　　　GP 2.10　Review Status with Higher-Level Management
Capability Level 3:
　GG3　Institutionalize a Defined Process

GP 3.1   Establish a Defined Process
GP 3.2   Collect Improvement Information
Capability Level 4:
  GG4   Institutionalize a Quantitatively Managed Process
    GP 4.1   Establish Quantitative Objectives for the Process
    GP 4.2   Stabilize Subprocess Performance
Capability Level 5:
  GG5   Institutionalize an Optimizing Process
    GP 5.1   Ensure Continuous Process Improvement
    GP 5.2   Correct Root Causes of Problems

Each capability level builds on the previous level. So, to be Capability Level 5, the organization must satisfy the specific practices for the selected process area (Capability Level 1), plus the generic practices for Capability Levels 2, 3, 4, and 5.

The following pages discuss each process area for Level 5. We use the abbreviations SG for specific goal and SP for corresponding specific practices.

The Process Areas for Maturity Level 5: Optimizing

Organizational Innovation and Deployment

The purpose of Organizational Innovation and Deployment (OID) is to select and deploy incremental and innovative improvements that measurably improve the organization's processes and technologies. The improvements support the organization's quality and process–performance objectives as derived from the organization's business objectives.

Specific Goals and Practices for This Process Area:
  SG1   Select Improvements
    SP 1.1   Collect and Analyze Improvement Proposals
    SP 1.2   Identify and Analyze Innovations
    SP 1.3   Pilot Improvements
    SP 1.4   Select Improvements for Deployment
  SG2   Deploy Improvements
    SP 2.1   Plan the Deployment
    SP 2.2   Manage the Deployment
    SP 2.3   Measure Improvement Effects

SP 1.4 has changed wording. The complete practice now reads, "Select process and technology improvements (not improvement proposals) for deployment across the organization." Well, whether you call them "proposals" or "improvements," it doesn't matter. This PA emphasizes instituting improving your organization, in a structured fashion, with improvements that stand a better chance of actually working in the organization. And, those improvements will be studied and analyzed against measurable criteria. If the reader reviews the Organizational Process Focus process area, he will find that process improvements are mentioned there as well. What's the difference? In OID, the proposals are subjected to quantitative analysis of proposed improvements. Metrics residing in the historical database, as well as defects and where they were introduced, are reviewed as well in order to determine where, when, and how to make improvements. Costs and benefits of the proposed versus actual improvements are also studied.

Some people have interpreted this PA as including both process and product improvements. This opens up a can of worms for appraisal teams. What was expected in the CMM for Software was process improvements *and* improvements in technology to support the processes. Technologies, such as a new requirements traceability tool or a new unit test tool, were included. Technologies that were to be part of a product, such as a new database management system or a new algorithm, were not included. With CMMI, these concepts become an even bigger issue. The systems that we may be building can include a lot of technologies. The question becomes how far should an appraisal team go? Is the organization expected to have a defined process to select technologies? When selecting the type of phones for its staff, is that covered by OID? When selecting which type of interface to put on their new phone system, is that covered by OID? Or is that covered in Technical Solution at Level 3?

The steps in this PA include:

- Submitting improvement proposals
- Reviewing and analyzing the proposals (including a cost-benefit review)
- Piloting the proposed improvement
- Measuring the improvement to see whether it has been effective in the pilot
- Planning the deployment of the improvement
- Deploying the improvement
- Measuring the effectiveness of the improvement across the organization or project

For example, a Level 1 organization will simply mandate that a certain change control tool is now to be used. There is no piloting of the tool, no requirements study to see which tools out there fit the organization, and no training is given. This introduction of the new tool causes chaos. A Level 5 organization will follow the steps above, and should the pilot prove effective, will probably deploy the tool one or a few projects at a time, not en masse into the entire organization. A go/no go decision will be made at each step.

Don't wait until Level 5 to introduce these concepts into your organization. The difference in introducing this approach at Level 1 or 2 versus Level 5 is that here at

Level 5 you absolutely know your organization's processes and can be more proactive about predicting the level of uncertainty that the tool (in the example used) will create. You can plan its introduction better and pinpoint areas that will need more attention, such as training and perhaps contracts.

Things that most organizations tend to forget about this process area:

- You must pilot your improvement! Only piloting will be able to accurately predict whether this improvement has a chance of being accepted and working in your organization. Most organizations do not want to take the time and trouble to pilot their improvements. Senior management does not understand, or does not want to understand, the importance of piloting. They feel, "Well, the stuff has been written—just throw it out to the projects. The project managers will make it work. That's why they are project managers." This is the wrong approach.
- You must plan the pilot and document critical success factors in a quantitative manner. Then a decision should be made, after reviewing the results against the critical success factors, whether the improvement should be implemented in the organization and what approach should be used to implement it (e.g., phased approach or en masse). More piloting may also be necessary.

The generic practice that directly maps to this process area is GP 5.1 Ensure Continuous Process Improvement.

Organizational Innovation and Deployment involves coordinating process improvement proposals submitted from the staff at various levels (improvement proposals may be related to innovative technology improvements); piloting selected improvements; planning and implementing the deployment of improvements throughout the organization; and measuring the effects of the improvements implemented.

Causal Analysis and Resolution

The purpose of Causal Analysis and Resolution (CAR) is to identify causes of defects and other problems and take action to prevent them from occurring in the future.

Specific Goals and Practices for This Process Area:
SG1   Determine Causes of Defects
      SP 1.1   Select Defect Data for Analysis
      SP 1.2   Analyze Causes
SG2   Address Causes of Defects
      SP 2.1   Implement the Action Proposals
      SP 2.2   Evaluate the Effect of Changes
      SP 2.3   Record Data

Proposals and plans to improve defects in the processes used to produce products are included here. Defect Prevention in the previous CMM for Software included integrating project work with kickoff meetings. This activity is no longer included here. We recommend this activity be performed as a best practice found in other organizations.

This process area looks at defects and determines their root cause. The simplest definition of a root cause is simply the one, most basic reason why the defect occurred (or the source of the defect) and if that cause is removed, the defect vanishes. This PA identifies the root cause(s) and addresses the cause using a structured approach. The steps in this approach are:

- Look at the defects and problems in the organization
- Select data to analyze
- Analyze causes
- Prepare proposals to address the problems
- Implement the proposals
- Evaluate the effects of the changes

You should already be analyzing defects and problems during Project Planning and Project Monitoring and Control at Level 2. Training to perform the more sophisticated studies required for Level 5 should be considered.

We recommend that users of the CMMI for process improvement also review the CMM for Software for more advice or suggestions on other activities to include in order to satisfactorily complete this PA. Kickoffs, sharing among projects, roles in the organization, rolling up project data/causes/problems into organizational-level data, and integrating changes into the processes are described somewhat in the CMM model, and may benefit the reader in understanding this PA.

Things that most organizations tend to forget about this process area:

- You are analyzing defects of the process. The defects of the process may result in product defects, which are probably more noticeable in your organization. For example, if your process for Unit Testing is broken, more defects may be released to the customer or more time may be spent in the entire Testing phase. What you may notice is that cost and effort are up, and defect rates are up. We worked with one organization that was just beginning the process improvement journey and were a very low, Level 1 organization. The director of software engineering, after hearing this process area explained, proudly announced, "Well, we are obviously a Level 5 organization! We use an automated debugger that finds defects in our code." Wrong. He was focusing on product defects and not on process defects. And there did not seem to be any analysis on what was causing the defects.
- The CMMI now makes very clear that the processes under review here should be quantitatively managed processes—that is, those processes that were

studied, produced, and implemented in the organization using the concepts discussed in the previous chapter on Maturity Level 4. So, the processes, subprocesses, models, and benchmarks that the organization developed and used as part of their statistical control effort are the primary ones that are scrutinized here. So, your outputs from Level 4 form your inputs to Level 5.

The generic practice that directly maps to this process area is GP 5.2 Correct Root Causes of Problems.

Causal Analysis and Resolution includes identifying defects and where in the process they were introduced; determining the causes of defects and their resolution; and defining methods and procedures to avoid introducing defects into the processes in the future.

Summary

The focus at Level 5 is on improving processes, but now the OSSP is the controlling document that provides the primary focus. By using the OSSP (which by now must surely reflect true organizational functioning), process improvement can be engineered into the organization in a much more reasonable and efficient manner.

Level 4 focuses on special causes of variation in the processes of the organization. Level 5 tries to find common causes and fix them, which will result in overall improvements. Measurements are used to select improvements and reliably estimate the costs and benefits of attempting the improvements. Measurements are used to prove the actual costs and benefits of the improvements. These same measurements can be used to justify future improvement efforts.

There are two types of improvement strategies—innovative and incremental. Incremental builds on the foundation of earlier improvements. Innovative tends to introduce more radical and drastic methods of improvement. Both can work in an organization, depending on the culture of the organization and the strength of its leaders, both politically and charismatically. However, most organizations have reported that incremental approaches to process improvement tend to have more long-lasting effects and lead to easier institutionalization.

At Level 5, the focus is on constantly reviewing and improving the processes, but these improvements must be introduced in a disciplined manner in order to manage and maintain process stability.

IMPLEMENTATION III

Chapter 9

Alignment of Multiple Process Improvement Initiatives

It is not uncommon to find multiple process improvement initiatives within even a moderately sized organization. These separate initiatives are going to be using different methods, techniques, and models as a basis for their work. Using CMMI has the potential to bring together existing process improvement initiatives covering software engineering, systems engineering, and hardware engineering activities within an organization.

Organizations that we work with have reported problems between groups because of different maturity levels of their processes; different expectations from senior management; different levels of training; and a mismatch of policies, processes, and procedures. These problems are often more difficult to resolve because of the separate initiatives occurring at the same time within the organization.

This chapter covers some of the things to consider when combining or aligning multiple process improvement initiatives. The topics covered are process improvement team structure, integration of existing procedures, measurement programs, and training programs. Following the topics, example real-world scenarios are described.

Process Improvement Team Structure

We often find different groups working on process improvement activities in an organization. For example, an organization may have a Software Engineering Process Group (SEPG) for software processes, a Systems Engineering Process Initiative (SEPI) for systems engineering processes, and an Engineering Process Group (EPG) for processes covering other disciplines such as electrical, mechanical, safety, and reliability. In addition to these explicit process improvement groups, organizations may have other existing groups, such as Quality Improvement Councils, Business Reengineering Teams and Six Sigma programs.

Given this wide range of groups interested in process improvement, it is not surprising that organizations find that, regardless of their current approach, they will need to clarify the roles and responsibilities of each team, increase communication between these teams, and often simplify the effort by eliminating some teams.

In order to address the structure, you need to know what structure already exists. Here are some questions to consider:

- What teams do you currently have?
  Take an inventory of the teams. Some organizations are surprised to find that they have a significant number of teams involved with process improvement across the organization. You may need to survey a number of people to identify all the teams. If it is difficult to identify all the teams, you will want to improve the communication and visibility of your teams. Process improvement teams need to be visible; stealth process improvement rarely works.
- How many teams are real?
  For a team to be real it should have a plan, a charter, a budget, and active members (see Chapters 11 and 12 for more information). In addition, teams should have an executive sponsor, and the team should have produced something. Look at the processes, procedures, templates, training materials, and so forth coming from each team.
- What overlap exists between your teams?
  It is not unusual to find multiple teams with many of the same members. This may not be a bad thing when the teams have a clear charter and know their responsibilities. If you have an overlap of team members and an overlap of responsibilities, it usually means nothing is going to get done or something will get done, but twice in slightly different ways.
- At what level do your teams communicate and how often?
  Even separate teams working in unique areas should be exchanging ideas and leveraging from one another. Ways to encourage communication include joint meetings on topics of mutual interest, peer reviews of team-developed work products across teams, and assigning a representative from a related team as a member of the team.

- Do your teams have an unhealthy competition?

  Multiple teams within an organization have been known to spend an unbalanced amount of time protecting their sphere of influence, their budget, and their unique processes. You need to be sensitive to this situation. If you are a member of one or more of these teams you may need an impartial third party to look at and evaluate your work and determine the value of what has been accomplished.

Once you collect this information about your teams you should be in a position to restructure your teams for better alignment. Make sure whatever teams you keep have a charter, a plan (not just a schedule; see Chapter 11), a budget, a management or an executive sponsor, and a communication plan. Later in this chapter, we discuss two scenarios related to team integration.

Integration of Existing Policies, Processes, and Procedures*

The separate process improvement initiatives in your organization are likely to have developed separate processes and procedures. Some organizations have written their policies, processes, and procedures to map directly to their process improvement model (e.g., CMM for Software, CMMI, SA-CMM), so one of the negative side effects of different process improvement models has been an incompatible set of policies, processes, and procedures. To resolve these problems, we offer the following questions and suggested approaches.

Questions you should ask regarding your process-related documentation include:

- Do your current policies cover your selected CMMI scope?
- Do you need more detailed procedures?
- Do you have overlap in your procedures?
- What procedures should be merged?
- What procedures should remain separate?

Following are some suggested approaches to integrating policies, processes, and procedures.

---

* Chapter 15 is our "meat and potatoes" chapter on policies, processes, and procedures and will give you more details on some of these concepts, along with Chapter 13 that discusses documentation guidelines.

Collect and Review the Policies, Processes, and Procedures

The first thing you need to do is collect in one place all the documentation that makes up your policies, processes, and procedures, and conduct a review. Hopefully, it will be as easy as it sounds. Make sure you have a good working definition of policy, process, and procedures—if in doubt look at Chapter 13 for documentation guidelines (this was written by one of the most intelligent people we know). Not everything you find will be labeled correctly. For example, we have seen lots of documents with the title "Process for X" that are really policies stating that you are expected to do X. These documents may still be helpful. Also look at your training courses; sometimes a process or a procedure is only documented in a training course. (Note: We do not recommend only documenting processes and procedures in training courses.) Identify the correct title, author, change authority, and sponsor of all documents. Create a document log with all the above information. Conduct a review and record your findings. Use the questions above and the rest of this section to give you ideas on what to look at.

Examine the Interfaces

Examine and consider the interfaces between procedures to ensure that artifacts produced in one process satisfy the requirements of the receiving process (for example, Systems Requirements flowing into Software Requirements, Systems Requirements into Acquisition, and Software Requirements into Acquisition). Each of these processes represents a producer and a consumer part. The producer needs to provide part of what the consumer needs to do his job. What can be done to make your interfaces clearer and more productive? In one organization, the addition of a formal design review step between the Systems Requirements and Software Requirements improved not only the artifacts, but also the working relationship between the groups. It also resulted in savings of a staff year for a 15-person project.

Review the Roles

Review the roles people perform and the various disciplines within your organization. For example, configuration management and quality assurance often perform similar roles. These two disciplines exist at both the systems level and the software level, perform similar activities regardless of the discipline, and may or may not be performed by the same individuals. Can your procedures for these roles be improved by sharing ideas? For example, in most organizations we work with, the software quality group has much more experience in reviewing and auditing process and the systems quality group has more experience in reviewing and auditing products. Sharing best practices has proven useful.

Consider Life Cycles

Consider the life cycle of the disciplines and scope of the procedures. Systems procedures may cover total life cycle "lust to dust" (that is, conception through to disposal), yet software and acquisition-related procedures may only cover the requirements phase to the test phase. How do these different life cycles affect your procedure integration? One example: some organizations find that systems engineering has a better technique for understanding customer needs and expectations. This technique can be borrowed and reused in software-only systems.

Consider the Level of Detail

Consider the level of detail of the written procedures. Some disciplines may have written procedures to just "pass the test" and be at such a high level that they provide very little value. Some disciplines, such as purchasing, may have developed detailed procedures and supporting checklists that help provide a repeatable and improvable activity. Now may be the time to leverage more practical process architectures and procedural approaches from other disciplines.

Consider the Format

Consider the format of the documentation you have produced, that is, process-related internal documentation and the documentation you turn over to your user. Again, now may be the time to implement consistent process architecture, formats, and styles.

Table 9.1 contains an example of what you might find existing across an organization. This example is based on documentation we have reviewed from organizations in the past. The three right columns indicate the disciplines of systems engineering, software engineering, and acquisition (or purchasing). Key characteristics for each discipline are identified in the policies, processes, and procedures in the left-hand columns.

Measurement Programs

If the organization has not developed an integrated measurement program, it is likely that measures* and measurement will be unbalanced across multiple process improvement initiatives. Different improvement models place different levels of

---

* Measures in this section refer to both base measures and derived measures. Base measures are simple values of some attribute, for example, size of a document in pages or effort to produce a document in hours. Derived measures are defined to be a function of two or more base measures, for example, productivity in hours per page to produce a document.

Table 9.1   Example Characteristics of Policies, Processes, and Procedures By Discipline

	Systems Engineering	Software Engineering	Acquisition (or Purchasing)
Primary Standard	Systems Engineering Handbook • focus on engineering practices • based on unique customer requirements and best practices from the organization	Standard Software Process • focus on project management practices • based on best practices and Project Management Institute	Buyer Guidelines • focus on open market acquisitions • based on government regulations, unique customer requirements, and corporate guidelines
Level of Tailoring	Very little tailoring allowed — requires contract change	Some tailoring done on most projects	Tailoring expressly forbidden
Process Architecture	Based on waterfall life-cycle phases plus unique phases for internal research and development	Based on CMM for Software Key Process Areas	Based on roles in acquisition process
Level of Detail	High-level process descriptions	Level of detail varies by process area • detailed management processes • high-level engineering processes	Very detailed guidelines with checklists
Review Approach	Formal reviews (with customer) — systems requirements review, preliminary design review, critical design review	Internal peer reviews (some involve systems engineering and acquisition participants)	Process execution review by managers, technical details reviewed by engineering, all activities audited by customer
Configuration Control	Data management for all formal work products — plans, drawings, specifications, and prototypes	Configuration management procedures around change control boards and software library	Contracts library with limited access containing specifications, requests for proposals, proposal responses, contract and contract status, vendor performance and preferred vendor lists
Quality	Verification and validation by 3rd party or with external witnesses	Both product and process review, emphasis on process assurance	All activities audited by customer or 3rd party representative

importance on measurements. To exploit some of the resulting differences, we offer the following questions and suggested approaches.

Questions you should ask regarding your measurement programs include:

- What measures are being collected for each discipline?
  Some measures can cover several disciplines, for example effort measures and earned value. Other measures would be unique to a discipline, such as number of late deliveries from vendor X or lines of code per hour.
- Are there measurement specifications defined for all measures?
  A measurement specification should contain a definition of the measure, source of the data, collection mechanism, criteria for counting, unit(s) of measure, and expected range value. In addition, guidelines on interpreting the measurement information including an analysis approach and criteria for decision making should be documented. Why do we need all this stuff? Well, measures are like many things in life; "if it ain't written down it ain't so." For example, when you ask someone, "How many requirements do you have in your system?" the only way to make sense of the answer, and for that matter the question, is to have a definition of what a requirement is.
- What measures are being presented to management on a regular basis?
  The approaches to presenting measurement to management vary widely across organizations. We have worked with groups that hold a formal monthly measurement review with senior management and we have worked with groups that simply provide measures at quarterly project status report. The key to success with measures is to provide accurate measurement data to management on a regular periodic basis—during both good times and bad—showing both good news and bad.
- How mature are the measurement systems for each discipline?
  Many of the organizations we work with began their measurement initiatives in the software area and have not placed as much emphasis in other disciplines. Therefore, software measurement in these organizations is often more mature. (We really do mean many, but not all. We have had the opportunity to work with both systems and programs that exhibit sophisticated measurement programs.) Measurement maturity shows up in several ways, such as how well measures are defined, how consistent measurements are taken and used, and how well the actual data collected reflects the processes being executed.
  You will want to understand these issues and the success individual disciplines have had in your organization in order to share best practices across the organization. Some organizations have software data identifying critical components, attributes, and measures of the standard processes based on critical business issues. If that is the case, showing the value the organization has gotten from more mature software measures may be helpful in getting buy-in from the other parts of your organization that have not been as

intensely involved in process improvement or are just starting their process improvement initiative.

■ How are the measures collected within the disciplines?

Again, we often find wide variation in how measures are collected across the disciplines. For example, you may use a manual method for calculating and collecting critical performance factors for formal reviews, or you may have a fully automated, integrated development and time-tracking environment that produces weekly and on-demand measurement charts. These charts may include effort, earned value, requirements changes, size (code and documents), number of reviews, number of defects, and productivity measures. As a rule, you should make collecting measures as painless as possible. Remember that "if it is too damn hard, people won't do it." Automate data collection as much as possible, but don't forget to verify, validate, and monitor collection to be sure you are getting the right stuff. A brain is required to analyze and comprehend information, and a brain is required to ensure the data collected makes sense. An automated tool does not have a brain.

Following are some suggested approaches for developing a measurement program.

Collect and Review the Related Documentation

The first thing you need to do is collect all the documentation related to measurement policies, processes, and procedures. Some of this may be imbedded in documentation for project planning and tracking or other process areas. Some disciplines will have developed measurement handbooks containing measurement specifications. Collect whatever you can find.

Collect Examples of Measures Presented to Management

Collect copies of status reports and briefings prepared for and presented to management. These include status from projects, major programs, functional areas, and the entire organization or division. Identify which measures are being reported and how often.

Identify All the Groups (or Individuals) with Measurement Responsibility

You need to know which groups and individuals are actually doing tasks related to measurement. You may find groups within individual disciplines, for example a Process Action Team for Measurement chartered by the SEPG. You may find groups or individuals responsible of collecting and maintaining time reporting data. You may find groups or individuals response for maintaining data used in bid and proposal activities. Go through the questions in the first section, "Process Improvement Team Structure," and answer them for the groups and individuals with measurement responsibility.

Identify How the Measures Are Being Collected

You may find how the measures are being collected in a measurement specification. You may find this information as part of the status report. You may have to interview the individuals responsible for the measures to see how they really do it. It is not unusual to find people guesstimating, that is, guessing at a number and calling it an estimate, or worse, presenting it as actual data. Note: We do not encourage this behavior; however, we recognize its existence. You need to be somewhat understanding and flexible during this data collection phase. In some cases, we have had to get senior management to declare an amnesty for all past behavior.

Create a Measurement Log

Create a measurement log summarizing the information identified above. At a minimum, this log should contain the measure; how it is documented; the group or individual responsible for collecting it; the tool or method used to collect it; and how often, to whom, and how it is reported.

Our experience is that if you go through all the steps above, you document your results, and review your findings with management, you will be able to identify the business case for merging your measurement programs, collection systems, and measurement databases. The primary business reasons that we have found for integrating measurement programs are removing duplication of effort, leveraging best practices, and establishing consistency.

Training Programs

Training programs need to include defining required training, planning the training, and executing the training plans. Different improvement models have placed different levels of importance on training. Some disciplines will have separate training programs, with some of them being more formal than others. With multiple training programs, it is not unusual to have several related courses. To exploit some of the resulting differences, we offer the following questions and suggested approaches.

Questions you should ask regarding your training programs include:

- Does your current training cover your selected CMMI scope?
- Do you need more detailed training in some disciplines?
- Do you have overlap in your training?
- What training should be merged?
- What training should remain separate?

Following are some suggested approaches to get to these answers.

Identify Which Training Programs Are in Scope

You need to know what training programs exist within the CMMI scope you have selected. These training programs may exist at the enterprise level, the organizational level, and within the disciplines (systems, software, and purchasing). For example, the enterprises through corporate human resources may train individuals in project management as they take their first management assignments; the organization may have orientation and training covering the specific domain of their major customers; and purchasing may have training in contract law and negotiations.

Identify All Sources of Training

Understanding the sources of the training courses helps make sure that you don't leave anything out. The sources of training are likely to include in-house training conducted within specific disciplines, enterprise- or organizational-level training (often within human resources), and training provided by specialist consultants (for example, if you have been using a process improvement consultant, he is likely to be doing your model training).

Identify and Collect All Training Plans and Schedule

Some training plans will be easy to identify, as they will have the title "Training Plan." Some training plans will only have a schedule. A schedule is not enough. Any training program should be managed as a project with a plan identifying what training is required, who needs the training, what resources (budget, participant hours, facilities, etc.) are required to perform the training, how training will be provided, and a schedule.

Identify All Training Courses

Create a course log summarizing the information identified above. You may need to survey the groups you have identified. At a minimum, this log should contain:

Course description and syllabus

- What form it is in (video, PowerPoint slides, or interactive computer training module)
- Group or individual responsible for course content
- Group or individual responsible for course materials
- Method used to deliver the training
- How often it is taught, to whom, and how it is recorded
- How the course is evaluated

Our experience is that if you go through all the steps above, and you document your results and review your findings, you will be able to identify two major opportunities for alignment:

- Merging training programs. For example, you might merge a systems engineering training program and a software engineering training program for the same reason you merge process improvement groups to eliminate overlap, simplify the efforts, increase communication, and focus your resources.
- Merging courses with similar content, roles, and level of detail. For example, you might merge data management and configuration management courses to eliminate redundancy, improve consistency, and increase knowledge across two similar groups. Caution: Some courses, for example, a quality assurance orientation and a quality assurance techniques course, are similar, but with a different level of detail for different audiences. Those would not be merged.

The other outcome of this effort is identifying courses that need to be developed to address the expanded scope of CMMI. For example, if you have a software project manager course but don't have a systems or purchasing project manager course, you will either want to expand the scope of the software course or create new courses for systems and purchasing.

Scenarios

Following are two scenarios to consider. Our lawyers tell us that we have to include the following statement: This is a work of the imagination depicting organizations and events that have not happened. Any resemblance to actual companies or persons, living or dead, is purely coincidental.

Scenario One: Merged Teams

Background: Road Runner Industries is a development organization with products that contain both custom hardware and software. It mainly produces embedded software for their primary products and some automatic test equipment software to test the final product. It does a lot of what it considers to be systems engineering, including the analysis of customer requirements, total systems design, and verification and validation activities throughout the development and installation life cycle. It has a large purchasing group that covers everything from buying paperclips to buying aircraft to use as test platforms.

Existing Teams: Road Runner Industries has been doing process improvement with the software CMM for over ten years and it has a classic Software Engineering Process Group (SEPG) sponsored by the director of embedded software. It has an ISO program in place for the hardware manufacturing activities that is part of its standard quality process that has been going on for five years managed by the vice president of quality. The company began a systems engineering process improvement activity two years ago using the Systems Engineering Capability Model (EIA/IS 731) and it has an Engineering Process Improvement Group (EPIG) that is sponsored by the director of engineering. The chairman of the EPIG is a member of the SEPG and the chairman of the SEPG is a member of the EPIG. Training comes from two sources—a Software Training Group and an organizational-level training function within the human resource department.

Approach: Road Runner Industries has defined its organizational scope for the CMMI initiative to include all of engineering (systems, software, mechanical, electrical, and avionics), training department, quality assurance, and purchasing. As part of the new initiative they have merged the SEPG and EPIG into a new group named the Engineering Process Group (EPG) and expanded its charter to cover all of engineering and purchasing plus related quality assurance functions. The company has assigned sponsorship of the EPG to the newly identified vice president of technology. It has renamed the Software Training Group to the Engineering Training Group (ETG) and given it responsibility for training unique to engineering and purchasing. The company decided to leave the ISO program as is, but has assigned the senior in-house ISO auditor as a full-time member of the EPG.

Rationale: The rationale for the merged team approach is that:

- The company found that it had many of the same members and stakeholders in the SEPG and EPIG.
- It has very similar processes and procedures for systems and software in requirements, design, integration, verification, and validation with some understandable differences in specialty engineering.
- The newly assigned VP of technology sees this merged EPG and ETG as a way to improve communications between systems, software, and purchasing and is looking for a way to reduce rework.

Scenario Two: Separate but Equal

Background: Wily Coyote Industries, a division of Kannotgetabrake, Inc., is an organization that produces major systems containing both custom hardware and software and significant amounts of purchased hardware and software. It produces a variety of custom software including embedded, information systems, and command and control applications. It does a lot of what it considers to be systems engineering including the analysis of systems requirements, specification writing for components and subsystems, verification and validation activities, and product integration. A group at corporate headquarters, over 900 miles away, performs most purchasing activities.

Existing Teams: Wily Coyote Industries has been doing software engineering process improvement with the CMM for Software for six years and has recently been assessed at Level 4 against that model. It has a classic SEPG sponsored by the director of engineering. The SEPG is responsible for all software processes, procedures, and training. It started a systems engineering process improvement initiative four years ago and formed a Process Improvement Group (PIG) sponsored by the senior engineering scientist. The PIG is responsible for systems process and procedures. The corporate training department covers systems engineering training activities. There is very little formal interaction between the SEPG and the PIG, but a lot of competition. Each group has its own logo, t-shirts, and coffee cups.

Approach: Wily Coyote Industries has defined its organizational scope for the CMMI initiative to include systems engineering and software engineering. It has left the SEPG and PIG separate, but has assigned a member of the SEPG to attend all PIG meetings and a member of PIG to attend all SEPG meetings. It has moved the responsibility for software training to the corporate training department and has transferred the old software-training group to corporate.

Rationale: The rationale for the separate teams is that:

- The SEPG is planning a Level 5 appraisal against the CMM for Software next year and sees this as priority over the CMMI initiative.
- The competition between the groups was determined to be healthy by executive management.
- The processes and procedures for software are quite varied with very different approaches in each domain (embedded, information systems, and command and control applications).
- The processes and procedures for systems engineering are very formal and unique to the major client.
- The move toward a total corporate training approach supports a corporate goal of leveraging training across divisions.

Summary

This chapter covers some of the things to consider when combining or aligning multiple process improvement initiatives. Considerations include process improvement team structure, integration of existing procedures, measurement programs, and training programs. Different improvement models have placed different levels of importance on some of these areas. This has naturally resulted in different levels of implementation across the disciplines.

None of the ideas presented in this chapter are difficult to understand. Mainly, they concern understanding the policies, processes, procedures, plans, courses, and people you currently have in place, understanding how they fit together within the expanded scope of the CMMI, and the vision the organization has created for their process improvement journey.

While we have presented these concepts in a simple, straightforward fashion, this effort actually will take many hours of hard work. Do not underestimate the level of effort required to successfully accomplish these tasks.

Chapter 10

Is CMMI Right for Small Organizations?

This chapter presents two viewpoints concerning implementing the CMMI within a small organization. A small organization is defined as an organization with 20 or fewer technical personnel developing systems. In a small organization, it is not uncommon for a project to consist of three people. One individual may serve as the project manager, developer, and tester; another individual may serve as a coder, tester, and database administrator; and the third individual may serve as a part-time quality assurance representative. The project may only last from three to six weeks.

A point–counterpoint approach is presented to discuss the pros and cons associated with various issues and their operational impacts. The reader should be somewhat familiar with both the CMMI effort and the previous models developed by the Software Engineering Institute (SEI).

The authors of this book do not make any claims as to these arguments. We believe the reader should be able to make up his own mind.

Definitions

Before continuing, let's discuss some basic terms to avoid any confusion later.

Systems Engineering

There seems to be no real agreement as to what Systems Engineering really is. The Systems Engineering Capability Maturity Model, version 1.1, states:

> Systems Engineering is the selective application of scientific and engineering efforts to:
>
> - Transform operational need into descriptions of the system configuration which best satisfies operational need according to measures of effectiveness
> - Integrate related technical parameters and ensure compatibility of all physical, functional, and technical program interfaces in a manner that optimizes total system definition and design
> - Integrate efforts of all engineering disciplines and specialties into total engineering effort

The definition of Systems Engineering from the draft version 0.5 of the Systems Engineering Capability Model EIA 731-1 states, "Systems Engineering is an interdisciplinary approach and means to enable the realization of successful systems." The CMMI v1.2 defines Systems Engineering as:

> The *interdisciplinary approach* governing the *total technical and managerial effort* required to *transform* a set of customer needs, expectations, and constraints *into a product solution*, and to support that solution, throughout the product's life. This includes the *definition of technical performance measures*, the *integration of engineering specialties* toward the establishment of a product architecture, and the *definition of supporting life-cycle processes* that balance cost, performance, and scheduled objectives.

What do these definitions mean as they relate to CMMI? Basically, Systems Engineering covers the development of total systems, which *may or may not include* software. Systems Engineering integrates all parts, areas, personnel, and characteristics of a project that are necessary to produce a completed system for delivery to the customer. Projects may begin with feasibility, cost/benefit, and concept of operations analyses to justify any subsequent software or nonsoftware activities.

Software Engineering

This discipline covers the development of software-focused systems. Projects begin once a software project manager is assigned and funding has been received.

Software Engineering may be a subset of Systems Engineering or it may stand alone as its own area of focus. It is possible to have some systems that are entirely made up of software-only tasks.

Integrated Product and Process Development

This discipline covers the usage of large product development teams, with each team member focusing on specific areas of expertise. Each team's results are then integrated into one product.

Acquisition

This discipline covers the identification of a need, selection of vendors, and monitoring the vendors' ability to produce the system according to contract constraints.

The Staged Representation (The Architecture in Use by the Software CMM)

This structure focuses an organization's improvement activities on undertaking the practices depicted in each process area within each level. For example, an organization would choose to attain Level 2 (by satisfying the goals for each process area in Level 2) before trying to undertake process areas in Levels 3, 4, or 5. Each level provides the foundation for further improvements. This model begins with basic management practices and continues with increasingly sophisticated focus areas that belong within a specific level. Practices reside within process areas within levels. There are five maturity levels, each serving as process boundaries.

The Staged approach provides guidance to organizations on the order of improvement activities they should undertake, based on (key) process areas at each stage/maturity level. Performing practices in the appropriate process area at a given level will help stabilize projects, thus allowing the execution of further improvement activities. Incremental improvement is supported in each maturity level/stage because that stage contains a collection of process areas on which to focus current activities.

The Continuous Representation (The Architecture in Use by the Systems Engineering Models)

This structure focuses process improvement on actions to be completed within process areas. Organizations are expected to select the process areas of interest to them.

Processes may span different levels and are grouped by functional categories. More sophistication in implementing the practices for each process area is expected at the different levels. There are six capability levels, which group process areas into functional categories of increasing evolution.

The Continuous approach provides more flexibility in defining process improvement programs. It recognizes that individual process areas are performed at distinct capability or maturity levels. Organizations need to perform an analysis of how the various process areas address the needs of the organization. This exercise also provides an opportunity to gain consensus on the sequence of improvement activities that are appropriate to the organization as a whole.

Maturity Levels

These belong to the Staged Representation. These apply to an organization's *overall* process capability and organizational maturity. Each maturity level comprises a predefined set of process areas and generic goals. There are five maturity levels numbered 1 through 5. These components suggest a recommended order for approaching process improvement in stages by grouping process areas into actionable groups.

Capability Levels

These belong to the Continuous Representation. These apply to an organization's process improvement achievement for *each* process area. There are six capability levels numbered 0 through 5. Each capability level corresponds to a generic goal and a defined set of generic practices. Capability levels focus on maturing an organization's ability to perform, control, and improve its performance in a process area. These levels enable an organization to track, evaluate, and demonstrate an organization's progress as it improves its processes associated within a specific process area. A recommended order of process improvement is also suggested by these levels, due to the groupings of the process areas into functional categories.

SCAMPI

SCAMPI stands for Standard CMMI Appraisal Method for Process Improvement. It is an appraisal technique that is similar to both the former CBA-IPI and Software Capability Evaluation methods. SCAMPI uses CMMI as its reference model. (See Chapters 20, 21, and 22 for more information.)

Small Organizations

This encompasses those organizations having 20 or fewer people, in total, supporting software or system development. Each member of a project may wear several hats (i.e., may perform several different roles) as part of normal daily tasks. Projects are short-lived, that is, between three to six weeks.

Point–Counterpoint

A point–counterpoint approach is presented to discuss the pros and cons associated with various issues and their operational impacts. The reader should be somewhat familiar with both the CMMI effort and the previous models developed by the Software Engineering Institute.

The authors of this book do not make any claims as to these arguments. We believe the reader should be able to make up his own mind.

Issue: No tailoring guidance is given for tailoring CMMI for small organizations.

Point: The previous CMM was often criticized as having been written by large, DOD (Department of Defense) organizations, for large, DOD organizations. Projects within the DOD realm generally consist of many people devoted full time to one project or many people devoted full time to one of several subprojects. These projects run for years and cost millions of dollars. This type of thinking is completely opposite to that of small organizations. One example of problems that small organizations currently have with the CMM is the number of "groups" suggested by the CMM to achieve Level 3. The number of groups suggested is 13. Even if a group may range from one person, part time, to several people full time, if your entire organization only consists of 20 people maximum, 13 groups become quite an expenditure of resources. CMMI, relying heavily on practices maintained by large organizations, will be even more difficult to implement in small organizations. CMMI has been slow to catch on in the commercial community. CMMI tends to attract DOD/aerospace organizations. The only tailoring guidelines given are called "Discipline Amplifications" or some "Hints and Tips," which reside in the margins of most process areas, and consist only of one or two sentences. These guidelines are often not clear or detailed enough to follow. The tailoring guidelines suggested are similar to those found in the original CMM for Software; that is, the more tailoring done, the less likely an organization is to improve. That warning seems to address only the possible negative aspects of tailoring. It seems as if tailoring is actively discouraged. Also, software shops are not necessarily interested in systems engineering; it just may not apply to them. So how/when can this be tailored out?

Counterpoint: There is a brief case study in the second edition of the CMMI concerning CMMI in small organizations. Fewer groups are explicitly defined in the CMMI, and this lack of group definition has actually been criticized by some organizations that preferred having more structure spelled out. The organization may determine how many groups are needed, if any, to implement the practices suggested in the CMMI. While it is true that more guidance is needed as to how to select those process areas and practices that are most relevant to a small organization, CMMI still allows the organization to tailor its process improvement objectives to the organization's business goals. The point of CMMI is to improve the processes of the organization, not to just worry about maintaining fidelity to the model for maturity level ratings.

Issue: CMMI is simply too big for small organizations to handle.

Point: The CMM was criticized for having too many key process areas and too many key practices. Just doing a visual comparison of CMMI against the CMM, CMMI appears to be three times as big! Also, the CMM was criticized for not containing everything necessary to promote development of effective, efficient systems. So, CMMI has removed the term *key* from its process areas and practices. It now seems as though the CMMI is trying to prescribe *everything* necessary to produce good systems. The CMM has over 300 key practices. Processes and supporting procedures needed to be written by the organization to describe how these practices were to be followed. This effort was seen by most organizations as a major part of the time it took for their software process improvement efforts. CMMI contains more practices, and most of these are not detailed enough to be understood in such as way as to promote consistent application across organizations. Writing procedures will be long and difficult. The time, resources, and costs associated with implementing CMMI appear to have expanded exponentially, compared to the already major investment required by the CMM.

One response heard at an SEPG conference was that an organization no longer had to write as many procedures! That response was based on the fact that the CMMI rarely uses the word *procedures*, whereas the CMM did rely on that word. However, a close reading of the CMMI will reveal that most of what an organization used to call "procedures" is now included in the "plans" that are a major part of each process area. Without the detail included in documented procedures, it is very difficult to ensure that processes are being followed in a consistent manner across your organization. So, whether they are called procedures or plans, an effective process improvement program still has plenty of documentation to prepare.

Counterpoint: CMMI allows small organizations, as well as large ones, to realize the benefits of following a structured process. CMMI allows for tailoring of the process and for aligning the process to the needs of the organization. However, this alignment requires more thought than was previously required with the CMM, as the CMM was directed specifically at software engineering. As stated previously, the SEI responded to the cries from the marketplace for more information regarding those areas where the CMM was lacking—specifically systems engineering. The organization can also choose how much of the model it wishes to follow. For example, if an organization is not interested in applying Systems Engineering guidelines cited in the model, that organization may select the continuous representation of the model or only the Software Engineering aspects. Rather than add more information to the CMMI version 1.2, the type of information contained in this model is also being distributed among the three CMMI constellations, that is, the CMMI for Development, the CMMI for Acquisition, and the CMMI for Services. The CMMI has been successfully applied in small organizations; care must be taken in interpreting the practices in a manner suitable to the environment. And all organizations, no matter what the size, must realize that a significant investment in time, resources, and money must be made to be successful.

Issue: Return on investment (ROI) from CMMI has not been validated, especially as it relates to small organizations.

> **Point:** The return on investment quoted by proponents refers to the ROI gained from the CMM, not for the ROI from CMMI. With some organizations reporting that it takes three to five years to realize its ROI from following the CMM, how long will it take an organization to realize its ROI from following the CMMI? Small organizations do not have the deep pockets and overhead of the larger organizations. Small organizations must worry about meeting payroll every two weeks. Expected ROI from using a model is often the argument used to justify the large expenditures necessary to institute and maintain a process improvement effort. Yet no real studies are available (at time of print) that can help a small organization calculate ROI from using this model.

> **Counterpoint:** This point is no longer relevant. When CMMI version 1.1 was released, the ROI statistics were mainly based on old figures using an older model. Now, however, many studies have been completed that show data depicting a strong ROI from organizations using the CMMI version 1.1. The "normal" ROI quoted is usually 5 to 1, that is, for every dollar invested, five dollars are returned. Some studies show an even greater increase. However, the point should be made that these figures do not occur overnight, and only occur when CMMI-based process improvement is implemented correctly. Actual results of studies concerning the benefits of CMMI usage (including ROI as well as other factors) in organizations can be found on the SEI Web site www.sei.cmu.edu.

Issue: CMMI emphasizes Systems Engineering over Software Engineering.

Point: Historically, the biggest seller of all the models was the CMM for Software. For those customers who bought into and applied the CMM for Software, Systems Engineering may not be part of their work and simply may not apply. The biggest growth sector in the marketplace right now for technical work is not large, bureaucratically structured organizations, but small, *software*-oriented shops. Why make taxpayers pay for a model that is not universally needed?

Counterpoint: Systems Engineering is necessary no matter how large or small the organization. Very few organizations develop just software—there are always systems issues to be taken into consideration, platform and hardware requirements, as well as interfacing with other groups or individuals responsible for some part of the system being built. Good systems engineering practices flowing into and out of software engineering tasks can only improve the software engineering effort. CMMI has been successfully adopted in many different types of organizations using many different development approaches. See Chapter 23, which discusses implementation of CMMI in an Agile development organization.

Issue: CMMI is too prescriptive for small organizations.

Point: The CMM was sold as being *what* to do, with the organization responsible for defining *how* to do the *whats*. CMMI is structured so similarly to large, bureaucratically controlled efforts that there seems to be little room to maneuver. For example, published results of CMMI pilot appraisals have reported that the appraisers had difficulty not asking interviewees leading questions because the model is basically black or white, yes or no, do you do this or not. As for examples in the process areas themselves, Risk Management seems to require a risk mitigation plan. Is this really necessary if you are a maintenance shop and your projects only last three weeks? Verification and Validation may be too rigorous for small teams. Can independent testing and configuration audits satisfy the tenets of these process areas instead?

Counterpoint: One of the criticisms of the previous CMMI version 1.1 was that there were too many process areas, especially at Level 3. CMMI version 1.2 has removed three process areas from that level and consolidated the information into other process areas. The CMMI is a balanced model, promoting not only Systems Engineering concepts, but also Software Engineering, IPPD, and Hardware Engineering. The organization may choose which areas to focus on, as well as the degree of focus that fits their business objectives. The developers of CMMI realized that small organizations, as well as those organizations not as mature as early adopters of the SEI's process improvement approach, should not be penalized. Because going from Level 1 to Level 2 is generally the hardest for most organizations, Level 2 remains basic. An organization may also choose to follow the Continuous approach. With this approach, an organization may select which process areas best fit their needs and concentrate on those areas only. Organizations may also elect to focus on only one discipline. So, CMMI is actually very flexible.

Issue: Small organizations are run differently from large organizations and face different challenges.

Point: The *primary* business driver in small, high-tech companies is time-to-market. Decisions must be made quickly and all relate to the bottom line. While CMMI promotes quality by elongating the process used to develop and deliver systems (because of preplanning and embedded checkpoint mechanisms), time-to-market does not seem to be considered. Ignoring time-to-market concerns is simply not practical in today's marketplace. Although the public decries poor-quality systems, it seems to prefer speed over functionality. And delivering products quickly is the lifeblood of small organizations.

Counterpoint: This is the reason models like the CMMI were written. What good does it do to deliver a system on time if it doesn't work? While small organizations may need to consider time-to-market questions, inevitably, if the organization cannot deliver good products, it will go out of business. CMMI is written based on the best practices of highly mature organizations that have used the various models and methodologies, and have learned from them. CMMI has leveraged this information, consolidated it, and presents it in a format that can be tailored to the needs of any organization. While several process areas within CMMI may prolong the development and delivery of systems, using the Process Areas of this model will result in better products delivered and better decision making by executives.

Issue: CMMI was written for already mature organizations.

Point: Early, introductory material from the Staged Representation of an earlier version of CMMI states that organizations currently rated at the higher maturity levels, or pursuing Malcolm Baldridge or ISO 9000 certification, should consider using the CMMI. These organizations are already working on, or have achieved, some notion of process improvement. But isn't it true that most organizations are still functioning at the lower levels? Is this an elitist model? Consider the following example. Measurement and Analysis is now a stand-alone process area. Measurement and Analysis used to be a common feature in the previous CMM. As such, it served as an effective check-and-balance for the entire key process area. If an organization had performed the activities preceding it, then that organization should be able to measure those activities. Then, the measurements could be reported to management and software quality assurance (as discussed in the Verifying Implementation Key Practices). The effectiveness of the processes for a particular key process area, as well as any deficiencies, could then be determined by reviewing the metrics collected. In CMMI, we now have Generic Practice 2.8 Monitor and Control the Process. This practice has far fewer examples of practical metrics. Although the Measurement and Analysis process area has useful information, much of this information seems to relate to higher maturity levels. If an organization is just beginning the road to process improvement, how much of this process area must be implemented? The reason this process area was pulled out of each key process area of the CMM and is now its own process area was as a result of input from higher maturity organizations. They all stated that measurement is the key to successful improvement efforts. But is creating this as a stand-alone process area the answer? Hindsight is a wonderful thing. Most organizations at Levels 4 and 5 are large organizations with deep pockets. Do these organizations really believe that they could institute this process area in their organizations back when their organizations were not quite as sophisticated as they are today? Do they believe that small organizations can implement this process area as written? Comprehensive metrics programs for small organizations, while beneficial, are too hard and expensive to implement at Level 2.

Counterpoint: Level 2 in CMMI still remains somewhat comparable to what it was in the CMM for Software. This should allow organizations, no matter what their size, to readily achieve this level if they had already been appraised at Level 2 or above using the CMM. Measurement truly is the key to focused improvement. As stated, if you have done it, you should be able to measure it. *Using* the measurements is also key. It does no good to simply collect the numbers and report them—the numbers must be used. At the lower levels and in less mature organizations, the metrics were not always used. Most organizations only began focusing on metrics when they were attempting to reach Level 4. And not all organizations continued in process improvement once they achieved Level 3. They dropped out before really turning their attention to measurement. By separating out this process area, emphasis is placed on collecting, analyzing, reporting, and using the measurements. Once again, the organization can tailor its process improvement efforts, and the usage of this process area, as related to business goals. The authors of this book were also surprised at how easily most organizations new to CMMI were able to implement this process area and how much the organizations seemed to appreciate the guidance given.

Issue: CMMI is too vaguely written to be used in appraisals.

Point: Organizations attempting to use the model for an appraisal report greatly extended timeframes. Interpretation seems to be based on personal experience, not on careful reading of the model. Most appraisal teams have difficulty interpreting the model and state that the model is too vaguely written. Therefore, they must rely on their own personal experience. Since individuals have different experiences, this reliance does not promote consistent appraisal results across organizations. While this consistency has always been a problem with CMM-based assessments and evaluations because of their dependence on the individuals who make up the appraisal teams, it is magnified with this model. Assessment teams could go to the CMM and read its practices and subpractices for guidance. Users of the CMMI report that this guidance cannot be found. Also, appraisal teams have been directed to appraise three projects from the Software area and then three different projects from the Systems area. Where is the integration? This is not just a problem for small organizations.

Counterpoint: These issues were raised by early pilot appraisals and have been addressed in the SCAMPI method. Early CMM-based assessments had significant interpretation issues, so this is nothing new. The sampling method is also prescribed for use in SCAMPI appraisals, reducing the time needed to conduct an appraisal. As for lack of guidance, some information has been added in the hints and tips in the margins of the CMMI book.

Summary

Regardless of an organization's size, process improvement must use a structured approach to be successful. CMMI includes more information and includes more areas that promote the development of high-quality systems. However, professional judgment in determining how to implement, interpret, and scale the model must be used.

One problem that still surfaces concerning CMMI and small organizations is cost. The costs of implementing CMMI in any organization are high. Costs include training your own organization, assigning personnel at least on a part-time basis to perform process improvement work that is nonbillable to your client, and perhaps hiring external consultants for process improvement and appraisal assistance.

Additionally, the SEI is enforcing conflict-of-interest rules governing who can conduct and participate in SCAMPI appraisals. Basically, those personnel who have been heavily involved in process improvement efforts for an organization (such as writing procedures or overseeing their implementation) cannot serve as Lead Appraisers or as members of the SCAMPI team. This places an additional cost burden on the organization should that organization need to hire or contract with personnel outside of its immediate organization or business unit in order to perform the SCAMPI and procure the additional formal training required for the SCAMPI. More training activities, more certifications and observations to authorize personnel, and the costs of such activities have also increased. Therefore, for those organizations that are small and are struggling just to meet their payroll requirements, the CMMI approach may be beyond your reach. You may have been priced out of the marketplace. While the concepts expressed in the CMMI are still beneficial, a formal implementation and appraisal of them may not be financially feasible for the truly small organization.

It can also be said that the CMM is always right for an organization; the CMMI is always right for an organization; SCAMPI/SCE/CBA-IPI is always right for an organization. What is *not* right for an organization is basing contract awards or contract bid opportunities solely on appraisal results.

Chapter 11

Establishing Your Process Improvement Organization

Whether you are using the CMM for Software, the CMMI, ISO, or any other process-focused guidelines, this chapter is for you. This chapter presents the four basic phases of process improvement:

- Set Up—Establishing a process improvement group and organizational infrastructure. This includes baselining your processes, initial planning, and securing funding and commitment throughout the organization.
- Design—Writing policies and procedures, and identifying and writing standards and processes.
- Pilot—Training participants and trying out the procedures in a few areas. The procedures are then updated, as necessary, based on the results of the pilots.
- Implement—Following the procedures on all projects and measuring their effectiveness.

Set Up

Set Up, or Initiation, involves selling the concept of process improvement to the organization, planning the effort, securing funds and staff, and structuring the effort. Most organizations become aware of process improvement through conferences, books, articles in industry magazines, or, most prominently, when achieving maturity levels become the basis for contract awards. An individual is usually chosen as the "champion" who literally promotes the process improvement effort throughout the organization. This promotion may entail doing research on Return on Investment, budget allocations within the organization, and cost-benefit analyses. For those of you tasked with this responsibility, the Software Engineering Institute (SEI) provides information on its Web site www.sei.cmu.edu. While the information in this Web site changes from time to time, you can find data under Community Profiles and under the Publications directory.

After the executives have been satisfied that process improvement should be attempted, initiate an Engineering Process Group (EPG). The EPG's role is to establish and prioritize process improvement actions, produce plans to accomplish the actions, and commit resources to execute the plans. It also either writes the processes or assigns personnel to write the processes, and then reviews and update them. More about roles and responsibilities can be found in Chapter 12.

Planning is critical, and during Set Up, planning is the primary activity. While the plans for each organization differ, there are certain plans that seem to be commonly used among different organizations. They are:

■ Process Improvement (PI) Plan—High-level strategic plans that document the organization's vision of process improvement and success factors and justify the initial budget for this effort.
■ Implementation/Operations Plan—Tactical-level plans that discuss the formation of specific groups and include deliverables and timetables.
■ Action Plans—Very specific plans that address specific weaknesses and organizational problems discovered during an appraisal or other organizational process baselining technique.

Guidelines and templates for these plans are included in Chapter 13.

SCAMPI

Somewhere between the PI Plan and the Implementation/Operations Plan, an appraisal is usually done. Before you can begin your process improvement effort, you really need to understand your organization. Most people would argue that they already know what is going on throughout their workplace. While that may be true for some folks, we have found that people know their *own* jobs; they don't necessarily know *other people's* jobs and roles and duties, and they certainly don't know how everything done throughout their departments *fits* into the entire organization. Most senior managers (at the executive levels of an organization) also think they know what is really happening. *But they don't.* Just because a flurry of memos has been written mandating something to be done, does not mean that it is being done. (Our experience shows that things need to be communicated at least seven times and in three ways before people even hear the message.) It also does not mean that everyone is doing it the same way. The thing about process improvement to remember is that consistency is the key. While we don't expect people to mindlessly follow instructions like some sort of robots, we are looking for consistent application of policies, procedures, processes, plans, and standards. So, in order to truly understand what is going on at your place of business, we recommend that the first step in process improvement be to conduct some sort of organizational process appraisal.

SCAMPI (Standard CMMI Appraisal Method for Process Improvement) is the appraisal method developed by the SEI. SCAMPI is an appraisal method for organizations that want to evaluate their own or another organization's processes using the CMMI as their reference model. SCAMPI consists of a structured set of team activities that includes conducting interviews, reviewing documents, receiving and giving presentations, and analyzing surveys and questionnaires. SCAMPI results are ratings and findings of strengths, weaknesses, and improvement activities using the CMMI. What are these results used for? To award contracts and to baseline processes for process improvement. Results are based on how the organization satisfies the goals for each process area. One or more projects, process areas, and maturity or capability levels are investigated, depending on the purpose of the SCAMPI. So, the steps in the SCAMPI are basically:

- Gather and review documentation
- Conduct interviews
- Discover and document strengths and deficiencies
- Present findings

And the primary components of a SCAMPI are:

- Planning and preparing for the appraisal
- Collecting and consolidating data, both before and during the appraisal
- Making judgments
- Determining ratings
- Reporting results

There are three classes of appraisals recognized by the SEI when using the CMMI: A, B, and C. Each class is distinguished by its degree of rigor. SCAMPI and other appraisals are discussed in greater detail in Chapter 20 and Chapter 21. A comparison of other assessment methods can be found in Appendix A.

The Design Phase

The Design phase focuses on establishing the Process Action Teams (PATs) to build the organization's processes. The initial steps for this effort are:

- Generate the PAT charters
- Review, modify, approve the charters
- Generate Action Plans
- Review, modify, approve plans
- Assign work per the Action Plans
- Do the work according to the Action Plans (generate policies/procedures/standards)
- Develop supporting metrics and measurement techniques
- Develop required training material
- Track status
- Review/recommend tools
- Facilitate/review/monitor work
- Update Action Plans
- Attend meetings/Support EPG

We discuss creating the documentation listed above in Chapters 14 and 16.

The Pilot Phase

After the Design phase is completed, the processes developed by the PATs should be piloted across two or more projects. The Pilot phase consists of the following steps:

- Select pilot projects
- Document success criteria and measurement techniques
- Orient and train pilot project members in CMMI concepts
- Orient and train pilot project members in the processes and procedures developed
- Perform the pilots
- Monitor the pilots
- Analyze results from the pilots
- Measure success
- Provide lessons learned
- Update procedures and repilot as needed

As described below, the piloting effort consists of a structured approach to implementing a selected number of procedures in project(s) throughout the organization and then evaluating the procedures throughout the project(s), as well as at the end of the pilot.

Select the Pilot Project(s)

The project or projects targeted for the pilots selected must be in the appropriate phase of the process and must be in the appropriate phase of the life cycle. For example, you cannot adequately pilot your test procedures if none of the selected pilot projects have reached the test phase yet. In order to adequately test the procedures during the pilot process, the pilots have to be of sufficient duration, size, and have an appropriate number of staff members. The pilots also must last long enough to test all of the procedures piloted. For example, if the procedures being piloted were written for regular projects that were made up of 50 people, lasted ten months, and consisted of over a million lines of code and involved systems engineering, software engineering, and software acquisition personnel, one would expect the pilot to take at least three months and involve members of those organizations mentioned. One would also expect the pilot projects to not be small, Web-based design projects, but match the type of projects for which the procedures were written. Typically, we request that the pilot project last for two to six months, and that at least five PI staff be involved with the pilot on an ongoing basis. Of course, the duration and number of people involved depends on the type of improvement being piloted and the type of development approach selected by the organization.

Document the Success Criteria

In order to determine whether the pilots performed are going to be successful, the organization needs a clear-cut vision of what success really means. The following are some of the criteria that can be used to determine the success of a pilot project:

- How long will the pilots last?
- How many pilots will there be?
- How will the use of the procedures be monitored?
- How will needed changes to the procedures be identified and implemented?

Train Pilot Participants

Project staff from the pilots must be trained in the policies/procedures to be followed and the purpose of the intended pilot. Training does not consist of simply handing the pilot participants the written procedures and telling them to read them! The EPG may assist in the training.

Monitor the Pilot Efforts

The EPG provides an ongoing program for monitoring and analyzing the pilot progress by monitoring and answering questions posed by the pilot project teams.

Refine Policies/Procedures Based on Pilot Results

The PATs must be prepared to make changes to the policies/procedures, both on an ongoing basis as the pilot progresses and afterward as the pilot is evaluated.

After the Pilots

The pilot projects will last as long as there are process areas to be piloted or significant changes to processes. The overall plan should be to use these initial pilot projects on as many PAs as possible. If the originally selected projects for piloting cannot be used again, then new pilot projects may need to be selected.

More information concerning checklists for the pilot effort may be found in the Appendices.

The Implementation Phase

Once the EPG and senior management have decided that the pilots have been successfully completed, the Implementation phase begins. This phase focuses on implementing the new processes across the organization in a phased manner; that is, one or two projects at a time. Each project will be monitored to determine success, and procedures and plans will be modified to reflect the lessons learned from each project. For each project, a go/no go decision will be made to determine whether the processes as written can be continued to be implemented across the organization. Any no go will result in review by senior management and will be considered for rewrites of the processes, retraining, or other remedial efforts.

The Implementation phase mirrors the Pilot phase, changing only in scope and duration. The Implementation phase consists of:

- Selecting one or more actual projects
- Documenting success criteria and measurement techniques
- Orienting and training project members in CMMI concepts
- Orienting and training members in procedures
- Assisting in implementation as needed (by the EPG, PAT members, and the writers of the processes)
- Monitoring and measuring success

- Providing lessons learned
- Updating procedures as needed
- Implementing across more projects as needed
- Signing off completion of the PATs

The EPG needs to determine whether the processes/procedures will be rolled out en masse or one project at a time. We do not recommend that all of the procedures for all of the process areas be rolled out for implementation on all of the projects at the same time.

Monitoring the Process Improvement Effort

The one area that makes upper management uncomfortable is the inability to see progress being made. To that end, we suggest the following measurements as a start to use as tracking mechanisms for PI efforts:

- Actual size of deliverables (based on processes to be developed, as well as standards to be devised; all track directly to the requirements in the CMMI)
- Actual effort (staff hours) expended for major activities
- Start and end dates for major activities
- Completion dates for identified milestones (Design–Pilot–Implementation for each process area)
- Number and type of changes to the PI strategy

In some organizations, the process improvement effort is the first implementation of a structured, disciplined approach for software or systems development. Tracking and reporting these measurements is one of the ways that the process improvement effort can serve as a model for future process improvement and non-process improvement projects. By tracking and communicating progress to upper management, the Process Improvement Program can lead through example. More tracking guidance is given in Chapter 14.

Sample Process Improvement Program

The following is a "typical" approach for process improvement.

ABC Corporation Process Improvement (PI) Program

- Baseline current processes—SCAMPI
- Implement Virtual Organization for ABC Corporation PI Program

- Establish Process Action Teams (PATs)
- Provide training for the Engineering Process Group (EPG) and PATs
- Conduct Process Area (PA) Workshops and Develop Action Plans
- Implement and manage Action Plans
- Perform a midpoint mini-appraisal (e.g., using a Class C Appraisal Method)
- Update plans
- Establish new baseline (conduct a SCAMPI) when mini-appraisal indicates readiness
- Update plans
- Continue

Why should you begin with an appraisal? Most organizations just starting out on the path to process improvement already know that they are Maturity Level 1 or Capability Level 0. Why do a SCAMPI appraisal? Because it is absolutely essential. You may not have to do a full SCAMPI, but at least do an appraisal against the CMMI practices. (The differences between SCAMPI and other CMMI Appraisal Methods are discussed in greater detail in Chapter 20.) This appraisal baselines processes and introduces the PI approach using the model. It helps the organization find, gather, and review existing documentation and standards, promotes team members learning about their organization, helps the organization learn about the CMMI, and helps direct PI efforts based on SCAMPI results (and not someone's idea about what process improvement should be according to whim). This appraisal must be done by trained, certified individuals.

The other thing that the appraisal results will lead to is devising a schedule for improvement activities. Based on SCAMPI results, and working with management, the EPG should devise the schedule, prioritize areas of weakness that need to be addressed and their sequence, and assign resources. Be prepared to change some of your approach as more knowledge of the organization becomes available and as the organization learns the CMMI.

As for the schedule, management is going to be very interested in the schedule and resources. Nowadays, they never give you enough time, resources, or staff. So, even though you just may be casually reading this book, start lobbying management now! Make sure everyone involved, including management, the sponsor, the EPG, PATs, and organization members have CMMI goals in their performance evaluations. Remember, if it is measured and reported to management, it will be done.

Different Approaches for Process Improvement

Now that we have presented the fundamentals of process improvement, let's compare two different approaches.

The Traditional Approach to PI

- Form EPG (35 or more members)
- Define the "AS IS" process
- Define the "TO BE" process
- Gain consensus across the organization
- Start up the PATs
- Continue

The benefits of the traditional approach are that it promotes communication across large organizations, promotes organizational consensus, gives the players in the organization the "big picture," and can expand the focus on areas of improvement not called out specifically in the CMMI.

The disadvantages are that it takes a long time (up to a year or more to define the AS IS process, and then another six months to define the TO BE process). It is hard to show progress to management (players leave before getting to the "real work," that is, the PATs), decision making with a large EPG is unwieldy and slow, funding runs out or the PI project is canceled, and ideas do not always map to the CMMI.

An Alternate Approach

- Do an appraisal (SCAMPI)
- Set up EPG (sometimes already done and it participates in the SCAMPI)
- Proceed based on SCAMPI findings
- Prioritize areas to concentrate on
- Prioritize PATs

The benefits of this alternative approach are that it gets the organization involved quickly, gets the organization CMMI-aware quickly, can show progress to management more easily, proves to the organization that everyone does *not* do everything the same way, documents how things are currently done and ties it directly to CMMI practices, and sells the idea of appraisals to management.

The disadvantages are that this approach takes the organization longer to get the "big picture" (interdependencies of the CMMI and current organizational processes), and some people feel the program is pushed down upon them with little input from the workforce.

Summary

There are four phases of process improvement:

■ Set Up
■ Design
■ Pilot
■ Implement

These four phases may be accomplished in as many ways as there are organizations. However, no matter which approach you take, or even which model you choose, planning the effort and tracking the effects of the effort are paramount. Process improvement must be planned and tracked as if it were a project. If not, slippage will occur and focus and momentum will be lost.

Chapter 12

People, Roles, and Responsibilities

This chapter discusses the major players involved with a process improvement (PI) task. Group and individual responsibilities are highlighted. However, your organization may require more—or fewer—groups. Also note that one person can fulfill many of these roles simultaneously or serially, depending on the size of your organization and the complexity of your process improvement effort.

Process Improvement Champions, Sponsors, and Groups

Process improvement efforts generally require the following individuals and groups:

- PI Sponsor—The person from the organization responsible for overseeing the entire PI effort. This person generally has the power to allocate funds and personnel. This person is usually at the directorate level or above.
- PI Champion—This is the public relations person for the PI effort. This person may or may not also serve as the EPG Lead. This person markets the idea, approach, and results of PI.
- Engineering Process Group (EPG) Lead—This person leads the group that reviews processes. This person assigns tasks to the EPG members, monitors their efforts, and plans the daily duties of the EPG.
- EPG Members—These individuals serve on the EPG as committee members. They are responsible for ensuring that process improvement documentation

is written and followed. They are also responsible for generating metrics to track the process improvement process. They lead the PATs.

■ Process Action Teams (PATs)—These teams generate the process improvement documentation—policies, processes, procedures, charters, and Action Plans.

■ Transition Partner—Usually one or two individuals who are outside consultants brought in to help set up, plan, lead, and monitor progress in organizational process improvement. These individuals bring experience doing process improvement from several other organizations and industries.

Engineering Process Group (EPG)

Previously, under the CMM, the group responsible for establishing the process improvement structure, directing, and monitoring its activities was called the SEPG (Software Engineering Process Group). Now, that group is referred to as the EPG (Engineering Process Group), as Engineering takes in more than just software efforts. Remember, CMMI no longer focuses only on software—it was designed to include many areas of your organization needed to produce a product. Figure 12.1

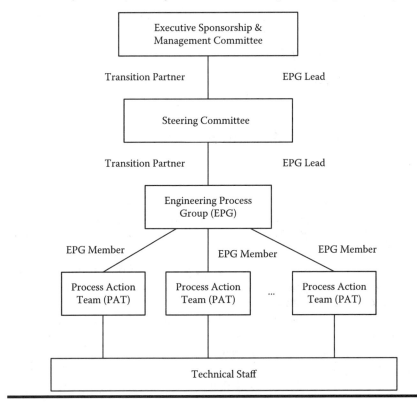

Figure 12.1   Implementing a virtual PI organization.

depicts a typical structure that has proven useful to us when we have instituted process improvement in other organizations. Notice that the Transition Partner and EPG Lead need to interact at multiple levels in the organization.

The EPG's primary role is to improve processes within the organization. This group needs to understand the current process (AS IS), develop a vision of the desired process (TO BE), establish and prioritize process improvement actions, produce a plan to accomplish actions, and commit resources to execute the plan. The EPG is formed from individuals within the organization. The head of the EPG—the EPG Lead—reports on process improvement activities to the Steering Committee. The Steering Committee is responsible for allocating resources, budget, and time to the EPG. The Executive Steering Committee is responsible for providing the initial funding, vision, and directives for process improvement. The PATs are individual teams that are created to address specific process improvement concerns or process areas. Generally speaking, they focus on the areas of weakness found during appraisals. The PATs are the "worker bees." They write the procedures, pilot them, and update them as needed. Members of the PATs are pulled from the technical staff from many projects throughout the organization. The technical staff may also include project managers, and we recommend that they also serve on PATs. Sometimes a Transition Partner is hired to help the organization structure, create, and track process improvement activities. This Transition Partner is usually an outside consultant with process improvement experience performed at several other organizations. An organization may have several EPGs in existence at the same time and several layers of EPGs. It all depends on size and complexity.

When establishing a PI organization, you need to identify a PI Champion. Usually, the champion will be responsible for gaining staff and resources to generate the PI program, and "push" the concept to all layers of the organization. The PI Champion may also serve as the EPG Lead or may appoint someone else for this duty. The EPG Lead is tasked with reporting to the Executive Steering Committee and with overseeing and directing the efforts of the EPG and the various PATs created to develop and implement change. The EPG Lead may also develop and maintain PI management plans. The plans need to document PI tasks, EPG schedules, resource utilization, and risks. Results are reported to senior management. The EPG Lead, before establishing the rest of the EPG, may need to work with senior management in order to address fundamental infrastructure needs. Typical infrastructure needs that should be addressed by the EPG Lead include:

- Setting up or stabilizing communication mechanisms throughout the organization
- Establishing and staffing the EPG, Steering Committee, and Executive Boards
- Establishing and maintaining a Configuration Control Board (CCB)
- Developing CCB control of PI documentation
- Creating mechanisms to present ideas and requests for improvement to the EPG and PATs

- Developing organizational policies for each process area
- Creating a measurement framework to assess success and progress made
- Providing appropriate training and support
- Evaluating and providing appropriate support tools

The EPG will be responsible for developing and implementing Action Plans that address the deficiencies discovered during the appraisal process. Action Plans are written by the PATs and reviewed by the EPG to address the deficiencies found during the appraisal. Action Plans must be reviewed to determine their thoroughness, completeness, and ability to be effectively implemented within the organization's environment. Action Plans are written and updated based on current appraisal results and in conjunction with site business objectives. While the EPG is responsible for these tasks, they may be performed by, or in conjunction with, other individuals within the organization.

One way to create Action Plans and to devise processes (and their associated procedures) is to institute process discovery and definition workshops. These workshops are where the steps necessary to document current AS IS processes and generate preliminary TO BE processes will occur. The participants of this effort generally include the EPG members, the members of the PATs, and any other respected subject-matter experts. The EPG monitor the results of the PATs' activities. If necessary, the Action Plans are updated to refine the approach taken, or to address new issues.

The organization should conduct an EPG-led process review that is performed at all project initiations (to get validation and buy-in of tailoring and process compliance), during major project reviews/milestones (to gather preplanned collection of process measurement data), and at project completion (for lessons learned collection and plan versus actual analyses). The EPG should also review current organizational methods in use for process and product measurement, determine if the right measurement data are being collected, and make necessary adjustments to the collection and analysis process. This step insures that metric reporting and follow-up actions are in place.

Every six months, we recommend that appraisals or mini-assessments be performed to determine the extent to which the deficiencies discovered during the baseline appraisal have been resolved. When it appears that most of the deficiencies have been addressed, a new, formal appraisal of all the process areas in the desired maturity or capability levels should be performed to establish a new baseline and prioritize follow-on activities.

Sounds like the EPG has a lot to do. Yes, it does. Most organizations find that being a member of the EPG is a full-time job. Those organizations that allow an individual to only charge this effort as part-time has usually started the process improvement death march. This death march is well known. It is caused by a general misunderstanding of what process improvement is about and why it is being undertaken. The death march usually begins by senior management announcing that a certain level of the CMMI will be achieved by a specific date. That date may be two years in advance but is generally only one year in advance. Unless you have been doing process improvement using the CMMI for at least two years, we would not recommend setting this date so close. Generally speaking, it took organizations at least 18 to 24 months to achieve Level 2 using the CMM. And most organizations reported a much longer time frame. If management is browbeating its workers into achieving a level in a shortened time frame, it is totally missing the boat. This sort of mentality shows that this organization does not understand process improvement, is not really dedicated to it, and will not reap lasting benefits from it. It just wants the rating. The death march approach has failed for many, many organizations. Even organizations that have successfully "passed" an appraisal have slipped back because of lack of a solid foundation and true institutionalization.

Process Action Teams (PATs)

How do the PATs work? An EPG member leads a specific PAT. The PATs are conducted like the EPG (charters, agendas, behaviors, tracking action items, etc.). No one sits on a PAT without receiving training in the process area under development, otherwise, the PAT member doesn't really know what is expected and what he is supposed to do, so he makes it up as he goes along, straying from the CMMI. PAT member qualifications are the same as for the EPG.

If the EPG has not developed templates, before beginning this effort, a PAT might be created to do just that so that all of the PATs follow the same structure, reducing the need to rewrite documentation. Search Web sites to get several examples of everything, including blank templates for procedures. It's OK to use a Department of Defense (DOD)-based Web site and examples, even if you are not working in a DOD-based organization. The CMMI brings structure to an organization. DOD thrives on structure. DOD has good stuff, their Web sites are free—take a look! Start with the Software Engineering Institute's (SEI's) two Web sites—www.sei.cmu.edu and seir.sei.cmu.edu. The latter Web site requires a password and logon ID. It contains a bulletin board and recent articles.

The PATs need to generate PAT Charters, PAT Plans, and a CMMI compliance matrix that tracks back to the practices for each process area they are developing. This matrix ties activities to practices and specific people and dates. The matrix is used for status tracking and to check on the extent of the documentation produced. PATs generally write the procedures and processes for the organization.

If I'm on a PAT, how do I determine where to start? The EPG will determine which process areas to focus on first, based on the results of the SCAMPI. The PAT Lead (an EPG member) will determine which practices and associated findings to attack in which sequence, by reviewing complexity, available staff, skill sets of staff, and so forth. The PAT Lead works with his group determining work assignments and sequence of the work. The PAT Lead, working with the PAT members and the EPG will ask the following questions: Can a practice be combined with another practice or practices into one document instead of several? What are the dependencies between the other practices in that process area and with other process areas? How do these activities tie in with activities of other PATs? Do we need to write procedures for all of the practices in the process area? Are we going to have a separate Metrics PAT that focuses on the Directing Implementation common feature?

Here is an example: Each process area has some sort of requirement for "objectively evaluating adherence." Are you going to have each PAT write a procedure documenting how this will be done, or will you try to write one overall, generic procedure for how to perform this function for all of the process areas, and a checklist for those items to review per process area? You can do this in whatever way makes sense for your organization, as long as the practices for each process area are covered.

Consider having each PAT initially write procedures for evaluating adherence reviews and for Directing Implementation. Then stop, gather what has been written, and keep the best, discard the rest. Start writing a generic tailoring procedure that can be used when deciding which procedures and which part of the procedures to use for which parts of your organization. The approach helps sell the procedures to the organization. You might define a large, medium, and small project, and what tailoring can be done based on this definition. Include a tailoring section in each procedure. However, little tailoring will be necessary if you write your procedures for the most common business practices. For example, if you are a large company that writes automobile insurance polices for millions of customers, and the programs that support this effort were written in the 1970s in COBOL, don't try to write procedures for tracking customer complaints via your brand-new intranet Web site. You are not in the Web site business—you are in the automobile insurance business. And the procedures you write must be specific enough to be followed. That means they must be detailed. You cannot write detailed procedures for Web site customer service that can be used by the rest of the automobile insurance departments. Another example: If you are building weapons systems using nuclear missiles, don't think you can use the procedures written for tracking financial accounts payable.

So, get the PATs working. After they get some experience with the CMMI, get all the PATs together. Discuss who is doing what. Draw a chart on how the work is fitting together. Draw a chart on what needs to be done and where the connections are. Don't get too detailed, and don't get too excited when you find duplication of effort or work deferred to other PATs.

Whatever you choose will be wrong and you will have to backtrack. The PATs love deferring work to other PATs. It's not always fair or workable to have one PAT write documentation for all of the PATs to implement. Remember, you should just choose an approach, start out doing it one way or another, and then stop and see what you have and whether it is working.

Training for PI Members

Train the EPG using the SEI-authorized Introduction to CMMI course, in Process Improvement Planning, and in the SCAMPI method. Before starting each PAT, get training in the PA or area the PAT is to focus on. Initial training for the rest of the organization can consist of receiving an overview of the CMMI. Be prepared for questions. If there are no questions, either the audience members do not understand your presentation, they do not care about your presentation, or they care very much but feel that they are being dragged into this effort and have no voice.

In order to avoid this scenario, have a well-respected member of your EPG give an overview of why they have started doing PI, what the organization can expect the EPG to do, why it is important, and what the organization (each individual) needs to do to support this effort. And concentrate on WIFM—What's In It For Me? Make sure to relate the benefits to something relevant for the people in your organization. Setting up a common drive where the staff can view what is being written and sharing information as it is being written will also aid in making individuals feel that they are part of this process.

EPG and PAT Member Qualifications

The members of these groups need to be motivated. We don't want lazy, deadweight, individuals who are just waiting for retirement to come. Neither do we want "BSers." A BSer is a person full of himself who talks a good game but can't deliver on his promises. An EPG/PAT needs imaginative, self-starters with a wide range of experience. Experience can include working in different jobs within the organization (which shows how such things as roles, duties, and other organizational departments fit together) and also working at other companies. This diversity provides other perspectives that may prove useful in your organization. Because writing will be such a large part of this effort, people who are able to write and like to write should be approached. Another big selling point for implementing the procedures written is if they were written by respected members of the organization (technically respected, as well as movers and shakers).

How many people should be on an EPG? According to articles published by the SEI over the years, 1 percent to 3 percent of your organization.

If you are in a large organization, that may be too big. If you are in a small organization, that may be too small. We find that between five to ten motivated people usually works well. However, they have to be prepared to write procedures and do work—not just review and comment on the work other people have produced.

Sometimes, in order to get buy-in, the director of this effort will recommend EPG and PAT members for political reasons. If you must, you must. But, buy-in does not come from politics. It comes from doing something good that makes life easier in the workplace. If forced to choose, choose quality over quantity, and talent over politics. Remember, you will never get total, 100 percent buy-in.

Conducting Meetings

This section holds true for both the PATs and the EPG. Hold meetings at least weekly, require attendance, and require timeliness. Take notes and publish the notes, but rotate who actually takes the notes; you don't need a secretary, and you want each person to contribute equally—not just have someone whose only role is to take notes. Send out an agenda at least one day before the meeting. Try to get the sponsor/executives to attend a meeting here and there. They are busy, but their attendance proves to the members that their efforts are being noticed. It also shows buy-in from the executives. The EPG meetings should consist primarily of reviewing the status of what is occurring on the PATs, and planning how to resolve issues that occur on the PATs. Discuss any problems, issues, or concerns. Allow for questions back and forth. Document and track action items. Store the meeting minutes in an online common drive (include dates of meetings).

There needs to be a simple and easy mechanism for the organization to present ideas and issues to the EPG. Whether this is done via your intranet, or whether you have Engineering Change Proposals or Process Improvement Proposals—it doesn't matter. What matters is that the people in your organizations feel that they are part of the process of process improvement. They need to be able to introduce ideas, as well as to challenge the ideas produced by the EPG currently under development. Also necessary is a mechanism to communicate to the organization what the EPG is doing. See the discussion elsewhere in this book concerning a communication plan for ideas. Remember you have to communicate things at least seven times and three ways just to be heard.

Quality Assurance (QA) and the EPG

What's the difference between Quality Assurance and the EPG? Can't we have QA do process improvement too? Can't we just structure the organization so that process improvement becomes another QA initiative? No, that is a recipe for disaster. If you set up your process improvement effort as part of QA's duties, process improvement will be seen as just another QA task. It will not receive the attention from management—and from the organization as a whole—that it requires. Can QA people serve as part of the EPG? Of course. But the EPG should be representative of your entire organization—not just the QA department.

Besides, QA and the EPG serve different functions. QA reviews both the products built and the activities that occur on a project. The EPG is responsible for reviewing processes that occur across the organization. Therefore, there is some overlap. However, QA's primary role focuses on the projects, while the EPG focuses on processes throughout the organization. The EPG does not concentrate on products—that is QA's job.

What about standards? Doesn't QA review products to see if they conform to standards? Yes. However, one of the flaws of both the CMM and the CMMI is that the authors of both models assumed that organizations had standards in place and were using them. While some of the older, larger, more mature organizations did have standards, the smaller, younger ones did not. So before they could focus on process, they had to back up and devise some product standards. In their search for standards, they often just usurped the standards written for DOD (MIL-STD-2167A, MIL-STD-498, IEEE, NIST, FipsPub) or they just copied standards from a previous workplace. This is also not a good idea. Standards must fit the type of work done and the culture of the organization. Standards should be tailored to work for everybody mandated to use them. Otherwise, they will not be used.

Summary

The organization needs to devise a method to assign resources, schedule the work, decompose activities to manageable size, trace requirements and contractual obligations, and measure success. We suggest that individuals be given certain roles to play to carry out these assignments. We suggest that a sponsor designate a champion, and that an EPG Lead be appointed to work with personnel from the organization to establish the process improvement infrastructure. The CMMI is tremendously interconnected. Your organization will want to know how everything fits together. Do not attempt to flowchart the CMMI. This exercise goes in one ear and out the other because people have little experience with the CMMI and can't equate it with anything relevant to them.

Try to do most of what the CMMI suggests. If it does not fit, document why and devise an alternative practice. Tailor your approach to your organization. For example, when writing procedures, DOD likes books, commercial organizations don't. Keep it simple and to the point.

Process improvement is continuous. Once you start, you will uncover more and more areas to be improved and issues to be resolved.

Chapter 13

Documentation Guidelines

This chapter presents our approach for generating the piles of documentation necessary for process improvement. The thing to remember is that this documentation is *necessary* documentation. You do not write BS just to get credit for finishing your assignment to write a particular piece of documentation. The old CMM tenet still applies, "If it isn't used, it doesn't exist." Process improvement is not a documentation drill. Generally speaking, if your procedures are not used throughout the organization, then *you have no procedures*!!! The whole purpose of the CMMI is to use what you have developed. Your documentation is not "for show."

Introduction

Why is documentation necessary? Consider this example. Say you are stuck at work one evening. You think you can get home in time to fix dinner, but doing some shopping beforehand is definitely out. So you call your teenage son and ask him to go to the store to buy some food for dinner. Would you leave it at that? Those of you who have teenagers know the answer is a resounding no. You decide that you will fix macaroni and cheese for dinner, and you tell him this over the phone. Consider all of the different options someone would have with only that requirement. Do you get the boxed stuff? If yes, do you get the name brand or the store generic? If you are fixing it from scratch, what kind of cheese do you get? How much? What kind of macaroni? How much? Do you need anything else, like maybe milk? Regular, skim, condensed, evaporated? Now, back to the teenager. If you tell him all of this over the phone, what else do you tell him? That's right—write it down! Why? Because you know he is more likely to get it right if he writes it down than if he just tries to remember it. Unless your teenager is some kind of genius.

Well, process improvement is the same way. If you want someone to do it right, and have everyone doing a task consistently, then write it down. And write it in enough detail that it is not open to interpretation. Understanding this concept is the heart of this chapter.

When writing documentation or making writing assignments, remember people hate it, people are not good at it, or they think they can do it until they try and then they can't. But they can be taught. When writing documentation, don't use documentation from your previous organization. You'll get to check off the Designing procedures part of your plan, but ...

- You won't get buy-in from the organization
- Your wonderful procedures will never be implemented across the organization
- You'll fail the SCAMPI

Doesn't the CMMI tell me how to do stuff? Can't I just copy what it says and reword it a little bit? No! The CMMI documents best practices from other organizations. It describes *what* to do, not *how* to do it. The organization's job is to document *how* to do things.

I know what you are thinking, "This is gonna be hard ..." Your organization members will figure out that this effort is more than they originally thought. They will start justifying why they can't or won't do something. Usually it boils down to it's too hard, they don't know how, it's a hassle, they don't want to do it. That is not a strong justification!

Don't worry—we provide some templates and guidelines as examples in Chapters 14 and 15.

Definitions

We are often asked to interpret the words in the CMMI. Part of that interpretation includes defining the different types of documentation required to implement an effective process improvement strategy.

What is a standard? What is a process? What's a procedure? What's the difference? A *standard* is a structure serving as a foundation to be used as a model for later development. It is recognized as an acceptable example and has been officially authorized for use. Its purpose is to promote uniformity and consistency of results, leading to a quality *product*. The IEEE defines a *process* as a sequence of steps performed for a given purpose. The CMMI definition is much more convoluted and discussed elsewhere in this book. What's the difference?

Standards are generally thought of as pertaining to products, specifically formats for deliverables. This is what the product should look like. Examples are a template for a System Requirements Specification, a Test Results Report format, a

System Implementation Plan boilerplate, Coding Standards (program layout and data naming conventions).

Processes consist of actual steps of what to do to build the product. *Procedures* consist of step-by-step instructions of how to perform the process. The examples relate to a Risk Management Process. In a Risk Management Process, we might simply list the steps as:

1. Identify the risk
2. Prioritize the risk
3. Mitigate the risk

Well, that's all right as far as it goes, but if you proudly handed these three steps to your project managers of several different projects, do you really think they would all follow this process the same way? Do you think they would all identify risks in the same manner? Would they prioritize them at the same level of criticality? Would they choose the correct approaches for controlling the risks? No. That's why we need procedures to support the processes—processes are at too high a level to be consistently applied. An example of a supporting risk management procedure might be something like:

■ If the risk affects safety of human beings, categorize it as level 1
■ If the risk will cause the site to shut down and all processing to stop, categorize the risk as level 2
■ If the risk will allow processing to continue, or consists of a simple fix, categorize it as level 3

And there would be examples and definitions to help flesh out the information listed in the bullets (like how to identify a level 1, 2, or 3 risk, and what to do about it). It's just a simple example for this discussion.

The point is that the CMMI requires processes to be *documented in enough detail to be followed*. A process is not just a high-level flowchart of *whats*. It needs supporting procedures to be effective.

In addition to processes, procedures, and standards, there are policies, charters, and plans. A *policy* is a high-level document, generated under senior management sponsorship, that directs the organization to perform. It is a high-level statement of what is to be done, and who is responsible to do it, and maybe even why it is to be done. A *plan* is a document specific to achieving a goal, objective, or producing a product. There can be many levels of plans, from high-level strategic vision plans, to low-level project plans that describe how the project will be run, to very detailed and specific Action Plans to address specific weaknesses found during a process appraisal. Plans should discuss estimates for size of the endeavor, the number of personnel needed to be assigned, the skill sets needed from those individuals, tasks divided into milestones, deliverables, training required, the time the task is scheduled to take, the general approach, risks, money, and assumptions. A *charter* is a document that describes why a group was formed and how a group intends to act. It discusses prescribed behaviors, when the group shall meet, the time of the meetings, rules of conduct, scope of the group, resolution of issues, and purpose.

Process Definition Approaches

This section describes our approach to supporting the Process Action Teams that are charged with developing processes and procedures to be implemented throughout the organization.

One way to develop processes and the rest of the documentation necessary is to begin with writing workshops. Those individuals tasked with creating documentation should attend these workshops where ideas concerning the area of documentation are discussed. Then after the workshop, the individuals tasked with the assignment go back to their desks and begin writing. *The documentation itself is not produced during the workshop.* That would take forever. However, the workshops are very useful in giving people ideas. Also consider assigning two people to write the document. However, make sure that each is writing the document or that they have worked out a deal where one writes it and the other reviews it and makes changes. Just don't assume that they are writing the document. We have found that sometimes when this dual approach is used, one person assumes (or wishes) that the other person is writing the document, and vice versa, and the document does not get written. And don't think that this documentation will be perfect, good, or even useable. Make sure you plan for rewrites and rereviews.

All workshops should be facilitated by someone who knows how to facilitate a workshop. A key to conducting an effective workshop is preparation. The workshop facilitator (who can be the Engineering Process Group [EPG] Lead, an EPG member, or an outside consultant) should begin working with the workshop sponsor to:

- Define the purpose of the workshop
- Develop a logical agenda and write a comprehensive outline
- Identify measurable objectives
- Identify potentially hot topics and controversial agenda items
- Review current policies, procedures, and processes

The general steps that occur in facilitating a functional workshop are described in the following sections.

Identify Workshop Parameters

The first step is to work with the EPG to define the objective(s) of the workshop and gain an understanding of the expected participants, for example, the participants' technical sophistication and relative interest in the issues at hand. Then determine the most suitable scope of activities and material contents to be prepared for the workshop stakeholders as well as the appropriate level of detail to be presented.

Prepare Workshop Activities and Materials

Prepare and publish a workshop agenda along with instructions to the anticipated participants. If the purpose of the workshop is to share information, prepare presentation slides. If the purpose is to collect information, construct exercises and data gathering templates. If the purpose is to make decisions, establish preliminary criteria, trade-offs, and scoring/ranking methodologies. Present the draft workshop materials for EPG review and approval. Make sure to have plenty of flip charts and markers available. Some organizations prefer to do this via computer or groupware, using a package such as Lotus Notes.

Manage Workshop Logistics

Work closely with staff to ensure the timely distribution of any read-ahead packets that outline the workshop's purpose and scheduled activities. Verify that adequate meeting space is reserved and properly set up in advance, all necessary materials and supplies are available, and equipment is in working order.

Facilitate Workshops

Facilitation support begins by making any necessary introductions, reiterating the purpose of the workshop, and reviewing the ground rules for an orderly, productive exchange of information. Then proceed to initiate and focus discussions on the planned topics while making ad hoc adjustments to allow issues requiring additional attention to be fully addressed. Always maintain control of the workshop at all times, taking the steps necessary to keep it on target and moving at an appropriate pace.

Document Workshop Outcomes

Consolidate all information discussed and collected during the workshop, and document major outcomes and decisions made. In coordination with organizational staff, distribute the resulting documentation to the workshop participants for their review and comment so that there is no misunderstanding with respect to workshop proceedings. Updates and clarifications are made as appropriate.

Analyze Workshop Findings

Conduct a thorough analysis of the workshop findings in conjunction with key organizational representatives. Analyze this information to determine its significance and implications, as well as to identify any constraints and opportunities for improvement. Supportable conclusions are drawn, and rational, justifiable recommendations are forwarded.

Plan for any schedule changes by developing contingency plans for workshop dates and facilitators. When reviewing any materials, the EPG should ensure that any workshop deliverables are CMMI-compliant.

Some organizations find the preceding workshops too lengthy, too formal, too time consuming, and too costly. If the organization does not desire to follow the above approach, there is another way. Identify knowledgeable people in the organization; interview them about how they do their jobs; write it down; compare what they do and how they do it to the CMMI; identify gaps; and fill in the gaps with your ideas on how to do things. Then present this to the EPG for approval and piloting. The EPG cannot really predict whether the procedures will work. Pilots have proved very helpful in this area. Another way to write procedures is to assign them to one individual, and have him go back to his desk and write them. While this may get you off the hook, and while it looks like something is being done, this method generally does not work. It is too much work for one individual. Even if you have several individuals writing procedures, they still will need help reconciling how they perform a function versus how *the rest of the organization* does it versus what the CMMI is recommending.

Summary

When writing any of the documentation discussed, remember to focus your efforts on:

- What is practical
- What is practicable
- What is tied to the CMMI
- What is tied to SCAMPI results

Make sure the people writing the procedures understand that they will also have to follow them. One of our client organizations calls this "Eat your own dog food." It's easy to write bad procedures if you think they will not pertain to you.

Chapter 14

Planning and Tracking the Effort

This chapter discusses the various plans needed to guide the process improvement effort and a few approaches to tracking the tasks involved. While the CMMI considers process descriptions and procedures to be part of the "plan" needed for each process area, this chapter defines a plan as the strategy necessary to prepare the organization for process improvement. Processes and procedures are discussed in Chapter 15.

Defining Plans

CMMI requires a "plan" for every process area (PA). However, these plans incorporate not only what one would normally expect in a plan (activities, time frames, general approach and strategy, estimated resource expenditures), but also what used to be called "procedures" (see Chapter 13 for a discussion of procedures). In order to add greater value to your Process Improvement (PI) program, we have separated out these concepts. In reality it does not matter whether you call these documents plans, procedures, George, or Shirley, as long as you generate some documentation that covers these concepts.

A plan is not a schedule! It is the documented strategy necessary to perform work. It generally includes a definition of the scope of the work, the resources needed, why the work is to be done, how the work will be tracked, how it will be reviewed, schedules, and costs. It also includes an explanation of why the work was planned the way it was, so that if errors occur or project managers change, the plan can be understood and updated to promote project continuation.

There are three types of plans in process improvement that must be addressed in your Design phase. They are:

1. Process Improvement (PI) Plan—Overall Strategic Plan used for funding, resources, justifying the PI program, and defining goals.
2. Implementation/Operations Plan—Tactical Plan, or more detailed plan, that defines the effort for the entire organization into manageable tasks based on the results of the SCAMPI. Also called a PI Action Plan.
3. Action Plans—Very detailed plans created by the Process Action Teams (PATs) that focus on what their PAT is supposed to do and how and when it will be done. PATs focus on one process area (PA) or one problem area noted as a weakness from the SCAMPI appraisal.

A Communication Plan is also popular. We discuss that plan at the end of the section on plans.

The PI Plan

Executives need a PI Plan. Its purpose is to get executive buy-in, generate a written contract for PI, and get money allocated for PI. Sometimes the sponsor will generate the plan, sometimes the Engineering Process Group (EPG) Lead will generate the plan, and sometimes the Transition Partner (outside consultant) will generate the plan. Whoever creates the plan must remember that PI must be managed like any other well-managed project—do a schedule, track against the schedule, assign staff, identify and track deliverables, and so forth. Process Improvement must be planned and tracked just like any other project. The PI plan should address and schedule the following activities:

■ Using a SCAMPI to baseline current processes
■ Establishing the EPG and PAT structure
■ Providing training in the CMMI and PAs
■ Measuring progress through mini-appraisals
■ Designing–Piloting–Implementing processes
■ Conducting full-blown SCAMPI for certification

The PI Plan defines the problem, the purpose of PI for this organization, and the purpose of this plan. This plan is used to sell the CMMI and process improvement to the organization—its executives, its managers, and its lower-level staff. The PI Plan must document the benefits and costs and define the business goals and objectives linked to business issues confronting the enterprise.

The plan also defines the scope of the work and how to manage changes to scope. It documents project resources and other support needed. Assumptions and risks are also addressed (most common are pulling staff away from PI to do "real work," emergent work, production emergencies, etc.).

As for tracking and controlling the effort, the PI Plan documents how you will track, control, measure, and report the status of the work. In the plan, present your schedule with milestones included at the lowest level of detail that you feel you can realistically accomplish and that you feel are necessary in order to track at a level that keeps the effort focused. Discuss rewards and include a "Miscellaneous" category for anything else that fits your organization or will politically motivate individuals who might prove to be obstacles in this effort.

We don't include an example PI Plan because these plans can be very different, depending on why an organization is undertaking process improvement, the culture of the organization, and the different levels of planning required. The PI Plan is often written by a Transition Partner (outside consultant), in conjunction with the proposed PI Champion and PI Sponsor. Because budgets and schedules are a large part of this plan, financial statistics for this program can be found on the Software Engineering Institute Web site, www.sei.cmu.edu. Also check with the budget/financial area of the enterprise for data on past improvement/quality/ measurement programs, as well as any major expenditures forecast for upcoming projects and organizational endeavors.

Implementation/Operations Plan

The Implementation/Operations Plan comes after the shock of the baseline SCAMPI has worn off. It is now time to get real. The PI Plan is a high-level, strategic vision type of plan. It makes a case for process improvement and calculates the initial, overall budget. The Implementation/Operations Plan is more detailed because it is based on the results of the SCAMPI appraisal that documented how close an organization is to a maturity or capability level, which process areas are satisfied or not satisfied or nowhere near to being satisfied, and the weaknesses found in how the organization implements the PAs. Therefore, this plan is based much more on reality and real issues. This plan may contradict the original PI Plan. Document any deviations from the original PI Plan.

The Implementation/Operations Plan discusses how to address and implement the results of the SCAMPI. Take those results, review and analyze them, and prioritize the PAs, issues, and concerns. Determine how to set up the EPG/PAT/ Configuration Control Board (CCB) infrastructure, which individuals to assign to these activities, training required, and an initial pilot strategy.

The PAs should be prioritized based on complexity, difficulty implementing or performing within this organization, amount of documentation needed, how close to attainment based on the SCAMPI, "bang for the buck," and where an early success may be achieved.

Format your plan based on the four phases of process improvement: Set Up, Design, Pilot, and Implementation (see Table 14.1).

The last section of the Implementation/Operations Plan discusses controlling the effort. Basic tracking mechanisms should initially focus on the following areas. As learning and sophistication increase within the organization, more metrics may be added. Basic metrics to track include:

- Actual size of deliverables
- Actual effort (staff hours) expended for major activities
- Start and end dates for major activities
- Completion dates for identified milestones
- Number and type of changes to this plan

Action Plans

Action Plans are usually produced by the PATs assigned to address the weaknesses found during the SCAMPI. Table 14.2 shows a sample Action Plan template. PATs are usually set up according to process areas (such as Requirements Management (REQM), Project Planning, Integrated Process Management). Action Plans should be based on the SCAMPI results. They also must be measurable. Tie them directly to the CMMI PAs and practices to maintain focus on the CMMI itself and to make tracking progress easier. Where the organization decides to deviate from the CMMI, build and document a strong case for why. Alternative practices may be substituted for the practices, when justified appropriately and strongly. Action Plans will focus on how to generate processes and procedures, and how to introduce them into the organization once produced. Tracking and measuring the effectiveness of the Action Plans and the processes and the procedures are usually functions of the EPG.

Communications Plans

Achieving success in process improvement programs requires more than good policies and procedures. The organization must "buy-in" to the effort, and support must be maintained throughout the implementation program, especially early on when costs are highly visible, but benefits are not. An effective Communications Plan may prove critical to PI program success. Whether your organization is small or large, whether your organization requires a formal or informal approach, you must determine a method for keeping everyone informed. A Communications Plan has four key objectives:

Table 14.1 Implementation/Operations Plan Template

1.0 Set Up
  1.1 SCAMPI Results
  1.2 Areas of Focus
  1.3 EPG Structure
  1.4 Process Action Team (PAT) Structure
  1.5 Configuration Control Boards
  1.6 Quality Assurance
  1.7 Schedule
  1.8 Tools
  1.9 Risks
  1.10 Reviews and Approvals

2.0 Design Phase
  2.1 Generate PAT Charter
  2.2 Review, modify, approve charter
  2.3 Generate Action Plan
  2.4 Review, modify, approve plan
  2.5 Assign work per Action plan
  2.6 Do the work (policies/procedures/standards)
  2.7 Develop metrics and measurement techniques
  2.8 Develop required training material
  2.9 Track status
  2.10 Review/recommend tools
  2.11 Facilitate/review/monitor work
  2.12 Update Action Plans
  2.13 Attend meetings/Support EPG

3.0 Pilot Phase
  3.1 Select pilot projects
  3.2 Document success criteria and measurement techniques
  3.3 Orient and train project members in CMMI concepts
  3.4 Orient and train members in processes and procedures
  3.5 Perform the pilots
  3.6 Monitor the pilots
  3.7 Analyze results from the pilots
  3.8 Measure success
  3.9 Provide lessons learned
  3.10 Update procedures and OSSP as needed

4.0 Implementation Phase
  4.1 Select one or more true projects
  4.2 Document success criteria and measurement techniques
  4.3 Orient and train project members in CMM concepts
  4.4 Orient and train members in procedures
  4.5 Assist in implementation as needed
  4.6 Monitor and measure success
  4.7 Provide lessons learned
  4.8 Update procedures and OSSP as needed
  4.9 Implement across more projects as needed
  4.10 Signoff completion of PATs

5.0 Control and Monitoring

Table 14.2 Sample Action Plan template.

EXECUTIVE OVERVIEW
1.0 Objective/Scope
1.1 Problem Statement
1.2 Vision After Success
1.3 Goal Statement
2.0 Entry Criteria
2.1 Management Sponsor(s)
3.0 Major Inputs
3.1 Relevant Appraisal Information (Results/Deficiencies)
3.2 Relevant Existing Work (Projects/Tasks/Pilots/PA Improvements and Results)
4.0 Summary of Approach
4.1 Steps/Tasks for PA (Based on Practices)
4.2 Short Term Scenario (Schedule for Implementation)
5.0 Major Outputs
6.0 Exit Criteria
DETAILED PLAN
7.0 Programmatic Issues
7.1 Constraints/Limitations
7.2 Assumptions/Dependencies
7.3 Risks
7.4 Alternatives
8.0 Schedule
8.1 Steps
8.2 Process Improvement Project (PERT/GANTT)
9.0 Required Resources
9.1 People (Who/How much of their time)
9.2 Training
9.3 Computer/Technological Resources
9.4 Other
MANAGEMENT OF PLAN
10.0 Reviews
10.1 Peer Reviews
10.2 Management Reviews
10.3 Other Reviews
10.4 Measurement Criteria
11.0 Roll Out/Implementation/Training Plan

- Achieve and maintain an enterprise awareness of the CMMI and the PI Program
- Maintain the PI Program focus and momentum
- Facilitate process implementation activities
- Provide a vehicle for rewards and recognition

There are numerous target audiences in any organization. Each audience is impacted differently and may have a different role to play. Communications need to be targeted to the various audiences. In addition, communications should utilize multiple vehicles for delivering the message to facilitate reaching a broader audience. Our experience shows that things need to be communicated at least seven times and three ways before people even hear the message. Communications mechanisms used include:

- Articles in monthly newsletters
- Articles by participants from the various divisions/departments, PAT members, Transition Partners, and EPG staff
- Intranet Web pages containing information on PI activities such as workshops and pilot projects, and which may include the Process Asset Library of procedures and best practices that may be of value to personnel
- Briefing to senior management at yearly management retreats
- Presentations at "all hands" meetings

Tracking the Documentation

Monitoring the process improvement effort is critical to stay focused and ensure progress is being made. To track the activities of the PATs, we provide a sample compliance matrix. This matrix is based on tracking the activities performed during the Design phase. Piles of documentation will be written. This table may help you track this effort. However, don't be fooled into thinking that once you have your procedures written, you are done. Remember, you still have to train the pilot participants, pilot the procedures, rewrite them based on the pilot results, train the organization in the procedures, roll out the procedures for implementation, and track adherence and changes. There is still a lot of work to be done. The Action Plans can track PAT efforts, and the PI Plan and Implementation/Operations Plan can be used to track EPG and organizational-level tasks.

Table 14.3 shows a sample CMMI compliance matrix for the Requirements Management process area. This matrix can be used as a checklist to track whether procedures have been written for a practice, what stage (or status) the documentation produced is in, and who is responsible. You can add more columns to insert comments, subpractice artifacts, or anything else you feel you need to help structure and track your efforts. It should be noted that in order to fully understand and implement the practice, the *subpractice* usually must be analyzed and incorporated into the procedure. This template can also be used for tracking infrastructure documentation, such as plans, charters, and standards preparation, as well as any other activities performed throughout the PI effort. Appraisal Teams can also use the completed checklist to help determine goal satisfaction.

We feel that most practices should be covered in some way by documentation—either a single document per practice, or more likely, a single document that describes how to do several practices.

It is also necessary to track how the procedures are being used in the projects and to what extent they are being used. For this task, we suggest talking to people to find out. If people will not talk and do not voice their displeasure, it doesn't

Table 14.3 Sample CMMI Compliance Matrix

No.	Practice or Activity	Associated Procedure or Document	Assigned To	Date Due	Date Reviewed	Status
	Process Area: Requirements Management (ReqM)					
	GG2 Institutionalize a Managed Process					
1	GP 2.1 Establish an organizational policy	Policy			3/2/2007	Approved
2	GP 2.2 Plan the process	1. Plan 2. Process description 3. Schedule 4. Estimates			3/2/2007	Complete
3	GP 2.3 Provide resources	See Plan				"
4	GP 2.4 Assign responsibility	See Plan				"
5	GP 2.5 Train people	See Plan and training materials				In progress
6	GP 2.6 Manage configurations	TBD; will integrate with CM PAT				In progress
7	GP 2.7 Identify and involve relevant stakeholders	See Implementation Plan				Complete
8	GP 2.8 Monitor and control the process	TBD				Deferred
9	GP 2.9 Objectively evaluate adherence	Procedure P15				Complete
10	GP 2.10 Review status wih higher level Management	Procedure P16				Complete
	SG1: Manage Requirements					
11	SP 1.1 Obtain an understanding of requirements	Procedure RM1				EPG review
12	SP 1.2 Obtain commitment to requirements	Procedure RM2				EPG review
13	SP 1.3 Manage requirements changes	Procedure RM3, RM4				Pending
14	SP 1.4 Maintain bi-directional traceability of requirements	Procedure RM4				Rejected
15	SP 1.5 Identify inconsistencies between project work and requirements	Procedure RM5				Pending

mean they are happy campers. It means they have concerns but feel that voicing the concerns will be of no use. They feel they have not been part of the process, and their opinions are worthless. So, *no news is not good news*. If people do not feel part of the process, they will not buy-in to it. And ultimately, they might sabotage the effort. So try to find out what is happening.

The opposite also holds true. People will complain ad nauseam about the procedures because:

- They have to read them. No one likes to read anymore—we wait for the movie or the video game to come out.
- They have to follow them.
- They have to change the way they work.
- Someone is monitoring how they do their jobs.

We won't go into changing the culture—there are already several books on the market about that. Suffice it to say, people do not like to change. So reward them for their efforts, and praise them.

Besides simply talking (and listening) to people, we suggest a report card. Simply create a checklist that can be e-mailed to each project manager and have him fill it out and return it to the EPG. It should track whether each project is using the procedures, which ones are used or not, and why or why not.

You may have to take a stand to stop the complaints. But before you do, you'd better check to see whether these folks are justified in their complaints. Are these procedures really a good fit for them or are they forced to use them just because the procedures took a long time to write and you need to get the maturity level to bid on contracts? Is the Appraisal Team on its way to conduct a SCAMPI appraisal for a rating? Is that why you haven't changed the procedures? Or is it because it took blood to write the procedures, so there is no way they will ever be changed? Was the organization forced to cut the time it took to produce the procedures? Was the Pilot phase skipped? Were people pulled from the PATs to do "real work"?

That brings us to management commitment. We usually have to set up a special one- to three-hour executive briefing for management because they are not willing to take the time to attend the full-blown class. True management commitment is shown through providing adequate resources and funding. That means enough of the right people, enough time, and enough money to do the job. While management might send out memos promoting the greater glory of the organization and why the organization should adhere to process improvement, real management commitment doesn't really happen, especially at first. Management (and we mean very senior management—the executive levels that decide process improvement must be done to garner future business) doesn't understand what process improvement really means and what it takes. We have taught nearly 200 introduction classes, and in all that time we have had only a few executives in our class. The rest of the students were usually process improvement people or developers. Management will say they are committed. It's up to you to make them prove it by following the concepts expressed in this book.

Summary

The CMMI combines procedures, process descriptions, and approaches into a document called a "plan." Chapter 15 discusses processes and procedures. This chapter broke out the parts of the CMMI plan into three major documents, or strategies. While there are many plans that can be written, the following plans are normally needed to promote a successful process improvement effort:

- A plan that documents why process improvement is being initiated and what it will cost
- A plan that specifies the areas of the organization and the issues to focus on and assigns personnel
- A plan to addresses each weakness found and builds a schedule with associated deliverables

Chapter 15

Defining Processes, Procedures, Policies, and Charters

This chapter is the "meat and potatoes" chapter. This chapter provides guidelines for creating process improvement documentation and presents templates. You do not have to use these templates! They are simply provided to help you get started. Find something that fits your organization's culture and use it.

Defining Processes

A process consists of:

- Roles and responsibilities of the people assigned to do the work
- Appropriate tools and equipment to support individuals in doing their jobs
- Procedures and methods defining *how* to do the tasks and the relationships between the tasks

A process is *not* just a high-level flowchart. A life-cycle standard (e.g., DOD-MIL-STD-498 or 2157a) is not a process. A tool is not a process. A process consists of sequential steps of *what* needs to be done, plus the procedures detailing *how* to do the *whats*.

The CMMI definition of *process* is found in the glossary. It states, "A process as used in the CMMI product suite consists of activities that can be recognized as implementations of practices in a CMMI model. These activities can be mapped to one or more practices in CMMI process areas to allow a model to be useful for process improvement and process appraisal." Although this definition does focus on implementing the practices of the CMMI, we find the definition unsatisfactory. We prefer to look at the definition in the CMMI for process description. A *process description* is "a documented expression of a set of activities performed to achieve a given purpose that provides an operational definition of the major components of a process. The documentation specifies, in a complete, precise, and verifiable manner, the requirements, design, behavior, or other characteristics of a process. It also may include procedures for determining whether these provisions have been satisfied. Process descriptions may be found at the activity, project, or organizational level." This definition seems to allude to the fact that processes must be detailed enough to be followed and that procedures can lead to that effect.

More about procedures later. Let's concentrate on how to define a process. With a defined process, you can see where to improve quality, productivity, cost, and schedule. A defined process is the prerequisite for process improvement. Without defining processes in an orderly fashion, sustained improvement is impossible. Defined processes improve communication and understanding of both the currently existing AS IS processes used in the organization, and the TO BE processes that constitute the desired end result. Defined processes aid in planning and execution of the plans, provides the ability to capture lessons learned, and help facilitate the analysis and improvement of organizationwide and enterprisewide processes.

When is a process defined? When it is documented, training is provided in the process, and it is practiced on a day-to-day basis. In order to create process documentation, the writers of the process at hand must understand the current process (AS IS) and have developed a shared vision of the desired process (TO BE).

Where to start? Translate your products and services into outcomes. That is, if you build B1 Bombers, your outcome would be the fully constructed bomber. However, you would also have to break down this outcome into its constituent parts—the body, the software, the hardware, and so forth. Then break those parts down into their parts. And so on. You will need a documented process (actually documented processes) for the work to be performed to develop each outcome. Now, take one outcome and divide it by all of the activities it takes to produce that outcome. Be sure to include organizational units and support areas. This involves figuring out the *tasks* associated with the work to be performed, the *inputs and outputs, dependencies*, and *roles and responsibilities*.

Yes, it's a lot of work, and yes, it is hard.

Most templates for defining processes include the following entities:

- Activity Entry Criteria
- Activity Exit Criteria

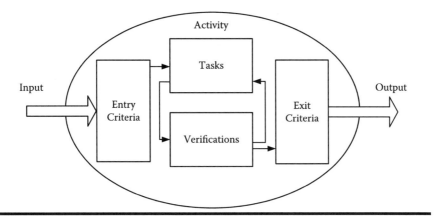

Figure 15.1   ETVX process model.

- Activity Input
- Activity Output
- Activity Performed By
- Task Description
- Verification Description
- What Activity Comes Next

This is called the ETVX model, and was created by IBM and used by the SEI (Software Engineering Institute) as part of its process framework. This generic method of transcribing activities, ETVX, stands for: Entry Criteria, Tasks, Verification, and eXit Criteria. Since IBM introduced the ETVX model in the 1980s, it has been adopted by a large number of users. Some users have made minor modifications over the years including differing representations, differing levels of detail, and differing focus on verification. Figure 15.1 is an example diagram showing the ETVX process model showing the flow between four major components.

Some terms used include:

- Work Product/Work Outcome—Any product, service, or result
- Task—The action taken to create or achieve the product, service, or result
- Agent—The person who accomplishes or performs the action to achieve or create the product, service, or result

Examples of Work Outcomes are the results or products of a process, such as a Project Plan, a project schedule, allocated requirements, management approval, management signoff, trained employees. The following paragraphs demonstrate a sequence to be used when defining processes, as well as questions to ask and examples.

Activity Entry Criteria

Question: When can this activity begin?

Entry criteria describe the conditions under which the activity can be started.

Answer: Jot down a verb describing the state of a product or its associated activity.

Examples: Approved Statement of Work, assigned responsibilities for creating the Project Plan, an approved Test Plan.

Activity Exit Criteria

Question: When is this activity completed?

Exit criteria describe the conditions under which an activity can be declared complete and may determine the next activity.

Answer: A verb about the state of the product, the person performing the activity, or the activity itself.

Examples: The Project Plan is ready for review, customer commitments are approved and incorporated into the project schedule, control mechanisms are in place for changes to the schedule.

Activity Input Criteria

Question: What interim work products are used by this activity?

Input is a relationship or link between an activity and a work result. Inputs are the results of a prior activity and used by the activity being described.

Answer: The name of the resultant work product.

Examples: Statement of Work, approved allocated requirements.

Activity Output Criteria

Question: What work results or products are produced by this activity?

Output is a relationship or link between an activity and a work result. Outputs are the results that are produced by the activity being described.

Answer: The name of the resultant work product.

Examples: A piece of code, a test procedure, a design specification, an approved Statement of Work.

Activity Performed By

Question: Who performs this activity?

"Activity performed by" is a relationship or link between an activity and an agent (the person performing the activity). It is the organizational unit, role, or automated agent responsible for performing the activity.

Answer: A list of the organizational units, roles, or automated agents that participate or are affected by the work.

Examples: The Quality Assurance (QA) group, a Project Manager, a Lead Software Engineer.

What Activity Comes Next?

Question: What activity is next?

Activity flow is a conditional relationship or link between activities. Activity flow defines the ordering of activities and is generally dependent on exit criteria.

Sometimes, Entry Criteria and Inputs are combined, and Exit Criteria and Outputs are combined. They are not really the same, as Entry and Exit Criteria are *triggers*. Inputs and Outputs are *products*. It's up to you how to do it. Most organizations currently combine the concepts.

Sometimes, the previous ETVX information is presented as a flowchart with accompanying verbiage describing what goes on. Sometimes it is presented as a list of sequenced steps. Sometimes it is presented as pages and pages of text. Whatever format fits the culture of the organization should be used.

After documenting the processes, the supporting procedures would be written, based on the process steps just documented. The procedures describe in detail *how* to perform the steps in the process.

Table 15.1 shows an example of a process for Requirements Management. This template was created by an organization that did not depend on a lot of verbiage in its documentation. It wanted just the facts, short and sweet. Even though the information looks short, if there are many steps to a process, this can get quite complicated.

Table 15.2 shows another example of the same process by the same organization when it decided to add more text to explain the process. Included in the text were the supporting procedures. The exhibit is simply the table of contents for the process. The complete process was 20 pages long. Even though it was called the Requirements Management Process, it only concentrated on creating the Requirements Specification, the Requirements Traceability Matrix, and changes to the requirements document itself.

Table 15.1   Requirements Management Process

Action or Task	Responsibility
Obtain Work Request from the customer	SM, PM
Review Work Request	PM
Create Initial Budget/Estimates/Schedule	PM
Initial planning	PM, project team
High-level requirements	PM, project team, customer
Risk identification and documentation	PM
Requirements Spec DRAFT	PM, project team
Technical review	PM, project team, QA
Customer review	Customer
Refine Requirements	PM, project team, customer
Create Requirements Traceability Matrix	PM, project team
Review requirements and RTM	PM, customer, project team, QA
Review/update risks	PM
Update estimates and schedules	PM
Review requirements and schedules and estimates	PM, project team, QA, customer
Requirements Spec FINAL	PM, analysts
Approvals and signoffs	Customer, QA, PM, SM, EPG
Baseline Requirements Spec	PM, CCB, EPG
Assess, track, and incorporate changes	PM, CCB, QA, EPG, Customer, project team

LEGEND:
    PM = Project Manager
    SM = Senior Management
    CCB = Configuration Control Board
    QA = Quality Assurance
    EPG = Engineering Process Group

Another way of documenting processes is by using a flowchart. Figure 15.2 is an example of a graphical representation called a Swimlane Process Flowchart. This example shows a Review Process with individual lanes for the four roles: Moderator, Reviewers, Authors, and Recorder. The tasks to be performed are in ovals with decisions in diamonds.

Defining Procedures

What are procedures? Procedures are step-by-step instructions on *how* to perform a task. To be repeatable, the steps need to be broken down to a level that anyone who needs to perform the task, with a general understanding of the work to be done, can perform the work adequately by following the instructions. Procedures are a subset of processes. The process is *what* to do; the procedures are *how* to do the steps in the process.

Procedures are step-by-step instructions of how your processes are performed. They include:

Table 15.2   Requirements Management (REQM) Process Table of Contents

1.0 INTRODUCTION
1.1 Purpose
1.2 Scope
1.3 Change Management
1.4 Roles and Responsibilities
2.0 PROCESS DESCRIPTION
2.1 Process Overview
2.2 Process Flow
2.3 Process Detail
2.3.1 Develop the Requirements Specification
2.3.1.1 Description
2.3.1.2 Input/entry criteria
2.3.1.3 Tasks/activities
2.3.1.4 Conduct reviews
2.3.1.5 Output/exit criteria
2.3.2 Develop the Requirements Traceability Matrix (RTM)
2.3.2.1 Description
2.3.2.2 Input/entry criteria
2.3.2.3 Tasks
2.3.2.4 Output/exit criteria
2.3.3 Changes to Requirements
2.3.4 Verification
2.3.4.1 Senior Management Involvement
2.3.4.2 Project Manager (PM) Involvement
2.3.4.3 Quality Assurance (QA) Involvement
2.3.4.4 Product Reviews
2.3.4.5 Management Reviews
2.3.4.6 Customer Reviews
3.0 RESOURCES AND FUNDING
4.0 MEASUREMENTS
5.0 TRAINING
6.0 REFERENCE DOCUMENTS
7.0 CHANGE HISTORY

- Sequence of activities
- Deliverables
- Controls
- Inspections/Reviews
- Guidelines and standards used

Table 15.3 is a template used by some organizations to capture these details.

Procedures are created the same way as processes. Once you have generated a process, the process becomes the major tasks or steps. Break down each process step into its constituent parts. Those activities become the steps in the procedure. Then consider roles, agents, products, and outcomes. Two things we might add to the procedure template are measurements to be taken (and then refer to the procedure that details how to take the measurements) and verification that the procedure has been followed (and refer to the verification procedure). When it comes to measurements

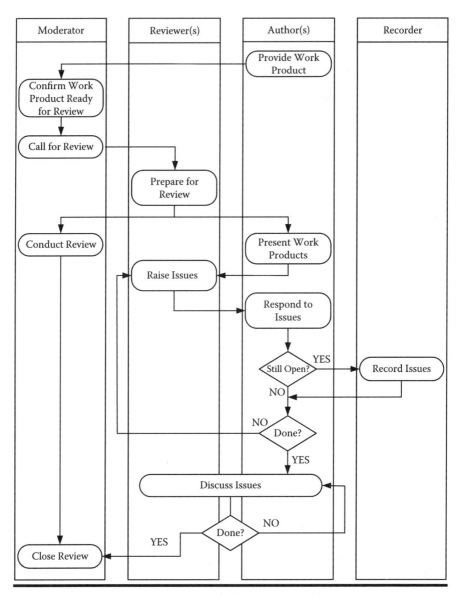

Figure 15.2 Review process using Swimlane Process Flowchart.

and verifications, most organizations write one overall measurement process and procedure and one overall verification process and procedure, as everything must be measured and verified. Measurement and verification are global activities that cross all process areas in the CMMI and all maturity and capability levels.

You do not have to use the suggested format for procedures. Some organizations prefer to be wordier. Some organizations prefer more graphics. You need the find the balance that works for you.

Table 15.3   Procedure Template

Document Number:	Date: Revision Number:
Description: This procedure involves … The activity's primary aim is to …	
Entry Criteria/Inputs:	Exit Criteria/Outputs:
Roles: Role Name: What does s/he do?	
Assets: Standards, reference material, deliverables, previous process descriptions …	
Summary of Tasks (List major tasks/process steps): 　Task 1 　Task 2 　Task 3 　Task 4 PROCEDURE STEPS 　Task 1 　　　Detail Step 1 　　　Detail Step 2 　　　Detail Step 3 　　　Detail Step 4 　Task 2 　　　Detail Step 1 　　　Detail Step 2 　　　Detail Step 3 　　　Detail Step 4 Continue…	

Defining Policies

Policies are high-level *whats*. They contain who is responsible for doing work, usually by position title, not by specific name of the individual. In some organizations, policies are very important. They are used to justify the initiation, continuance, and termination of work.

In other organizations, policies are not greatly valued. In these organizations, the organizational culture is that each individual has a responsibility to do what-

Table 15.4   Requirements Management (REQM) Policy

1.0 Purpose
The purpose of Requirements Management (REQM) is to manage the requirements of the project's products and product components and to identify inconsistencies between those requirements and the project's plans and work products.
2.0 Scope
This policy applies to software projects within the xxx Division of the xxx organization. The term "project", as used in this policy, includes system and software engineering, maintenance, conversion, enhancements, and procurement projects.
3.0 Responsibilities
The project manager shall ensure that the REQM process is followed. Each project will follow a process that ensures that requirements will be documented, managed, and traced.
4.0 Verification
REQM activities will be reviewed with higher level management, and the process will be objectively evaluated for adherence by the Quality Assurance (QA) staff.
5.0 Signoffs
The following shall review and approve this policy. Associate Director Quality Assurance EPG Chairman

ever it takes to get the job done. To strictly delineate responsibilities and tasks is an unnecessary step in organizational bureaucracy. However, the CMMI requires policies. So, it depends on your organizational culture as to how important and how in depth the policies should be. In any case, make sure that your policies follow the guidelines stated in the CMMI and that they are comprehensive enough to direct an organization's efforts toward implementing process improvement.

Most United States federal government agencies substitute official agency directives for policies. Other organizations that used the CMM for Software copied the Commitment to Perform and Ability to Perform Common Features and used them as policies. This approach is not recommended for the CMM or CMMI, as the information contained is not comprehensive enough to effectively manage and implement a process improvement program. Policies are addressed in the first generic goal in the CMMI.

Table 15.4 is an example of a policy used in an organization. Notice that it summarizes the goals for Requirements Management as listed in the CMMI.

Charters

Charters are usually generated for the Engineering Process Group (EPG) and Process Action Teams (PATs), and are often very similar in format; their scope is different, depending on the roles and responsibilities of each group. Charters contain statements addressing the following:

- Customer—Who are the customers?
- Sponsor—Who is sponsoring this effort?
- Start date—When does this PAT begin? If this is the EPG, how long will this EPG focus on the goals and objectives defined?
- End date—See previous.
- Purpose—Why are we here? What problem are we to address?
- Scope—How long, what results are expected, what is included and not included and why/why not?
- Deliverables—Action Plans, processes, charters, other plans, training materials, procedures, policies
- Members—Who are the members? By name and title.
- Percentage of their time—This is mandatory. Use this measure to track if anyone is overallocated. As a member of this team, can you really devote this much time to your task? Is the EPG full time? PATs are usually only part of the time of the members. The rest of the time, they work on their normal tasks.
- Role of each team member—What position do they fill? What deliverables are they expected to write?
- Authority of the PAT/EPG—Define problem resolution here. Does this PAT have the right to overrule another project manager?
- Assumptions—All members will attend and actively participate in all meetings.
- Ground rules—On time attendance.
- Attendance—100 percent attendance or may someone attend in your place? Will quorums be used? What constitutes a quorum?
- Decision process—Usually done through consensus. Consensus is that all members agree with the decision and can publicly support it. If you don't choose consensus, what constitutes a majority?
- Expected behaviors.
- Unacceptable behaviors.

Table 15.5 shows a PAT charter template and Table 15.6 shows an example EPG charter.

Summary

How many diagrams should you use when building your documentation? Consider the trade-off between diagrams and text. People are different—some are more graphically oriented and some more textually oriented. Some organizations use

Table 15.5   Process Action Team (PAT) Charter Template

Customer: Sponsor: Start: End: Purpose of the PAT:
Linkage to Business Objectives (from strategic or business plan if we have it):
Scope:
Deliverables:
PAT Members: Name   % of Time   Role 1 2 3 4
PAT Authority:
Assumptions:
Ground Rules: Attendance:
Decisions:
Behaviors:
Signoffs:

diagrams like the ETVX Process Model (Figure 15.1) and the Swimlane example (Figure 15.2) as work aids on a laminated card or wall chart that people use every day. These organizations often supplement the diagram with a more detailed textual representation to use during initial training and as a desk reference. You need to find the right balance for your organization.

Process Improvement is continuous. You will never get the perfect procedure written, so try for something workable. Communicate that you don't want something awful, but perfection is out of reach. Get something and pilot it. The

Table 15.6a Example Engineering Process Group (EPG) Charter.

Title: Engineering Process Group Charter
Rev B, March 14, 2007

This document describes the mission, objectives, and preliminary tasks necessary to establish the Engineering Process Group (EPG) at the xxx organization. This charter will apply to all members of the EPG.

Mission

The mission of the EPG is to implement process improvement (PI) at xxx. PI activities include fostering an understanding of the Software Engineering Institute's (SEI) Software Capability Maturity Model Integration (CMMI); conducting a baseline SCAMPI; generating Action Plans based on the results of the SCAMPI; implementing the activities documented in the Action Plans; and monitoring results.

Objectives

The objectives of PI are to achieve all goals of the Process Areas (PAs) for Level 2 and Level 3. Level 2 achievement is projected for xxx date. Level 3 achievement is projected for xxx date. These objectives will be accomplished by reviewing and augmenting existing documentation; conducting periodic appraisals; performing training and orientation as needed for personnel; participating on teams established to institute PI; incorporating planned activities into existing practices; and monitoring and measuring results.

EPG Membership and Operating Procedures

The EPG will consist of senior members of the systems and software development staff, will be managed by the PI project leader, and will be facilitated by an onsite PI consultant. The EPG will meet once a week. This weekly meeting will serve as the focal point for reporting the status of the Process Action Team (PAT) tasks. The EPG will serve as a forum to discuss and resolve issues occurring during PI project activities, to introduce information and new technologies or methods into xxx, and to review material generated during project process improvement activities.

PI Structure

The PI reporting structure is as follows. Each member of the EPG (except for the PI project leader and PI consultant) will serve as the chairman (or lead) of each PAT. This structure allows for an effective flow of information from the EPG to each PAT, from each PAT to the EPG, and for sharing information among the different PATs. Each PAT will exist only on a temporary basis. As the activities detailed in the Action Plan for each PAT are accomplished, that PAT will be dissolved. The members of that PAT will then be assigned other PI tasks. PAT teams will consist of the EPG representative (as PAT lead) plus other members of the organization, as necessary. For example, if one of the tasks in the Action Plan is to generate Configuration Management standards, a PAT will be established for that purpose.

Pilots will show where the gaps are more effectively than yet another EPG review. That doesn't mean don't have EPG reviews! It means don't keep rereviewing and rereviewing. Let the organization show you what works and what doesn't.

Table 15.6b (Continued)

Title: Engineering Process Group Charter
Rev B, March 14, 2007

Continued:

The PAT lead may request help in this area from other organizational individuals knowledgeable in configuration management standards used both at xxx and across the industry. Those individuals may be temporarily drafted on a part-time basis to assist in generating those standards. After the standards have been documented and approved by the EPG, those individuals will no longer be needed, the PAT will be disbanded, and the PAT lead will be used either on another PAT or as needed elsewhere for PI duties.

Steering Committee Obligations

The EPG chairman (the PI project leader) will in turn report EPG activities to management and an Executive Steering Committee. Senior management determines the budget and is responsible and accountable for the ultimate direction of PI at xxx.

EPG Tasks

Initial EPG tasks will include training in the CMMI and the SCAMPI process, generating business meeting rules, setting up PATS, developing detailed Action Plans on a PA by PA basis, and instituting a PI infrastructure.

As a result of the SCAMPI presented to management on February 6, 2006, the following tasks were generated.

Generate an OSSP to structure further PI efforts.

Search for Standards, where a standard will provide organizational focus and support, enforced by our QA personnel.

Implement Requirements Management (REQM) and Configuration Management (CM) through establishing PATs to generate policies, procedures, with the EPG monitoring the results.

Implement a Configuration Control Board (CCB) with the EPG performing this function until resources become available to perform this function separately from the EPG.

Project Planning (PP) and Project Monitoring and Control (PMC) will be planned and acted upon once the results of the pilots for the preceding PAs (REQM, CM) have been reviewed.

Level 2 PAs should be the primary focus at this time. All efforts must be supported by training. Training must be received, not only in the CMMI, but also in the PA assigned to the various PAT Team members. PAT Teams cannot be expected to write procedures for performing a PA if they have not been trained in what the CMMI requires and what the PA consists of.

Pilot projects need to be selected to pilot the CMMI procedures and instructions. The monitoring of CMMI-related activities will be performed by the EPG.

MEASUREMENT

Chapter 16

Measurement within the CMMI

This chapter discusses the general topic of measurement within the CMMI. This chapter serves as an introduction to our next three chapters about measurement: Chapter 17, "A Boatload of Metrics"; Chapter 18, "Statistical Process Control"; and Chapter 19, "A High Maturity Perspective." Chapter 9, "Alignment of Multiple Process Improvement Initiatives," also discussed measurement by describing an overall Measurement Program.

The CMMI has increased its focus on measurement by creating the Measurement and Analysis process area (PA), emphasizing measurement within the Engineering process areas, and expanding the importance of high-maturity concepts in Level 4 and Level 5. We discuss each of these areas and summarize the decisions organizations make that lead to success or failure when implementing measurement programs.

The Measurement and Analysis Process Area

Organizations that used the family of CMMs learned that measurements need to be aligned to business objectives to provide benefit, used regularly to justify effort and cost, well defined so people could understand and use measurements correctly, and communicated in an unbiased manner. Some organizations just went through the motions or paid lip service to collecting measurements. They performed measurement activities superficially (in order to pass an appraisal of some type or to impress the boss that a measurement program was in effect in his organization) with little or no benefit resulting from these activities. The Measurement and Analysis PA refocuses that effort into mapping measurement collection and analysis to the ability of those measures to support management information needs; that is, not doing measurement for measurement's sake but in order to achieve some value from the measurements. Specific goals of the Measurement and Analysis PA are that measurement objectives must be aligned with identified information needs and objectives, and that measurement results address these needs. Great. But what are information needs? While there is no strict definition (because what is needed is specific to what is needed in your organization), a review of the following documents will provide clues as to what information is needed by your organization:

- Plans—Project plans, strategic plans, business plans, and process improvement plans
- Results of monitoring project performance
- Management objectives
- Formal requirements or contractual obligations
- Recurring or troublesome management or technical problems

By reviewing these documents, you can craft measurement specifications that map to the needs implied in the documents. So, after conducting the review, define measures that align to the organization's information needs. Provide detailed measurement definitions (also called specifications) of what is to be measured (precisely and unambiguously), how it is to be measured, and how the measures will be analyzed. A measurement specification should contain a definition of the measure, source of the data, collection mechanism, criteria for counting, units of measure, and expected range value. Make sure that when you conduct this exercise that you actually analyze what is actually needed and that you don't simply develop a rationale for continuing to collect the measures that you have always collected. Information needs usually focus on cost, quality, schedule, customer satisfaction, or generating new business. Few organizations really analyze how their measurement programs support business objectives and information needs. Most organizations do not invest serious time and effort into developing meaningful measurement specifications. Therefore, their results continue to disappoint them.

The Engineering Process Areas

The Engineering PAs include:

- Requirements Management (REQM)
- Requirements Development (RD)
- Technical Solution (TS)
- Product Integration (PI)

- Verification (VER)
- Validation (VAL)

Additionally, the CMMI states or implies the need for measures in Generic Practice 2.8 Monitor and Control the process area, Generic Practice 2.10 Review Status with Higher-Level Management, Generic Practice 3.2 Collect Improvement Information, and the Project Planning, Project Monitoring and Control, Organizational Process Performance, and Quantitative Project Performance PAs. Table 16.1 shows some example measures that can be used to monitor development.

Measuring the development process (i.e., the Engineering PAs), can lead to better products. The Engineering PAs appeal most to the techies in your organization. Generally, techies do not care about measuring their results. They care about coding and testing and producing software, learning the latest technology and the latest upgrades to packages, and trying out all of this stuff in their programs. Identifying and tracking measures is the least of their worries and the least of their interests. Therefore, those people most interested in the Engineering PAs (i.e., the techies) often see the amount of measurement in these PAs as overwhelming (and unnecessary and a bit scary). Why focus on additional engineering measures? Because customers are demanding higher and better quality in a shorter amount of time to increase reliability.

Table 16.1 Example Measures for Engineering Process Areas

Process Areas	Measures to Monitor and Control the PA (GP 2.8)
REQM	Requirement volatility (percentage of requirement changes)
RD	Cost, schedule, and effort expended for rework
	Defect density of requirement specifications
TS	Cost, schedule, and effort expended for rework
	Percentage of requirements addressed in design
	Size and complexity of product, product-component, interfaces and documentation
	Defect density of technical solutions work products
PI	Product-component integration profile (e.g., assemblies planned and actual, and number of exceptions found)
	Integration evaluation problem report trends (e.g., number written and number closed)
	Integration evaluation report aging (i.e., how long each problem report has been open)
VAL	Number of activities planned versus actual
	Validation problem report trends
	Validation problem report aging
VER	Verification profile (e.g., number activities planned versus actual, and the defects found)
	Number of defects detected
	Verification problem report trends
	Verification problem report aging

Most organizations use effort measures to satisfy the requirements for monitoring and controlling their projects. This focus on one measure has shown little benefit. Some organizations use measures similar to the examples shown in Table 16.1 and have demonstrated significant improvements in product quality and reductions in rework. Most of the organizations that implement measurement programs successfully develop their own in-house tools that provide measurement data as an add-on or side effect of performing normal work.

The CMMI Measurement Focus

The CMMI focuses on measures throughout the model. For example:

- In the Project Planning, and Project Monitoring and Control process areas, planning parameters and indicators (e.g., cost, effort, schedule, size, complexity, and weight) for the projects are defined, measured, and monitored.
- In the Measurement and Analysis process area, measurement capability is developed and sustained by establishing measurement programs to support information needs.
- In the Verification and Validation process areas, results from reviews, tests, inspections, demonstrations, and evaluations are measured and analyzed.
- In the Organization Process Definition process area, the organization's measurement repository is established and maintained.
- In the Integrated Project Management process area, data from the organization's measurement repository is used for planning projects.
- In the Organizational Process Performance and Quantitative Project Management process areas, a quantitative understanding of processes is established. Process Performance Baselines (PPBs) and Process Performance Models (PPMs) are established and used to manage quality and process performance objectives (see Chapter 19).
- In the Organizational Innovation and Deployment process area, a quantitative understanding, specifically PPBs and PPMs, is used to analyze prospective and piloted innovations.

The generic practices (GP) used in all of the process areas also support the expanded focus on measurement. For example:

- GP 2.8 Monitor and Control the process area. Actual process performance is measured against the plan.
- GP 2.10 Review Status with Higher Level Management. Measures support the "appropriate visibility" asked for in the GP and provide clear, objective status reporting.

■ GP 3.2 Collect Improvement Information. Measures and measurement results are collected for the organization's processes and products to support improvement.

Evolution of Measurement

There is a natural evolution of measurement implied in the CMMI. This "natural" evolution may not seem so natural as an organization improves its processes across the levels. Most organizations encounter confusion because of what appears to be abrupt differences in scope and terminology. People struggle with the apparent paradigm shifts between the levels as they transition from Level 2 to Level 3, from Level 3 to Level 4, and from Level 4 to Level 5.

Measurement concepts are actually consistent and simply evolve through the levels. Level 2 primarily focuses on status measures (e.g., planned versus actual size, effort, cost, and schedule; number of changes, and number of nonconformances in products and processes). Level 3 adds measures for process improvement and quality, including defect density and productivity. Level 4 creates and uses PPBs and PPMs. While the introduction of these baselines and models looks like a drastic change, the data in these models are drawn from historical data found at the lower levels of the CMMI model. What changes is their analysis and depiction. Level 5 requires that quantitative improvements be made based on the baselines and models created. The PPBs and PPMs are used to plan and demonstrate actual improvement.

Successful organizations have shown the value from lower level measures to justify the transition to more mature measures. They have created useful measurement specifications that work through all the levels. Successful organizations start using simple PPBs and PPMs early in their improvement efforts. Unsuccessful organizations have gone through the motions of collecting measures, without understanding the measures they need to collect or how quantitative analysis of the measures works. Unsuccessful organizations often just produce "pretty pictures."

Summary

Measurement should start on the first day of your process improvement journey. Successful organizations analyze how their measurement programs support business objectives and information needs. Successful organizations communicate their process improvement goals and why measurement is being done. They invest serious time and effort into developing meaningful measurement specifications. They don't set unreasonable goals and then measure performance against those unreasonable goals. Measures are collected "painlessly," that is, as automatically as possible, and as a side effect of performing work. Successful organizations focus on a small number of PPBs and PPMs that are used to make real decisions to improve the projects and the organization. And they perform real, continuous quantitative improvement.

Chapter 17

A Boatload of Metrics

This chapter offers some guidelines for metrics to use in your organization. It presents some metrics that are commonly collected in organizations, some tips on how to devise metrics, and some advice on structuring your metrics process.

We could not possibly discuss everything necessary to set up and administer a top-notch metrics program in one small chapter. To that end, we have listed several books on the subject at the end of this chapter.

For a discussion on the importance of collecting consistent data, and when and how to collect that data, please read Chapter 18, "Statistical Process Control," and Chapter 19, "A High Maturity Perspective." By the way, you will find that we use the terms *measurement* and *metric* interchangeably. We are sorry if this offends you, but we decided that we really don't want to weigh in on the war of words around measurement.

Background

When beginning a process improvement effort in an organization, invariably a project manager (PM) or the executive in charge will pull one of us aside and ask, "What metrics should we collect?" We hate that question. We hate it because it shows that the person asking has no clue about what process improvement is and generally only wants a quick fix for his organization. "Just tell us what to collect, we'll do it, and then we're done." We don't think so. Now, true, this judgment is harsh—after all, these people are only beginning the process improvement journey. However, one of the first deliverables requested by management from us for any organization is a list of metrics to collect. The managers then mull over the metrics and decide not to collect them anyway because by collecting the metrics, we can really track and report on what is going on in the projects, and, heaven knows, we just can't have that! So, much moaning and groaning takes place—we don't have the people to do this, we don't collect these numbers, we don't need these numbers, the staff won't stand for it, and so on. And then, after discussing the pros and cons of each metric, we begin with a very small list. After seeing that the metrics really do help an organization (after several very difficult months), the managers are glad that we collect those metrics. Then we begin to suggest that there are more metrics that will help them, and we must begin the battle all over again.

The purpose of metrics is not to drive everybody crazy. It's to look at the numbers as indicators of how your project is doing and how all of the projects are doing. If the numbers are not what you expected, is there a problem? Where did the problem occur? Where was that problem injected originally? Understanding the metrics and what they mean are critical elements for successfully running an organization.

Selecting Metrics for Your Organization

One place to begin looking for metrics to collect that will benefit your organization is the CMMI. In the CMMI, an entire process area is devoted to metrics; that is Measurement and Analysis. It resides at Maturity Level 2 in the staged representation, and in the Support process category in the continuous representation. In addition, one of the common features—Directing Implementation—also addresses measurement. Just like the CMMI presupposes that you have standards and are using them, the CMMI also presupposes that you are collecting appropriate metrics about your project (for example, schedule and cost overruns, people turnover on your project, number of errors in deliverables submitted and returned from the client, etc.). This is often not the case. In fact, in some organizations just beginning the process improvement journey, no metrics are kept! While that may shock some of you, there are large state and local agencies that have no timekeeping systems; there are some publicly held companies that do not track dollars spent on projects that are contracted out; and the reverse, companies that only track contractor work, not their own, internal commitments.

The CMMI specifically relates its metrics to the process area (PA) activities; for example, how long it took you to plan your planning activities (in the Project Planning PA), how long it took to write the Quality Assurance Plan (in the Product and Process Assurance PA), and so forth. Well, what good is tracking how long you took to write a project plan if you don't also track late delivery of products and late milestones? So use the metrics mentioned in the CMMI only as a guideline when deciding which metrics would be appropriate for your organization.

We also recommend the metrics listed in the Measurement and Analysis common feature of the original CMM for Software. We find that these metrics make sense, are directly tied to each key process area, are commonly collected and used in organizations, and are straightforward. Although it is called the CMM for Software (actually its real name is *The Capability Maturity Model: Guidelines for Improving the Software Process*—and most folks have just added the "for Software" appellation), if you go through the book and take the word *software* out, you will find that most of the concepts and metrics described can be used in almost any organization, software-based or not.

There is another way to determine which metrics would be the most beneficial for your organization. It is called the Goal–Question–Metric (GQM) technique. We discussed this approach previously when discussing tying process improvement efforts to business goals. We basically said that this approach sounds good, but is difficult to implement successfully in low-maturity organizations because their business objectives are generally not documented in enough detail to really tie directly to the CMMI (their business objectives are basically described as "to make money"). However, when it comes to metrics, once organizations have seen the list of measurements they can collect, they become apprehensive and overwhelmed. So, using a list of possible measures and using the GQM technique to decide which metrics to select, if facilitated correctly, can be useful.

The basic G–Q–M approach is to:

- Determine the Goal: What business goal are you trying to support? Why are you collecting these numbers? What will they do for you? Why is it important to collect metrics?
- Determine the Question that is most closely associated with achieving the goal.
- Determine the Measurements that help answer the question or metrics that would provide you with the response to the question.

So a simple example of using the G–Q–M approach is the following:

- Goal: Reduce the time it takes for our requirements definition process (while maintaining quality)
- Question: Where is the most time spent?
- Metric(s): Refer to our list here. Some suggested metrics are:
  - Number of requirements changes proposed versus number approved and number implemented
  - Time it takes for the different phases of our requirements process
  - Number of users interviewed per job function and category
  - Number of errors traced back to the Requirements phase
  - Time it takes for requirements sign-off
  - Quality of the delivered product

Obviously, more refinement of the question and metrics are needed. For example, what metric (number) can you use to quantitatively define *quality*? What part of the requirements process is broken? Do we really need to reduce the time it takes to gather, refine, document, and manage changes to our requirements? Or would it be better to reduce the time spent somewhere else in our life cycle?

Be sure to clearly define what is being measured. For example, if you are measuring the time to perform the requirements process, does that only include time to write and review requirements, or does that also include the time to attend status meetings to discuss the requirements process?

It is also critical that the purpose of each metric be explained and understood. Everyone should understand:

- Why the metrics are being collected
- How the metrics will be used
- What is expected from each person as to gathering, reporting, interpreting, and using the metrics

After you have selected metrics, please pilot them in your organization. When selecting pilot projects, make sure the projects selected are already following whatever "best practices" your organization has. If not, then this project is probably not going to be successful piloting anything. In fact, some organizations will deliberately choose a dysfunctional project to pilot improvement efforts because:

- They vainly hope that trying anything on these projects will somehow automatically improve the projects.
- They really don't want the improvement efforts to work so they can go back to doing things the way they used to.

Also make sure that these projects are not piloting everything in your organization, and that they are not going to be overburdened by collecting and piloting the metrics. There are more recommendations for planning and tracking pilots in previous chapters, as well as in the Appendices section.

One more reminder: metrics should not be collected and used to judge anyone's work on a personal basis. In other words, metrics should not be used to justify a person's salary or justify some other sort of personal abuse. Metrics are used to determine how your project-level or organizational processes are working—not whether your people are "good" or "bad."

List of Metrics

Every organization we have ever assisted with process improvement efforts has always asked, "What metrics should we collect?" Well, once again, define your metrics to your business needs and the problems you face. Having said that, most executives and managers still want and need examples. So here they are.

The following metrics are arranged according to the maturity levels and process areas in the CMMI. We have tried to present metrics that might be found more commonly and used more effectively at certain stages of organizational sophistication.

However, just because a metric appears in a process area at Level 3, and you are just trying to reach Level 2, if that metric will help you, then use it. This list is arranged somewhat arbitrarily. Some readers will say, "Hey, that metric goes better in a different process area (process area X)!" That's OK, since this list is just to get you thinking about measurements that can be of help to you and your organization.

These are by no means the only measurements to collect in an organization. They are simply representative of those measures we have found collected most frequently. We used Generic Practice 2.8 Monitor and Control the Process of the CMMI as the basis for these metrics, supplemented by metrics our users have used in their own organizations. You should also note that most of the organizations we have assisted in their process improvement efforts and in their metrics programs began by reviewing the metrics documented in the CMM and CMMI, and then decided whether these metrics would work for them.

For the most part, this list represents base measures to collect. *Base measures* are simple values of some attribute, for example, size of a document in pages or effort to produce a document in hours. To get value from your measurement, you will most likely want to compare actual performance (often referred to as "actuals") to planned performance (often referred to as "planned") and to produce derived measures from your base measures. *Derived measures* are a function of two or more base measures, for example, productivity in hours per page to produce a document. Another comparison of base versus derived measures follows. The base measure we have listed is "3. Cumulative number of changes to the allocated requirements, including total number of changes proposed, open, approved, and incorporated into the system baseline." The derived measure that can be produced from this base measure is "the percentage of changes incorporated compared to the total number of changes proposed." Most organizations also want to compare actuals to benchmarked industry data.

Remember, this list is just a start. With a little creativity, we are sure you can come up with even more.

Level 2

Requirements Management

1. Requirements volatility (percentage of requirements changes)
2. Number of requirements by type or status (defined, reviewed, approved, and implemented)
3. Cumulative number of changes to the allocated requirements, including total number of changes proposed, open, approved, and incorporated into the system baseline
4. Number of change requests per month, compared to the original number of requirements for the project
5. Number of, time spent, effort spent, cost of implementing change requests

6. Number and size of change requests after the Requirements phase is over
7. Cost of implementing a change request
8. Number of change requests versus the total number of change requests during the life of the project
9. Number of change requests accepted but not implemented
10. Number of requirements (changes and additions to the baseline)

Project Planning

11. Completion of milestones for the project planning activities compared to the plan (estimates vs. actuals)
12. Work completed, effort expended, and funds expended in the project planning activities compared to the plan
13. Number of revisions to the project plans
14. Cost, schedule, and effort variance per plan revision
15. Replanning effort due to change requests
16. Effort expended over time to manage the project compared to the plan
17. Frequency, causes, and magnitude of the replanning effort

Project Monitoring and Control

18. Effort and other resources expended in performing monitoring and oversight activities
19. Change activity for the project plan, which includes changes to size estimates of the work products, cost estimates, resource estimates, and schedule
20. Number of open and closed corrective actions or action items
21. Project milestone dates (planned vs. actual)
22. Number of project milestone dates made on time
23. Number and types of reviews performed
24. Schedule, budget, and size variance between planned versus actual reviews
25. Comparison of actuals versus estimates for all planning and tracking items

Measurement and Analysis

26. Number of projects using progress and performance measures
27. Number of measurement objectives addressed

Supplier Agreement Management

28. Cost of the commercial off-the-shelf (COTS) products
29. Cost and effort to incorporate the COTS products into the project
30. Number of changes made to the supplier requirements
31. Cost and schedule variance per supplier agreement

32. Costs of the activities for managing the contract compared to the plan
33. Actual delivery dates for contracted products compared to the plan
34. Actual dates of prime contractor deliveries to the subcontractor compared to the plan
35. Number of on-time deliveries from the vendor compared with the contract
36. Number and severity of errors found after delivery
37. Number of exceptions to the contract to ensure schedule adherence
38. Number of quality audits compared to the plan
39. Number of senior management reviews to ensure adherence to budget and schedule versus the plan
40. Number of contract violations by supplier or vendor
41. Effort expended to manage the evaluation of sources and selection of suppliers
42. Number of changes to the requirements in the supplier agreement
43. Number of documented commitments between the project and the supplier
44. Interface coordination issue trends (i.e., number identified and number closed)
45. Number of defects detected in supplied products (during integration and after delivery)

Process and Product Quality Assurance (QA)

46. Completions of milestones for the QA activities compared to the plan
47. Work completed, effort expended in the QA activities compared to the plan
48. Numbers of product audits and activity reviews compared to the plan
49. Number of process audits and activities versus those planned
50. Number of defects per release and/or build
51. Amount of time/effort spent in rework
52. Amount of QA time/effort spent in each phase of the life cycle
53. Number of reviews and audits versus number of defects found
54. Total number of defects found in internal reviews and testing versus those found by the customer or end user after delivery
55. Number of defects found in each phase of the life cycle
56. Number of defects injected during each phase of the life cycle
57. Number of noncompliances written versus number resolved
58. Number of noncompliances elevated to senior management
59. Complexity (McCabe, McClure, and Halstead metrics)

Configuration Management (CM)

60. Number of change requests or change board requests processed per unit of time
61. Completions of milestones for the CM activities compared to the plan
62. Work completed, effort expended, and funds expended in the CM activities
63. Number of changes to configuration items
64. Number of configuration audits conducted
65. Number of fixes returned as "Not Yet Fixed"
66. Number of fixes returned as "Could Not Reproduce Error"
67. Number of violations of CM procedures (noncompliance found in audits)
68. Number of outstanding problem reports versus rate of repair
69. Number of times changes are overwritten by someone else (or number of times people have the wrong initial version or baseline)
70. Number of engineering change proposals proposed, approved, rejected, implemented
71. Number of changes by category to code source and to supporting documentation
72. Number of changes by category, type, and severity
73. Source lines of code stored in libraries placed under configuration control

Level 3

Requirements Development

74. Cost, schedule, and effort expended for rework
75. Defect density of requirements specifications
76. Number of requirements approved for build (versus the total number of requirements)
77. Actual number of requirements documented (versus the total number of estimated requirements)
78. Staff hours (total and by Requirements Development activity)
79. Requirements status (percentage of defined specifications out of the total approved and proposed; number of requirements defined)
80. Estimates of total requirements, total requirements definition effort, requirements analysis effort, and schedule
81. Number and type of Requirements changes

Technical Solution

82. Cost, schedule, and effort expended for rework
83. Number of requirements addressed in the product or product-component design

84. Size and complexity of the product, product components, interfaces, and documentation
85. Defect density of technical solutions work products (number of defects per page)
86. Number of requirements by status or type throughout the life of the project (for example, number defined, approved, documented, implemented, tested, and signed off by phase)
87. Problem reports by severity and length of time they are open
88. Number of requirements changed during implementation and test
89. Effort to analyze proposed changes for each proposed change and cumulative totals
90. Number of changes incorporated into the baseline by category (e.g., interface, security, system configuration, performance, and usability)
91. Size and cost to implement and test incorporated changes, including initial estimate and actual size and cost
92. Estimates and actuals of system size, reuse, effort, and schedule
93. The total estimated and actual staff hours needed to develop the system by job category and activity
94. Estimated dates and actuals for the start and end of each phase of the life cycle
95. Number of diagrams completed versus the estimated total diagrams
96. Number of design modules/units proposed
97. Number of design modules/units delivered
98. Estimates and actuals of total lines of code—new, modified, and reused
99. Estimates and actuals of total design and code modules and units
100. Estimates and actuals for total CPU hours used to date
101. The number of units coded and tested versus the number planned
102. Errors by category, phase discovered, phase injected, type, and severity
103. Estimates of total units, total effort, and schedule
104. System tests planned, executed, passed, failed
105. Test discrepancies reported, resolved, not resolved
106. Source code growth by percentage of planned versus actual

Product Integration

107. Product-component integration profile (e.g., product-component assemblies planned and performed, and number of exceptions found)
108. Integration evaluation problem report trends (e.g., number written and number closed)
109. Integration evaluation problem report aging (i.e., how long each problem report has been opened)

Verification

110. Verification profile (e.g., the number of verifications planned and performed, and the defects found; perhaps categorized by verification method or type)
111. Number of defects detected by defect category
112. Verification problem report trends (e.g., number written and number closed)
113. Verification problem report status (i.e., how long each problem report has been open)
114. Number of peer reviews performed compared to the plan
115. Overall effort expended on peer reviews compared to the plan
116. Number of work products reviewed compared to the plan

Validation

117. Number of validation activities completed (planned vs. actual)
118. Validation problem reports trends (e.g., number written and number closed)
119. Validation problem report aging (i.e., how long each problem report has been open)

Organizational Process Focus

120. Number of process improvement proposals submitted, accepted, or implemented
121. CMMI maturity level or capability level
122. Work completed, effort expended, and funds expended in the organization's activities for process appraisal, development, and improvement compared to the plans for these activities
123. Results of each process appraisal, compared to the results and recommendations of previous appraisals

Organizational Process Definition + IPPD

124. Percentage of projects using the process architectures and process elements of the organization's set of standard processes
125. Defect density of each process element of the organization's set of standard processes
126. Number of on-schedule milestones for process development and maintenance
127. Costs for the process definition activities
128. Parameters for key operating characteristics of the work environment

Organizational Training

129. Number of training courses delivered (e.g., planned vs. actual)
130. Posttraining evaluation ratings
131. Training program quality surveys
132. Actual attendance at each training course compared to the projected attendance
133. Progress in improving training courses compared to the organization's and projects' training plans
134. Number of training waivers approved over time

Integrated Project Management + IPPD

135. Number of changes to the project's defined process
136. Effort to tailor the organization's set of standard processes
137. Interface coordination issue trends (i.e., number identified and number closed)
138. Performance according to plans, commitments, and procedures for the integrated team, and deviations from expectations
139. Number of times team objectives were not achieved
140. Actual effort and other resources expended by one group to support another group or groups and vice versa
141. Actual completion of specific tasks and milestones by one group to support the activities of other groups and vice versa.

Risk Management

142. Number of risks identified, managed, tracked, and controlled
143. Risk exposure and changes to the risk exposure for each assessed risk, and as a summary percentage of management reserve
144. Change activity for the risk mitigation plans (e.g., processes, schedules, funding)
145. Number of occurrences of unanticipated risks
146. Risk categorization volatility
147. Estimated versus actual risk mitigation effort
148. Estimated versus actual risk impact
149. The amount of effort and time spent on risk management activities versus the number of actual risks
150. The cost of risk management versus the cost of actual risks
151. For each identified risk, the realized adverse impact compared to the estimated impact

Decision Analysis and Resolution

152. Cost-to-benefit ratio of using formal evaluation processes
153. Number of formal evaluations performed on the project (planned vs. actual)

Level 4

Organizational Process Performance

154. Number of Process Performance Baselines established and maintained
155. Number of Process Performance Models established and maintained
156. Number of processes and subprocesses included in the organization's process–performance analyses
157. Trends in the organization's process performance with respect to changes in work products and task attributes (e.g., size growth, effort, schedule, and quality)

Quantitative Project Management

158. Time between failures
159. Critical resource utilization
160. Number and severity of defects in the released product
161. Number and severity of customer complaints concerning the provided service
162. Number of defects removed by product verification activities (perhaps by type of verification, such as peer reviews and testing)
163. Defect escape rates
164. Number and density of defects by severity found during the first year following product delivery or start of service
165. Cycle time
166. Amount of rework time
167. Requirements volatility (i.e., number of requirement changes per phase)
168. Ratios of estimated to measured values of the planning parameters (e.g., size, cost, and schedule)
169. Coverage and efficiency of peer reviews (i.e., number/amount of products reviewed compared to total number of defects found per hour)
170. Test coverage and efficiency (i.e., number/amount of products tested compared to total number of defects found per hour)
171. Effectiveness of training (e.g., percent of planned training completed and test scores)
172. Reliability (e.g., mean time-to-failure usually measured during integration and systems test)

173. Percentage of the total defects inserted or found in the different phases of the project life cycle
174. Percentage of the total effort expended in the different phases of the project life cycle
175. Profile of subprocesses under statistical management (e.g., number planned to be under statistical management, number currently being statistically managed, and number that are statistically stable)
176. Number of special causes of variation identified
177. The cost over time for the quantitative process management activities compared to the plan
178. The accomplishment of schedule milestones for quantitative process management activities compared to the approved plan (e.g., establishing the process measurements to be used on the project, determining how the process data will be collected, and collecting the process data)
179. The cost of poor quality (e.g., amount of rework, rereviews, and retesting)
180. The costs for achieving quality goals (e.g., amount of initial reviews, audits, and testing)

Level 5

Organizational Innovation and Deployment

181. Change in quality after improvements (e.g., number of reduced defects)
182. Change in process performance after improvements (e.g., change in baselines)
183. The overall technology change activity, including number, type, and size of changes
184. The effect of implementing the technology change compared to the goals (e.g., actual cost saving to projected)
185. The number of process improvement proposals submitted and implemented for each process area
186. The number of process improvement proposals submitted by each project, group, and department
187. The number and types of awards and recognitions received by each of the projects, groups, and departments
188. The response time for handling process improvement proposals
189. Number of process improvement proposals accepted per reporting period
190. The overall change activity including number, type, and size of changes
191. The effect of implementing each process improvement compared to its defined goals
192. Overall performance of the organization's and project's processes, including effectiveness, quality, and productivity compared to their defined goals

193. Overall productivity and quality trends for each project
194. Process measurements that relate to the indicators of the customer's satisfaction (e.g., surveys results, number of customer complaints, and number of customer compliments)

Causal Analysis and Resolution

195. Defect data (problem reports, defects reported by the customer, defects reported by the user, defects found in peer reviews, defects fond in testing, process capability problems, time and cost for identifying the defect and fixing it, estimated cost of not fixing the problem)
196. Number of root causes removed
197. Change in quality or process performance per instance of the causal analysis and resolution process (e.g., number of defects and change in baseline)
198. The costs of defect prevention activities (e.g., holding causal analysis meetings and implementing action items), cumulatively
199. The time and cost for identifying the defects and correcting them compared to the estimated cost of not correcting the defects
200. Profiles measuring the number of action items proposed, open, and completed
201. The number of defects injected in each stage, cumulatively, and overreleases of similar products
202. The number of defects

OK, there it is. We're glad that's over.

Questions to Ask When Generating and Reviewing Metrics

Most organizations collect some sort of measurements, even if they are only when projects start and finish, or how much money has been spent so far. When structuring your metrics process, you can consider asking the following questions of your project managers:

■ What metrics do you collect?
■ How to they track to the cost–effort–schedule metrics needed by senior management or other corporate activities?
■ Do you use and understand earned value?
■ Do you track the time it takes to enter, track, and report metrics?
■ Do you use any graphs or automated tools?
■ Which metrics work for you and which ones do not work for you? Why/why not?

- How have you used the metrics?
- What problems do you see in entering, collecting, analyzing, and reporting the metrics?
- How do you use the WBS? Does it tie back to the activities tracked by the metrics?
- How are the metrics you collect tied to business goals and the business problems in this organization?
- How do you analyze the metrics data?
- How do you verify that the data are correct and accurate?
- As for trends, what problems did/does your project have? Do the metrics reflect this finding? Did using the metrics help you identify this problem?
- In which phase of the life cycle did these problems occur?
- Do the metrics collected reflect or help you identify the phase of the life cycle where the problem occurred, or the cause of the problem?

Selection of the metrics to be used on the projects should take into consideration the size of the project (both in dollars, personnel, and product size); project classification (Development, Enhancements, or Maintenance); and complexity of the system being built. In addition, metrics should reflect the needs of the projects that represent the main functional areas in your organization. This approach will help to ensure coverage of representative projects of the organization.

Planning the Metrics Process

Metrics programs must also be planned. A simple Measurement Plan outline is shown in Table 17.1.

The exhibit is admittedly, a very simple outline for your metrics planning. Be sure to discuss how each metric will be collected, why, how it ties back to business objectives or problems, the format to be used to define and document each metric, and why everything discussed is relevant to the reader. The list of measurements

Table 17.1   Measurement Plan Outline

I.   Introduction (Purpose, Scope)
II.   Organizational and Project Issues
III.   Overall Measurement Approach
IV.   Approach for Project Management Metrics
V.   Approach for Technical Metrics
VI.   Approach for Introducing Metrics into the Organization
VII.   How Metrics Will Be Collected and Used
VIII. Roles and Responsibilities
IX.   Communication/Feedback Plan
X.   List of Measurements

in the Measurement Plan needs to include your project's and/or organization's definition of each measure. Don't assume that because you know what a "defect" is that everyone else has the same definition in mind. Be sure to keep your definition practical. Defining metrics is not an academic exercise.

Some Problems You May Encounter

The following is a list of problems we have encountered in metrics programs found in organizations. This list may be used as a checklist for any metrics or metrics programs you have implemented in your organization.

- Metrics are collected but not used
- No mechanism exists to distribute project performance metrics for review, comparison, and use
- Project-level metrics do not appear to be used to help project managers manage their projects
- No understanding of the value of metrics or how to use them is found
- No formal feedback loop found on the quality of the metrics, questions about them, and so forth
- Metrics reports are hard to review for trends
- Metrics data are inconsistent
- Personnel collect and input data that they think are right but are unsure
- A standard work breakdown structure (WBS) (a basic building block for management activities) is not followed consistently, and metrics cannot be traced back to WBS activities
- No one reviews the metrics data in the various databases for data integrity
- Training and communication are not occurring throughout the organization
- Procedures need to be devised to document metrics generation, collection, review, and use
- Existing procedures need to be updated to reflect changes
- Automated tools are not used, or the wrong automated tool is used, or the automated tool is used incorrectly
- The metrics reports are hard to read and understand
- Procedures are not well defined or consistently followed (usage of "may ... if desired ... at PM's discretion")
- The time it takes to identify, track, collect, and report the metrics is not measured
- Redundant data entry is rampant

Recommendations

Recommendations fall into two main categories:

1. Recommendations to improve the metrics identification and collection process itself
2. Recommendations to improve actual performance on projects

Recommendations to Improve the Metrics Identification and Collection Process Itself

The Number One, overall recommendation is to *automate the process and make it seamless and simple!* If it is too hard, the metrics collected will be useless. If it's too *damn* hard, people won't do it.

Other recommendations include:

- Involve your project managers and process owners with designing the metrics to be collected. Help them to understand why metrics are collected and how to use them to help run their projects.
- Collect metrics that the project managers need. Other metrics (i.e., corporate-level metrics used for executive reviews) can be generated automatically, based on the project-level data, and rolled up into a corporate report.
- Metrics should not be used punitively. They should be used to help assist the project managers in running their projects more effectively and to help improve estimating and tracking techniques.
- Facilitate workshops to derive meaningful metrics. Involve the project managers, directors, supervisors, metrics team, quality assurance personnel, process improvement specialists, technicians, budget and finance representatives, and any other interested individuals. Try to map your project-level and senior management-level metrics to business objectives and problems the organization faces.
- Provide feedback to the project managers and staff on the metrics collected so that they may see how they are doing compared to other projects in the organization and to other projects throughout the different business units.

Recommendations to Improve Actual Performance on Projects

Train the project managers and anyone else who generates, collects, reviews, or uses the metrics. First of all, make sure your PMs have received detailed, effective training in basic project management. Some managers simply do not have the skill sets required for the increasingly sophisticated tasks that their jobs require. For example, it is not uncommon to find PMs who are not really administrative-type managers concerned with costs and budgets. They more closely resemble technical leads. These PMs do not focus their energies on administrative tasks, such as documentation, planning, tracking, and reporting. They mostly concentrate on the technical fixes required for design and coding. Therefore, training on earned value—what it is, how to use it, how it can work for them—must be undertaken, as well as true training in how to do the job in your organization.

Metrics must be used. Instruct your staff (especially the PMs) in how the metrics can be used to help them manage their projects. Basically answer the question, "What's in it for me?" Just mandating that the metrics be used and to follow the procedures, will not work.

Besides estimating, most projects seem to fumble when it comes to requirements. Teams need to be formed to write instructions that are easy to read and understand, and on *how* to analyze and decompose requirements. The Standish Group, an organization devoted to collecting metrics summarizing performance of software organizations, has stated that up to 85 percent of all errors can be traced back to the Requirements phase. Therefore, most organizations can benefit from improving their requirements definition and analysis efforts, in that the Requirements phase appears to be where most errors are injected.

Summary

Generating metrics is not really that difficult—just look at the list we have presented! However, generating meaningful metrics that can be used in your organization is a little bit more complicated. Getting buy-in for the metrics effort will take some time and persuasion, and collecting and understanding the metrics will also present a challenge.

Do not give up! Most process improvement books (the CMMI among them) do not expect you to get it right the first time. In fact, the one thing that you will find is that, as you use the metrics, you will need to update them and make changes as your business needs change and as your staff becomes more knowledgeable.

Make sure you understand each metric selected for use, why it was selected, how it will be used, and how and when it will be collected. If not, ask. Maybe someone who generated the metrics decided that since these numbers worked at his previous place of employment, they should work here. Or maybe the metrics were designed for some other department or type of work or level in the corporation that does not meet your needs.

There are many, many books on metrics and metrics programs available. Although we make no recommendations, the ones most of our customers have used the most are:

Measuring the Software Process, William Florac and Anita Carleton, Addison Wesley, 1999.

Practical Software Measurement, John McGarry, David Card, Cheryl Jones, Beth Layman, Elizabeth Clark, Joseph Dean, and Fred Hall, Addison Wesley, 2002.

Metrics and Models in Software Quality Engineering, Stephen Kan, Addison Wesley, 1995.

Understanding Variation: The Key to Managing Chaos, Donald J. Wheeler, SPC Press, 2000.

Chapter 18

Statistical Process Control

This chapter is about Statistical Process Control, or SPC. This topic is often the most dreaded of all subjects when discussing process improvement. Why? Because it involves numbers and then scrutinizing the numbers to determine whether the numbers are correctly collected, reported, and used throughout the organization. Many organizations will collect metrics "because the book says we have to in order to get our rating." Well, we have to admit that is a good reason, but it is not the best reason. When used correctly, metrics can help decision-makers make good decisions. When used incorrectly, they can help decision-makers justify their boo-boos. Metrics can also be used by managers to abuse their people. So, this chapter spends a lot of time discussing metrics and the data that go into them.

It would be absurd to think that one small chapter in this book could teach you all about SPC. What we have tried to do in this book is to distill the knowledge you need to implement process improvement activities in your organization. So, this chapter also tries to do that; that is, to summarize what can sometimes be difficult concepts into something you can use right away. We have tried to summarize the information we have learned over the years and to summarize the best practices we have found in other organizations.

This chapter introduces different types of charts and discusses reasons for using the charts and reasons for collecting data. You will not be an expert in SPC once you have read this chapter. You will, however, have a very basic understanding of what SPC is about and where your organization might start.

Those of you who are experts at SPC can skip this chapter. However, for those of you who are experts who decide to read this chapter, we ask a little leeway. Everyone has a different approach to SPC—what should be used, what works best, definitions. We also have our own opinions, which may differ from yours. This chapter is also written to be understood, not to impress anyone with high-falutin' terminology or inscrutable examples, so the terminology used may be somewhat irritating to a few of you.

One more thing. *Data* are plural. Although most folks generally say, "the data *is* not yet available," proper grammar is to say, "the data *are* not yet available." So it may sound a little funny when you read it.

Background Information

What is Statistical Process Control? SPC consists of some techniques used to help individuals understand, analyze, and interpret numerical information. SPC is used to identify and track variation in processes. All process will have some natural variation. Think about it this way: Let's say you get into your car and drive to work every weekday. What can vary about that? Well, assuming that you don't change the route you take, the natural variation can be the number of stoplights you hit (that means the lights you must stop at—not that you hit them with your car), the number of cars waiting at the stoplight, the number of cars that are making turns at the stoplight, and so on. It can also include the number of accidents (if accidents are a normal part of your drive into work), the number of school buses you get behind, and on a really good day when everything seems to irritate you, the number of trash trucks you follow that you just can't seem to pass. All of these frustrations are those that you currently, normally encounter on your way to work. While the number of trash trucks may change, and the number of cars turning may change, the basic process of driving to work has not changed. Those variations are *normal* variations. The *exceptional* variation would be when you decide to drive into work, again on a weekday, that just happens to have a holiday fall on that day. Let's say that, due to a crushing workload, you decide to drive into work on Labor Day (which for those of you not familiar with the United States' holidays, always falls on the first Monday of September). Hopefully, you do not always go to work on a holiday, so this is an exception. You follow the same route, but it doesn't take as long, you don't hit as many stoplights, and the number of cars in front of you is lessened.

Due to normal variation in any process, the numbers (in our example, the number of cars waiting at the stoplight, the number of accidents that may occur) can change when the process really has not. So, we need to understand both the *numbers* relating to our processes and the *changes* that occur in our processes, so that we may respond appropriately.

Other terms that you may see are *common causes* of variation and *special causes* of variation, and *common cause systems* and *special cause systems*. Common causes of variation result from such things as system design decisions and the use of one development tool over another. This variation will occur predictably across the entire process associated with it and is considered normal variation. Special causes of variation are those that arise from people-type errors and unplanned events. This variation is exceptional variation. Other terms you will hear are *in control* for predictable processes or *steady-state*; and *out of control* for unpredictable processes that are "outside the natural limits."

When a process is *predictable*, the process exhibits routine variation as a result of common causes. When a process is *unpredictable*, it exhibits exceptional variation as a result of assignable causes. It is our job to be able to tell the difference and to find the assignable cause. When a process is predictable, it is performing as consistently as it can (either for better or for worse). It will not be performing "perfectly"; there will always be some normal, routine variation. Looking for assignable causes for processes that are running predictably is a waste of time because you won't find any. Work instead on improving the process itself. When a process is unpredictable, that means it is not operating consistently. It is a waste of time to try to improve the process itself. In this case, you must find out why it is not operating predictably, and detail the *whys* as specifically as possible. To do that, you must find and fix the assignable cause(s); that is, the activity that is causing the process to behave erratically.

An example of fixing an assignable or special cause of variation in our driving to work example would be if your car breaks down on the way to work. If this happens once, you might not take any action. However, if your car is old and breakdowns occur frequently, you might decide to remove this special cause by buying a newer car.

In contrast to predictability of a process, we may want to consider if a process is capable of delivering what is needed by the customer. Capable processes perform within the specification limits set by the customer. So, a process may be *predictable* but not *capable*.

Seven Common Tools

SPC takes numbers and presents the numbers pictorially in order to tell a story. The story that is told demonstrates what is happening within the process. That story is often called "the voice of the process." The pictures produced must be explained and must be accurate. To that end, there are seven commonly recognized tools for statistical process control. They are the:

- Check sheet
- Run chart
- Histogram
- Pareto chart
- Scatter diagram/chart
- Cause and effect or fishbone diagram
- Control chart

Table 18.1 Check Sheet

Student Name	In Class This Week?
Jane	√√√√
Robert	√√√√
Jennifer	√√√
Puff Daddy	

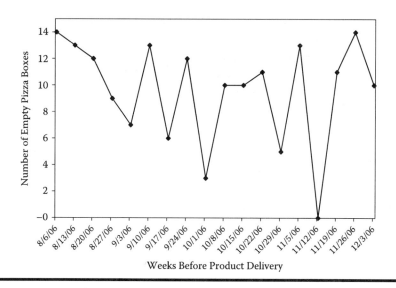

Figure 18.1 Run chart.

Some basic examples follow. These examples are for illustration only; we don't go into how to derive the values for each chart and then how to translate the values into meaningful representations.

Check Sheet

The check sheet, shown in Table 18.1, is used for counting and accumulating data.

Run Chart

The run chart, shown in Figure 18.1, tracks trends over a period of time. Points are tracked in the order in which they occur. Each point represents an observation. You can often see interesting trends in the data by simply plotting data on a run chart. A

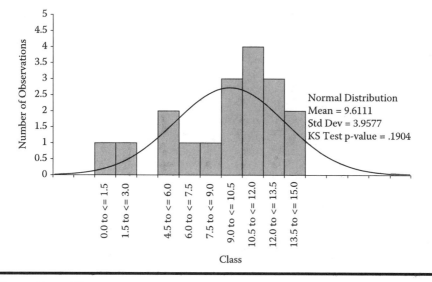

Figure 18.2 Histogram.

danger in using run charts is that you might overreact to normal variations, but it is often useful to put your data on a run chart to get a feel for process behavior.

Histogram

The histogram, shown in Figure 18.2, is a bar chart that presents data that have been collected over a period of time and graphically presents these data by frequency. Each bar represents the number of observations that fit within the indicated range. Histograms are useful because they can be used to see the amount of variation in a process. The data in the histogram in Figure 18.2 are the same data as in the run chart in Figure 18.1. Using the histogram, you get a different perspective on the data. You see how often similar values occur and get a quick idea of how the data are distributed.

Pareto Chart

The Pareto chart, shown in Figure 18.3, is a bar chart that presents data prioritized in some fashion, usually either by descending or ascending order of importance. Pareto charts are used to show attribute data. Attributes are qualitative data that can be counted for recording and analysis, for example, counting the number of each type of defect. Pareto charts are often used to analyze the most often occurring type of something.

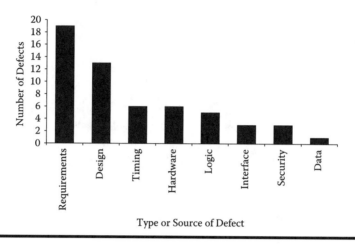

Figure 18.3 Pareto chart.

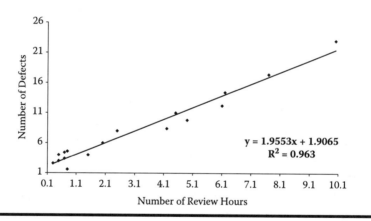

Figure 18.4 Scatter diagram.

Scatter Diagram/Chart

The scatter diagram, shown in Figure 18.4, is a diagram that plots data points allowing trends to be observed between one variable and another. The scatter diagram is used to test for possible cause-and-effect relationships. A danger is that a scatter diagram does not prove the cause-and-effect relationship.

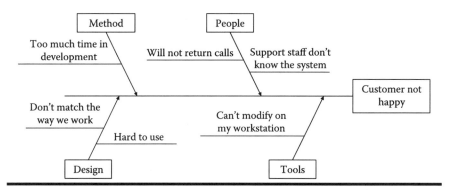

Figure 18.5   Cause and effect/fishbone diagram.

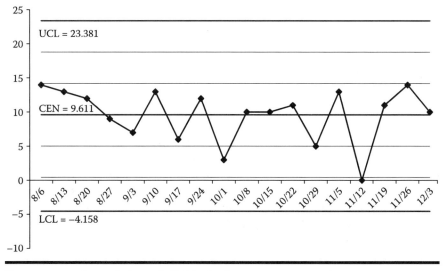

Figure 18.6   Control chart (individuals chart).

Cause and Effect/Fishbone Diagram

The cause and effect or fishbone diagram, shown in Figure 18.5, is a graphical display of problems and causes. This is a good way to capture team input from a brainstorming meeting, from a set of defect data, or from a check sheet.

Control Chart

The control chart, shown in Figure 18.6, is basically, a run chart with upper and lower limits that allows an organization to track process performance variation. Control charts are also called process behavior charts. The data in the control chart in Figure 18.6 are the same data as in the run chart in Figure 18.1 and in the histogram in Figure 18.2. We will discuss control charts in more detail in the following sections.

Figure 18.6 is labeled as an individuals chart, which is shorthand notation for individual values chart. Some of you may have reviewed the charts above and said, "Wait a minute! That's not a histogram! That's a Pareto diagram!" or "That's not a control chart! That's a run chart!" The names of these diagrams are a result of "book learnin'" over actual usage. Your organization may call these charts and graphs something totally different. Just make sure you use the right calculations for the charts, know where the data come from, know what the data represent, and how to interpret the charts.

While some people include the fishbone diagram as a "statistical" tool, others do not because the fishbone does not necessarily focus on quantitative data. We have included it because we often use it during data gathering workshops.

Why aren't pie charts listed? Pie charts are the most commonly found charts in organizations and are used frequently in newspapers and articles across this country. Why aren't they included as statistical tools? We believe it is because pie charts simply take counts of data that could be (or actually are) listed in tables, either just by raw count or by percentages, and display these data as parts of the pie. We like pie charts—they are easy to understand. But, we don't believe that they allow the viewer to understand the voice of the process better than other types of charts.

These seven graphical displays can be used together or separately to help gather data, to accumulate data, and to present the data for different functions associated with SPC. For example, we like to use the fishbone diagram when conducting brainstorming sessions with our clients. We select a problem that has occurred in the organization and brainstorm the causes and effects of the problem. We then draw a scatter diagram to spot trends in the gathered data. In any event, most people prefer to review data represented pictorially than by data listed in endless tables. While tables can list the values or results found, they cannot show the relationships between the values and between each table, or illustrate areas that are not performing in a statistically predictable way.

Representing and Reporting Data

Charts are based on data. In order to produce accurate charts, the data must be consistent and accurate. Those of you operating in low-maturity organizations (Maturity Levels 1 or 2) will not be able to produce accurate charts. Why not? Because at your current level of functioning, your processes are not yet stable enough to produce consistently accurate data. That is why SPC is not broached in the CMMI until Maturity Level 4. So do not jump right into producing statistical charts and graphs when initiating a process improvement effort. You are not ready for it—yet.

Data must be consistent! What does that mean? It means it was collected at the same time in the process and in the same manner. We once appraised an organization that had proclaimed itself to be a Level 4 organization; that means that they were able to quantitatively predict their quality, productivity, and schedule ability in statistically accurate terms, and manage with the data. The data we found were in no way shape or form statistically accurate. Yes, the organization had been collecting data for 18 years. But what did the data say? What did they look like? For the past 17 years, the organization had collected data on all of their projects for only when the project started and when the project ended. That's it. Each project lasted from five to eight years. These data tell you just about nothing. Because the customer had requested an outside, external appraisal, the organization for the last (one) year collected data according to their system development life cycle. So they collected data relating to when each project started the Requirements phase and when each project ended that phase. Then, they collected start and end dates for the Design phase, the Construction phase, the Testing phase, and the Implementation/Delivery phase. They mixed all this data in with the previous data from the previous 17 years. This is not an example of consistent data.

Another example of inconsistent data that we run across quite often is that collected from peer reviews. It is a good idea to collect data from peer reviews. If these data are collected during peer reviews for, say, code, these data can be used to show trends in programming errors found that might be solved via increased training in coding techniques or in improving the processes used for eliciting and documenting requirements, and then designing systems. But once again, the data must be consistent. For example, suppose a peer review is done on a program comprising 8,000 lines of code, and 8 errors are found. Another peer review is done on a program comprising 8 lines of code, and 6 errors are found. The second peer review found fewer errors. Does that mean that the person who coded the second program is a better coder than the person who coded the first program? Of course not. You also need to consider the complexity of the programs, the length of the programs, the type of language, and so forth. Just collecting data for the sake of collecting data and populating your brand-new database with numbers is not a good enough reason to jumble all of these numbers together.

What questions should you ask yourselves when reviewing the data for your charts? The following seven questions are a start:

1. Who collected these data? (Hopefully, the same people who are trained in proper data collection techniques.)
2. How were the data collected? (Hopefully, by automated means and at the same part of the process.)
3. When were the data collected? (Hopefully, all at the same time on the same day or at the same time in the process—very important for accounting data dealing with month-end or year-end closings.)

4. What do the values presented mean? (Have you changed the process recently? Do these values really tell me what we want/need to know?)
5. How were these values computed from raw inputs? (Have you computed the data to arrive at the results you want or to accurately depict the true voice of the process?)
6. What formulas were used? (Are they measuring what we need to measure? Are they working? Are they still relevant?)

And the most important question of all:

7. Are we collecting the right data, and are we collecting the data right? (The data collected should be consistent, and the way data are collected should be consistent.)

Much of the data reported to senior management is contained in some sort of report, usually produced and presented monthly. These data are usually aggregated data; that is, data that have been collected from various processes and various parts of the processes. These data are then summarized and combined into percentages of something or other. Do not trust these data. They are just that—data (numbers), not meaningful information. While on the surface these data may seem logical and accurate, they really aren't. For example, most financial/budget/cost data are collected at month-end closing. However, month-end closing within several departments often follows inconsistent processes. Each department follows processes that vary at least somewhat throughout the organization. Each department is collecting different data that measure *its* work and the cost of the work done in *that* department. The month-end process, therefore, varies. It varies in the processes used to collect the data, the data collected, the persons collecting the data, and the time when the books are actually closed and the accounts reconciled. These data from all of the departments are then aggregated and summed, making them look accurate. The point is, the data cannot be used as a basis of any sort of reasonable predictions because they consist of a mixture of apples and oranges. A control chart, based on this aggregated data, would be of no value. If you really wanted to improve your month-end closing process, you would need to chart the process for each individual department, and then determine where improvements are needed.

Know your data. Make sure they represent actual activities that occur, and not just counts of how many times something or other happened.

The Tyranny of Control Charts

Every organization we have ever worked for or appraised ends up using control charts. At first, we didn't understand why. The reason for our not understanding was because the charts were not generated correctly, and the numbers were never explained. It was simply enough to draw pretty pictures that made management happy. One organization we worked for produced 127 control charts. We were called in to help them reduce the number of charts produced. Our analysis of the charts revealed one stunning conclusion: although 127 charts were produced, there were really only 3 charts, produced many times over. The charts produced tracked productivity of contractor labor, cost of contractor labor, and CPU uptime versus downtime. The reason so many charts were produced was that some managers wanted them in color; some managers wanted them for the month ending on the 15th of the month; other managers wanted them ending on the 30th of the month; others wanted them produced weekly; and others wanted them produced monthly and quarterly. But they were basically the same charts! Once this observation was reported to senior management, the lower-level managers were told to only view the charts for data reported at the end of the month and no more color representations.

Another organization that we appraised did the following "dog and pony" show for the appraisal team. We were given a presentation by the Metrics Team of the metrics and control charts used in this organization. Several members of the Metrics Team got up and presented their charts on the overhead projector, and then sat down. After the presentations were over, the appraisal team had a chance to ask questions. Our team members were silent. They had been suitably impressed by the length and depth of the metrics collection and reporting. The charts were pretty, in color, and seemed sophisticated. We were not impressed. Our job was to help our team determine whether the metrics collected were appropriate enough to use to measure the stability and predictability of the processes used in this organization. So, we began asking questions of the leader of the Metrics Team. Our question was, "How did you collect the data?" He told us the data were collected using an automated tool. We asked for a demo of the tool. During the demo, we asked, "What data were collected? How was it determined to collect these data? How were the charts used in the organization? What did all of the charts show? Where were the data that could backup the information on the charts? What story were the charts really telling?" He could not answer our questions. Instead, he had us talk to the programmer who had coded the program used to collect the data. The programmer could not tell us why the programs used the formulas to collect and calculate data values. He only knew that he was responsible for updating the program. When was the last time he did that? Well, he had been there 12 years and had never updated the program. He told us to talk to the strategic planning manager who was responsible for creating the Master Schedule. So we did. She also could not tell us why these data were selected and what the charts showed. She told us to talk to the contracting officer who was in charge of the budget and billing the client. She also could not tell us the answers. Nor could she explain how the budget was derived or how the billing was calculated. She referred us back to the strategic planning manager. She referred us back to the Metrics Team. Basically, no one in this organization really knew where the data came from, how they were collected, and whether they were still relevant or not. No one had bothered to ask. They were happy producing pretty pictures. No decisions were being made based on these charts.

The two organizations discussed used control charts to display their data. We soon learned that control charts are a wonderful means of displaying data to use to identify information, *when people understand what the data mean and how to interpret the charts.* So while we have titled this section "The Tyranny of Control Charts," that is really a misnomer. We will discuss control charts at length.

Control charts are used to identify process variation over time. All processes vary. The degree of variance and the causes of the variance can be determined using control charting techniques. While there are many types of control charts, the ones we have seen the most often are the:

- c-chart. This chart uses a constant sample size of attribute data, where the average sample size is greater than 5. It is used to chart the number of defects (like 12 or 15 defects per thousand lines of code). c stands for the number of nonconformities within a constant sample size.
- u-chart. This chart uses a variable sample size of attribute data. This chart is used to chart the number of defects in a sample or set of samples (like 20 out of 50 design flaws were a result of requirements errors). u stands for the number of nonconformities with varying sample sizes.
- np-chart. This chart uses a constant sample size of attribute data, usually greater than or equal to 50. This chart is used to chart the number defective in a group. For example, a hardware component might be considered defective regardless of the total number of defects in it. np stands for the number defective.
- p-chart. This chart uses a variable sample size of attribute data, usually greater than or equal to 50. This chart is used to chart the fraction defective found in a group. p stands for the proportion defective.
- X and mR (XmR) charts. These charts use variable data where the sample size is 1. This is the chart we use the most often. X stands for individual value and mR stands for moving range. More on this later.
- X-bar and R (XbarR) charts. These charts use variable data where the sample size is small. They can also be based on a large sample size greater than or equal to 10. X-bar stands for the average of the data collected. R stands for the range (distribution) of the data collected.
- X-bar and s (XbarS) charts. These charts use variable data where the sample size is large, usually greater than or equal to 10.

So, as you can see, you can sometimes use several of the charts, based on types of data and on the size of the sample, and the size of the sample may change. While some folks will quote hard and fast rules for the use of these charts, we have found that organizations often modify when they are used and how they are used, based on the preferences of someone influential in the organization. In any case, when using these charts, look for trends or patterns in the data collected. Try to collect 20 to 25 groups of samples to be statistically correct, although 5 or 6 may prove useful in detecting initial trends.

The control chart definitions use the terms *attribute* data and *variable* data. Attribute data are data counted as discrete events or occurrences. For example, yes/no, good/bad, is/is not defective. These data are usually counts of something. For our purposes, examples are number of CMMI process area goals attained, percent of defects found per month, number of trained people on a project team, and percent of projects using function points to calculate size. Variable data are data that vary and must be measured on a continuous scale. These measurements are usually quantitative measures. Examples are length, time, volume, height, effort expended, memory utilization, and cost of rework.

Control charts help detect and differentiate between *noise* (normal variation of the process) and *signals* (exceptional variation that warrants further investigation). An everyday example of noise in a process is the "white lab-coat effect." This effect is what happens when you go to the doctor to get your blood pressure checked. Anyone who has a tendency to high-blood pressure will generally become a little nervous during this procedure. Therefore, the blood pressure reading taken by the medical professional (in the white lab coat) has been known to skew higher than if the reading had been taken in the comfortable surroundings of your own home. Another example is for those of us trying to maintain our weight. Even those persons who are successfully maintaining their weight notice fluctuations throughout the month—especially women. But tracking our weight over the period of a year, we will find that the average stays about the same—unless we start supersizing our meals and indulging ourselves in ice cream desserts or key lime pie. In fact, if we do indulge ourselves several days (or months) in a row, we know that we will gain weight. That indulgence is therefore a signal to watch our intake of food, exercise more, and do all that other stuff we know we should do.

Individuals and Moving Range Control Chart (XmR)

Which chart should I use? Although others may disagree, we recommend that you use the individual values and moving range (XmR) chart for most situations because:

- It is easy to use.
- It is easy to understand.
- It is easy to implement.
- It is most often the most appropriate for use in an organization.
- It is the most often found and most often used chart in high-maturity organizations.

Table 18.2   Count and Moving Range Values for 2002

	Jan	Feb	Mar	Apr	May	Jun	Jul	Aug	Sep	Oct	Nov	Dec
Count values	10	15	20	14	12	25	12	12	18	22	25	25
mR values		5	5	6	2	13	13	0	6	4	3	0

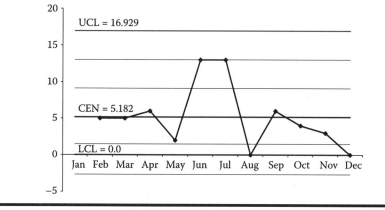

Figure 18.7   Moving range chart for 2002.

■ There are automated tools that can support building and displaying these charts. But remember, a tool does not do the thinking for you. It is up to you to collect the data correctly, to collect the correct data, and to interpret the results correctly.

Another suggested reason for using the XmR chart: Do you understand the terms *binomial probability* and *Poisson probability*? Do you know how to verify these probability models? If the answer is no or "What kinda language are you talking?" then stick with the XmR. Life is complicated enough.

The task we need to undertake is to figure out how to tell the difference between noise and signals in our process data. Properly generated control charts, specifically the XmR chart, can help us in this task. Past data (historical data) are critical for generating accurate control charts and for correct SPC analyses. To determine whether the results found are normal noise or true signals, comparisons of past data limits must be made and moving ranges determined. What's a moving range? Variation between successive values. Table 18.2 shows the count and mR value for each month of the year 2002. The mR values (moving range) shown are the absolute value of the difference between the count value for one month and the month immediately prior.

We can then average the moving range, as shown on Figure 18.7. Add up all of the moving ranges and divide by the number of months differentiated (11), and we

Table 18.3 Count and Moving Range Values for 2001

	Jan	Feb	Mar	Apr	May	Jun	Jul	Aug	Sep	Oct	Nov	Dec
Count values	10	12	20	18	11	22	15	18	20	22	25	25
mR values		2	8	2	7	11	7	3	2	2	3	0

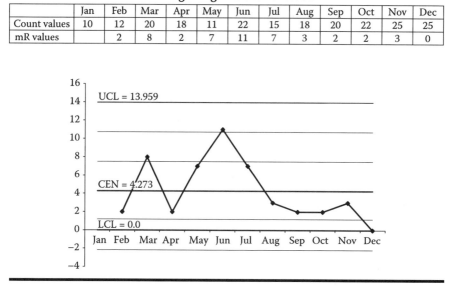

Figure 18.8 Moving range chart for 2001.

come up with 5.18 for our average moving range. The center line shows the average moving range for Table 18.2. The upper limit is 16.93. The lower limit is always 0.0 for the moving range chart, since mR is an absolute value and an absolute value is always either positive or zero.

Table 18.3 shows the count and mR value for each month of the year 2001. We then average the moving ranges. Add up all of the moving ranges and divide by the number of months differentiated (11), and we come up with 4.27 for our average moving range. The center line, see Figure 18.8, shows the average moving range. The upper limit is 13.96.

Table 18.4 shows the count and mR value for each month of the year 2000. We then average the moving ranges. Add up all of the moving ranges and divide by the number of months differentiated (11), and we come up with 2.64 for our average moving range. The center line, see Figure 18.9, shows the average moving range. The upper limit is 8.61.

While these charts are clear and easy to understand, they don't tell us enough of the story. To make these charts more relevant, we need to include a corresponding chart for the individual values represented by the individual months for each year in order to show a correlation or relationship between the values displayed.

Table 18.4 Count and Moving Range Values for 2000

	Jan	Feb	Mar	Apr	May	Jun	Jul	Aug	Sep	Oct	Nov	Dec
Count values	8	10	12	14	15	18	12	15	18	22	25	25
mR values		2	2	2	1	3	6	3	3	4	3	0

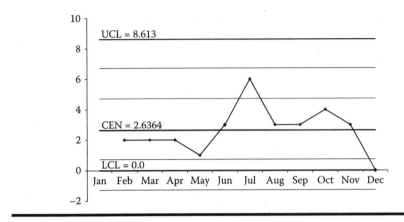

Figure 18.9   Moving range chart for 2000.

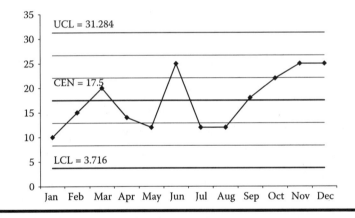

Figure 18.10   Individuals chart for 2002.

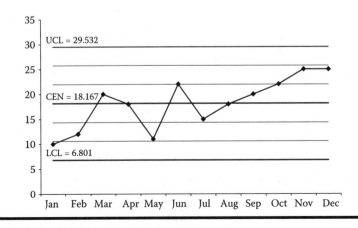

Figure 18.11   Individuals chart for 2001.

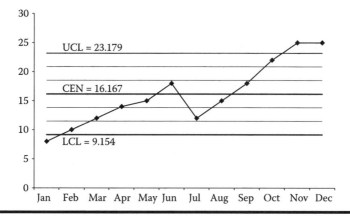

Figure 18.12   Individuals chart for 2000.

Are these good numbers or bad numbers? The charts will help us decide. These individual values, or counts, are shown by year in Figures 18.10, 18.11, and 18.12 on what is called an individuals chart.

The center line shows the average of the individual values (the sum of the values for the individual months divided by 12).

Using the count values for 2002 from Table 18.2, we produce the chart shown in Figure 18.10. The center line is 17.5. The upper limit is 31.28. The lower limit is 3.72.

Using the count values for 2001 from Table 18.3, we produce the chart shown in Figure 18.11. The center line is 18.17. The upper limit is 29.53. The lower limit is 6.8.

Using the count values for 2000 from Table 18.4, we produce the chart shown in Figure 18.12. The center line is 16.17. The upper limit is 23.18. The lower limit is 9.15.

So far, we have not really gotten the most value from our data. Now, we can combine the values for all of the charts for all three years into two charts: one for individual values for all three years and one for the average moving ranges for all three years, then compare the two. We can further combine them into the stacked XmR chart shown in Figure 18.13. By stacking or aligning the individuals chart on top of the moving range chart you can better compare the monthly data.

In the moving range chart at the bottom of Figure 18.13, the center line is 4.66. The upper limit is 15.21. In the individuals chart at the top of Figure 18.13, the center line is 17.28. The upper limit is 29.67. The lower limit is 4.89. You can clearly see cycles in the individuals chart. The line for December to January shows a precipitous drop that appears to occur every year. The line for February begins a climb back up. The line for March to April goes downward. The line for May goes back up. June and July are down. July to December is up. These cycles also show up in values for the moving range. Note the spikes for moving range values in January

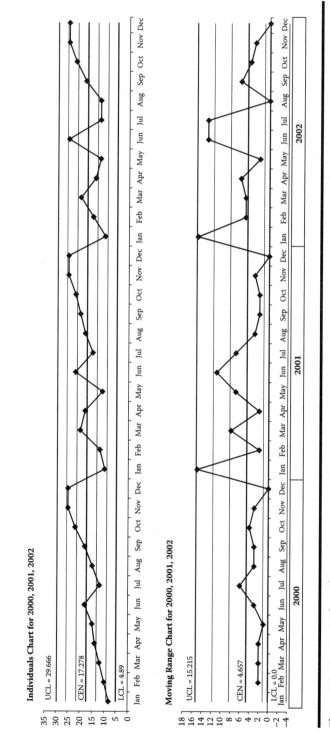

Figure 18.13 XmR chart for 2000, 2001, and 2002.

and June. The charts do not tell us why, but we can clearly see that *something* is happening. We need to investigate that something to determine what is going on.

Computing Limits for the XmR Chart

We know that the values for the center lines for each chart were computed by simply taking the average of the values displayed (that is, by adding up the values for each month and then dividing by the number of months/values to compute the average). How were the upper and lower limits for the charts shown calculated? We can calculate the limits for both the X (individual values) chart and the average moving range (mR) chart as follows:

- For the mR (moving range) chart. The upper range (or upper control limit, or upper natural limit) is computed by multiplying the average moving range (the center line of the mR chart) by 3.27.
- For the X (individual values) chart. The upper range for the X chart is computed by multiplying the average moving range of the associated chart by 2.66 and then adding the value for the center line of the X chart. The lower range for the X chart is computed by multiplying the average moving range by 2.66 and then subtracting the value for the center line of the X chart.

Notice that values for both representations (individual values and average moving range values) must be gathered and computed. The upper and lower limits for the individual values chart (X chart) depend on the average variations calculated for the center line of the average moving range chart. Therefore, these charts are interdependent and can be used to show relationships between the two types of charts and the two types of data.

When you present these charts to management, they may decide that the variation looks a little too big for their comfort. So, they may suggest moving the limits to plus or minus some value. No! The only way to change the limits is to change the process itself. Remember, the charts show the voice of the process. So if management desires to improve the limits, they must improve the process. The numbers shown in the charts reflect results of the process. Our job is to find what caused these results. When analyzing the causes, and adjusting the process, remember that the inputs and outputs of the process may be affected, as well as any other processes that are dependent upon the original process under review. So, focusing on one or two causes will have downstream ramifications and will probably affect parts of your process, as well as other processes.

We have also seen the limits for the XmR charts calculated using median ranges instead of average ranges. The median moving range is often more sensitive to assigned causes when the values used contain some very high range values that inflate the average. Remember, the median range is that range of numbers that hover around the middle of a list sequenced in ascending or descending order. So the median range chart will automatically "throw out" the very high-end or low-end values. Use of the median moving range approach is valid; however, the formulas (constants) change. The constant value 2.66 changes to 3.14, and the constant value 3.27 changes to 3.87. If you decide to use both methods on your data, you will find some slight differences in the limits but not much. Try it and see.

Don't panic over computing these numbers. Most of the automated tools out there will do it for you and draw the charts. While we make no recommendations, the tool we used to generate the charts in this chapter is an add-on to Microsoft Excel.

Hints on How to Read the Charts

The most obvious interpretation is when one or more data points fall outside your control limits (either upper or lower). Those values should be investigated for assignable causes, and the assignable causes should be fixed. If your control chart shows three out of four consecutive points hovering closer to the limits than to the center line, this pattern may signal a shift or trend and should be investigated (because predictable processes generally show 85 percent to 90 percent of the data closer to the center line than to the limits). Remember, useful limits can be constructed with as few as five or six consecutive values. However, the more data used to compute the limits, the greater the certainty of the results.

Another way to spot trends is to look at the data points along the center line. If eight or more consecutive data points are clustered on the same side of the center line, a shift in the original baseline or performance of the process has probably occurred, even without a data point falling outside the limits. This is a signal to be investigated.

Also look for 6 consecutive points either increasing or decreasing in value. These points could signal a trend. Other points to notice are 14 points in a row alternating up and down; or 15 points clustered around the center line, both above and below the line.

Notice that we don't say, "This is a problem." We don't know yet. We *do* know that something has happened that needs more focus.

c-Charts

While XmR charts are the most often applied in organizations and are the most appropriate charts to use most often, they are not infallible. Sometimes an event will occur that skews the norm; that is, a rare event way outside of the average has occurred. When this happens, a c-chart is better used. A c-chart is used for rare events that are independent of one another.

The formulas for c-charts are different from XmR charts. First, calculate the average count of the rare occurrence over the total time period that the occurrence happened. That number becomes the center line. The upper limit is calculated by adding the average count to three times the square root of the average count. The lower limit is calculated by subtracting the average count from three times the square root of the average count.

The questions to ask yourself are, "Why am I charting rare events? What do I hope to discover?" Charting the number of times a rare event occurs is pretty useless. But charting the time periods between recurring rare events can be used to help predict when another rare event will occur. To do this, count the number of times the rare event occurs (usually per day per year) and determine the intervals between the rare events. Convert these numbers into the average moving ranges and voilà, you can build an XmR chart.

u-Charts

The u-chart is based on the assumption that your data are based on a count of discrete events occurring within well-defined, finite regions/areas, and that these events are independent. The u-chart assumes a Poisson process. You may want to consider a u-chart when dealing with defects (counts) within a group of pages (region/area), for example, number of errors per page or the number of defects per 1,000 lines of code.

The u-chart differs from the XmR in that the upper and lower control limits of the u-chart change over time. The ū in u-chart is the weighted average of the count (ū = Σcountj / Σsizej). The upper control limit is calculated by adding ū to three times the square root of the ū divided by the last size (sizej). The lower control limit is calculated by subtracting ū from three times the square root of the ū divided by the last size (sizej).

Now then, let's go back and look at our example of inconsistent data gathered from peer reviews. We said, "Suppose a peer review is done on a program comprising 8,000 lines of code, and 8 errors are found. Another peer review is done on a program comprising 8 lines of code, and 6 errors are found. The second peer review found fewer errors. Does that mean that the person who coded the second program is a better coder than the person who coded the first program? Of course not. You also need to consider the complexity of the programs, the length of the programs, the type of language, and so forth." A u-chart is sometimes used for just this example because it takes into consideration the size of the program reviewed. However, we still do not recommend using a u-chart in this case. It is too easy to misinterpret the results and too easy to use the wrong data to construct the charts.

OK, so if this all sounds too complicated, and you don't like the idea of your limits changing with each observation, then just go ahead and use the XmR chart with your count-based data. The XmR chart's behavior will resemble the c-chart and the u-chart, since these are special cases of the individuals chart.

Summary

Keep it simple! If collecting and analyzing data are too hard, it won't be done. Don't try to chart every metric you have. Start by identifying where the problems are in your organization, and devise metrics to track and monitor your current processes and improvement efforts. Or you may start with a list of metrics that you currently collect and use, and decide which ones (two or three) might relate to the problems your organization faces.

SPC depends on historical data. It also depends on accurate, consistent process data. If you are just beginning the process improvement journey, do not jump into SPC. You (your data) are not yet ready for it. That's why the CMMI waits until Maturity Level 4 in the staged representation to suggest the application of SPC techniques. At Level 2, processes are still evolving. At Level 3, they are more consistent. Level 4 takes process information from Level 3 and analyzes and structures both the data and their collection. Level 5 takes predictable and unpredictable processes, and improves them.

Don't just show pretty pictures. Know what they mean, and where the data come from. Use the information provided in the charts to identify areas of improvement and to measure whether improvements are really taking place.

Chapter 19

A High-Maturity Perspective

This chapter discusses several concepts associated with high-maturity organizations and offers some suggestions on how to transition to a high-maturity organization. We discuss how to create and use Process Performance Baselines and Process Performance Models. We define a high-maturity organization as an organization operating at CMMI Maturity Level 4 or Level 5 or Capability Level 4 or Level 5. While there are many high-maturity concepts we could tackle, we focus on those concepts that most people consider confusing.

The most fundamental high-maturity concept is how measurements are handled at high maturity. Measures in this chapter refer to both base measures and derived measures. Base measures are simple values of some attribute of interest; for example, the size of a document in pages or the effort to produce a document in hours. Derived measures are defined to be a function of two or more base measures. An example of a derived measure is productivity. Productivity is a function of the size of a produced work product divided by the time to produce it (for example, design document productivity in pages per hour is the number of pages in the document divided by the hours to produce the document).

The high-maturity measurement concepts that we are going to cover are Process Performance Baselines, Process Performance Models, and Event Level Measurement. Event level measures are used to build Process Performance Baselines. Process Performance Baselines are used to build Process Performance Models. The Process Performance Baselines and Process Performance Models rely on the predictable and stable processes that we described in our Chapter 18 on statistical process control.

Table 19.1 Example Event Level Measures

Objective	Event	Measures
Productivity	Requirement (defined)	Hours, Complexity
	Requirement (designed)	Hours, Complexity
	Interface Implemented	Hours
	Object Coded	Hours
	Subsystem Integrated	Hours
	Test Scenario Executed	Hours
Product Quality	Design Review (completed)	Defects, Pages, Hours
	Inspection (completed)	Defects, Lines, Hours
	Test Scenario Executed	Defects, Hours, Coverage
Schedule	Task Completion	Days (no. late or early)

Event Level Measurement

One of the things that people overlook with high-maturity measurement is the level of detail that you want in your measures. Relating measures to events gives you this detail. An *event level measure* is a measure taken at the completion of an event, for example, definition of a requirement, implementation of an interface, performance of an inspection, or execution of a test. Most organizations initially collect total hours at the phase level, that is, total hours in the requirements phase, and therefore can only monitor and control at the phase level. That means that only at the end of the Requirements phase can they see how they have done. With measures taken at the event level, more detailed monitoring and controlling can be done and data can be used to manage throughout the phase. You don't have to wait until the end of the phase. You can adjust predictions within a phase at the completion of each event, in some cases, and take corrective actions as appropriate. In addition, event level measures can be used within different life cycles. For example, the event of defining a requirement is the same within a waterfall life cycle or within most iterative life cycles.

Examples of event-level measures are shown in Table 19.1. The table is divided into three potential objectives that an organization may consider important to meet its business goals. Those objectives are productivity, product quality, and schedule. The second column identifies some potential events of interest, for example, Requirement (defined), which would indicate that an individual requirement was defined. The third column identifies measures that would be collected and identified that relate to the event. In the case of Requirement (defined), the hours for the task and the complexity of the requirement (complex, nominal, or simple) are noted.

Process Performance Baseline

A *process performance baseline* (PPB) documents the historical results achieved by following a process. Once a PPB is developed, it is then used as a benchmark for comparing actual process performance in a project against expected process performance.

Table 19.2 is an example of a PPB containing the historical productivity results from executing the process used for new development within an organization. There are PPB elements for each of the five phases that this organization has in its life cycle: Requirements Definition, Design, Implementation, Integration, and Systems Test. Implementation for the example organization includes both the classic code and unit test of a software system, plus implementation of individual nonsoftware components. The first line under Requirements Definition is the number of hours to define a complex requirement. There are elements for complex requirements, nominal requirements, and simple requirements with values for the upper limit, mean, and lower limit for each. The Design PPB elements are based on requirements and follow the same structure. Implementation, Integration, and Systems Test PPB elements are based on the work products most important to those phases.

In addition to productivity for new development, an organization would want to develop additional PPBs covering other processes, for example, productivity for maintenance. In addition to productivity, other important organizational goals (e.g., product quality and schedule) would be covered in separate PPBs.

This example PPB points out one of the most important issues with using measures, particularly with using measures at higher maturity levels—that is, the need for clear definitions of measures. In this case, what the organization means by a complex requirement, a nominal requirement, and a simple requirement must be clearly defined so that the people collecting the data can tell how to count them. Most organizations start with a working definition and refine the definitions over time. In addition to defining what a requirement is, you also need to define what is included in the number of hours: Is it only hours sitting at your desk writing a requirement? Does it include hours for attending status meetings to discuss your work? How do you count time for review of requirements? These are questions that need to be answered in your organization to ensure that the data are collected consistently.

So How Do You Use a PPB with Your Projects?

New projects could use the example PPB for estimating their effort based on estimates of the number of requirements, number of interfaces, number of design pages, and so on. The range of values (upper, mean, and lower) allows the estimators to determine the most likely, worst case, and best case estimates of not only productivity, but also the staffing levels that are needed.

We have personally witnessed the positive change in organizations when they have PPBs that people believe. The estimation and planning process becomes much more of a professional activity and less emotional. Project managers armed with PPBs based on historical process performance are less likely to fall victim to unfounded pressure to lower estimates and reduce schedules.

After planning, the PPB can also be used to monitor and control the project's work by comparing the actual number of hours to perform the work against expected range of values for the PPB element. Remember, if the actual number of hours is outside the expected range, it is only meaningful if your process is already stable. Stabilizing your process takes time. Look for the cause, but don't overreact. Your process may have a lot of variation, and the tendency early on is to shoot the messenger. If people believe that bad things happen to people when the data are not what is expected, the people will find ways (devious and nefarious ways) to make the data acceptable. This is not what you want.

Process Performance Model

A closely related concept to the PPB is the *Process Performance Model* (PPM). The PPM describes the relationships among attributes of a process and its work products, and is used to estimate or predict a critical value that cannot be measured until later in the project's life—for example, predicting the number of delivered defects or predicting the total effort. Attributes of a *process* include productivity, effort, defects produced, defects detected, and rework. Attributes of a *product* include size, stability, defects contained, response time, and mean time between failures. PPMs are built on historical data and are often built from PPBs. PPMs can be developed for a wide range of project objectives. Example PPMs include Reliability Models, Defect Models, and Productivity Models.

Table 19.3 is an example of a simple PPM for predicting effort based on both the PPB shown in Table 19.2 and organization historical effort distribution. The PPB elements at the top of the second column (Number of Complex Reqs, Number of Design Pages, Number of Components, etc.) come from the Unit of Measure column in Table 19.2. The Estimated Number of Elements column in Table 19.3

Table 19.2 Process Performance Baseline (PPB) for New Development Productivity

PPB Elements	Upper Limit	Mean	Lower Limit	Unit of Measure
Requirements Definition	50.8	35	19.2	Hours/Complex Requirement
	29.2	21	12.8	Hours/Nominal Requirement
	13.4	8.6	3.8	Hours/Simple Requirement
Design	81.4	49.8	18.2	Hours/Complex Requirement
	44.4	31.7	19.0	Hours/Nominal Requirement
	18.6	13.3	8.0	Hours/Simple Requirement
Implementation	13.4	8.6	3.8	Hours/Interface
	35.4	21.0	6.6	Hours/Design Page
	6.54	4.3	2.1	Hours/Object
Integration	301.5	175.5	49.5	Hours/Subsystem
	32.5	23.5	14.5	Hours/Component
Systems Test	18.5	12.4	6.3	Hours/Test Scenario

Table 19.3 Process Performance Model (PPM)—Effort for New Development

Line Number		Est'd Number of Elements	Req Phase	Design Phase	Implement Phase	Integration Phase	System Test Phase	Total Effort
			mean	mean	mean	mean	mean	
1	**PPB Elements**							
2	**Number of Complex Reqs**	75	35	49.8				
3	**Number of Nominal Reqs**	100	21	31.7				
4	**Number of Simple Reqs**	200	8.6	13.3				
5	**Number of Interfaces**	TBD			8.6			
6	**Number of Design Pages**	TBD			21.0			
7	**Number of Objects**	TBD			4.3			
8	**Number of Subsystems**	TBD				175.5		
9	**Number of Components**	TBD				23.5		
10	**Number of Test Scenarios**	TBD					12.4	
11								
12	**Historical Effort Distribution**		20%	30%	20%	15%	15%	100%
13								
14	**Estimates**							
15	**Based on PPB Elements**		6,445	9,565	0	0	0	
16	**Based on Effort Distribution**		6,445	9,668	6,445	4,834	4,834	32,225
17								
18	**Actuals by Phase**		6,752	0	0	0	0	0
19								
20	**Prediction Based on Actual When Available or Best Estimate**		6,752	9,565	6,445	4,834	4,834	32,430

is derived from project information gathered and from the organization's metrics database. The mean value for each PPB element by phase comes from the Mean column in Table 19.2. The Historical Effort Distribution on line 12 of Table 19.3 comes from project actuals stored in the organization's metrics database.

The purpose of the example PPM for effort shown in Table 19.3 is to predict the total effort for the new development project. This model is designed to predict the total project effort throughout the life cycle, using more and better estimates and data as they become available. The example is divided into the following five sections.

PPB Elements (Lines 1–10)

For each of the elements, the model contains an estimated number of elements and the mean effort in hours for each applicable phase from the example PPB shown in Table 19.2. For example, line 2 shows that 75 complex requirements are estimated, that the mean number of effort hours in the Requirements phase for a complex requirement is 35, and that the mean number of effort hours in the Design phase for a complex requirement is 49.8. At this time, only the number of complex, nominal, and simple requirement elements have been estimated; therefore, line 5 through line 10 show the remaining estimated number of elements as TBD (to be determined). Later in the project's life cycle, as estimates for these other elements become available, they would be added to the model.

Historical Effort Distribution (Line 12)

This shows that, historically, projects have taken 20 percent of total staff effort in the Requirements phase, 30 percent in the Design phase, 20 percent in the Implementation phase, 15 percent in the Integration phase, and 15 percent in the Systems Test phase. (We have simplified the effort distribution percentages to make the example easier to follow.)

Estimates

The model has two estimates:

1. The first estimate on line 15 is based on the estimated number of PPB elements that most affect each phase. You can see how this is computed by looking at the value under the requirement phase. This value is computed by multiplying the estimated number of requirements by the mean number of effort hours for that type of requirement:
   - Number of complex reqs × mean effort req phase for complex reqs = 75 × 35 = 2,625

- Number of nominal reqs × mean effort req phase for nominal reqs = 100 × 21 = 2,100
- Number of simple reqs × mean effort req phase for simple reqs = 200 × 8.6 = 1,720
- Summing those three values, we get 6,445.

The total estimate based on PPB elements is calculated by summing the value for all phases. Since only the first two phases are estimated, we don't have a total estimate on line 15.

2. The second estimate on line 16 is based on the requirements phase estimate (6,445 from line 15) proportionally propagated across the life cycle. We use the ratio of historical distribution for requirement effort to the historical distribution for effort of the other phases. Using the historical effort distribution from line 12 in the following values:

- Design effort = 6,445 × (.30 / .20) = 9,668
- Implementation effort = 6,445 × (.20 / .20) = 6,445
- Integration effort = 6,445 × (.15 / .20) = 4,834
- System Test phase effort = 6,445 × (.15 / .20) = 4,834
- Total effort is then the sum of all phases = 32, 225

Actuals by Phase (Line 18)

This line captures the actual hours per phase. This example is shown at the completion of the requirements phase where 6,752 actual hours were used. No other actuals for this project are yet available.

Prediction Based on Actual When Available or Best Estimate (Line 20)

This is the real purpose of this model. The values on this line are selected from Actuals by Phase (line 18) if available. These are actuals for this project. If Actuals by Phase is not available, then the value from Estimate Based on PPB Element (line 15) is used, if available. Use the Estimate Based on Historical Effort Distribution (line 16) if no other values are available. The prediction is then 32,430, which is the sum of all phases. (Not to be confused with the *Sum of All Fears*, which is a book by Tom Clancy.)

So how do you use a PPM with your projects?

You use PPMs to estimate or predict a critical value that cannot be measured until later in the project's life. Our example showed a model to predict total effort throughout the project life cycle. No one really knows what the total effort will be until the project is over.

We have seen a model similar to our example used to accurately predict total effort. The PPM used came within 5 percent of the total effort following the completion of the requirements phase. We have also seen models built that successfully predict number of delivered defects, mean time between failures, and number of system failures during integration testing. The exciting thing about the use of the models is that the focus of project management becomes trying to find defects and trying to accurately measure performance, and not on dysfunctional interoffice politics.

Not to confuse the issue, but Table 19.3 is a simplification of a PPM. The basic flaw in this model is that, by using the mean (or average) value of the historical data points, we disregard the distribution between the upper and lower levels of the phase. This means that if a project were to use this model to predict its effort throughout the life cycle, the project would most probably never hit the actual mean for each phase. Instead, the project effort would fall somewhere between the range of upper and lower limits. This is a problem that can be corrected by incorporating the upper and lower control limits into the model. The flaw in the model could be corrected by producing a best case estimate and worst case estimate by substituting the upper limits or lower limits, respectively, for the mean value.

Transitioning to Level 4

Level 4, either capability level or maturity level, is about managing quantitatively. It includes both organizational- and project-level quantitative management. When you read the CMMI, you realize that it is written from the perspective of an organization and its projects executing at a steady state. The Organizational Process Performance process area describes an organization that has in place both the PPBs and PPMs that will be useful to the projects. The Quantitative Project Management process area describes projects that have selected processes that will satisfy the project's objectives, that are executing stable processes, and that are managing process performance to best satisfy the project's quality and process–performance objectives using PPBs and PPMs.

OK, so how do you transition to Level 4?

Following are some steps that we recommend. You will most likely need to perform multiple iterations through these steps as you become more experienced and your data become better.

Select the Measures That Will Be the Basis for Your PPBs and PPMs

An organization needs to develop the PPBs and PPMs that will be used by the projects. These baselines and models are built around what is important to the goals of the organization and the projects. We mentioned in earlier chapters that the only goals some organizations have are "to make money." *And so why is this a bad thing, you say?* Well it's not, but we need to decompose that goal into something that the engineering, product development, and support groups can directly contribute to. Identify what the critical components and attributes are, and identify measures of the standard processes and their work products. Measures related to product quality, cost, and schedule are often your best bet.

In Chapter 17, "A Boatload of Metrics," we identified a little over 200 measurements. We are not advocating that you collect anywhere near that number for your baselines and models, but you can use that list as a resource.

An example of using a single measure to build a PPM occurred in an organization we worked with that was able to do some impressive forecasting work based on only one measurement (the number of defects expected per thousand lines of code based on a similar project). The organization used that single number, its project's rate of defects found, and its project's rate of defects closed over the last four weeks to build an initial prediction model of when they would finish testing. They improved the model over the project's life cycle and got real customer buy-in and support. The organization's simple prediction model allowed them to better manage both the project schedule and customer expectations, turning a problem project into a success story. Before you ask, no—we are not saying this one success story makes the organization Level 4. But it did create an initial success that they were able to build upon and demonstrate the value of Quantitative Management to the organization.

Be sure to select measures that cover the life cycle for the types of projects that you want to quantitatively manage. For example, if you have maintenance projects, don't just measure the development life cycle. You might measure the number of problem reports, time to review problem reports, time to implement problem reports, time to test, number of retests, and so forth.

You need to consider both breadth and depth. *Breadth* means the measures across the entire life cycle, for example, cost, schedule, defects, and effort; and *depth* means the details in areas that are critical to your organization, that is, number of customer returns by release and number of subcontractor failures by vendor.

Collect the Measures Identified from the Projects

Often the hardest part of measurement is to get good data. Again don't be disheartened if you find problems with the data. Even if your standard process requires that your projects collect certain metrics, you may find that the data are missing and/or incorrect. You may need to "mine the data"; this means dig them up. The data may be in lots of different forms—in paper records, Excel spreadsheets, Word documents, or PowerPoint slides. They may only be in project status reports. They may be in many separate systems in many separate departments—finance, engineering, human resources, and so forth. Don't be surprised if you need to invest a lot of time and money to uncover old data.

Work with the projects early and often to make the data better. You may decide to take more time to collect new and better data.

Analyze the Data from the Projects

Chapter 18, "Statistical Process Control," shows a number of tools that you can use to analyze the data. In some organizations, this will be the first time anyone outside the project has really looked closely at the data. You are most likely going to find missing data, incorrect or dirty data, and the data are likely to show that not all projects are really following the standard process. Your analysis activities should include the following steps:

1. Review and fix the data. Investigate and correct missing data, zeros (for things like number of hours to perform a task), really large or really small numbers.
2. Look for ways to normalize data across projects. For example, use "defects by size" not just "defects."
3. Plot the data. Use a histogram to see if you have a normal or Poisson distribution. Use a scatter diagram to see any correlations. Use a run chart to view any trends. Use control charts once you find data that show promise.
4. Investigate the out of control points for their root cause. It is best to get project team members involved with this analysis, since the recorded data are likely to be incomplete. Put corrective actions in place to address the root causes. (This is a good place to use the approach described in the Causal Analysis and Resolution process area.)

Establish Organizational PPBs and PPMs from the Project Data

Calculate the current and predicted process performance and capture that in a PPB. Be sure to establish baselines that cover the life cycle for the types of projects that you want to quantitatively manage. You will most likely want baselines that cover cost, schedule, and product quality. Be sure to identify the profile of the projects used to create the baseline, for example, large development projects using a waterfall life cycle and formal peer reviews, medium development projects using iterative life cycle and informal peer reviews, or small maintenance projects using quality assurance-led reviews.

From the baselines, produce predictive models that will allow your projects to manage to the goals that are important to your organization. You will most likely want models that predict productivity, defect insertion and detection, and schedule.

Derive Project Goals

The steps up to now have been organizational, and while that may be important, we need to remember that, as defined by the CMMI, the projects within the organization produce and deliver the products and services.

So it is important to realize that the project has some goals to satisfy. These often include on-time delivery, implementing all the technical requirements of the project, and staying within cost and schedule. Goals may come from the customers. Goals may also come from the organization—if you are reading this book, it is likely that the organization wants to improve or at least wants to get a rating. Those are organizational goals.

You need to derive the project goals so that you know what to quantitatively manage to get to those goals.

Select Critical Subprocesses to Be Managed by the Project

Ensure that you have a set of subprocesses that cover the life cycle (breadth) of the project, and ensure that the critical subprocesses go into enough detail (depth) on the things truly critical to your project.

Select the measures and define what needs to be done to collect and store the measures for the project. OK, here is where you may have a problem if the project goals are not covered as part of your organizational goals. Investigate adding these project goals to the organizational goals, but only if appropriate. Some projects truly are unique. You may need to identify unique measures, baselines, and models to satisfy these project goals. However, we have found that most projects are not truly unique from other projects; therefore, the goals of the projects should have been incorporated into organizational goals.

Select the Process Performance Baselines to Be Used by the Project

You need to compare the profile of your project to the profile of projects used to create the baselines, and select a PPB or set of PPBs to use. OK, here is where you may have another problem if the projects used to create the PPB are nothing like your project. But, don't give up just because things appear different. Here is an example: We were working recently with a large enterprise with multiple groups around the United States. This company had been comparing the average number of hours to fix problem reports. It found maintenance data in three separate organizations of widely separated geographic locations, using different processes and separate collection activities. To its surprise, the values came back as 12 hours per problem report, 13 hours per problem report, and 15 hours per problem report. These organizations had not compared notes, yet they came within 20 percent of one another. While you may want much closer ranges, these data proved useful in initial quantitative management of the maintenance projects.

Select the Process Performance Model(s) to be Used by the Project

Once you have selected the project's goals, measures, subprocesses, and PPBs, you can select the PPMs to use on your project. These may include:

- Schedule and Cost Models
- Progress Models
- Reliability Models
- Defect Models (defect identification and removal rates, defect removal effectiveness, latent defect estimation)
- Productivity Models

You will need to calibrate the models to match your project's performance. For example, your project will have its own defect and identification and removal rates that may be different from what is in the defect model. Be sure you understand the basis of the models before you do any calibration.

Manage the Project Quantitatively

The project can now use the PPBs and PPMs to manage process performance and to work toward achieving the organization's and projects' goals. This work includes:

- Maintaining control charts of the subprocesses and identifying the root cause of out of control points
- Adding the actual performance data to the prediction models
- Taking corrective actions throughout all phases of the project's life cycle to best achieve the project's quality and process–performance objectives

Start Early to Level 4

It takes some time for most organizations to collect the kind of data we have shown in the examples. If you don't have this much data, don't become disheartened. One of the things that we have found in working with organizations moving to high maturity is that even a little good data go a long way.

Transitioning to Level 5

The people we work with don't have as much of a problem with the concepts at Level 5 as we have seen with Level 4. But there are a few points that need to be made with each of the process areas, that is, Organizational Innovation and Deployment (OID) and Causal Analysis and Resolution (CAR).

The OID process area contains a reasonable set of steps for a Level 5 process improvement function in the following seven specific practices as written:

SP 1.1   Collect and analyze process- and technology-improvement proposals.

SP 1.2   Identify and analyze innovative improvements that could increase the organization's quality and process performance.

SP 1.3   Pilot process and technology improvements to select which ones to implement.

SP 1.4   Select process- and technology-improvements for deployment across the organization.

SP 2.1   Establish and maintain the plans for deploying the selected process and technology improvements.

SP 2.2   Manage the deployment of the selected process and technology improvements.

SP 2.3   Measure the effects of the deployed process and technology improvements.

A key to the OID process area that does not come out at the specific practice level is the assumption that the organization's processes are quantitatively managed. This is a key assumption since stable processes and quantitative data are the basis for several of the practices.

Following are some steps that we recommend for implementing OID in your organization.

Create an Organizational Group Responsible for the Collection of Improvement Suggestions for Both Process and Technology

It is critical to the success of OID that you collect improvement proposals from across the organization and that these proposals are handled in a professional way. Establishing a group responsible for reviewing improvement proposals is not an explicit CMMI requirement (the CMMI's OID introductory notes refers to an infrastructure, not a group), but a responsible group is the only way we have seen OID work. People need feedback on their proposals. We go into a lot of organizations where the staff has given up making suggestions because "nobody listens anyway." You also need to make sure the group is not dysfunctional. We worked with one organization where the primary author of the organization's standard process chaired the committee to review improvement suggestions. He saw all suggestions as a personal attack. The year after he was replaced as committee chair, the organization documented savings of over $700,000 from implementing process improvement proposals.

Establish a Well-Defined Process for Improvement Proposals

The process or procedures for improvement proposals need to include details on the improvement proposal content, the routing, the analysis, the reviewing, the initial approval of proposals, the feedback, the piloting methods, measurement methods, the review of piloting results, and final approval to roll out to the organization. The process or procedure should document the formats, the steps, and the authority. It should also identify the metrics to collect on the proposals, for example, number of proposals, how many from each group, time to respond, the number by status, and so forth. In addition, clear responsibility for independent process reviews and audits needs to be established to ensure the process is followed.

The analysis of improvement suggestions needs to be based on the data collected as part of the Level 4 activities. Use your PPBs and PPMs to calculate return on investment of the improvement proposals. To answer your question: no, we don't believe you can do real OID before you do Level 4.

Be sure to estimate a return on investment before running any pilot of the improvement. Update these estimates as the understanding of the improvement increases. Record historical data on all estimates. The pilot procedures and plans need to include evaluation techniques, for example, walkthroughs, prototypes, and human simulations along with documented methods for measuring savings.

Establish Process Improvement Goals

Your organization should have improvement goals and manage to them. The organization needs to consider establishing three types of strategic process improvement goals:

1. Incremental Improvements
2. Innovative Improvement
3. Targeted Improvements

Incremental improvements are stepwise improvements accomplished by making the current processes and tools a little better. A source of incremental improvement opportunities can be found by analyzing the organization's common defects from reviews and testing and other common causes of variation. The approach described in the Causal Analysis and Resolution process area works well for finding these kinds of improvements. These improvements are often the responsibility of the Process Improvement Group or a special team chartered to find incremental improvements.

Innovative improvements are major leaps in performance accomplished by bringing into the organization a significantly different process or technology. A good place to look for this type of improvement is from an external organization or specialists. These improvements are often the responsibility of a Process Action Team chartered to address a particular area or problem.

Targeted improvements are specific areas that have been identified as problematic. Senior management may establish an area of improvement as an organizational goal; for example, an organizational goal might be to reduce delivered defects by 20 percent. These goals are used to solicit improvement suggestions from across the organization.

The goal derivation, refinement, planning, and retirement process needs to be defined and understood by everyone involved in these activities. Be sure everyone participating is trained in goal derivation and process improvement including senior management. Consider establishing a Process Action Team(s) to create the process and create a draft set of goals. Use caution in defining the goals so that they don't belittle individuals or disciplines.

Clearly Communicate Process Improvement Activities and Goals to the Staff

Senior management is responsible for clear and positive communication to the staff of the goals, why the goals are important, and their personal commitment to improvement. This can be a very positive activity for the organization, but only when senior management takes the lead and describes the positive reasons for improving the process and technology.

Goals need to be considered part of the project commitment process. Imposing annual organizational goals on ongoing, preexisting projects is a change in requirements that needs to be managed as any other requirements change. Don't let your organization revert to Level 1 behavior by imposing uncommitted requirements on projects.

Remember to communicate seven times and three ways. The three ways might be the company Web page or newsletter, staff meetings, and "all hands" meetings. We worked with one organization where the goal definition activity was not clearly communicated to the staff, and the rumor mill had decided that senior management was meeting with the project managers and technical leads in order to plan a massive layoff. The morale was turned around only after the chief technical officer called a special engineering-wide meeting to communicate what was really going on.

The other process area described in Maturity Level 5 is Causal Analysis and Resolution. The CAR process area is a high-level description of identifying causes of defects and other problems and taking action to prevent them from occurring. The steps identified in the five specific practices are:

SP 1.1 Select the defects and other problems for analysis.

SP 1.2 Perform causal analysis of selected defects and other problems and propose actions to address them.

SP 2.1 Implement the selected action proposals that were developed in causal analysis.

SP 2.2 Evaluate the effect of changes on process performance.

SP 2.3 Record causal analysis and resolution data for use across the project and organization.

As we discussed in Chapter 8, "Understanding Maturity Level 5—Optimizing," you can be doing these CAR activities much sooner than Level 5. However, from a high-maturity perspective, these activities become mandatory for a useful Level 5 implementation and very desirable for a successful Level 4.

When transitioning to Level 4, use the steps described as part of CAR to investigate special causes of variation for their root cause. As stated previously, it is best to get project team members involved with this analysis, since the recorded data are likely to be incomplete. Put corrective actions in place across the organization to address the root causes, as appropriate.

At Level 5, use the steps in CAR when looking for incremental improvements. These steps can be the basis to investigate common causes of variation in your standard processes and technology usage, and to establish a plan to remove some of the undesirable common causes.

If you are looking for statistical techniques to use with CAR consider the run sheet, Pareto Chart, and Cause and Effect Diagram from our Statistical Process Control Chapter (Chapter 18).

Summary

This chapter describes our perspective and recommendations on high maturity. The high-maturity approaches described here take time and effort. We have seen the significant success that some organizations have with these approaches. We have also seen organizations attempt high-maturity behavior too soon before defining a solid set of organizational processes and working through the change management issues of Level 3. Those organizations have not been successful.

This chapter described both organizational and project-level high-maturity activities. We have a special word of caution here: be careful that in your organization you don't build a wall between the projects and the organization. We have seen some companies where there is such a strong "we–they" approach to quantitative management that it has become dysfunctional. The projects point to the organizational group members building the baselines and models and say it is their fault we can't do quality management because they have not given us what we need. And the organizational group members point to the projects and say it is their fault because we don't have clean data. Don't let this happen in your organization. Work from the beginning to establish organization-wide cooperation.

Transitioning to high maturity can be overwhelming. When in doubt, an organization should hire outside, expert help. This assistance is offered in the form of classes, mentoring, supervising data collection and reviews, and building models. Of course, as consultants we support this approach. However, some organizations are loathe to hire consultants. The most important thing to remember about hiring consultants is that you can always fire consultants if you are not happy with them. So if you need help, get it.

APPRAISALS

V

Chapter 20

Appraisals Using the CMMI

This chapter discusses the Software Engineering Institute's (SEI's) defined approaches to CMMI-based appraisals. Appraisals, assessments, and evaluations are by no means a new subject. There are a number of appraisal methods* that have been developed to measure and evaluate an organization against the family of Capability Maturity Models (CMMs) in addition to other models and standards. A community of appraisers, assessors, and evaluators has grown around these methods. The CMMI product suite introduces some new concepts, but mostly builds on the history of these previous methods and the best practices of the assessor and evaluator community. There are three classes of CMMI Appraisal Methods: Class A, Class B, and Class C.

The SEI has released three guiding documents for CMMI appraisals:

Appraisal Requirements for CMMI®, Version 1.2 (ARC, V1.2)—This technical report contains the requirements for three classes of appraisal methods Class A, Class B, and Class C. These requirements are the rules for defining each class of appraisal method.

Standard CMMI® Appraisal Method for Process Improvement (SCAMPISM) A, Version 1.2: Method Definition Document (MDD)—This handbook contains

---

* Not all these methods are called appraisals. Some are called assessments. Some are called evaluations. We use the term appraisal in an attempt to be consistent with the CMMI product suite. Appendix A provides a comparison of CBA-IPIs to SCEs to SCAMPI.

the only approved Class A appraisal method. This method satisfies the Class A requirement of the ARC.

Handbook for Conducting Standard CMMI Appraisal Method for Process Improvement (SCAMPI) B and C Appraisals, Version 1.1—This handbook contains the approved methods for Class B and C appraisals. These methods satisfy the Class B and C requirement of the ARC.

This chapter is based on version 1.2 of both the ARC and the SCAMPI MDD that were released in August 2006 and version 1.1 of the B and C Handbook released in December 2005.

We need to emphasize one point. SCAMPI A is currently the only approved CMMI Class A Appraisal Method. In other words, SCAMPI A satisfies all the requirements of an ARC Class A Appraisal Method and has been approved by the SEI. Since the writing of our first version of this book, the SEI has defined the method for SCAMPI Class B and SCAMPI Class C Appraisals in the technical report, *Handbook for Conducting Standard CMMI Appraisal Method for Process Improvement (SCAMPI) B and C Appraisals, Version 1.1, CMU/SEI-2005-HB-005,* released December 2005. SCAMPI B and C Appraisals satisfy all the requirements of an ARC Class A Appraisal Method and have been approved by the SEI.

Definitions

The following definitions may be helpful when considering this subject. These come from the ARC and the MDD.

- Assessment—An appraisal that an organization does to and for itself for the purpose of process improvement.
- (Process) Appraisal—An examination of one or more processes by a trained team of professionals using an appraisal reference model as the basis for determining, at a minimum, strengths and weaknesses.
- Evaluation—An appraisal in which an external group comes into an organization and examines its processes as input to a decision regarding future business. (Note: This definition is somewhat misleading since evaluations can be either Acquisition/Supplier Selection or Process Monitoring. Process Monitoring includes incentive/award fee decisions or risk management planning.)
- Organizational unit—That part of the organization that is the subject of an appraisal (also known as the organizational scope of the appraisal). An organizational unit deploys one or more processes that have a coherent process context and operates within a coherent set of business objectives. An organizational unit is typically part of a larger organization, although in a small organization, the organizational unit may be the whole organization.

- (Appraisal) Rating—The value assigned by an Appraisal Team to (1) a CMMI goal or process area, (2) the capability level or a process area, or (3) the maturity level of an organizational unit. The rating is determined by enacting the defined rating process for the appraisal method being employed.
- Strength—Exemplary or noteworthy implementation of a CMMI model practice.
- Weakness—The ineffective, or lack of, implementation of one or more CMMI model practices.
- Objective Evidence—Documents or interview results used to indicate implementation or institutionalization of model practices. Sources can include instruments (surveys), presentations, documents, and interviews.
- Rules of Confidentiality and Non-attribution—Information gained during appraisal activities is not disseminated outside of the Appraisal Team when this information could result in negative consequences or be attributed to any person, team, group, or project. The purpose of confidentiality and non-attribution is to allow free and open discussions of activities, decisions, results, and issues. These rules also apply to company proprietary or sensitive data. Members of the Appraisal Team cannot be compelled to divulge confidential appraisal information.

We offer some words of caution. Even though the definition of an assessment says "to and for itself for the purpose of process improvement," we will see that SCAMPI can also be for purposes other than process improvement.

There is also no clear definition of what it means for "the organizational unit to be part of a larger organization," under the definition of an organizational unit. Some companies game the appraisal by defining the organizational scope to be only a small number of well-managed projects for the appraisal to fit their agenda for securing the level rating and "passing" the appraisal. With all appraisals, some planning must be done to align model scope and method details to the organization's business needs and objectives. However, it is up to the Lead Appraiser to keep the organization honest and to ensure that the organizational unit is clearly identified in the appraisal report.

As we discussed in earlier chapters, appraisals consider three categories of model components as defined in the CMMI:

1. Required: Specific Goals (SGs) and Generic Goals (GGs)
2. Expected: Specific Practices (SPs) and Generic Practices (GPs)
3. Informative: Everything else in the model. This includes subpractices, typical work products, goal titles, practice titles, amplifications, and elaborations.

The Appraisal Team must find an indication that projects and organizational groups within the organization unit are satisfying the required specific and generic goals. Appraisal Teams generally look at the practices associated with the goals to decide whether the goals have been met. This is done through examination of project and organizational practices to see that they are "compliant with" or support the specific and generic practices. All of the practices are really expected. Since a lot of the practices are written to cover all kinds of situations, the informative material provides clarification. The Appraisal Teams use subpractices and typical work products to clarify the meaning of the practices and goals.

SCAMPI Fundamentals

As identified earlier, SCAMPI is an acronym that stands for Standard CMMI Appraisal Method for Process Improvement. A SCAMPI Class A Appraisal must be led by an SEI Authorized SCAMPI Lead Appraiser. SCAMPI Class B and C Appraisals must be led by an SEI Authorized SCAMPI B&C Team Leader. SCAMPI is supported by the SCAMPI Product Suite that includes the SCAMPI Method Description, work aids, and templates. Currently, SCAMPI A is the only method that can provide a rating, the only Class A method recognized by the SEI, and the method of most interest to organizations.

SCAMPI is based on experience from previous methods, including:

- CBA IPI—CMM Based Appraisal for Internal Process Improvement
- SCE—Software Capability Evaluation
- EIA/IS 732.2—the interim international standard titled Systems Engineering Appraisal Method
- Software Development Capability Evaluation (SDCE)
- Federal Aviation Administration (FAA) Appraisal Method (FAM)

Non-process Improvement Appraisals

A stated goal of SCAMPI A is to support two non-process improvement uses often associated with Software Capability Evaluations:

- Acquisition/Supplier Selection
- Process Monitoring (often contract monitoring)

Note: SCEs may be, and have also been, used for Internal Process Improvement.

Table 20.1 shows usage modes for SCAMPI A appraisals.

SCAMPI v1.2 does not make the use of only external team members a requirement for these non-process improvement types of evaluations. It would be reasonable to expect that this external-only requirement will continue to be imposed by both Federal, individual corporate and other acquisition policies to avoid conflict of interest. Some organizations, in an attempt to avoid the appearance of possible

Table 20.1 SCAMPI A Modes of Usage

Usage Mode	Description
Internal Process Improvement	Organizations use appraisals to appraise internal processes, generally to either baseline their capability/maturity level(s), to establish or update a process improvement program, or to measure progress in implementing such a program. Applications include measuring process improvement progress, conducting process audits, focusing on specific domains or product lines, appraising specific parts of the organization, and preparing for external customer-led appraisals. In this manner, SCAMPI A appraisals supplement other tools for implementing process improvement activities.
Supplier Selection	Appraisal results are used as a high-value discriminator to select suppliers. The results are used in characterizing the process-related risk of awarding a contract to a supplier. The appraisal results are typically only one criterion among many used to select suppliers. Results are often used as a baseline in subsequent process monitoring with the selected supplier.
Process Monitoring	Appraisal methods are also used in monitoring processes (e.g., after contract award, by serving as input for an incentive/award fee decision or a risk management plan). The appraisal results are used to help the sponsoring organization tailor its contract or process monitoring efforts by allowing it to prioritize efforts based on the observed strengths and weaknesses of the supplying organization's processes. This usage mode focuses on a long-term teaming relationship between the sponsoring organization and the development organization (i.e., buyer and supplier).

conflict of interest, and to obtain a fresh perspective of their processes, require one or more appraisal team members to be external to the organization.

All Class A SCAMPI v1.2 appraisals that will become public record (e.g., announced in a press release or on an organization's Web site, or posted on a published SCAMPI appraisals results Web page) or used in a proposal in response to U.S. Department of Defense requirements must be led by an SEI-authorized SCAMPI Lead Appraiser from an external, third-party organization. The external, third-party organization can be another SEI Partner company or a separate business unit from the one containing the appraised organization (e.g., from corporate or from a different division, group, or other organizational business type, which is under separate management).

Appraisal Classes

As mentioned earlier, there are three classes of CMMI Appraisal Methods. Each class is distinguished by the degree of rigor associated with the application of the method. Class A is the most rigorous. Class B is slightly less rigorous. Class C is the least rigorous. Table 20.2 gives you some idea of the expected differences between the methods in each class. The paragraphs that follow describe some of the details.

Table 20.2 Appraisal Class Characteristics

Characteristics	Class A	Class B	Class C
Amount of Objective Evidence Gathered (relative)	High	Medium	Low
Organizational Unit Coverage	Required	Not Required	Not Required
Rating Generated	Allowed (Goal Ratings Required)	Not Allowed	Not Allowed
Resource Needs (relative)	High	Medium	Low
Team Size (relative)	Large (minimum 4)	Medium (minimum 2)	Small (minimum 1)
Types of Objective Evidence Gathered	Documents and Interviews Required	Documents and Interviews Required	Documents or Interviews Required
Appraisal Team Leader Requirement	Authorized Lead Appraiser	Person Trained and Experienced	Person Trained and Experienced

Class A Appraisal Methods must satisfy all ARC requirements. A Class A Appraisal Method is the only method that can provide a rating. It requires two sources of data: interviews and documents. An interview is a formal meeting between one or more members of the organization and the Appraisal Team or mini-team. During this interview, the interviewee represents the organization in some capacity, based on the role he performs. For example, the Appraisal Team may interview a project manager, a quality assurance representative, and the director of systems engineering. Many interviews are held with many members of the organizational unit. A document is just that—a written work product or artifact that is used as evidence that a process is being followed. It can be a plan, meeting minutes, or a process description. The document may be either hard copy, electronic, or information captured in a tool.

A Class A Appraisal Method can additionally be either EIA 15504 conformant or non-EIA 15504 conformant. EIA 15504 is an international standard covering software process assessments. When an EIA 15504-comformant appraisal method is desired, there are additional requirements introduced to document how well processes perform. These include process profiles and product quality characteristics. Process profiles summarize the performance of processes found in the reviewed projects. Quality characteristics summarize the quality of the products and services provided, (e.g., defect density, reliability). Measuring and reporting process performance and quality characteristics is a fundamentally different approach to appraisal from previous CMM-related approaches.

A Class B Appraisal Method has fewer requirements than a Class A. A Class B still requires two sources of data and a consensus-driven process. Team consensus refers to a technique of team decision making regarding observations and findings that results in decisions that all team members are willing to support. However, the team size can be as small as two people. Data sufficiency and the draft presentation are optional with a Class B. Data sufficiency means, that for all specific and generic practices reviewed, validated observations exist. These observations are adequate to understand the extent of implementation of the practice, are representative of the organizational unit, and are representative of the life-cycle phases in use within the organizational unit. A draft presentation of findings (strengths and weaknesses based on valid observations) is used to get feedback from the people interviewed by formally presenting the draft findings before finalizing the findings. Data sufficiency and a draft presentation are optional in Class B in order to reduce the amount of time needed for the appraisal. The result of an appraisal without data sufficiency and a draft presentation is an appraisal done in a shorter amount of time and effort, but with possibly less confidence in the findings.

A Class C Appraisal Method has even fewer requirements than a Class B. A Class C requires only one source of data (interviews, instruments, or documents). Team consensus, observation validation, observation corroboration, data sufficiency, and draft presentation are optional. Team size can be as small as one person. Making observation validation and observation corroboration optional means the team does not need to agree that enough data has been gathered for an observation and that observations need not be consistent with other observations. The result of an appraisal without team consensus, observation validation, observation corroboration, data sufficiency, and draft presentations is an appraisal done in a shorter amount of time and effort, but again, with much less confidence in the findings. A Class C can be done on documentation of a process that has not yet been implemented. No implementation evidence is required. The result is an understanding of how well the process documentation satisfies the CMMI.

Which Class Appraisal Method Should I Use?

Organizations that are involved in process improvement often use a range of methods to appraise their improvement progress.

Many organizations undergo process improvement using the CMMI in order to be rated at a particular level. Therefore, these organizations will need a Class A Appraisal Method at some time and today that means a SCAMPI. The usage of a Class B or Class C appraisal will depend largely upon the organization's process improvement and appraisal strategy. Examples follow.

- Strategy One: A Class B appraisal is used to initiate an organizational-level process improvement program by identifying the majority of weaknesses against the CMMI. The process improvement plan is based on the identified weaknesses. Class C appraisals would then be performed periodically to measure progress against the process improvement plan and to determine readiness for a follow on Class B appraisal or a Class A appraisal.

■ Strategy Two: Class C appraisals are used on subsets of the organization. These subsets are based on business areas or project size. The process improvement plan is based on the aggregation of the weaknesses found. Since the Class C appraisal is less detailed, the weaknesses are addressed across the organization, not just in the subset where found. A Class B appraisal would be performed after six months or a year of performing against the process improvement plan to determine readiness for a Class A appraisal.

■ Strategy Three: A Class A appraisal is used to initiate an organizational level-process improvement program, as in Strategy One. The process improvement plan is based on the identified weaknesses. A Class B appraisal would be performed after six months or a year of performing against the process improvement plan to determine readiness for a second Class A appraisal for an official rating.

In most situations, Strategy Three would be recommended because:

■ The most weaknesses are found in a Class A with the highest confidence level.
■ More organizational learning occurs through the formal appraisal process.
■ More organizational buy-in is possible, particularly for internal team members.

Using SCAMPI A in the Field

Pilots of SCAMPI v1.0 indicated that the appraisals took too much time. As a result, a performance goal of SCAMPI v1.1 (and v1.2) was defined as follows:

> Onsite activities should be completed within 2 weeks or 100 hours (excluding training and pre-onsite activities) for an appraisal covering CMMI, through Maturity Level 3. Four projects would be *reviewed that represent the organizational unit*. Both the systems engineering and software engineering disciplines would be included.

"New" approaches taken to meet this goal included the development of the Practice Implementation Indicators (PII) that are collected prior to the onsite review in a PII Description (PIID). This approach is based on the best practice from many process improvement specialists, Lead Evaluators, and Lead Assessors of having the organization generate and maintain a compliance matrix showing how practices are performed in the organization. Table 20.3 shows a sample PIID Element containing the three types of PII information collected: Direct Work Product, Indirect Work

Table 20.3 Sample PIID Element for Project Planning Specific Practice 1.1

Practice ID	Project Planning (PP) Specific Practice (SP) 1.1 *"Establish a top-level work breakdown structure (WBS) to estimate the scope of the project."*		
PII Type	**Direct Work Product**	**Indirect Work Product**	**Affirmations**
Organizational Implementation Evidence	Top-level WBS, with revision history	Minutes of meetings at which WBS was generated or used to develop project estimate.	Developer 1 — "We used the WBS"
	Task Descriptions		Project Manager 2 — "I worked on the WBS team"
	Work product descriptions	Project estimates aligned with WBS elements	
Appraisal Team Notes	WBS found for all projects	Minutes found for two projects	

Product, and Affirmations. Direct Work Product and Indirect Work Product come from documents. Affirmations come from interviews. This example contains information and Appraisal Team notes that have been collected for a Specific Practice of the Project Planning process area.

The initial PIIDs contain the direct and indirect work products that are prepared by the organization and demonstrate how the practices of the CMMI are implemented in their organization via organizational documentation. In practice, often the PIID will contain the location of the work products, either hard copy or electronic. Development of the PIIDs is nontrivial. This PIID development puts additional work on the organization to prepare for an appraisal.

The SCAMPI A team is required to conduct a Readiness Review of the PIIDs prior to the start of the onsite SCAMPI A. The Lead Appraiser is responsible for giving the go-ahead at the Readiness Review to begin the onsite interviews. This go-ahead statement means that the SCAMPI A team feels the organization is ready to have the SCAMPI A team show up at the organization and begin the interview process. This step proved necessary because, in pilots, several false starts occurred, costing the organization and the SCAMPI A teams time, money, and frustration.

SCAMPI A v1.2 is designed to support a verification-based appraisal using the PIID to focus the team resources in areas needing further investigation. The SCAMPI A team will need to verify the contents of the PIID. This is in contrast to an observation-based or discovery-based appraisal where the team writes observations for all practices and discovers the existence of documentation through interviews and document reviews as part of the onsite review period. The SCAMPI A authors acknowledge that some legacy appraisal methods encouraged organizations to provide traceability and mapping tables from the models to their organizational processes and project work products to minimize this discovery process.

The verification of the PIIDs may result in a more hostile environment being created between the organization and the SCAMPI A team. The organization and the developers of the PIIDs may state that "X" on the PIID shows they are compliant. The SCAMPI A team is now in the position of saying, "No, you are not compliant because X does not match the intent of the CMMI practice."

The SCAMPI A method also encourages mini-teams, a subset of the entire team, to interview independently. Mini-teams are optionally given authority to reach consensus on practice implementation for each instance. The entire team remains responsible for consensus at the organizational unit-level. This is a change over most previous methods that required the entire team to conduct interviews. Allowing mini-teams to interview independently may result in low quality or inconsistent results during late-night roll ups of findings. The mini-teams must be formed based on trust and experience working with the SCAMPI A team members. It is not unusual for a mini-team to interview an individual, and come back and report to the rest of the SCAMPI A team. The SCAMPI A team may then respond by asking, "Well, did you then follow-up with a question about x or y or z?" The mini-team says no. The mini-team may also be allowed too much freedom. For example, the SCAMPI Lead Appraiser may allow the mini-team to interview one project manager, and another mini-team to interview another project manager and another mini-team to interview yet another project manager. Each mini-team, if not immediately consolidating their results with the entire team, may find that the first project manager does something in agreement with a practice, the second one does not, and the third manager was not even asked a question relating to that practice. During the late-night, last-night onsite roll up of results to produce final findings, the teams may be surprised to learn that they have inconsistent findings on a number of practices. So, while the concept of mini-teams sounds like it will promote time savings by allowing more people to be interviewed in a shorter timeframe, the mini-teams must be managed closely by the Lead Appraiser. Which puts yet another burden on the Lead Appraiser.

Some of the older assessment and evaluation methods had more specific guidance in some areas, for example, the number of focus projects and the appraisal team size. This guidance is not as clear in the ARC and SCAMPI. This leads the user of these new methods to make more decisions. And while one of the stated purposes of the ARC and the SCAMPI is to ensure more consistent results in appraisals, this lack of guidance may in fact result in less consistent results. The SEI now states that the minimum number of team members is four and the recommended maximum number is nine.

All SCAMPI A v1.2 appraisals that will become public record (e.g., announced in a press release or on an organization's Web site, or posted on a published SCAMPI appraisals results Web page) or used in a proposal in response to U.S. Department of Defense requirements must be led by an SEI-authorized SCAMPI Lead Appraiser from an external, third-party organization. The external, third-party organization can be another SEI Partner company or a separate business unit from the one containing the appraised organization (e.g., from corporate or from a different division, group, or other organizational business type, which is under separate management).

Additional Requirements for High Maturity SCAMPI A Appraisals

For all SCAMPI A v1.2 high maturity appraisals, that is, Capability or Maturity Levels 4 and 5, two significant additional requirements have been added:

1. An SEI-certified High Maturity Lead Appraiser must lead the appraisal. This requirement is in addition to the standard requirement that an SEI-Authorized Lead Appraiser must lead all SCAMPI A appraisals. The SEI defines *certification* as the acknowledgement that an individual has attained a well-defined level of understanding and ability in a particular body of knowledge or skill set. In particular, High Maturity Lead Appraisers must have received training in high maturity topics, for example, statistical process control and probability and statistics, have high maturity appraisal experience, have developed/implemented high maturity processes, and have built/taught courses in high maturity topics. Applicants for this certification must also pass an exam given by the SEI.

2. The Appraisal Team Leader (i.e., the Lead Appraiser) must validate that a substantial portion of the organization's and projects' quality and process–performance objectives and statistically managed subprocesses can be mapped directly to and support: (a) the established business objectives as stated and disseminated to key employees of the organization, and (b) the needs and priorities of customers, end users, and other stakeholders. This validation is required to prevent the granting of high maturity ratings for trivial improvements. The Appraisal Team Leader documents in the Appraisal Disclosure Statement (ADS) that all SCAMPI A requirements were satisfied.

Reusing Previous Appraisal Results

Organizations often want to use previous appraisal results when beginning a CMMI initiative. This has proven to be extremely difficult for many organizations, and in our experience, has led to inappropriate actions. By previous appraisals, we mean results from non-CMMI appraisals (CBA IPIs, SCEs, EIA 732, etc.). The reason for these problems in reuse include the following:

- Different levels of detail in appraisal approach
- Some appraisals did not consider institutionalization of practices
- Not all weaknesses were documented

Don't assume that since you did not have a weakness, that you have a strength. Often only level-threatening weaknesses are documented. A threat to a level is only known after hours of consensus and team negotiations. Some appraisal methods don't require these findings to be captured and documented. In order to use old results for any purpose, you need to understand the key differences between appraisal methods and their results.

Most organizations using the CMMI will need a baseline SCAMPI appraisal to obtain a consistent understanding across the expanded scope of the organization and of the model.

Frequently Asked Questions for Planning and Conducting a SCAMPI A

The following are the most frequently asked questions that we have been asked to address. We have pulled them from lists of questions that prospective clients for SCAMPIs have sent us.

1. How will you determine the number of focus projects to include in an appraisal?

   Response: The primary criteria are that the focus projects are a representative sample of the organizational unit's overall behavior, provide at least two instances of the processes being investigated as sources of objective evidence, and provide representative coverage of the life cycles in use within the organization.

   Our goal would be to keep the number of focus projects small (usually four). If the scope of your appraisal includes systems engineering and software engineering or you have a large organization it may be difficult to meet the stated criteria with four projects.

2. What is the minimum number of projects (we have three core businesses)?

   Response: We consider the minimum to be four projects, however as stated in question 1, this may be difficult to accomplish. For example, if the three core business units use significantly different processes, methods, and tools to produce their products or provide their services, this could expand into a need for considering 12 projects.

   The MDD states, "If the organization unit includes more than 3 projects, then the organizational scope must include sufficient focus projects and non-focus projects to generate at least 3 instances of each practice in each project-related PA in the model scope of the appraisal." Given this statement, the hard minimum is three. However, for a useful appraisal in your organization, you may want to consider more than the minimum.

3. Do you consider the organization as a separate project?

Response: We don't understand exactly what this question means. As far as planning goes, we will need to interview organizational managers—middle managers responsible for technical development, process improvement, training, quality, and measurement.

The SCAMPI A Appraisal Team must have data for each practice in the reference model, in other words, for CMMI, each specific practice or generic practice within scope of the appraisal. For example, if the Organizational Training process area is in scope, then the parts of the organization responsible for training would be treated similarly to a project with interviews and other data collection requirements.

4. Can projects that are partially through the product development life cycle be included in the appraisal? How many projects will have to provide full life-cycle coverage?

Response: Yes, most projects should be ongoing and therefore are most likely partially through the product development cycle or some phase or iteration. There is no exact answer to the second part of this question. The selected projects need to provide representative coverage of the life cycles in use in the organization. In other words, the sum of the selected projects' life cycles needs to cover the organization's life cycle.

5. How is model coverage determined?

Response: If by "model coverage" you are referring to verifying and validating objective evidence, this is determined by reviewing documents and artifacts and affirmations for each practice.

If by "model coverage" you are referring to reference model scope, this is determined by the Lead Appraiser reviewing appraisal goals with the sponsor and ensuring the sponsor makes an informed choice.

6. Do you characterize implementation of model practice instantiation on the basis of specific and generic practices, or at the subpractice level?

Response: Appraisals consider three categories of components as defined by the CMMI:

- Required—Includes specific and generic goals
- Expected—Includes specific and generic practices
- Informative—Includes subpractices, discipline amplifications, generic practice elaborations, and typical work products

So to be compliant with the model, we would characterize implementation based on specific and generic practices and use subpractices to guide interpretation of the practices.

7. Are typical work products, discipline amplifications, or generic practice elaborations listed in the model included in the instantiation decision?

Response: Yes, as stated in question 6, these are informative and would guide interpretation of the practices.

8. Can you conduct a two-week, eight-hour day, onsite CMMI target profile 5 appraisal, covering systems engineering, software engineering, and hardware engineering with six Appraisal Teams (including the lead appraiser)? Please be specific.

Response: No, based on no additional knowledge of the organization and the time it takes to conduct a SCAMPI A. Our estimate for a SCAMPI Class A Appraisal covering 22 process areas through Capability/Maturity Level 5 with six Appraisal Teams that have received team training to include Introduction to CMMI, SCAMPI Appraisal Team Member Training, and High Maturity Appraisals is 13 days. In addition to the Lead Appraiser, we base our estimate on at least one additional external appraiser on the team. Even with 13 days, it is probable that some days may be longer than eight hours.

Only when we have worked with the organization and have a better understanding of the organization's processes, organizational structure, and qualifications of the Appraisal Teams would it be possible to decrease the proposed schedule.

9. How many participants do you plan to interview for an appraisal covering software engineering, systems engineering, and hardware engineering? Please use a matrix to indicate by function, the total number of staff involved, and estimate the total number of labor hours (e.g., project manager, middle manager, test, quantitative measurement specialists, etc.).

Response: Since we have not performed detailed planning and don't have an understanding of your organization's processes, roles, and structure, this is very difficult to answer with any certainty. However, the example matrix in Table 20.4 will give you an idea of what to expect.

10. How many follow-up interviews do you anticipate? Please estimate the level of effort (e.g., total number of labor hours).

Response: Our goal is to have nearly no follow-up interviews. For planning purposes, you may want to consider allowing time for two one-hour follow-up interviews with four people each for a total of eight labor hours for the interviewees.

11. Do Lead Appraisers interpret the CMMI (key) practices as required or expected? Please elaborate. Under what conditions is an "alternate practice" acceptable in satisfying the CMMI?

Response: Specific practices and generic practices are expected model components. Expected components are practices an organization will typically implement when it is trying to satisfy a set of specific and generic goals. Ordinarily, an alternative practice has to contribute an equivalent effect toward satisfying the goal associated with the practice. In some cases, an alternative practice may not explicitly contribute an equivalent effect because a project's characteristics are different from the characteristics assumed in the

Table 20.4 Expected Organizational Participation During Appraisals

Role	Estimated Number of Interviews	Per Interview		Estimated Total Hours
		Hours	Number of Interviewees	
Project Managers	4	2	1	8
Measurement Group (assumes separate organization and project groups)	2	1.5	4	12
Middle Manager Groups (assumes separate systems and software groups)	2	2	4	16
Training Group	1	2	3	6
Requirements Representatives	1	2	4	8
Development Representatives	1	2	4	8
Test Representatives	1	2	4	8
Integration Representatives	1	2	4	8
Process Improvement Group (assumes separate leads and specialists)	2	2	4	16
Quality Assurance Groups (assumes separate systems and software)	2	2	4	16
Hardware Engineering Group	1	2	4	8
Tool Group	1	2	3	6
		Total Estimated		120

model. An example of this might be where the project's customer performs requirements management. The alternative practice might be to review the customer's requirements management process and activities. The practices implemented by the project in this example might not contribute an equivalent effect toward the goals. The decision as to whether an alternative practice is acceptable is an Appraisal Team decision. The Lead Appraiser's role in that decision is to ensure the integrity of the SCAMPI process and help the team correctly interpret the model.

12. How do Lead Appraisers interpret "institutionalization" of a process area? Is it expected that all generic practices be performed? How is the generic goal judged in the absence of one or more generic practices? Is there any required

time duration that a practice must be performed to consider it institutionalized? Please elaborate.

Response: Institutionalization in the CMMI is interpreted as satisfying the requirements of the generic goals. For the staged representation this means that GG 2 Institutionalize a Managed Process is satisfied for Level 2. In addition, GG 3 Institutionalize a Defined Process is satisfied for Level 3.

Yes, we expect generic practices to be performed. If one or more generic practices are not performed, the Appraisal Team will determine the impact of the missing practice upon satisfying the required generic goal. Although each generic practice is expected to be performed, the implementation of the generic practices to individual process areas is often not distinguishable (one process area versus another), and they may appear to be absent for a process area or areas. This may be acceptable, but the Appraisal Team would have to understand and determine whether the implementation is reasonable.

While the SEI has not published specific guidelines for institutionalization, a number of appraisers consider a minimum of six months as a demonstration of basic institutionalization. Other appraisers expect to see that practices have been performed through several cycles. And some other appraisers have considered the requirement to be a demonstration that the practices have been performed in the past and will continue after the appraisal. In addition, some Lead Appraisers consider how often a process can be performed. For example, on a 20-year-old legacy system, they would not consider it reasonable to expect that the initial customer requirements were captured using today's process; however, they would expect new requirement changes to use today's process. With no stated institutionalization requirement, a Lead Appraiser and Appraisal Team may consider any or all of the above guidelines.

13. How do Lead Appraisers interpret the need for documented procedures in the CMMI, now that the phase "according to a documented procedure" is not used? Are documented procedures required, or can an acceptable alternative practice be to perform the practice without a documented procedure? Explain in terms of both organization-level and project-level procedures. Please elaborate.

Response: For any process area to satisfy Level 2, GG 2 Institutionalize a Managed Process, a Lead Appraiser would expect that "GP 2.2 Establish and maintain the requirements and objectives, and plan for performing the process" is performed. Although documenting the process is only a subpractice of GP 2.2, it is quite implicit in the statement of GP 2.2, and hence is expected. The clearest way to meet the expectations of GP 2.2 is to have a documented process and plan covering the process area. An alternative practice of "just doing it" is generally not acceptable. The term *plan* in the CMMI has been expanded to include such documentation as processes and procedures.

Part of an acceptable process description is that it contains an appropriate level of detail. In some areas of the process, this means that a documented procedure is appropriate, but neither "expected," nor "required" in CMMI terminology. Note that there are only a very few mentions of "documented procedures" in the informative parts of the CMMI model. The test that the Appraisal Team will have to apply is not whether there is a documented procedure for "x," but whether the process, the plan, and/or supporting procedures are adequate in the area of "x." This is the same for both the project-level and the organization-level processes.

For any process area to satisfy GG 3 Institutionalize a Defined Process, a Lead Appraiser would expect that "GP 3.1 Establish and maintain the description of a defined X process" is satisfied. The expectation is that a process from the organization's set of standard processes is tailored to address the needs of a specific instantiation. As defined in the Model Terminology section of the model, the phrase "Establish and Maintain" connotes a meaning beyond the component terms; it includes documentation as well as a usage component. In other words, documented and used throughout the organization.

14. In which situations is the Supplier Agreement Management process area applicable/nonapplicable? Please address Integrated Product/Process Teams ("badgeless" teams of multiple contractors), tool vendors, and hired labor (bodyshop workers). Please address customer-directed subcontractors.

    Response: The Supplier Agreement Management process area states that it is applicable to a "contract, a license, or a memorandum of agreement" for acquired products that are "delivered to the project from the supplier and becomes part of the products delivered to the customer." It applies primarily to both internal and external "arm's length" relationships where the prime contractor lets an identifiable piece of customer deliverable work to a subcontractor and the project manager is not directly involved in managing the activities of the supplier.

    The Supplier Agreement Management process area does not apply to products that are not delivered to the project's customer, such as nondeliverable development tools. It does apply to commercial vendors if their product is included in the product delivered to the customer. It does not apply to hourly contract workers who are managed in the same way as any other member of the project team.

    For all deliverable work not covered by the Supplier Agreement Management process area, the project management process areas (PP, PMC, RSKM, IPM, and QPM) and the additional IPPD goals (if IPPD is implemented and that part of the model is used in the organization) will apply.

15. What are the minimum contents of an organization's set of standard processes?

    Response: The OSSPs (Organization's Set of Standard Processes) must cover the processes for the engineering, project management, engineering support (e.g., QA and CM), and organizational activities (e.g., training and process group; limited to software if the appraisal is limited that way). The

OSSPs describe the fundamental process elements that will be part of the project's defined processes. It also describes the relationships (for example, ordering and interfaces) between these process elements. Often the OSSPs for the organizational processes are one and the same as the defined processes. The OPD process area provides specific information as to what might be in the process descriptions and how they might be defined. This information is reasonable for most organizations and would be considered by the Appraisal Team. But there are no hard and fast rules as to the minimum content.

16. Some projects' defined software processes may predate the establishment of the organization's standard software process. Is a matrix showing the traceability sufficient? Please elaborate.

    Response: It is expected that the majority of the organization's projects would be using the OSSP. However, an organization that is improving its OSSP is likely to have some number of long-term projects that predate the establishment of the current OSSP. For business reasons, these projects may not migrate to the new OSSP. All projects' defined processes should however be recognized as alternative processes by the organization. A Lead Appraiser would expect to see rationale for why projects were exempted from using the OSSP. A Lead Appraiser would expect to see an analysis of the existing process against the OSSP that may take the form of a traceability matrix. However, the existence of such a matrix would not in and of itself be sufficient to exclude a project from using the OSSPs. Furthermore, it should be recognized that a project's defined process that is not tailored from the OSSPs will have an impact on organizational learning and any efforts to establish performance baselines for the organization and for these projects. The organization would have to make appropriate accommodations for these shortfalls.

17. Some of our projects require special security clearances for access to any project documents. A subset of the internal appraisal team members has these accesses. What is your approach for appraising such projects?

    Response: If the issue is limited to gaining access to the project documents, or if this also includes limiting the access during interviews, then we need to discuss this situation further. This represents a high risk that the team will not be able to achieve consensus on some process areas, that sufficient data collection may not be performed, and certain PAs would have to be not rated. "Not rated" does not satisfy SCAMPI rating requirements and will result in the organization not receiving a level rating. What we have done in the past is make sure that all members of the team have the appropriate security clearances. Team members could also sign a nondisclosure agreement.

18. What metrics are required for each process area? Must separate time accounting be performed for every process area?

    Response: There is no simple list of required metrics for each process area. The requirement is for sufficient metrics to monitor and control the processes at Level 2, sufficient metrics to support the organization's needs at Level 3, and sufficient metrics to achieve reasonable predictability of the project's processes (relative to the critical business issues) at Level 4. Metrics should not be defined around CMMI process areas, they should be defined around the projects' and organization's process and their need for metrics. Separate time accounting is not required and certainly not for each CMMI process area. Hours to perform the individual processes is often not very useful, however, many organizations provide this metric because it is easy compared to collecting more interesting metrics. Some organizations at a lower maturity level also find this metric initially helpful in reviewing the time spent and dollars expended in doing process improvement work. It helps them build a preliminary case for return on investment.

19. How is the generic practice for collecting improvement information interpreted? What is the minimum information that must be collected?

    Response: This generic practice represents the "supplier" or input to several practices of the OPF and OPD process areas. There is no clear specification of the minimum information that must be collected. The types of information collected are defined in the model: the organization's common set of measures plus other measures, lessons learned, process improvement proposals, and process artifacts. For measures, the "minimum" is the organization's common set of measures applicable to the processes performed. The Appraisal Team will have to judge whether what is collected, stored, and, more importantly, used is appropriate to the OSSPs, the projects, and the organizational and support groups. Too much can be as big a problem as too little.

20. How long is an organization's level rating good for?

    Response: The SEI has defined an *Appraisal Validity Period* as part of the release of CMMI v1.2 and SCAMPI A v1.2. The period is defined as follows:

    ■ SCAMPI A v1.2 appraisal results are valid for a maximum of 3 years from the date of the SCAMPI A Appraisal Disclosure Statement (ADS). The ADS is generated and approved following the onsite period.

    ■ SCAMPI A v1.1 appraisal results expired on August 31, 2007, or 3 years after the date the appraisal was conducted, whichever is later.

Summary

Appraisals require planning. When planning an appraisal of your organization, determine the scope of the organizational unit, which disciplines to include, whether the Appraisal Team will consist of members internal or external to your organization, projects to be included, individuals to be interviewed, and the type or class of appraisal necessary. Remember that team training does not include CMMI training, and this training must be completed prior to the onsite visit. Plan enough time into your schedule for completing all of the necessary documentation required before the team appears onsite.

Chapter 21

The SCAMPI A Approach

This chapter discusses our approach for performing SCAMPI (Standard CMMI Appraisal Method for Process Improvement) Class A appraisals. This chapter should be read subsequent to reading our Chapter 20, which offers an overview of the different appraisal types available for CMMI process improvement. Chapter 22 on PIIDs (Practice Implementation Indicator Descriptions) should also be read, as it discusses required appraisal documentation. These chapters are complicated and should not be read by the faint of heart.

We usually recommend using the formal, full-blown SCAMPI Class A appraisal, as the SCAMPI A provides more information with less risk of inaccuracy then the smaller, "quick-look" Class B and Class C appraisals. Class B and C appraisals offer a greatly condensed and accelerated set of activities than SCAMPI Class A. The time it takes to conduct a SCAMPI A depends on the scope of the SCAMPI Class A appraisal, that is, the number of process areas to be reviewed, number of projects to be reviewed, the organization's exposure to previous appraisals, the organization's experience with process improvement, the type of resulting documentation to be produced, and whether a rating (maturity level or capability level) is desired. This chapter summarizes the steps involved and should not be perceived as replacing SCAMPI A training or the SCAMPI A Method Definition Document.*

---

* This chapter is focused on using the SCAMPI A appraisal with the CMMI as a reference model. SCAMPI A is also being used with other reference models, for example, the People CMM.

Our Perspective

This chapter summarizes most of the concepts in the MDD, which is a long and complicated document of 242 pages. We cannot possibly discuss all of the different interpretations and decisions that must be made when deciding when, how, and why to conduct a SCAMPI in this chapter. (Maybe that can be our next book.) So, we took the approach that this SCAMPI A is being conducted by an organization that needs a level rating to determine where the organization is relative to its process improvement efforts, and to advertise its level rating for further contract-award consideration. The SCAMPI A is being sponsored by and paid for by the organization. This SCAMPI A is conducted by a trained Lead Appraiser external to the organization being appraised, with an Appraisal Team consisting of members from that organization. This is our experience. However, we have heard that some organizations are performing totally external SCAMPI A appraisals, meaning that the entire Appraisal Team is external to the organization, that is, no members of the appraised organization are on the Appraisal Team.

What Is a SCAMPI A Appraisal?

A SCAMPI A is an intensive look at how an organization has implemented its processes and process improvement activities based on a detailed review of a selected subset of an organization's projects and related support groups. These selected projects, which are called focus projects, must represent the type of projects that the organization normally supports. These selected projects must demonstrate the methods used to institutionalize the processes used throughout the organization, as well as the process improvement approach used. The related support groups are groups that are within the model scope for your appraisal, for example, the Training Group for the Organizational Training process area or the Quality Assurance Group for the Process and Product Quality Assurance process area. Other "groups" that might be included as part of the appraisal can be grouped by their function, for example, project managers, programmers, or test personnel.

SCAMPI A appraisals must be performed by a formally trained Appraisal Team and be led by an SEI-Authorized SCAMPI Lead Appraiser. Some team members may be from your organization. Process documentation is reviewed by the Appraisal Team. The format normally used to present this material is called a PIID. We discuss PIIDs in Chapter 22.

A SCAMPI A is a formal Class A process appraisal method documented in the *SCAMPI A, Version 1.2: Method Definition Document* (MDD). The MDD defines three phases of the SCAMPI A:

1. Plan and Prepare for Appraisal
2. Conduct Appraisal
3. Report Results

Table 21.1 Plan and Prepare Appraisal Phase

Processes	Activities
1.1 Analyze Requirements	1.1.1 Determine Appraisal Objectives 1.1.2 Determine Appraisal Constraints 1.1.3 Determine Appraisal Scope 1.1.4 Determine Outputs 1.1.5 Obtain Commitment to Appraisal Input
1.2 Develop Appraisal Plan	1.2.1 Tailor Method 1.2.2 Identify Needed Resources 1.2.3 Determine Cost and Schedule 1.2.4 Plan and Manage Logistics 1.2.5 Document and Manage Risks 1.2.6 Obtain Commitment to Appraisal Plan
1.3 Select and Prepare Team	1.3.1 Identify Appraisal Team Leader 1.3.2 Select Team Members 1.3.3 Prepare Team
1.4 Obtain and Inventory Initial Objective Evidence	1.4.1 Obtain Initial Objective Evidence 1.4.2 Inventory Objective Evidence
1.5 Prepare for Appraisal Conduct	1.5.1 Perform Readiness Review 1.5.2 Prepare Data Collection Plan 1.5.3 Replan Data Collection

Table 21.2 Conduct Appraisal Phase

Processes	Activities
2.1 Prepare Participants	2.1.1 Conduct Participant Briefing
2.2 Examine Objective Evidence	2.2.1 Examine Objective Evidence from Documents 2.2.2 Examine Objective Evidence from Interviews
2.3 Document Objective Evidence	2.3.1 Take/Review/Tag Notes 2.3.2 Record Presence/Absence of Objective Evidence 2.3.3 Document Practice Implementation 2.3.4 Review and Update the Data Collection Plan
2.4 Verify Objective Evidence	2.4.1 Verify Objective Evidence 2.4.2 Characterize Implementation of Model Practices
2.5 Validate Preliminary Findings	2.5.1 Validate Preliminary Findings
2.6 Generate Appraisal Results	2.6.1 Derive Findings and Rate Goals 2.6.2a Determine Process Area Capability Level 2.6.2b Determine Satisfaction of Process Areas 2.6.3a Determine Capability Profile 2.6.3b Determine Maturity Level 2.6.4 Document Appraisal Results

These phases are grouped into *processes*. The processes are grouped into *activities*. Tables 21.1, 21.2, and 21.3 list the formal processes and activities for each phase as shown in the MDD. The formal processes and activities from the MDD imply a fixed sequence of activities, but as with most processes, there is more iteration between the activities then implied in the exhibits.

The following information summarizes the SCAMPI A phases, processes, and selected activities.

Table 21.3   Report Results Phase

Processes	Activities
3.1 Deliver Appraisal Results	3.1.1 Deliver Final Findings 3.1.2 Conduct Executive Session(s) 3.1.3 Plan for Next Steps
3.2 Package and Archive Appraisal Assets	3.2.1 Collect Lessons Learned 3.2.2 Generate Appraisal Record 3.2.3 Provide Appraisal Data Package for CMMI Steward 3.2.4 Archive and/or Dispose of Key Artifacts

Plan and Prepare for Appraisal Phase

During this phase, the SCAMPI A Lead Appraiser, working with the appraisal sponsor from the organization and members from the organization composing the Appraisal Team, performs preappraisal tasks. These tasks are really steps in the appraisal and are called processes. These processes are completed prior to conducting the onsite phase of the appraisal. These appraisal tasks (or processes) include:

■ Analyze Requirements
■ Develop the Appraisal Plan
■ Select and Prepare the Team
■ Obtain and Inventory Initial Objective Evidence
■ Prepare for Appraisal Conduct

Table 21.1 lists the formal processes and activities of this phase as shown in the MDD.

Analyze Requirements Process

The SCAMPI A involves the appraisal sponsor from the organization to be appraised in order to determine his objectives and business goals. Why is this appraisal being done? Does he want a level rating or not? Will the rating be used for a contract award? Answers to these questions and others form the information that the MDD calls the Appraisal Input. The Appraisal Input is required at both the beginning and the end of the appraisal. The Appraisal Input is the basis for detailed planning for the appraisal. The Appraisal Input may be generated incrementally throughout the planning phase; however, a completed baseline version must be approved prior to the start of data collection. This Appraisal Input document is normally signed off by the Appraisal Team Leader (i.e., the Lead Appraiser) and the sponsor from the organization being appraised. The Appraisal Input document is submitted to the Software Engineering Institute (SEI) as part of the appraisal data package at the end of the appraisal. The MDD allows for various levels of formality for this document, from a formal signed document to simple meeting minutes. Your Lead

Table 21.4   Appraisal Input (Information Expected)

Appraisal Sponsor	Identification and Contact Information
	Relationship to the Organizational Unit Being Appraised
Appraisal Purpose	Reason for Appraisal
	Alignment with Business Objectives
Appraisal Scope	Organizational Unit being Appraised
	Organizational Scope of the Appraisal (Project and Support Groups)
	Critical Factors Affecting the Appraisal
Process Context	Organizational Unit Size and Demographics
	Application domain(s), Size, Criticality, and Complexity
	Characteristics of the Products and Services of the Organizational Unit
Appraisal Constraints	Availability of Key Resources (e.g., staffing, funding, tools, and facilities)
	Schedule Constraints
	Maximum Amount of Time
	Specific Process Areas or Organizational Entities to Exclude
	Maximum, Minimum, or Specific Sample Size/Coverage Desired
	Ownership of Appraisal Results and Any Use Restrictions
	Controls on Information Resulting from a Confidentiality Agreement
	Non-attribution of Appraisal Outputs to Individuals
Reference Model Used	Model, Version, Discipline(s), and Representation
SCAMPI Lead Appraiser	Identification and Contact Information
	Organizational Affiliation
Appraisal Team Members	Identification and Contact Information
	Organizational Affiliation
	Specific Appraisal Responsibilities
Appraisal Participants	Identification and Contact Information
	Organizational Affiliation
	Specific Appraisal Responsibilities
Support Staff	Identification and Contact Information
	Organizational Affiliation
	Specific Appraisal Responsibilities
Additional Information	Other Information to Support Achievement of Appraisal Objectives
Appraisal Outputs	Planned Ratings and Other Outputs
Follow-on Activities	Planned Reports, Action Plans, and/or Re-appraisals
SCAMPI A Tailoring	Planned Tailoring and Tradeoffs
Appraisal Usage Mode	Internal Process Improvement, Supplier Selection, or Process Monitoring

Appraiser can provide an Appraisal Input document template from the SEI. An outline for the Appraisal Input is shown in Table 21.4.

Develop the Appraisal Plan Process

The Appraisal Plan documents the appraisal purpose and focuses on discovering the processes, standards, and technologies in use. Team logistics, the schedule, roles and responsibilities, project characteristics, and expected outcomes are defined. The Appraisal Plan describes in detail all required data collection and analysis activities in the appraisal. The plan also documents the appraisal scope, that is, what part of the organization is to be appraised, which site or sites, which projects, who will participate, what are their roles, which process areas are to be investigated, and

Table 21.5 Appraisal Plan (Information Expected)

Appraisal Input	Includes all the data from the Appraisal Input (see exhibit 4)
Activities	Actvitites to be performed in Conducting the Appraisal
Resources	Appraisal Team Members (and Backups)
	Appraisal Participants
	Equipment and Facilities
	Other Resources Needed
Estimates	Cost
	Effort
	Duration
Schedule	Pre-On-site Activities (Training and Coordination)
	Detailed On-site Schedule (by hour and for all individuals)
	Final Report and Appraisal Package to SEI
Appraisal Logistics	Facilities, Badging, and Access to Rooms, Equipment, and Supplies
	Workstations Support and Access
	Security/Classification of Materials
	Transportation and Lodging
	Meals
	Communication Channels
Risk Management	Risks and Mitigation Plans
There must be a signature block for the appraisal team leader and the sponsor to indicate in writing their commitment to the plan. If minor updates are made to the plan, signatures do not have to be obtained again except when one or more elements of the appraisal input have been changed.	
At a minimum, the appraisal team members are considered relevant stakeholders and should receive a copy of the approved appraisal plan.	

whether a level rating will be produced. The plan should also capture the nonattribution and confidentially rules for the appraisal.

The Appraisal Plan document is submitted to the SEI as part of the appraisal data package at the end of the appraisal. An outline of the information expected in the Appraisal Plan is shown in Table 21.5. Your Lead Appraiser can provide an Appraisal Plan document template from the SEI that can be used as a starting point.

Some of the more important activities in this process include decisions affecting tailoring of the SCAMPI method and developing a realistic schedule. Do not get carried away with the idea that you can tailor the SCAMPI. There are strict rules about what can be tailored and what cannot. Factors that can be tailored focus on number of members of the Appraisal Team, their experience (e.g., process improvement, project management, development, etc.), number of organizational sites visited, which process areas will be appraised, and so forth. The MDD indicates specifically which aspects of the method are required and which are tailorable. All tailoring decisions are made by the trained Lead Appraiser.

This is where your organization's commitment to process improvement really shows. Did you have enough time to do process improvement, or did you take shortcuts? Did you have enough of the right people involved, or did you just staff it with whoever was available? Did your management really commit to this effort or just send out memos? The Lead Appraiser does not tailor the SCAMPI method to match your expectations for a level rating or to cover for any inadequacies in the process improvement approach taken.

Another important aspect of this process is developing the schedule. Because the SCAMPI A is time intensive, a rigid schedule must be followed. This schedule information is included as part of the Appraisal Plan. The information in the schedule includes date and time of the appraisal, individuals involved, and other logistics.

To maximize the team's time, the process areas of major concern will be clearly identified and prioritized. The format for the outputs of the appraisal will be finalized to match the goals of the appraisal (not to ensure that a specific-level rating is achieved) and to help ensure that the outputs and results of the appraisal are used for further process improvement or other organizational objectives.

Select and Prepare the Team Process

The activities of this process are to identify the Appraisal Team Leader, select team members, and prepare the team.

Selecting your Appraisal Team Leader is an important step. Your team leader must be an SEI-Authorized SCAMPI Lead Appraiser. An additional requirement for high maturity appraisals, that is, Capability or Maturity Levels 4 and 5, is that the Lead Appraiser must be an SEI-certified High Maturity Lead Appraiser (see Chapter 20 for more information). Not only are you looking for a qualified Lead Appraiser with the right authorizations and certifications, you want someone that will be respected by the people in your organization and someone that can work with all levels of the organization from the boardroom to the cubicles.

The Lead Appraiser must receive advanced training from the SEI, report his results in a standardized fashion, pass a test on the CMMI and the SCAMPI A method, be observed by the SEI, pay licensing fees, and adhere to SEI-proclaimed standards. The point of this diatribe is to warn any organizations that are looking to "buy a rating" that this entire process is heavily scrutinized in order to maintain the quality and integrity of the ratings process.

The Lead Appraiser *does not* determine the findings, the rating, or whether you pass or fail the SCAMPI. The Lead Appraiser leads the appraisal by helping to devise the schedule, the activities, and offering interpretation of the model where needed. The point is, the appraisal is a team effort. The Lead Appraiser is responsible for the quality of the SCAMPI A. SCAMPI A results are reported to the SEI and the results undergo review by the SEI.

The Appraisal Team also may include representatives from the organization being appraised. The overall team size, skills, and experience should result in a professional, nonbiased team capable of working together and telling the truth. As early as possible in the planning phase, the Lead Appraiser works with the internal coordinator from the appraised organization to select appropriate internal

Appraisal Team Members from the organization. The size of the team varies based on the scope of the appraisal, but generally ranges from four to six people. The official minimum number of team members is four, with a recommended maximum of nine.

What other issues should be considered when selecting team members? Each team member should have experience in the areas he will investigate (such as project planning or requirements development), and should have been doing this type of work "for a while." What this means is, do not assign a member of your organization to this team if he is directly out of college or is not considered an experienced member of the organization or is just someone who is failing on his project, so you want to get rid of him for a while and make him someone else's problem. This assignment of incorrect people to an Appraisal Team is also used when lower-level, dysfunctional organizations know they will not "pass" the SCAMPI A, so they try to assign incompetent staff to the team. That way, the organization's leaders can discredit the findings. Also, do not assign spies to the team. If any team member relays any information to nonteam members, either during or after the SCAMPI A, the results of the SCAMPI A are nullified, and the organization still must pay the bill. This is a violation of the confidentiality and nonattribution rules. The only variation of this rule is after the findings have been delivered to the organization. Team members may then disseminate information on what the finding means and where the organization did not meet the intent of a practice in order to develop action plans for continuing the process improvement effort. However, team members cannot reveal who said what during interviews and who said what during Appraisal Team discussions. Not revealing what is said by individuals is part of the confidentiality and nonattribution concepts of the SCAMPI.

When selecting team members, the Lead Appraiser must consider the roles and responsibilities that each team member must fulfill. The Lead Appraiser will assign specific roles and responsibilities to each Appraisal Team Member. Each team member is usually assigned one or more process areas (PAs) to investigate. The team member reviews the documentation, scripts questions, and after conducting interviews and participating in team consensus activities will prepare preliminary findings for his assigned PAs. The Lead Appraiser may also structure the Appraisal Team into mini-teams (a subset of the entire team) to independently conduct interviews of project members and other organizational representatives. The information these mini-teams discover is relayed back to the entire Appraisal Team for consideration.

Each team member must receive mandatory training from an SEI-authorized Instructor in preparation for participating on the team. The required courses are:

■ Introduction to the CMMI
■ SCAMPI Class A Team Training

In our appraisals, we recommend that all team members go through the SCAMPI course together, even if they have been trained previously. This approach helps build team cohesion and allows everyone to gain an initial understanding of the personalities and habits of the individual team members. It also allows the team to begin to behave as a "real" team. Once this training is completed, the Appraisal Team participates in the Readiness Review and the onsite appraisal period. The Appraisal Team may also be expected to participate in PIID development.

Obtain and Inventory Initial Objective Evidence Process

Based on the fundamental assumption that an executed process will produce artifacts (both intermediate work products and end products), the organization and the Appraisal Team will identify specific products available from each focus project and from the organization as a whole. Prior to arriving onsite, the Lead Appraiser distributes a package to the organization's technical point of contact (POC) requesting information needed for the SCAMPI A. This information usually includes:

- An organization questionnaire documenting the general characteristics of the organization
- PIIDs to be completed

In some cases, the organization will have its own format for PIIDs. If so, it is critical that the Lead Appraiser approve the format early in the planning phase to avoid rework. The Appraisal Team will ensure that all of the information requested from the organization has been provided in the proper format.

Prepare for Appraisal Conduct Process

The SCAMPI A method has incorporated an activity into its official methodology that the authors of this book consider to be a great idea. It is called the Readiness Review.

The purpose of the Readiness Review is to determine whether the organization to be appraised is ready to conduct the appraisal as planned. Without this review, organizations were sometimes surprised that they were going to "fail" their appraisal because they had selected the wrong projects (not representative of how their organization really does business), had selected the wrong people for interviews (the strategic thinkers or the salesmen, not the workers who had actually implemented the processes), or had produced the wrong documentation (processes not related to the CMMI, or no processes, procedures, or details on *how* to conduct an activity). This step, while not ensuring that the organization will "pass" the SCAMPI A, greatly increases the odds. The Lead Appraiser and Appraisal Team Members review the documentation and also check to make sure that any logistical problems have been solved (adequate facilities, the schedule has been approved, team members have received the required training, no one is planning to give birth during the appraisal, etc.).

The main point to focus on in this review is the PIIDs. Most organizations have trouble generating the PIIDs properly, so we devote Chapter 22 to those. For now, let's just say that the Appraisal Team, with the Lead Appraiser, reviews the PIIDs to see that the right type of information has been documented and can be accessed. The PIIDs record the documentation on a per practice–per process area–per project–per organization format. Most organizations create hotlinks to this information from the PIID to the actual document. The team may not review the documentation in-depth, as there is not that much time to do that in this step, and documentation is reviewed iteratively in the SCAMPI A method. This review is the team's introduction to the type of documentation produced as objective evidence to show that the organization has implemented each process area. The information is arranged by direct and indirect artifacts (also discussed in the PIID chapter). The Readiness Review will result in a decision to continue as planned, replan, reschedule, or cancel the appraisal. The authors of this book conduct this review as an addition to the required Appraisal Team training.

The PIIDs are reviewed to determine what data are available, what data are still needed, and how and where additional data will be obtained. The Appraisal Team looks for process area coverage gaps (documentation missing either for direct or indirect artifacts per practice or process area). During this readiness review, the Appraisal Team does not look for "goodness" of the data. The Appraisal Team simply looks to see if something that might be appropriate and relevant to the CMMI practice has been included in the right place in the PIID. The more time devoted to this review, the more closely the Appraisal Team can review the documentation in depth, the more information can be gained prior to the start of the onsite interviews, and the better the chance that the organization is ready for the full-blown appraisal.

Conduct Appraisal Phase

This phase focuses on collecting data to judge the extent to which the model has been implemented in the organization. This phase is also where findings and ratings are generated. This is the phase where the Appraisal Team does the bulk of its work. The steps (or processes) of this phase include:

- Prepare Participants (Onsite Appraisal In-Briefing)
- Examine Objective Evidence (Presentations, Interviews, and Documents)
- Verify Objective Evidence
- Validate Preliminary Findings
- Generate Appraisal Results

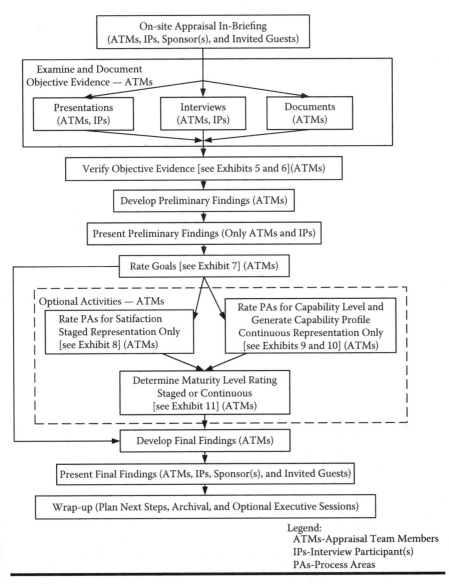

Figure 21.1 Onsite appraisal flow.

Table 21.2 lists the formal processes and activities of this phase as shown in the MDD. In this phase we begin the Onsite Appraisal. Figure 21.1 shows the flow of activities of the Onsite Appraisal that covers this phase and part of the next phase.

Prepare Participants Process

The SCAMPI A Lead Appraiser presents a tailored opening briefing of the appraisal to all participants. It describes the interview process, focus areas, examples of typical questions, and the information the Appraisal Team expects to obtain from the responses. It is used to set the expectations of the participants in the prospective interviews. The rules of confidentiality and nonattribution and the expected use of the appraisal data are communicated. Details regarding the schedule are also presented.

Examine and Verify Objective Evidence Processes

During the appraisal, the Appraisal Team examines evidence of process implementation from the organization. Sources of objective evidence can include presentations, documents, and interviews. Objective evidence can also be in the form of affirmations. An affirmation can be an oral or written statement about a CMMI practice within a process or can be a presentation or demonstration. Example statements might be, "I wrote a project plan for ABC project" or "I never use the standard process." A presentation could be a project manager's presentation on how he uses measures within the ABC project. An example of a demonstration could be showing how to use the online Process Asset Library to define new projects.

Presentations are used in our appraisals to increase the efficiency of the appraisal. Presentations allow organizational personnel to explain their processes. These presentations are limited to no more than 15–30 minutes to keep the presenters focused on important information. Presentations can be at the organizational level or the project level.

The briefing at the organizational level should consist of:

- What the organization does
- The organizational structure
- How responsibility, accountability, and authority are managed
- What problems were overcome during the process improvement initiative

The organization should be defined by showing and discussing an organizational chart that shows where the projects that were selected for the appraisal reside in the organization and where those projects not selected reside. This chart helps confirm that these projects are representative of how the organization normally performs work. (Remember, the Appraisal Team is supposed to review *representative projects*). Any terminology that is special to the organization or different from the CMMI is presented and defined. This presentation is usually given by a senior member of the organization, such as the director of software engineering or the vice president of quality. Please refer to Appendix D for more information that may be appropriate to include in your organization's presentation to the Appraisal Team.

Each focus project should deliver a briefing about the project. This briefing should include:

- A short description of the project, key product(s), and customer description
- Critical Success Factors—Key parameters to success, such as schedule, customer satisfaction survey, defect removal rate
- Project team membership and roles
- Project communications (team meetings, status reports, and frequency)
- Approach to planning and estimating
- Approach used to run the project (monitoring and controlling)
- Overview of methodology and/or life cycle used
- Tailoring decisions made and why (what makes your project special)
- Measurements collected and used

- For high maturity appraisals, that is, Capability or Maturity Levels 4 and 5, you might also include the:

- Projects' quality and process–performance objectives
- Projects' statistically managed subprocesses
- Projects' Process Performance Baselines
- Projects' Process Performance Models

These presentations are usually given by the managers of the focus projects. All Appraisal Team Members listen to the presentations and take and tag their notes relative to the CMMI process areas and practices.

Probably the most time-consuming and revelatory activity in the appraisal is reviewing documentation. The purpose of this activity is to collect data by examining artifacts. The artifacts examined are those that your organization probably has stored in your Process Asset Library. The Appraisal Team requests a list of which documents satisfy each practice of the CMMI. This list is a formal document required by the SCAMPI A process, has a formal structure, and is usually contained in a PIID. This document review activity is an iterative process and is repeated several times throughout several phases of the appraisal. It is undertaken to understand processes as actually implemented in the organization. Through these reviews, the Appraisal Team either confirms that the work being done is performed in accordance with the documented processes and procedures, and that those processes and procedures map back to the practices in the CMMI; or the team determines the contrary. The first documentation reviewed is the documentation listed in the PIIDs. However, if more documentation is needed, that documentation may be requested before, during, or after an interview by the Appraisal Team.

What would an appraisal be without interviews? The purpose of conducting interviews is to collect data by interviewing managers and project members of the selected projects to verify that the processes are followed as documented. The Appraisal Team conducts interviews by individuals, functional groups, project teams, project managers, or by process area. Interviews with project managers are usually conducted with the project manager interviewed by the entire Appraisal Team. Project members (other than the project manager) are usually interviewed as part of a group. However, individual interviews may be conducted for specific, detailed information, as needed. Each Appraisal Team Member may ask questions, or one member of the Appraisal Team may be designated to ask the questions. Appraisal Team Members may follow up with subsequent questions that deviate slightly from their previously scripted questions in order to help the interviewee understand and interpret the question or to gain more specific information. All Appraisal Team Members listen and take and tag their notes relative to the CMMI process areas and practices. Interviewees are not allowed to take notes. Interviews are used to gain insight into how processes are followed, decisions are made, and documentation is used. After each interview, or after a series of interviews, the Appraisal Team Members discuss what they heard and what they have read, and map these observations back to the CMMI.

Two related topics are consolidation and consensus. Consolidation is the activity of collecting and summarizing information collected into a manageable set of useful data. Consensus is a method of decision making that allows team members to develop a common understanding and agreement that all team members are willing to support.

Findings and ratings require team consensus. What that means is that the entire team must agree on the intent of the finding and the wording of the finding. There must be no strong disagreement. If the team has been consolidating data and discussing objective evidence and findings all along during the appraisal, then this consensus step is usually not a problem. However, if the team leaves this activity until the night before the ratings are due *there is a big problem.*

The Appraisal Team determines the extent to which a CMMI practice has been performed in an organization. The team begins by determining whether the practices have been implemented and to what extent they have been implemented at the lowest level possible, called the instantiation level (at the project or support group level). Each practice is verified to ensure that corroborated objective evidence has been found. Remember, the practice we are referring to is the practice's implementation in a focus project or support group. Each practice is characterized as Fully Implemented (FI), Largely Implemented (LI), Partially Implemented (PI), Not Implemented (NI), or Not Yet (NY, as in Not Yet Implemented) according to the rules in Table 21.6.

The CMMI subpractices and examples are used to help guide the team members in determining the degree of adequacy of the artifacts. There is room for discussion, as no organization ever implements every subpractice within a practice

Table 21.6 Rules for Characterizing Instantiation-Level Implementation of Practices

Label	Meaning
Fully Implemented (FI)	• One or more direct artifacts are present and judged to be adequate, • at least one indirect artifact and/or affirmation exists to confirm the implementation, and • no weaknesses are noted.
Largely Implemented (LI)	• One or more direct artifacts are present and judged to be adequate, • at least one indirect artifact and/or affirmation exists to confirm the implementation, and • one or more weaknesses are noted.
Partially Implemented (PI)	• Direct artifacts are absent or judged to be inadequate, • one or more indirect artifacts or affirmations suggest that some aspects of the practice are implemented, and • one or more weaknesses are noted. **OR** • One or more direct artifacts are present and judged to be adequate, • no other evidence (indirect artifacts, affirmations) support the direct artifact(s), and • one or more weaknesses are noted.
Not Implemented (NI)	• Direct artifacts are absent or judged to be inadequate, • no other evidence (indirect artifacts, affirmation) supports the practice implementation, and • one or more weaknesses are noted.
Not Yet (NY)	• The project or support group has not yet reached the stage in the life cycle to have implemented the practice.

and may not have completely implemented the practice itself. Alternative practices may also substitute for the actual CMMI practice, but only when the alternative practice meets the intent (as decided by the Appraisal Team) of the original CMMI practice. Alternative practices are not necessarily one-for-one replacements for the specific or generic practice, so this can become somewhat complicated. So, be careful when deciding to substitute your own practice.

Weaknesses are explicitly identified. A weakness is defined as the ineffective, or lack of, implementation of one or more CMMI model practices.

While it is required that you identify weaknesses, you may find it useful to capture information on strengths. A strength is defined as an exemplary or noteworthy implementation of a CMMI model practice. But, if you are not careful, you can waste unnecessary time and effort documenting strengths. *Not every implemented practice is a strength.* This statement is highlighted because in previous types of assessments, some teams considered any implementation of a practice to be a strength. We emphasize that the definition of a strength has been ... well... strengthened.

Once you have applied the rules of Table 21.6 to all the objective evidence for a particular practice for your focus projects and/or support groups in appraisal scope, then you can roll up the lower, instantiation-level data to the organizational unit-level following the rules shown in Table 21.7. The entire team is responsible for consensus at the organizational unit–level.

Table 21.7 Rules for Characterizing Organizational Unit–Level Implementation of Practices

Instantiations	Outcome	Remarks
All FI or NY, with at least one FI	FI	All instantiations are characterized FI or NY, with at least one FI.
All LI or FI or NY, with at least one LI	LI	All instantiations are characterized LI or FI or NY, with at least one LI.
At least one LI or FI and at least one PI or NI	LI or PI	There is at least one instantiation that is characterized as LI or FI and at least one instantiation that is characterized as PI or NI. Team judgment is applied to choose LI or PI based on whether the weaknesses, in aggregate, have a significant negative impact on goal achievement.
All PI or NI or NY, with at least one PI	PI	All instantiations are characterized PI or NI or NY, with at least one PI.
All NI or NY, with at least one NI	NI	All instantiations are characterized NI or NY, with at least one NI.
All NY	NY	All instantiations are characterized NY. There are no projects or support groups within the organizational unit that have yet reached the stage in the life cycle to have implemented the practice. (NOTE: If literally *all* projects and support groups in an organizational unit have not reached the stage in the life cycle to have implemented the practice, but will in the future, no rating can be given for the associated goal and PA.)

Validate Preliminary Findings Process

The most common approach to Validate Preliminary Findings, and the one we recommend, is for the Appraisal Team to prepare a briefing of Preliminary Findings covering each process area in scope. The Lead Appraiser delivers the briefing and actively solicits feedback from the participants.

To create the preliminary findings briefing, you need to have sufficient coverage of the CMMI model and organizational unit, meaning that you have:

- Completed your data collection, including interviews and document reviews
- Characterized all the expected instances of practices at the organizational unit
- Identified associated weaknesses and strengths

All weaknesses (i.e., from practices that have not been determined to be FI [Fully Implemented]) need to be presented in the findings in order to allow for the participants from the organization to comment.

A minimum of one session is required to present the preliminary findings. We often hold two sessions: one for managers and one for nonmanagers. No maximum number of sessions is specified by the MDD, but use common sense. These sessions must not violate the confidentially and nonattribution rules of the appraisal, and these rules and the expected use of the appraisal data must be communicated to participants in each presentation.

So, who should attend these presentations? Only those personnel who participated in the interviews may attend this preliminary findings presentation. You must not allow anyone who has not been interviewed to attend, period—it is a requirement of the SCAMPI A Method. To ensure this, you need to keep an accurate record of all the actual interviewees and the project or support group they represent—not just the people you invited to interview. It is not required that all interviewees attend a presentation; however, there must be at least one participant from each project or support group that provided objective evidence. Why can't just anyone attend? Because they have not been part of the appraisal, they have not participated in the appraisal, they probably have not attended the informational presentations given by the organization and by the Appraisal Team, they don't understand the process, they won't understand the findings, and they are probably there as management spies to deliver a heads-up to management about the level rating and to argue the results. Do not let this happen. The rules for attendance are very clear and are the result of many years of appraisals and findings presentations.

The Appraisal Team takes notes on the information found during this presentation. An important aspect of the preliminary findings session is that it is both a data validation and data collection activity. The Appraisal Team is presenting its draft—not final—findings. It is checking to see if it missed something or if it misunderstood something. This presentation gives the organization one last chance to deliver any information the Appraisal Team needs.

The standard briefing consists of weaknesses only. This approach optimizes time limitations and ensures that the majority of the time is spent validating weaknesses and collecting additional information to validate these weaknesses and potentially new items. But, by presenting only weaknesses, the organization may get nervous about whether it has passed the SCAMPI A. Make sure you have explained why only weaknesses are presented (i.e., to save time and that this approach is the preferred method in the MDD).

In our appraisals, we find that only listing and presenting weaknesses can be counterproductive and discouraging to the organization. To overcome this problem, we make use of the optional practice for including statements of strengths for exemplary implementations of model practices to present a number of strengths along with the weaknesses in order to provide a more balanced view to the organization. This inclusion of strengths does not take a lot of extra time because organizations will argue the weaknesses found, but have never (in our experience) argued the strengths found. It also prevents lynchings of the Appraisal Team.

There are other methods that may be used to validate preliminary findings. They are the use of focus groups and survey instruments. We do not go into these alternatives in this chapter. Those individuals interested in these methods may review them in the MDD.

Generate Appraisal Results Process

In this process, the Appraisal Team generates the final SCAMPI A Appraisal results. The activities of this process are to:

- Derive Final Findings and Rate Goals
- Determine Satisfaction of Process Areas (Staged Representation Only)—Optional
- Determine Process Area Capability Level (Continuous Representation Only)—Optional
- Determine Capability Profile (Continuous Representation Only)—Optional
- Determine Maturity Level Rating (Staged or Continuous)—Optional
- Document Appraisal Results

As you can see, four of the activities in this process are optional. These four activities depend upon the rating objectives defined in the appraisal plan and the CMMI model representation selected (either staged or continuous; see Chapter 4 for the differences between the representations).

The Derive Final Findings and Rate Goals step is *not optional* and is used with both the staged and continuous representations. In this step, the Appraisal Team must:

- Derive final findings from the preliminary findings and participant feedback and/or any other Preliminary Finding Validation Activities (such as focus groups or surveys). Final findings are goal-level statements that summarize the gaps in practice implementation.
- Rate both specific and generic goals for the process areas within the model scope of the appraisal using the rules shown in Table 21.8.

Table 21.8 reveals the importance of having practices rolled up into goals and rated at the organizational level, and in ensuring sufficient data coverage (for

Table 21.8 Goal Rating Rules (Staged and Continuous)

A goal must be rated Not Rated if there are any associated practices that are not characterized at the organizational unit level or that are characterized as Not Yet at the organizational unit level.
A goal is rated Not Rated if the associated set of objective evidence does not meet the defined criteria for sufficient data coverage.
The goal is rated Satisfied if and only if • all associated practices are characterized at the organizational unit level as either Largely Implemented or Fully Implemented, and • the aggregation of weaknesses associated with the goal does not have a significant negative impact on goal achievement.
For a goal to be rated as Unsatisfied, the team must be able to describe how the set of documented weaknesses (or single weakness) led to this rating.

Table 21.9   Process Area Rating Rules (Staged Representation Only)

Process Areas (PAs) must be assigned rating values of Satisfied, Unsatisfied, Not Applicable, Out of Scope, or Not Rated.
A PA is rated Satisfied if and only if all of its specific and generic goals associated with a given maturity level and below are rated Satisfied.
If even one of the goals associated with a given maturity level in a PA is rated Unsatisfied, then the PA is rated Unsatisfied for that maturity level and above.
When a PA is determined to be outside of the organizational unit's scope of work, the PA is designated as Not Applicable and is not rated. The identification of a PA as Not Applicable must occur during the planning of the appraisal.
When an applicable PA is outside the scope of the appraisal reference model used for the appraisal, the PA is designated as Out of Scope and is not rated.
If even one of the goals in a PA is rated Not Rated and none of the other goals are rated Unsatisfied, then the PA is rated Not Rated.

Table 21.10   Process Area Capability Level Rules (Continuous Representation Only)

Capability Level	Process Areas
0	Default Rating
1	Generic goal for capability level 1 is rated Satisfied. All specific goals are rated Satisfied.
2	Generic goals for capability levels 1 and 2 are rated Satisfied. All specific goals are rated Satisfied.
3	Generic goals for capability levels 1, 2, and 3 are rated Satisfied. All specific goals are rated Satisfied.
4	Generic goals for capability levels 1, 2, 3, and 4 are rated Satisfied. All specific goals are rated Satisfied.
5	Generic goals for capability levels 1, 2, 3, 4, and 5 are rated Satisfied. All specific goals are rated Satisfied.

example, appropriate number and types of projects, interviews, process areas, and practices investigated). If these conditions are not met, the goal will be rated Not Rated.

When using the staged representation, if the Determine Satisfaction of Process Areas option was selected during appraisal planning, then the Appraisal Team rates the satisfaction of each PA in the scope of the appraisal based on the ratings of the specific and generic goals within each PA. This step is done according the rules shown in Table 21.9.

When using the continuous representation, if the Determine Process Area Capability Level rating option was selected during appraisal planning, then the Appraisal Team rates the capability level of each PA in the scope of the appraisal based on the ratings of the specific and generic goals within each PA. This step is done according the rules shown in Table 21.10. Capability levels are only defined for process areas.

Table 21.11 Capability Profile Rules (Continuous Representation Only)

A simple bar chart is used for this display. Each PA is represented in a single bar along the horizontal axis, and the vertical axis represents the capability-level dimension. The height of each bar communicates the capability level of the PA represented.
Capability levels take only the values 0, 1, 2, 3, 4, or 5. Intermediate values (e.g., 2.7) are not defined for this appraisal outcome, and any embellishment of the Capability Profile with such values is outside the boundaries of SCAMPI A.

Table 21.12 Maturity Level Rating Rules (Staged and Continuous)

When using the staged representation, the maturity level determined is the highest level at which all PAs contained within the maturity level, and within all lower maturity levels, are rated as Satisfied or Not Applicable. The single exception to this rule is that generic goal 3 for applicable maturity level 2 PAs must also be rated Satisfied for a maturity level rating of 3 or higher to be determined.
When using the continuous representation, the appraisal reference model provides for equivalent staging, whereby a Capability Profile can be used to derive an equivalent maturity-level rating. A maturity level for a continuous representation is achieved if the Capability Profile is at or above the target profile for all PAs for that maturity level and all lower maturity levels in the equivalent staging, excepting those PAs that are designated as Not Applicable. The equivalence of particular Capability Profiles and particular maturity levels is addressed in Chapter 3 of the reference model.
To determine a maturity level as an output of the appraisal, the model scope of the appraisal must include the minimum set of PAs required by the appraisal reference model.

When using the continuous representation, if the Determine Capability Profile option was selected during planning, then the Appraisal Team generates a capability profile depicting the capability level attained for each PA in the scope of the appraisal. This step is done according the rules shown in Table 21.11.

When using either the staged or continuous representation, if the Determine Maturity Level rating option was selected during planning, the Appraisal Team generates a maturity-level rating. Maturity levels are defined for the entire organizational unit being appraised. A maturity level rating can be assigned using either the staged representation or the continuous representation. When using the continuous representation, the team uses what is called Equivalent Staging. If using the staged representation, satisfaction of the process areas must have been determined. If using the continuous representation, a Capability Profile must have been generated.

This step is done according the rules shown in Table 21.12.

The Appraisal Team documents final findings and ratings, and prepares the Appraisal Disclosure Statement (ADS) for the SEI.

At this point, having gone through all the steps above, documenting the Final Findings and Rating Outcomes should be straightforward. One new requirement with SCAMPI v1.2 is that the Appraisal Team Members are required to sign the

Table 21.13   Section 1: Appraisal Identification from ADS (Annotated Outline)

Organization Name	Legal entity for which this appraisal is being conducted.
Organizational Unit (OU)	Part of organization that is subject of appraisal.
Excluded Projects and Groups	List projects, categories of projects, or groups/functions that were specifically excluded from this appraisal and a justification for their exclusion.
Organizational Scope	Portion of the organizational unit that participates in the appraisal.
Organizational Projects and Support Groups	Specify all of the projects and support groups that are included within the scope of this appraisal and from which objective evidence has been obtained and analyzed.
POC for Any Non-disclosed Information	Option for Sponsor to identify a Point of Contact for any sensitive or proprietary project/group.
Org Sample Size	Percent of people, projects, and support groups of org unit included in the scope.
Critical Factors	Identify factors critical to the implementation of practices in projects with percentage of each critical factor identified in appraisal planning.
Appraisal Schedule	Start Date Completion Date Activity/Event for Phase 1 (Plan and Prepare for Appraisal), Phase 2 (Conduct Appraisal), and Phase 3 (Report Results).
Appraisal Expiration Date	The findings and results from a SCAMPI A Appraisal are valid for a period of not more than three years from delivery of the appraisal findings.
Appraisal Method Used	For example, SCAMPI A Version 1.2.
Representation Used	For example, CMMI Staged V1.2 or CMMI Continuous V1.2.
Appraised Functional Areas	For example, Software, Systems Engineering, Hardware, Program Management, Supply Chain Management, Logistics.
Constellation Used	Indicated constellation of CMMI v1.2 DEV, DEV+IPPD, ACQ, or SVC.
CMMI Model Scope	Indicates all process areas within scope of the appraisal.
Key Appraisal Participants	Appraisal sponsor, Appraisal team leader, and Appraisal team members.
Goal Ratings	For each goal, Satisfied(S), Unsatisfied (U), Not Rated (NR).
Process Area Ratings (OPTIONAL)	For each Process Area, Satisfied(S), Unsatisfied (U), Not Rated (NR), Not Applicable to Org Unit (NA), Out of Scope of Appraisal (OS).
Appraisal Ratings (OPTIONAL)	Maturity Level Rating(s) for Staged Representation Capability Level Rating(s) for Continuous Representation.
Additional Information for Appraisals Resulting in Capability or Maturity Level 4 or 5 Ratings	Describe which processes or subprocesses are under statistical management and were included in the objective evidence for this appraisal. Also list the PA(s) and organizational quality and process-performance objective(s) these processes or subprocesses pertain to Process/Subprocess, Process Area(s) and Quality/Process Performance Objective(s).

final findings. After the Final Findings are completed, the ADS can be completed and signed by the Lead Appraiser and the sponsor. The ADS has two sections:

- Section 1: Appraisal Identification provides for the disclosure of information, which meets the minimum requirements for the appraisal disclosure statement as defined for the SCAMPI appraisal method.
- Section 2: Affirmations provides for the affirmation of the accuracy of this ADS by the SEI authorized SCAMPI Lead Appraiser and the sponsor. These affirmations are required. There are also options that can be initialed by the sponsor to request and provide authorization for information in this ADS to be published on Web sites.

Table 21.13 contains an annotated outline for Section 1 of the ADS. Table 21.14 shows Section 2 of the ADS.

Table 21.14   Section 2: Affirmations from ADS

Appraisal Team Leader (required)
For all appraisals
I affirm that the information in this statement is accurate and that the appraisal described herein was conducted in full accordance with the requirements of the SCAMPI A appraisal method and the provisions of my authorization as a SCAMPI Lead Appraiser. I also verify that, to the best of my knowledge, the organizational scope as depicted herein is representative of the organizational unit for this.
For High Maturity Appraisals (Capability or Maturity Level 4 or 5)
I validate that a substantial portion of the organization's and project's quality and process performance objectives and statistically managed subprocesses can be mapped directly to and support the established business objectives as stated and disseminated to key employees of the organization, and the needs and priorities of customers, end users, and other stakeholders.
This validation is required to prevent the granting of high maturity ratings for trivial improvements.
Appraisal Team Leader Must Provide — Name, Signature, and Date

Appraisal Sponsor (required)
I affirm that the organizational scope described above is representative of the organizational unit for this appraisal.
I further affirm that the information in this statement is accurate and that the SEI may review the appraisal record and/or conduct interviews deemed necessary upon request.
I agree to maintain the appraisal record through the date of expiration of this appraisal as documented in this Appraisal Disclosure Statement.
I understand that, for the period of validity of this appraisal, it is my responsibility, with consideration of non-attribution (see MDD activity 3.2.2), to ensure that the appraisal record is stored under appropriate levels of control to support reviews and/or audits by the CMMI Steward.
Results of this appraisal will not be made public record or used in response to any request for proposal, etc., until I have been notified that the appraisal has been reviewed and accepted by the SEI.
Sponsor Must Provide — Name, Signature, and Date

The Appraisal Sponsor can also select the following:
____ Initial here if you are authorizing and requesting that the information from this ADS be published on the Published Appraisal Results System (PARS), a Web site providing public notice of appraisal results.

Report Results Phase

This is the final phase for the SCAMPI A appraisal. The two processes of this phase are Deliver Appraisal Results, and Package and Archive Appraisal Assets. Packaging the results and planning for next steps may be finished offsite. Table 21.3 lists the formal processes and activities of this phase as shown in the MDD.

Deliver Appraisal Results Process

Delivering the Appraisal results includes delivering the Final Findings, conducting optional executive sessions, and planning the next steps. The Final Findings are delivered to the organization as presentations. We usually do two presentations: one to the sponsor and executive in charge of the organization, and then one to the rest of the organization. The organization determines how many people should attend.

Some organizations like to have a separate Executive Session following the Final Findings presentation to allow the executives and other invited guests to ask the Lead Appraiser and the Appraisal Team more detailed questions than would be appropriate in a larger group. Of course, confidentially and non-attribution of data sources must be maintained. This session is also an opportunity for the Lead Appraiser to explain the roles of the Appraisal Team Members in any further process improvement efforts the organization may decide to undertake. This session also may be the place to provide general information to the executives concerning the next steps in the organization's process improvement efforts and how the results of the appraisal can help focus those efforts.

Next steps may include planning for the development of a final report, submission of Appraisal Team recommendations, and generation of action plans. A final written report may also be delivered to the organization, but we generally find that the organization prefers just the PowerPoint presentation. This presentation summarizes each process area and is enough for the organization to base continuing process improvement efforts upon.

Sometimes, an organization also requests that recommendations based on the findings be provided. The organization should be aware that the findings are based on satisfaction of the process area goals in the CMMI and not on recommendations that are offered by the Appraisal Team. Recommendations are optional. The authors of this book prefer to keep the generation of findings separate from the making of recommendations. We prefer to offer recommendations as part of follow-on activities involving generating action plans.

Package and Archive Appraisal Assets Process

This final process covers packaging and archiving appraisal assets. This process includes collecting lessons learned, generating a permanent record of the appraisal, providing the Appraisal Data Package to the SEI, and archiving and/or disposing of key artifacts.

The Appraisal Record is the organization's permanent record of the appraisal documenting the appraisal conduct and results. When generating this record, appraisal data must be cleansed or sanitized to comply with non-attribution and confidentiality rules (for example, no references to specific sources, such as individuals, projects, or support groups). The Appraisal Record includes just about everything from the appraisal: the Appraisal Input, Appraisal Plan, the objective evidence, the instantiation-level practice characterizations, the organizational unit–level characterizations, the Final Findings, and the ADS. Your Appraisal Sponsor agrees to maintain the Appraisal Record through the expiration of the appraisal to allow the SEI (also known as the CMMI Steward) to audit the appraisal should they decide that an audit is necessary (see Table 21.14).

The Appraisal Data Package is forwarded to the SEI (CMMI Steward) for record keeping and statistical purposes to track trends of process implementation and efforts worldwide. The Appraisal Data Package is a subset of the Appraisal

Record. The Appraisal Data Package includes the approved Appraisal Input, the approved Appraisal Plan, the approved ADS, and the Final Findings.

Summary

The SCAMPI A is a Class A appraisal technique used to measure satisfaction of the institutionalization of process area practices and activities in an organization. The SCAMPI A is a very intensive, high-pressure activity that should not be undertaken by sissies. It is a highly formal, structured set of activities that are defined by the Software Engineering Institute and reviewed by them for adherence to the method. There are no shortcuts to pass the appraisal and get your rating. The best way to do well on a SCAMPI A is to try to implement as many of the CMMI practices that make sense to your organization (which is most of the practices), to not rely on alternative practices to satisfy the intent of the practices, and to not rely on organizational constraints (lack of time, lack of personnel, lack of training, lack of real management commitment) to influence the rating. Do not think you can write some useless documentation and have it pass for meaningful processes. Do not rely on thinking that you can just write a check to the Lead Appraiser and get your rating. Really implementing CMMI into your organization takes time and money. The results are worth it, but it is not easy.

Chapter 22

Those Damn PIIDs!

The title of this chapter, if our publisher let's us get away with it, is "Those Damn PIIDs!" All of the organizations that we have performed SCAMPI A's on have complained endlessly about having to complete the PIIDs. One organization reported a total in manhours of 60 days spent completing these forms. Why the problem? Because the PIIDs are not arranged in the same way as the documentation is stored in your organization, and thought must be paid to what goes into them. Because of this confusion (and constipation), we have added this chapter. It is based on a class we teach.

This chapter should be read only after reading Chapter 20, "Appraisals Using the CMMI," and Chapter 21, "The SCAMPI A Approach." This chapter is written from the perspective of a SCAMPI A, however, it is also applicable to PIIDs used in SCAMPI B and C.

What Are PIIDS and Why Must I Use Them?

PIID stands for Practice Implementation Indicator Description. The PIIDs are forms used to capture the documented evidence of how each CMMI practice has been implemented. The easiest way to envision a PIID is to think of a table. Depending on the CMMI practice, the PIID may contain references or pointers to documented processes, procedures, meeting minutes, revision histories, change logs, or any other such proof of practice implementation. The PIIDs are divided into direct and indirect evidence (called direct and indirect artifacts). Appraisal Teams are required to seek evidence that each CMMI practice has been implemented. The fundamental idea of the Practice Implementation Indicators is that the conduct of an activity or the implementation of a practice results in "footprints," that is, evidence of the activity or practice. This evidence is required for both organizational-level and project-level implementation. PIIDs are the mechanism used for capturing objective evidence for direct and indirect artifacts. PIIDs are key to successful SCAMPI appraisals. There is no "required" format or implementation for a PIID. PIIDs can be implemented in Excel, Word, or a specialized database.

The SCAMPI Method involves:

■ Collecting process data to understand the current implemented process (through PIIDs, interviews, and presentations)
■ Identifying process weaknesses and strengths
■ Determining the degree of satisfaction of the goals investigated
■ Assigning ratings (if requested by the appraisal sponsor)

SCAMPI is designed as a verification-based appraisal method. What does that mean? What are we verifying? The first thing we verify is that we have PIIDs for each specific practice for each process area (PA) and for each generic practice for each process area. We look to see that each PIID is complete (no blank spaces) and contains documentation that shows how the CMMI practice has been implemented at the organizational level and in each project being appraised.

So what really is a PIID? A PIID is a form that points to evidence that each CMMI practice has been implemented in your organization. If you don't do the PIIDs, you will fail the SCAMPI. Period.* PIIDs are inputs to the SCAMPI process, so if you don't have them, you are not ready for the SCAMPI. If you are not ready, the SCAMPI is canceled. Now, go tell the executive in charge of your organization that you failed the SCAMPI because you don't like the PIIDs. See what happens next.

The PIIDs were developed to help organize the documentation reported to the Appraisal Team and to help minimize the time that the team spends on site. Previous assessments under different models often let the organization provide the documentation according to that organization's format. What we often found was that the documents listed in this documentation checklist were missing, not appropriate, or unable to be accessed for review. Remember, the SCAMPI is the Standard CMMI Appraisal Method for Process Improvement. Part of the standardization includes the usage of PIIDs.

Normally, the SCAMPI Lead Appraiser furnishes the empty PIIDs to the organization. The Engineering Process Group (EPG) usually completes the PIIDs or delegates someone to complete them. Completing the PIIDs is a big job, so do not appoint just one person to do the job. Select the people who know the most about

---

* As we mentioned in Chapter 20, the SCAMPI method is designed to be a verification-based approach. A discovery-based approach is an option with a SCAMPI A appraisal. Discovery-based appraisals are much more difficult, error prone, and time consuming. We *do not* recommend discovery-based approaches with SCAMPI A.

the process area. For example, an EPG member will probably know the most about organizational-level process areas (like Organizational Process Focus or Organizational Training), while the project managers of each project to be appraised probably know the most about project-level documentation (like the project plan and specific project metrics).

Make sure you have someone objective review the resulting PIIDs before you turn them over to the Appraisal Team. We have found that PIIDs are often filled out incorrectly because the person filling them out is also the person who wrote the documentation or was heavily invested in implementing the information in the documents. PIIDs are also completed incorrectly because the person filling them out doesn't understand them, doesn't want to understand them, or doesn't have the time to think about what is actually required, so he just puts something in to fill in the blanks.

Be sure your organization schedules enough time to complete the PIIDs, review the PIIDs, and correct the PIIDs. The Appraisal Team is not onsite to help you correct your PIIDs. They are there to determine if the information documented in your PIIDs maps to CMMI practices that are actually implemented in your organization. If the PIIDs are wrong, the Appraisal Team may assume that your implementation of the CMMI is also wrong. You fail.

One important concept to understand is that, while the PIIDs are mandatory in verification-based appraisals, their format is not. The information that must be contained in each PIID is organizational- and project-level documentation, categorized as either a direct or indirect artifact, that maps to each CMMI practice. The documents must show how the practice was implemented and at what level of the organization. Why must the information be arranged according to direct and indirect artifacts? Because you must have both types of artifacts to satisfy the goals for each process area in the CMMI, and without correct direct and indirect artifacts, you will fail the SCAMPI. Having direct and indirect artifacts for each practice, plus interviews (affirmations) that each artifact has been implemented in the organization and is used as documented, just about ensures passing the SCAMPI.

There are direct and indirect artifacts used to provide evidence that helps prove practice implementation. Direct artifacts are basically the expected or direct outcome from implementing the practice. For instance, Project Planning has a specific practice that reads, "Establish and maintain the overall project plan." The direct evidence listed in the PIID for Project Planning would be the overall project plan. That makes sense. Wouldn't you expect the direct output of planning a project to be a project plan? Also included as direct evidence is the revision history of the plan. This artifact may not seem as direct as the plan. The revision history shows that the plan has actually been used, and maps to the phrase "Establish and maintain" in the practice. (Remember, the phrase "Establish and maintain" means to create and use what has been created.) The indirect artifact example is listed as "issues and conflicts identified across subordinate plans." The basis of these artifacts comes from the Typical Work Products displayed under each practice within each process

Table 22.1   Practice Implementation Indicator Types

Indicator Type	Description	Examples
Direct Artifacts	The tangible outputs resulting directly from implementation of a specific or generic practice. An integral part of verifying practice implementation. May be explicitly stated or implied by the practice statement or associated informative material.	Typical work products listed in reference model practices. Target products of an "Establish and Maintain" specific practice. Documents, deliverable products, training materials, etc.
Indirect Artifacts	Artifacts that are a consequence of performing a specific or generic practice or that substantiate its implementation, but which are not the purpose for which the practice is performed. This indicator type is especially useful when there may be doubts about whether the intent of the practice has been met (e.g., an artifact exists but there is no indication of where it came from, who worked to develop it, or how it is used).	Typical work products listed in reference model practices. Meeting minutes, review results, status reports, presentations, etc. Performance measures
Affirmations	Oral or written statements confirming or supporting implementation (or lack of implementation) of a specific or generic practice. These statements are usually provided by the implementers of the practice and/or internal or external customers, but may also include other stakeholders (e.g., managers and suppliers).	Instruments Interviews Presentations, demonstrations, etc.

area. So, the direct artifact is what is usually a direct output of the practice. The indirect artifact is an indirect product of the practice, such as minutes of meetings that review the direct output. Usually, but not always. One thing we have discovered with PIIDs is that there really is no one hard and fast rule for defining direct versus indirect artifacts. Direct artifacts, indirect artifacts, and affirmations are called PII (Practice Implementation Indicator) Types.

Table 22.1 contains descriptions and examples of direct and indirect artifacts from the SCAMPI Method Definition Document.

Don't try to figure out the rationale for what is a direct or indirect artifact. The PIIDs already tell you that. Also, sometimes, the direct and indirect artifacts are interchangeable. Don't try to figure out the rationale. Just fill in the PIID.

Some organizations have also tried to use the PIIDs as their Process Asset Library (PAL). Please do not do that. There should be more information in your PAL than in the PIID, and this information should be organized in such a way that makes it easy to find and easy to retrieve by the people in your organization that need to use it. Remember, the PIID is developed for the Appraisal Team and is a summary of only the most pertinent and most relevant information mapping to specific and generic practices.

What Do the PIIDs Look Like?

Each PIID begins with the title of the process area. You will then see rows that display the Goal, the associated (specific) practice, and the type if evidence requested (Direct Artifact, Indirect Artifact, or Affirmation). You will see that one row has the phrase "Example Evidence (Look Fors/Listen Fors)" in it. These examples are based on the Typical Work Products in the CMMI. Under each example Direct Artifact and Indirect Artifact column is room for Organizational Evidence, Project 1 Evidence, Project 2 Evidence, up to as many projects as will be part of the appraisal. You will also see a column for Affirmation. That is when the Appraisal Team confirms during an interview that the artifact is implemented as written. The authors of this book usually do not have the organization fill in this affirmation area because the Appraisal Team members have their own spreadsheets to document interview responses and findings. When the organization fills out the PIIDs, the organization should just fill in the Direct and Indirect Artifacts portion. Leave the Affirmations blank. However, some organizations use this column as a reference to the person who developed and delivered the PIID for this practice or for a reference to the person they plan to interview for this practice.

Most organizations set up hotlinks from the document referenced in the PIID to the actual document itself. This allows the Appraisal Team to easily access and read the information to determine the degree of implementation in the projects and in the organization.

Don't forget that the PIIDs for the generic practices also must be completed for each process area for each project. Although the PIID format remains the same, the information listed in the PIID will change to reflect the implementation for each process area.

Do not put every artifact you have in the PIID! We usually ask for the most recent example or the last three instances that show usage (such as updates or meeting minutes). In some PIIDs, there is a long list of artifacts that can be input to the form. We suggest that you use your brain when selecting what to put in. For example, ask yourself, "What is the purpose of this practice?" If it is to track changes, perhaps you would like to show evidence of a change that has actually been tracked throughout the life cycle. Just don't fill in the PIID with junk. You will be judged not ready for the SCAMPI to continue.

Tables 22.2, 22.3, and 22.4 show example PIIDs. We have included one project-level process area PIID (Requirements Management), one organizational-level PIID (Organizational Training), and one generic practice PIID (Generic Practice 3.1 Establish a Defined Process). Notice that each PIID has both organizational evidence and evidence pertaining to the focus projects only. What does this mean?

Table 22.2   Example Requirement Management Specific Practice 1.1 PIID

Goal ID	REQM SG1 Requirements are managed and inconsistencies with project plans and work products are identified.		
Practice ID	REQM SP 1.1 *Develop an understanding with the requirements providers on the meaning of the requirements.*		
PII Type	Direct Artifacts	Indirect Artifacts	Affirmations
Example Evidence (Look Fors/ Listen Fors)	• Allocated Requirements Document • Allocated Requirements Database • Review Report of Requirements • Commitments from affected groups on Allocated Requirements • Defined criteria for evaluation and acceptance of Requirements	• Evidence of early (before committing to develop the corresponding software) system requirement allocated to software review (e.g., meeting minutes, reports...) • A list or characterization of requirements providers authorized to provide direction	
Organizational Implementation Evidence			
Project 1			
Project 2			
Project 3			
Appraisal Team Notes			
Assessment Considerations	Consider existence of requirements at multiple levels (e.g., product and product component requirements).		

It means that there is information that is used both at the organizational level and at the project level on a particular project. You may be using organizational-level documentation that relates to the Organization's Set of Standard Processes (OSSP) and also using information that relates to project-specific documentation. For example, you may be using a Configuration Management process for managing changes to a document that works for both an organizational document (like a strategic, overall project plan) and a project document (like a project tactical plan).

However, sometimes organizational-level PIIDs are truly organizational. One example is Organizational Process Focus. This PA usually does not contain project-specific references, as this PA pertains mostly to the EPG or the people who have managed the process improvement effort. Organizational Training, however, may have both organizational training plans that focus on the budget and high-level schedules, and project-level training that focuses on specific classes held and who attended from the project. Or the information in this PIID can point to the appropriate specific practice in the Project Planning PA that discusses training. So, there may be some overlap.

Table 22.2 is an example project-level process area PIID that must be completed for Specific Practice 1.1 of the Requirements Management process area. This PIID focuses on one specific practice of one process area (Requirements Management [REQM]) and must be completed by each project that will be investigated by the SCAMPI. There may be organizational-level artifacts used (such as an organizational-level process for the specific practice), plus processes used by each project to implement the specific practice on that project (for instance, a tailored version of the organizational level process).

Looking at Table 22.2 you can see there are empty cells to insert the direct and indirect artifacts for both the organizational-level artifacts and the artifacts for the three different projects. As you can see, this a lot of information to fill out. And this is just one PIID for one Specific Practice for one Process Area.

An example of an organizational-level process area PIID is shown in Table 22.3.

Table 22.4 is a PIID for Generic Practice 3.1. Although each process area is listed separately, remember that each project must complete this form. So each project must complete this form for each process area listed below for both organizational-level artifacts and project-level artifacts. Each PA in this example is listed by process category from the continuous representation.

Table 22.4 has many references to the General Evidence row. The General Evidence asks for process descriptions for each PA and changes to the process description or its implementation. Some organizations will break up this PIID and attach it to its respective PA. For example, an organization will fill out the PIIDs for Requirements Management (REQM), including all the specific practices, organizational information, and project information for each project (as in Table 22.2), and then skip a line or two and attach the PIIDs for all generic practices applied to REQM. This approach helps by not repeating the PIID entries over and over.

Table 22.3   Example Organizational Training Specific Practice 1.1 PIID

Goal ID	OT SG 1 A training capability, which supports the organization's management and technical roles, is established and maintained.		
Practice ID	OT SP 1.1 *Establish and maintain the strategic training needs of the organization.*		
PII Type	Direct Artifacts	Indirect Artifacts	Affirmations
Example Evidence (Look Fors/Listen Fors)	• Training needs • Review and revision history of the strategic training needs of the organization	• Assessment analysis • Documented rationale for strategic training objectives • Organization's strategic business plan or process improvement plan • Identification of roles and skills needed • List of required training courses needed	
Organizational Implementation Evidence			
Appraisal Team Notes			
Assessment Considerations	Note that the typical work products for this SP are at the organizational level, not project level		

Table 22.4 Example Generic Practice 3.1 PIID

Goal IDt	GG3 The Process is institutionalized as a defined process.	
Practice ID	*GP 3.1 Establish and maintain the description of a defined process.*	
PII Type	**Direct Artifacts**	**Indirect Artifacts**
General Example Evidence across Pas (Look Fors/Listen Fors)	• Defined process description (purpose, inputs, entry criteria, activities, roles, measures, verification steps, outputs, exit criteria) tailored from the organization's set of standard processes. • Change records for the defined process descriptions.	• Records of how the organizational standard process was tailored for a particular project or process application. • Artifacts showing that the defined process, as tailored, is followed.
Organizational Implementation Evidence		
Appraisal Team Notes		
Assessment Considerations	"The purpose of this generic practice is to establish and maintain a description of the process that is tailored from the organization's set of standard processes to address the needs of a specific instantiation." • Review definition of a "Defined Process." • A family of process descriptions may exist for use in different situations. • Separate process description need not exist for every PA; process descriptions may cover multiple PAs or part of a PA. • "Establish and maintain" implies usage, so it is expected that the defined processes are used by the projects or organization, tailored as appropriate, and revised as necessary.	
Process Management		
OPF	(see general evidence)	(see general evidence)
Organizational Implementation Evidence	(see general evidence)	(see general evidence)
Notes	This is an organizational process description for an organizational process and may be included in the plan.	
OPD (*IPPD)	(see general evidence)	(see general evidence)
Organizational Implementation Evidence	(see general evidence)	(see general evidence)
Notes	This is an organizational process description for an organizational process and may be included in the plan.	
OT	(see general evidence)	(see general evidence)
Organizational Implementation Evidence	(see general evidence)	(see general evidence)
Notes	This is an organizational process description for an organizational process and may be included in the plan.	
OPP	(see general evidence)	(see general evidence)

Table 22.4 (Continued)

PII Type	Direct Artifacts	Indirect Artifacts
Organizational Implementation Evidence		
Notes	This is an organizational process description for an organizational process and may be included in the plan.	
OID	(see general evidence)	
Organizational Implementation Evidence		
Notes	This is an organizational process description for an organizational process and may be included in the plan.	
Project Management		
PP	(see general evidence)	(see general evidence)
Project Implementation Evidence		
Notes		
PMC	(see general evidence)	(see general evidence)
Project Implementation Evidence		
Notes	This generic practice establishes and maintains a defined integrated project management process.	
SAM	(see general evidence)	(see general evidence)
Project Implementation Evidence		
Notes		
IPM (with IPPD)	(see general evidence)	(see general evidence)
Project Implementation Evidence		
Notes	This generic practice is different from the Establish the Project's Defined Process specific practice in this process area. The Establish the Project's Defined Process specific practice defines the project's defined process, which includes all processes that affect the project.	
PII Type	**Direct Artifacts**	**Indirect Artifacts**
RSKM	(see general evidence)	(see general evidence)
Project Implementation Evidence		
Notes		

Table 22.4 (Continued)

QPM	(see general evidence)	(see general evidence)
Project Implementation		
Evidence		
Notes		
Engineering		
REQM	(see general evidence)	(see general evidence)
Project Implementation		
Evidence		
Notes		
RD	(see general evidence)	(see general evidence)
Project Implementation		
Evidence		
Notes		
TS	(see general evidence)	(see general evidence)
Project Implementation		
Evidence		
Notes		
PI	(see general evidence)	(see general evidence)
Project Implementation		
Evidence		
Notes		
VER	(see general evidence)	(see general evidence)
Project Implementation		
Evidence		
Notes		
VAL	(see general evidence)	(see general evidence)
Project Implementation		
Evidence		
Notes		

Table 22.4 (Continued)

Support		
CM	(see general evidence)	(see general evidence)
Project Implementation		
Evidence		
Notes		
PPQA	(see general evidence)	(see general evidence)
Project Implementation		
Evidence		
Notes		
MA	(see general evidence)	(see general evidence)
Project Implementation		
Evidence		
Notes		
DAR	(see general evidence)	(see general evidence)
Project Implementation		
Evidence		
Notes		
CAR	(see general evidence)	(see general evidence)
Project Implementation		
Evidence		
Notes		

So Why Do PIIDs Take So Much Time?

The reason the PIIDs take so much time is that you need to collect a lot of data. To give you an idea, up to now in Tables 22.2, 22.3, and 22.4 we have seen blank PIIDs covering two specific practices and one generic practice covering 22 process areas for a total of 24 practices. For Maturity Level 2, the number of practices (specific and generic practices) for all 7 process areas comes out to 126 practices. So, that is 126 practices times the number of focus projects being appraised and that is just for Level 2. Table 22.5 shows the total number of practices for all the maturity levels.

Since there is so much data to collect in the PIIDs, you need to be sure that when your people fill them out they understand what is expected.

How Can I Screw Up a PIID?

Apparently, it's easy. Because so many organizations have trouble with PIIDs, this section contains some guidance on attributes of a good PIID, problems we have encountered with them, and solutions to those problems.

Critical attributes of a good PIID include:

- PIIDs clearly point to the artifacts
- PIIDs do not have blank entries
- PIIDs clearly address what the practice is asking for
- PIIDs demonstrate a history of consistent usage over time
- PIIDs list a specific document or artifact, not a repository or database
- PIIDs list a page or section in a large document with a specific reference to page number and section number
- PIIDs are under Version and Configuration Control
- PIIDs can be accessed via working hyperlinks in an electronic PIID repository

We discuss each of these concepts in turn.

PIID Attribute: PIIDs clearly point to the artifacts.
    Problem: If the reference is not clear, then the Appraisal Team cannot find the artifacts, resulting in wasted time and an unsuccessful appraisal.
    Solution: The entry needs to point to the actual, exact location of the artifact, and an artifact repository needs to be maintained. (The artifact may be paper or electronic.)
PIID Attribute: PIIDs do not have blank entries.

Table 22.5 Number of Practices By Maturity Level

	Maturity Level	Process Area	Number of Specific Practices
1	2	Requirements Management	5
2	2	Project Planning	14
3	2	Project Monitoring and Control	10
4	2	Supplier Agreement Management	8
5	2	Measurement and Analysis	8
6	2	Process and Product Quality Assurance	4
7	2	Configuration Management	7
		Total SPs for Maturity Level Two	**56**
8	3	Requirements Development	10
9	3	Technical Solution	8
10	3	Product Integration	9
11	3	Verification	8
12	3	Validation	5
13	3	Organizational Process Focus	9
14	3	Organizational Process Definition (with IPPD) (6 SPs without IPPD)	9
15	3	Organizational Training	7
16	3	Integrated Project Management (with IPPD) (9 SPs without IPPD)	14
17	3	Risk Management	7
18	3	Decision Analysis and Resolution	6
		Total SPs for Maturity Level Three	**148**
19	4	Organizational Process Performance	5
20	4	Quantitative Project Management	8
		Total SPs for Maturity Level Four	**161**
21	5	Organizational Innovation and Deployment	7
22	5	Causal Analysis and Resolution	5
		Total SPs for Maturity Level Five	**173**
		Total GPs for Maturity Level 2 (7 PAs * 10 GPs)	**70**
		Total GPs for Maturity Level 3 (18 PAs * 12 GPs)	**216**
		Total GPs for Maturity Level 4 (20 PAs * 12 GPs)	**240**
		Total GPs for Maturity Level 5 (7 PAs * 12 GPs)	**264**
		Total Practices (SPs and GPs) for Maturity Level 2	**126**
		Total Practices (SPs and GPs) for Maturity Level 3	**364**
		Total Practices (SPs and GPs) for Maturity Level 4	**401**
		Total Practices (SPs and GPs) for Maturity Level 5	**437**

Problem: If a PIID contains blanks, the Appraisal Team cannot tell if a blank entry is because the PIID is not finished or if the practice is not implemented.

Solution: Mark the entries as either "no evidence found" or "practice not implemented."

PIID Attribute: PIIDs clearly address what the practice is asking for.

Problem: The Appraisal Team cannot take time to go through materials that are not relevant and specific to the practice being investigated.

Solution: Understand the practices before you start completing the PIID form. Use the CMMI model book. Provide what is asked for on the PIID form.

PIID Attribute: PIIDs demonstrate a history of consistent usage over time.

Problem: Without historical data or multiple examples, the Appraisal Team cannot tell if the practice has only been done once or is in common usage.

Solution: Provide the last several occurrences (for example, the last three status reports or last two yearly training plans) to show trends. Provide the change log for a document.

PIID Attribute: PIIDs list a specific document or artifact, not a repository or database.

Problem: If the PIID does not contain the actual document, but simply a reference to where it may be found, the Appraisal Team will not know what document is relevant, resulting in wasted time and an unsuccessful appraisal.

Solution: Identify the individual document or file within the repository and specifically reference it. The more specific the reference, the better (see the next attribute).

PIID Attribute: PIIDs list a page or section in a large document with a specific reference to page number and section number.

Problem: The Appraisal Team does not have a lot of time to conduct its investigation. If the team must review a large document, the Appraisal Team may not know what page or section is relevant. They will not find the artifact or the correct evidence of implementation, resulting in wasted time and an unsuccessful appraisal.

Solution: Read the documents when building the PIIDs and capture page or section numbers.

PIID Attribute: PIIDs are under Version and Configuration Control.

Problem: The Appraisal Team can waste a lot of time by working on out-of-date PIIDs or the wrong versions.

Solution: Define a responsible person to maintain version and configuration control. Do not change the PIIDs after the onsite portion of the appraisal starts. Changing the PIIDs during the appraisal causes all of the information gained, investigation conducted, and SCAMPI steps performed up to this point to be nullified.

PIID Attribute: PIIDs can be accessed via working hyperlinks in an electronic PIID repository.

Problem: If the links do not work, the Appraisal Team can waste a lot of time and not find the required artifacts.

Solution: Have someone test every link. Verify that they are not broken and that all Appraisal Team Members have correct access rights. Make sure the Appraisal Team has the correct security to access the information required.

Data Consolidation Worksheets

What are Data Consolidation Worksheets? These are the worksheets used by the Appraisal Team Members to perform data consolidation. Data consolidation is the activity of collecting and summarizing all the appraisal information into a manageable set. We talked about data consolidation at length in Chapter 21, so we will not repeat that discussion here.

In our consultancy, we keep the PIIDs separate from the Data Consolidation Worksheets. It is the responsibility of the organization and projects to complete the PIIDs. It is the responsibility of the Appraisal Team Members to complete the Data Consolidation Worksheets. The Appraisal Team Members are individually, and as a team, responsible for reviewing the data in the PIID to ensure that the information is complete, correct, and it satisfies the expectation of the practice. We think this is important! Having separate Data Consolidation Worksheets helps keep the right focus. So, the organization enters the information into the PIIDs. The individual Appraisal Team Members review the information in the PIIDs and transfer only the correct and verified PIID information into the Data Consolidation Worksheets. The Appraisal Team Members then work together, as discussed in Chapter 21, to consolidate and reach consensus on the verified information.

Just like PIIDs, there is no "required" format or implementation for a Data Consolidation Worksheet. A Data Consolidation Worksheet can be implemented in Excel, Word, or a specialized database.

Table 22.6 is an example Data Consolidation Worksheet for the Requirements Management process area in a Maturity Level 2 appraisal. You will see that the example contains all five specific practices, SP 1.1 through SP 1.5, and all ten generic practices, GP 2.1 through GP 2.10. For each practice, you will see that there is space for an organizational-level entry and three other entries usually used for the focus projects. The column headings have the following meaning:

- Observations Strengths (Optional)/Weakness—Enter a textual observation about the data. You only need to enter text if it is a weakness.
- ATM Notes—Just a space to capture notes from the Appraisal Team Members.
- Direct—Use this to indicate a reference to a direct artifact (S for strength or W for weakness).
- Indirect—Use this to indicate a reference to an indirect artifact (S for strength or W for weakness).

Table 22.6 Example Data Consolidation Worksheet (REQM PA Maturity Level 2)

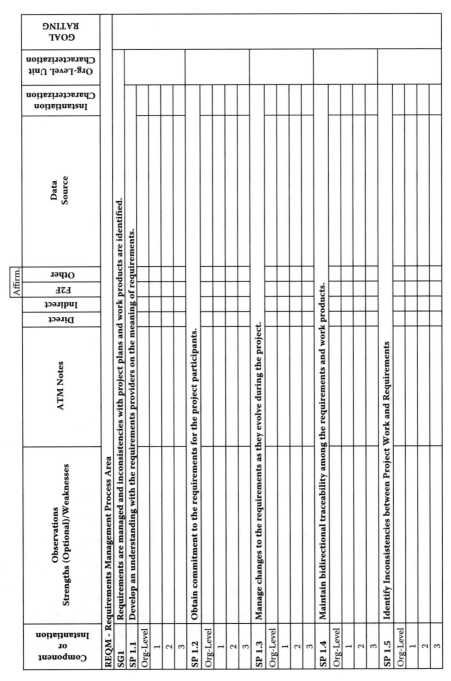

Component or Instantiation	Observations Strengths (Optional)/Weaknesses	ATM Notes	Direct	Indirect	F2F	Other	Data Source	Instantiation Characterization	Org-Level Unit Characterization	GOAL RATING
REQM – Requirements Management Process Area										
SG1	Requirements are managed and inconsistencies with project plans and work products are identified.									
SP 1.1	Develop an understanding with the requirements providers on the meaning of requirements.									
Org-Level										
1										
2										
3										
SP 1.2	Obtain commitment to the requirements for the project participants.									
Org-Level										
1										
2										
3										
SP 1.3	Manage changes to the requirements as they evolve during the project.									
Org-Level										
1										
2										
3										
SP 1.4	Maintain bidirectional traceability among the requirements and work products.									
Org-Level										
1										
2										
3										
SP 1.5	Identify Inconsistencies between Project Work and Requirements									
Org-Level										
1										
2										
3										

Affirm.

Table 22.6 (Continued)

Installation or Component	Observations Strengths (Optional)/Weaknesses	ATM Notes	Direct	Indirect	F2F	Other	Data Source	Instantiation Characterization	Org-Level Unit Characterization	GOAL RATING
GG2	The process is institutionalized as a managed process.									
GP 2.1	Establish and maintain an organizational policy for planning and performing the requirement management process.									
Org-Level										
1										
2										
3										
GP 2.2	Establish and maintain the plan for performing the requirements management process.									
Org-Level										
1										
2										
3										
GP 2.3	Provide adequate resources for performing the requirements management process, developing the work products, and providing the services of the process.									
Org-Level										
1										
2										
3										
GP 2.4	Assign responsibility and authority for performing the process, developing the work products, and providing the services of the requirements management process.									
Org-Level										
1										
2										
3										
GP 2.5	Train the people performing or supporting the requirements management process as needed.									
Org-Level										
1										
2										
3										

Affirm.

Table 22.6 (Continued)

Instantiation or Component	Observations Strengths (Optional)/Weaknesses	ATM Notes	Direct	Indirect	F2F	Other	Data Source	Instantiation Characterization	Org-Level, Unit Characterization	GOAL RATING
GP 2.6	Place designated work products of the requirements management process under appropriate levels of control.									
Org-Level										
1										
2										
GP 2.7	Identify and involve the revelant stakeholders of the requirements management process as planned.									
Org-Level										
1										
2										
3										
GP 2.8	Monitor and control the requirements management process against the plan for performing the process and take appropriate corrective action.									
Org-Level										
1										
2										
3										
GP 2.9	Objectively evaluate adherence of the requirements management process against its process description, standards, and procedures, and address non-compliance.									
Org-Level										
1										
2										
3										
GP 2.10	Review the activities, status, and results of the requirements management process with higher-level management and resolve issues.									
Org-Level										
1										
2										
3										

Affirm

- F2F—Use this for a face-to-face affirmation, usually an interview. This is also known as an oral affirmation. (S for strength or W for weakness)
- Other—Use this for any other kind of affirmation, for example, a presentation or a demonstration. (S for strength or W for weakness)
- Data Source—Description of the data source. What it is and where it came from. This can be a document by section or page, an interview by session code, or whatever clearly indicates the source. May be a hyperlink. (We recommend you avoid names of individuals.)
- Instantiation Characterizations—FI for Fully Implemented, LI for Largely Implemented, PI for Partially Implemented, NI for Not Implemented, NY for Not Yet (see Chapter 21, Table 21.6 for details).
- Org-Level Unit Characterizations—FI, LI, PI, NI, NY (see Chapter 21, Table 21.7 for details for the organization).
- Goal Rating—S for Satisfied, U for Unsatisfied, and NR for Not Rated (see Chapter 21, Table 21.8 for details).

Summary

PIIDS can be painful to complete because they are arranged differently from what resides in the organization's and projects' repositories, and because the arrangement of the information in the PIID may not be logical to the person completing the PIID. And yes, PIIDs are confusing and time consuming. Ask your Lead Appraiser for help in interpreting them as needed. Remember, your Lead Appraiser usually furnishes the PIIDs. If you find that you do not have the information requested by the PIIDs, you are in trouble. The evidence requested is based on the Typical Work Products and examples used in the CMMI. Perhaps you need to ask yourselves, have we really implemented our processes correctly? Direct and indirect artifacts are required for satisfaction of practices and process areas in the SCAMPI. Without having adequate documentation in your PIIDs, you will not have a successful SCAMPI.

ODDS AND ENDS VI

Chapter 23

Agile and the CMMI

This chapter discusses using Agile Methods with CMMI processes. Some of you will think we are crazy; that the two should never, and could never, mix. Au contraire. One of our clients, recently awarded CMMI Maturity Level 5, has blended the two approaches and seen significant benefits. Our client reports that productivity on Scrum teams (an Agile Method) is almost twice that of traditional teams. Projects demonstrated that using a story-based, test-driven approach to software development reduced defects found during final test by 40 percent. Another project finished early and reduced the number of coding defects in final test by 38 percent. Most organizations using Agile Methods do not report these figures because, since they chose Agile, most do not have the rigorous measurement processes in place to really prove these benefits. However, a CMMI Maturity Level 5 organization, with its databases of historical measurements, process performance baselines, and process performance models *must* be able to prove and defend their measures. So, we believe that the two approaches to software development can work, and do work, quite well together. However, like anything else, the devil is in the details. When reading this chapter, we ask that those of you who are experts in CMMI or Agile or both keep an open mind. There is no point in continuing turf wars. Can't we all just get along?

What Is Agile?

Well, if you have gotten this far in our book, and haven't skipped too many of the chapters, you probably have a good idea of what the CMMI is. So, we will not explain that. However, those of you reading a chapter on Agile in a book about the CMMI may be new to the idea of Agile. So, what is Agile all about? There are many names for Agile Methods and many types of Agile Methods. Agile is based on the tenets of something called the Agile Manifesto. The Agile Manifesto of the AgileAlliance (www.agilemanifesto.org) states:

> We are uncovering better ways of developing software by doing it and helping others do it. Through this work we have come to value:

> **Individuals and interactions** over processes and tools
> **Working software** over comprehensive documentation
> **Customer collaboration** over contract negotiation
> **Responding to change** over following a plan

That is, while there is value on the items on the right, we value the items on the left more.

The principles behind the Agile Manifesto are as follows:

1. Our highest priority is to satisfy the customer through early and continuous delivery of valuable software.
2. Welcome changing requirements, even late in development. Agile processes harness change for the customer's competitive advantage.
3. Deliver working software frequently, from a couple of weeks to a couple of months, with a preference to the shorter timescale.
4. Business people and developers must work together daily throughout the project.
5. Build projects around motivated individuals. Give them the environment and support they need, and trust them to get the job done.
6. The most efficient and effective method of conveying information to and within a development team is face-to-face conversation.
7. Working software is the primary measure of progress.
8. Agile processes promote sustainable development. The sponsors, developers, and users should be able to maintain a constant pace indefinitely.
9. Continuous attention to technical excellence and good design enhances agility.
10. Simplicity—the art of maximizing the amount of work not done—is essential.
11. The best architectures, requirements, and designs emerge from self-organizing teams.

12. At regular intervals, the team reflects on how to become more effective, then tunes and adjusts its behavior accordingly.

Agile Methodologies are usually implemented on small- to medium-sized teams that generate software in an environment with rapidly changing requirements or requirements that have not been defined in detail. Agile teams are usually colocated, usually with fewer than ten members. Agile Methods are also generally not used when developing life-critical, safety-critical systems. One reason is that Agile runs many tests during the development of the system. If you are developing nuclear bombs, testing the bomb again and again to see how well it works in this iteration is probably not a good idea. Other issues to consider when deciding if or how to implement Agile are requirements stability, geographical dispersion of the workforce, size of the application, and technical complexity.

Agile Methods

Some of the better known Agile Methods are:

- Extreme Programming (XP)
- Scrum
- Lean software development
- Adaptive Software Development (ASD)
- Dynamic Systems Development Method (DSDM)
- Feature Driven Development (FDD)

Most of our clients use Scrum as their Agile Method, so Scrum is the example Agile Method we used for this chapter.

What Is Scrum?

Scrum is a methodology that organizes projects into small, cross-functional teams. Work is organized and prioritized according to Product Backlogs. These backlog items are grouped into a series of short iteration tasks called Sprints. A brief meeting held daily (called a Scrum) communicates to the team the work that has been accomplished, what work needs to be done, and asks for input concerning possible barriers or problems that the team sees in accomplishing the work. These are generally standup meetings where each team member is asked, "What have you done since yesterday? What are you planning to do by tomorrow? Do you have any problems preventing you from accomplishing your goal?" A planning session is held that defines backlog items to be grouped into a Sprint. Sprint Retrospectives are held where team members discuss issues, accomplishments, and lessons learned about the previous Sprint. Customer input is highly sought, and customers may become part of the team. The customers must be able to provide the time and energy required to produce a good product. Working, intermediate products are verified by the customer or verified internally in increments; that is, as pieces or parts of the entire final product. These intermediate products are delivered as part of the development cycle in stages, not waiting to be delivered in whole at the end of the entire development cycle. Each delivery builds more and more functionality into the product. It should be noted that this incremental development approach relies on brevity—brief meetings, brief planning sessions, and brief customer commitment time periods. It also relies on frequency—frequent meetings, frequent planning and replanning, and frequent customer interaction.

Complementary Approaches

When we first read the Agile Manifesto we said, "That sounds like a well-executed CMMI project." One of the many misconceptions concerning CMMI is that you must write baskets and baskets of documentation that is only necessary to pass an appraisal. As we have cited often in this book, if you don't *use* the documentation you wrote, then you don't *have* any documentation. And we would also ask, "Why did you bother to write documentation that you have no intention of using?" We know why. Because it is hard to write something simple and straightforward, and easy to write something complicated and dense. (We know. We have done it ourselves and greatly struggled with this book to keep it simple when discussing difficult concepts.) We have tried to stress that you write documentation that you need and use. Other criticisms of the CMMI approach is that CMMI is often misunderstood as being strictly used in large, Department of Defense developments that take years, require massive documentation, require many layers of personnel, and use a rigid waterfall system development life cycle. Regarding Agile, we have all heard Agile Methods described by some as just another disguise for undisciplined hacking or by others as "we don't document." We know that this is not true. If your organization is basically cranking out code without any planning and without any documentation, you are *not* Agile. You are hackers. Other criticisms of Agile are that the methods lack structure, do not produce necessary documentation, require senior-level staffing, do not produce sufficient design architectures, are difficult to manage at a contract level, and place too much of a cultural-change burden on an organization. Each of these criticisms can be argued, as each has some degree of truth. But remember, all software development projects require talented personnel, all organizations undergo culture change, all software projects must be managed correctly, and all projects produce some sort of documentation somewhere for something.

We believe the value from Agile Methods can only be obtained through disciplined use. Our clients have found that using CMMI and Scrum together result in significantly improved performance while maintaining CMMI compliance. For Agile companies, we believe that using CMMI to institutionalize Agile practices is a big plus over undisciplined hacking.

How CMMI Can Be Used with Agile

An Agile company may implement Scrum or other Agile Methods but fail to achieve the benefits due to lack of institutionalization, or because of inconsistent or insufficient execution of engineering or management processes. CMMI can help Agile companies to institutionalize Agile Methods more consistently and understand what processes to address.

We believe that to fully realize all of the benefits of Agile Methods, a disciplined approach should be used. That is what we have seen with our customers. The CMMI concept of institutionalization can help establish this needed discipline. *Institutionalization* is defined in CMMI as "the ingrained way of doing business that an organization follows routinely as part of its corporate culture." Others have described institutionalization as simply "this is the way we do things around here." Note that institutionalization is an organizational-level concept that supports multiple projects. CMMI supports institutionalization through the generic practices (GP) associated with all process areas. For the purposes of our discussion, we will look at the 12 generic practices associated with Maturity Levels 2 and 3 in the CMMI, and how they might help an organization use Agile Methods.

Establish and Maintain an Organizational Policy for Planning and Performing Agile Methods (GP 2.1)

The first step toward institutionalization of Agile Methods is to establish how and when they will be used in the organization. An organization might determine that Agile Methods will be used on all projects or some subset of projects based on size, type of product, technology, or other factors. This policy is a way to clearly communicate the organization's intent regarding Agile Methods. In keeping with the Agile Principle of face-to-face conversations, an "all hands" meeting or a visit by a senior manager during a project's kickoff could be used to communicate the policy.

Establish and Maintain the Plan for Performing Agile Methods (GP 2.2)

This practice can help ensure that Agile Methods do not degrade into undisciplined hacking. The expectation is that Agile Methods are planned and that a defined process exists and is followed. The defined process should include a sequence of steps capturing the minimum essential information needed to describe what a project really does. The plan would also capture the essential aspects of how the other ten generic practices are to be implemented in the project. In Scrum, some of this planning is likely to be captured in a Product Backlog and/or Sprint Backlog, most likely within a tool as opposed to a document.

Provide Adequate Resources for Performing Agile Methods (GP 2.3)

Every project wants, needs, and expects competent professionals, adequate funding, and appropriate facilities and tools. Implementing an activity to explicitly manage these wants and needs has proved useful. In Scrum, for example, these needs may be reviewed and addressed at the Sprint Planning Meeting and reconsidered when significant changes occur.

Assign Responsibility and Authority for Performing Agile Methods (GP 2.4)

For a project to be successful, clear responsibility and authority need to be defined. Usually this includes a combination of role descriptions and assignments. The definitions of these roles identify a level of responsibility and authority. For example, a Scrum Project would assign an individual or individuals to the roles of Product Owner, ScrumMaster, and Team. Expertise in the Team is likely to include a mix of domain experts, system engineers, software engineers, architects, programmers, analysts, quality assurance experts, testers, user interface designers, and so forth. Scrum assigns the team as a whole the responsibility for delivering working software. The Product Owner is responsible for specifying and prioritizing the work. The ScrumMaster is responsible for assuring the Scrum process is followed. Management is responsible for providing the right expertise to the team.

Train the People Performing Agile Methods (GP 2.5)

The right training can increase the performance of competent professionals and supports introducing new methods into an organization. Institutionalization of the Agile Method being used requires consistent training. This practice includes determining the individuals to train, defining the exact training to provide, and performing the needed training. Training can be provided using many different approaches, including programmed instruction, formalized on-the-job training, mentoring, and formal and classroom training. It is important that a mechanism be defined to ensure that training has occurred and is beneficial.

Place Designated Work Products under Appropriate Level of Configuration Management (GP 2.6)

The purpose of a project is to produce deliverable products. This product is often a collection of a number of intermediate or supporting work products (code, manuals, software systems, build files, etc.). Each of these work products has a value and often goes through a series of steps that increase its value. The concept of configuration management is intended to protect these valuable work products by defining the level of control, for example, version control or baseline control and perhaps multiple levels of baseline control to use within the project.

Identify and Involve the Relevant Stakeholders as Planned (GP 2.7)

Involving the customer as a relevant stakeholder is a strength of Agile Methods. This practice further identifies the need to ensure that the expected level of stakeholder involvement occurs. For example, if the project depends on customer feedback with each increment, build, or Sprint, and customer involvement falls short of expectations, it becomes necessary to communicate the problem to the appropriate level, individual, or group in the organization. This group or individual will provide corrective action, as corrective action may be beyond the scope of the project team. In advanced Scrum implementations, this is often formalized as a MetaScrum where stakeholders serve as a board of directors for the Product Owner.

Monitor and Control Agile Methods against the Plan and Take Appropriate Corrective Action (GP 2.8)

This practice involves measuring actual performance against the project's plan and taking corrective action. Direct day-to-day monitoring is a strong feature of the Daily Scrum Meeting. The Release Burndown Chart shows how much work remains at the beginning of each Sprint, and the Sprint Burndown Chart shows total task hours remaining per day. Scrum enhances the effectiveness of the plan by allowing the Product Owner to inspect and adapt to maximize return on investment, rather than merely assuring plan accuracy.

Objectively Evaluate Adherence to the Agile Methods and Address Noncompliance (GP 2.9)

This practice is based on having someone not directly responsible for managing or performing project activities evaluate the actual activities of the project. Some organizations implement this practice as both an assurance activity and a coaching activity. The coaching concept matches many Agile Methods. The ScrumMaster has primary responsibility for adherence to Scrum practices, tracking progress, removing impediments, and resolving personnel problems, and is usually not engaged in implementation of project tasks. The Product Owner has primary responsibility for assuring software meets requirements and is of high quality.

Review the Activities, Status, and Results of the Agile Methods with Higher-Level Management and Resolve Issues (GP 2.10)

The purpose of this practice is to ensure that higher-level management has appropriate visibility into the project activities. Different managers have different needs for information. Agile Methods have a high level of interaction. For example, Scrum has a Sprint Planning Meeting, Daily Scrum Meetings, a Sprint Review Meeting, and a Sprint Retrospective Meeting. Management needs are supported by transparency of status data produced by the Scrum Burndown Chart combined with defect data. Management responsibilities are to (1) provide strategic vision, business strategy, and resources, (2) remove impediments surfaced by Scrum teams that the teams cannot remove themselves, (3) ensure growth and career path of staff, and (4) challenge the Scrum teams to move beyond mediocrity.

Establish and Maintain the Description of Agile Methods (GP 3.1)

This practice is a refinement of GP 2.2 described earlier. The only real difference is that the description of Agile Methods in this practice is expected to be organizationwide and not unique to a project. The result is that variability in how Agile Methods are performed would be reduced across the organization; and therefore more exchange between projects of people, tools, information, and products can be supported.

Collect the Results from Using Agile Methods to Support Future Use and Improve the Organization's Approach to Agile Methods (GP 3.2)

This practice supports the goal of learning across projects by collecting the results from individual projects. The Scrum Sprint Retrospective Meeting could be used as the mechanism for this practice.

All of these generic practices have been useful in organizations implementing other processes. We have seen that a number of these generic practices have at least partial support in Scrum or other Agile Methods. We believe that implementing these practices can help establish needed discipline in any Agile Method.

Using Agile in High-Maturity Organizations

Introducing Agile into an organization that is already functioning at a high maturity or capability level requires a cultural change. Our experience is that this culture change is easier to institute at the higher maturity organizations than at lower ones. Resistance to change has been (somewhat) overcome, as a high maturity organization has become used to introducing change in a controlled manner.

One of the changes when introducing Agile is to recalculate the process performance baselines and models to incorporate new measurements resulting from the new approach to structuring projects and receiving and analyzing the data these projects produce. There will be more instances of meetings, more intermediate work products, more testing and test results. All of these activities should generate more data that need to be fed into your measurement databases, baselines, and models. Most of the data that organizations collect and focus on seem to revolve around the cost of development and maintenance activities, effort distribution, defects, productivity calculations, and estimation and prediction capabilities. While all of this work appears overbearing, please remember that at the higher maturity organizations, these metrics are usually collected by automatic tools and at least initially reviewed and analyzed by the tools. These tools must be reset to incorporate the new data and the timing of the new data (both for collection and analysis). And updated review and analysis processes need to be generated.

Agile Approach to Process Improvement and SCAMPI

Two other issues remain to be addressed. One issue is using an Agile method as your process improvement approach. We have said in previous chapters that you should run your process improvement effort like any other project. That means that you have assigned a responsible person to manage it, you have devised a schedule with manageable milestones, you have organized tasks to produce deliverables, and you conducted frequent status reviews looking for progress or the lack thereof. Our clients have used Scrum for this effort, especially where Scrum can be used for Engineering Process Group (EPG) and Process Action Team (PAT) meetings.

The other issue is SCAMPI appraisals. Well, this book is about CMMI, not Agile, but suffice it to say that trying to explain using SCAMPI appraisals to rate an Agile implementation is very complicated and opens up a can of worms. However, we believe that some Scrum artifacts may serve as objective evidence during appraisals. Depending on the Scrum implementation, Product Backlogs might serve as requirements artifacts, and the Scrum meetings might satisfy some of the

Project Planning and Project Monitoring and Control practices. However, Scrum may not cover all the things that a project needs to do. Adopting Scrum (or any other Agile method) does not excuse an organization from following the rules of the appraisal. Agile adoption also does not allow broad appraisal tailoring decisions to be made (such as, "We don't do this because we are Agile."). If you are using Agile and desire a level rating of some sort, we suggest you choose your Lead Appraiser with care. Make sure your Lead Appraiser has a lot of experience in the CMMI approach to process improvement, SCAMPI appraisals, and Agile methods. Remember, SCAMPI appraisal results are subject to review by outside authorities, and it is not unreasonable to expect a reversal of ratings.

Summary

The key to blending Agile with CMMI is to build an organizational culture with a balance between discipline and change readiness. Companies in defense, aerospace, and other industries that require high maturity of processes, or those companies that require safety-critical or life-critical systems, should carefully consider introducing Agile practices into their existing development approaches using CMMI. While neither promoting nor discouraging the incorporation of Agile into your existing CMMI efforts, we have seen this approach work when properly managed. Our recommendation to the Agile community is to use the CMMI generic practices from CMMI Level 2 and Level 3 to amplify the benefits from Agile Methods. Our recommendation to the CMMI community is that Agile Methods can fit into your CMMI framework and will provide exciting improvements to your organization.

Chapter 24

Closing Thoughts

This chapter talks about odds and ends that we have either skipped over or not discussed in much detail. The purpose of this chapter is to give you some things to think about and to offer some final words of what we hope can be construed as wisdom.

Process Improvement Invades Your Life

It is amazing how your job becomes ingrained in your perceptions of everyday life. We have often spoken at the European Software Engineering Process Group (ESEPG) Conference in Amsterdam, and we also have often worked in Amsterdam. In all our years of working there, we have always talked about going to a comedy club but never managed to make it there. This past year, we did. The comedy club is Boom Chicago and presents improvisational comedy. While watching the performance (very funny—we recommend viewing a show), our process analysis viewpoint kicked in. What we discovered was that the improvisation part of the comedy really wasn't. The performers have predetermined skits that they perform, with predetermined roles, predetermined gags, and predetermined characters. In fact, one of the authors was selected to participate in the comedy act because he apparently fit all of the above set criteria. He is fat, gray bearded, and wears big glasses. He was also wearing a checked shirt, dark pants, and dark shoes. When the comedians saw him, they made up a character based on his looks and performed the associated skit. Was this coincidence? No. He matched their predetermined criteria. They already had a checked shirt, dark pants, dark shoes, gray wig, gray beard, big glasses, and a pillow to stuff into the shirt.

And what about the content of the comedy skits? Consider the venue for these shows:

- Tourists
- Amsterdam
- Drugs
- Sex
- Attitudes

So, whenever the comedians asked for situations and suggestions from the audience, these were the suggestions they received. The comedians also rejected any that they "didn't like," that is, did not have skits for. The point is, although this show was billed as "improvisational," they already had a set structure (a set of standard processes) in place. Without it, they would not be successful. True, there is room for improvisation, just as there is room for interpretation and tailoring of organizational processes in process improvement. But you have to have something to begin with.

Gee, aren't we a lot of fun? You can't take us anywhere.

Change Management

We have avoided talking about change management in this book. By "change management," we don't mean managing change as discussed in the CMMI process areas (PAs). The CMMI talks about managing changes to requirements in the Requirements Management PA; about managing systemic changes in Configuration Management; and about managing changes to management plans in Project Planning and in Project Monitoring and Control. That is not the kind of change management we need to discuss.

The type of change management that needs to be addressed is that of changing the culture in your organization. There are many books on this subject, most of which will have you determine what type of organizational paradigm you match (e.g., open, closed, random, synchronous), the type of management style prevalent (e.g., dictator, collaborative, charismatic), and the category of change implementation you prefer (e.g., early adopter versus late adopter). Most of these books are written by social scientists, not by engineers. This is actually a good thing because most engineers prefer a carefully laid-out, step-by-step game plan that addresses technical problems in the organization, not people problems. And people can be a problem. Just think how much easier it would be to make this process improvement stuff work if you didn't have to bother with the people you run into everyday in your workplace. Well, that's the same kind of thinking that suggests that systems would be a lot easier to build and deliver if it weren't for all of those damn users out there.

The same holds true for process improvement. Process improvement is all about change. If you don't really want to change, then don't start this journey. Period. The Software Engineering Institute has a line that goes, "If the level of discomfort is not high enough, then change will not occur." So, while people might complain about the way things are done, if the way things are done is not totally intolerable, you will have a fight on your hands to implement and institutionalize the changes that come with process improvement. Because people *hate* change.

How can you overcome this resistance to change? Well, there are several approaches, but most boil down into two methods:

- Force change (the hammer principle)
- Reward change (the dangling carrot principle, using benefits and bonuses)

The first method, called the hammer technique, is when the head honcho in your place of work (the president, the CEO, your boss) says, "either we get that level or you lose your job." Anyone found not following the newly written procedures (even if the procedures don't fit the organization) is punished. This technique, while draconian, has been known to work.

The second method, where change is rewarded, is when the organization comes up with awards, bonuses, promotions, positive attention, and proof that the new way of doing things creates a better work environment where the person doing the work has more control over his day-to-day duties. This approach has also been known to work.

Wait a minute! *Both* approaches work? Of course. As you will find with most anything in process improvement, every time you ask a question the answer begins with "it depends." While some of the people responding might be trying to give you a snow job, "it depends" is often the best answer. So what does "it depend" on:

- The size of your organization
- The culture
- The budget
- The type of work
- The history of introducing and accepting new ideas
- The type of people
- Personalities and egos
- Politics
- Consistent approach and commitment

And many more issues. So, take into consideration the type of place in which you work, and tailor and customize your process improvement efforts to it. And then start over again because you will be wrong. Expect missteps and stumbling blocks. There is no true step-by-step approach that works brilliantly each and every time. We have tried to summarize best practices that we have seen applied effectively in organizations that we have worked with. So take these lessons learned, and try them on for size. As with anything you try on, you may need to go up or down a size, and maybe the color isn't quite right for you. But at least it's a start.

If we had to pick one overall initial stumbling block that we have run into, it is that some people see their world through rose-colored glasses or prefer living in denial, to wit, "there are no problems in my organization/project." Well, guess what? It's called process improvement. If there are no problems, if everything is perfect, then you don't need to improve. But since you have already decided (or someone has decided for you) to do process improvement (probably for the mandated rating for business contract awards), then you will have to change. To prove it, do an appraisal using the CMMI as the reference model. That first appraisal is always an eye-opener. When you match your organization's practices against the CMMI's practices, you will find that there are gaps. Those gaps can be considered problems, or areas of improvement. Start there.

It's great to talk about the need for change, and accepting that change is part of process improvement. But how do we get from here to there?

Which brings us to Dr. Phil. Dr. Phil currently hosts his own television show, which, among other things, is about change. Now, Dr. Phil concentrates on changing people's personal lives; that is, losing weight, overcoming past slights, and becoming a better person overall. While we like Dr. Phil's no-nonsense approach (which seems to be what attracts most people to his show, as well as his folksy humor and country-boy ways of turning a phrase), we sometimes disagree with him on his solutions for problem resolution.

Dr. Phil makes no bones about the fact that he is not offering psychological counseling for the long term. Dr. Phil offers people what he calls "a wakeup call." This wakeup call is supposed to change your life, and apparently in most cases it does. However, he did one show where he offered solutions. In this case, we don't think he really accomplished what he set out to do.

On this one show, Dr. Phil interviewed a woman who was upset about her young daughter's weight. The mother, intending to motivate her daughter to lose weight, would call her daughter names, like fat and stupid. Did this inspire her daughter to lose weight? Of course not. Did the mother know she was not really helping? Yes. The reason the mother went on the show was for help in stopping her diatribes against the daughter and for help in replacing her (the mother's) bad habits with good, new ones.

What did Dr. Phil do? He said he gave her steps to help. He basically had her review the tape to see how she was hurting her daughter and destroying any positive self-image the girl might have once had. The mother then said, "I know what I am doing is wrong, but I can't stop. What should I do?" Dr. Phil responded by asking if she hadn't heard him correctly. Didn't watching the tape and hearing the discussion between Dr. Phil, the mother, and the daughter give her any insights?

Well, we guess it did for her, but we felt cheated. We didn't hear any sequenced steps of how to change her behavior. We would have liked something like the following (and we are not psychologists—this is just an example):

- Take a deep breath, and let it out slowly when you feel like criticizing.
- Look at your daughter and try to see her as the beautiful, young girl she is.
- Tell her something nice, something that you like about her.
- If you can't think of anything, lie. Come up with something. Use your imagination.

What does this have to do with process improvement? Everything.

What this woman had learned from her short time with Dr. Phil was the process of her actions. What she wanted was procedures detailing what to do, when, and how. If you want change to occur in your organization, you must not only give wakeup calls, but follow through with instructions that support the changes needed.

Rewards and Punishment

Sociological and psychological studies have been done that conclude that the best way to ensure long-lasting change is through positive, not negative, reinforcement. To that end, your organization needs to devise a new reward system. Instead of rewarding the guy who always stays late when a new system is going into production or is to be shipped to the customer, why not ask yourself, "Why is this guy staying late? Is he incompetent? Does he purposely wait to start his duties until the last minute? Does he enjoy the attention he gets from 'saving the show'? Did he do anything to obstruct the system going in more smoothly that necessitated his staying late? Did he not plan his work correctly? Did I not plan the work correctly? Did we not adequately staff this job?" The point is, the reward system must change. Reward people for doing their jobs right the first time, not for acting like saviors and pulling all-nighters. Our motto is "Dare to Be Dull." Or another way to think of it is "No Surprises."

One of the best "rewards" to demonstrate to process improvement novices, and to your organization as a whole, is the WIFM effect; that is, what's in it for me. If you can tie process improvement activities to potential benefits that people in your organization can realize and respond to, then more people will be able to overcome their fear of change and be co-opted into the process improvement challenge.

It is naïve to think that only positive reinforcement will promote process improvement. It would be wonderful if your organization hired only truly altruistic people who would put everyone else's needs and desires above their own so that process improvement could occur, the organization could get its ratings, business contracts would ensue, and everyone would live happily ever after in fairyland.

It doesn't happen that way. Yes, you should be open to changing your very hard-written procedures if they don't work. They will always need modification. But, if people are not following the procedures, and not contributing to improving them, then these people need to have what we have heard called a "come to Jesus meeting" with senior management, and get told to "get with the program."

People need a way to clearly communicate when the procedures are not working. A well-managed improvement proposal process serves two primary purposes: one, to capture real problems with the processes and procedures; and two, it gives people a way to complain. Face it, change is hard. We have worked with a lot of people that just need to voice their complaints and then they get on with the work. Don't overlook this human need to have their voices heard and to feel as if they are part of the process of process improvement.

Management Commitment

We were once at a conference where Watts Humphrey (who many people consider to be the father of process improvement using the CMM) was the featured speaker. At the end of his lecture, he asked for questions. One brave soul stood up and launched into a dissertation about the lack of support his organization was getting from senior management. Senior management expected the organization to achieve a certain level rating by a specific date, yet it had not adequately staffed and funded the effort. Whenever there was a problem in production, the process improvement people were told to return to their old jobs and do "real work." Basically, there was no management commitment to this effort. The poor soul then asked Watts Humphrey, "What should I do?" Watts responded by saying, "Quit."

When we heard this response, we were furious. This poor man had bared his soul to the assembled crowd and was desperate for a plan of attack that would yield positive results, and quite probably, help him keep his job. And all he had received was a terse, one-word answer—"Quit." How arrogant of Watts Humphrey to respond in such an unhelpful manner.

Well, after thinking about it for a while (and being placed in similar situations many times), we can't help but agree. True management commitment is absolutely necessary. How can you measure true commitment? Easy, put your money where your mouth is. In other words, ask your management and your sponsors the following questions:

- Have you given us enough time to do this?
- Have you given us enough money in the budget to do this?
- Have you given us enough people to do this?
- Have you given us the right people to do this?
- Have you given us authority to act, not just made us responsible?
- Have you really developed a vision of what the true problems are?

- Have you really developed a vision of what you want this organization to do?
- Have you made this effort *the* priority in your organization?
- Do you really understand what process improvement is and how it will affect everyone—including management—in the organization?
- Do you realize that *you* have to change, not just your people?
- Do you realize that *your* work will be scrutinized, as well as your lower-level managers?

If the answers are yes, then maybe you have a chance. One of the things that we have learned over the years is that an organization takes on the behavior characteristics of its leaders. We have seen this at all levels in the organization. If management won't change, then the organization can't change. *Period.*

Quality Assurance Is the Key

An independent and objective quality assurance (QA) department is the key to implementing and institutionalizing change management and process improvement. By independent and objective, we mean that the people performing the QA activities are not under undue influence to just let things slide. They also have a reporting chain that is separate from the managers and individuals whose work they are reviewing. Job performance and evaluation of QA personnel should also be independent of individuals associated with the work being reviewed.

This battle for establishing a separate QA office is one of our most frequent. Organizations simply do not want to budget for staff that does not directly contribute to building the product. Smaller organizations have difficulty budgeting for this duty, and those organizations that cannot shift the cost onto the customer also stall this effort. Some organizations decide that they will have the programmers from one team perform QA reviews on the work of programmers from another team. While this sounds OK at first, it often doesn't work out that way. Why not? Because people start making deals: "If you pass my stuff, I'll pass yours." Also, most of these people have not been trained in QA, don't understand what QA is really about, and don't realize the importance of QA activities. They'd rather be programming, building, or testing things.

Let's talk about human nature. Most of us try to do a good job. But, when we know that someone will be looking at and reviewing what we do, and how we do it, we tend to pay a little more attention to the details and maybe try a little bit harder to make sure everything works right. QA also enforces following procedures and notifies the process group and management when the procedures don't work. Most organizations are under a lot of schedule pressure. Scheduling often gets attention because it is easy to see, that is, the date is here and the product did not ship. Quality is harder to see.

Another advantage of having independent, objective QA staff is when things go wrong or are about to go wrong. If your procedures say that the product cannot be delivered until certain defects have been fixed and the tests show that these defects have not been fixed, QA can step in and notify/argue with senior management and delay shipment. If shipment is not delayed, QA can at least make sure that senior management signs off on the shipment with the understanding of all the defects and their ramifications. So, when customers receive products that don't work as expected, finger-pointing back to the worker bees can be reduced. (There are reasons why shipping a defective product may be a good idea and a wise executive decision, but we won't go into that here.)

In previous chapters, we discussed metrics and data collection. QA is a great place to report metrics that measure how things are working or not working in the projects, and then have QA report its findings to management. So, if one project manager tells senior management that this project is "on track," QA can dispute that by showing the milestones missed and expected project delays. QA can also report the metrics that track the results of peer reviews and testing that demonstrate the quality of the product (or lack thereof). The metrics collected as part of the normal QA activities cited in the Process and Product Assurance process area of the CMMI can be used to accurately measure progress and quality, and should be reported as part of management reviews.

A last point on QA. You need to staff QA with enough qualified people to get the work done. We have seen a lot of organizations that go through the motions and create a QA group out of the people that "can't do real work." And of course this approach fails. QA needs to be staffed by professionals that will be respected across the organization for their contributions. And the QA staff needs to be large enough to do the work. For most organizations, we recommend at least 5 percent of the development and maintenance budget be allocated to QA staffing and activities.

CMMI Perspective

Not too long ago, we met with a senior executive. The executive had been given the task by his board of directors to lower software costs in his company. We asked the man what we thought were two simple questions: "How much are your software costs?" and "What do you include in software costs?" You may be surprised to know that he did not have an answer to either question. He was talking to us—and as many experts as he could find—to help come up with a plan. What was interesting was that he told us that our plan based on the CMMI was the most logical and complete that he had heard. He felt that while the plans from other experts (representing Six Sigma, Lean, and specific design approaches) provided some good techniques, they were not as well suited to his total problem. The other plans focused too closely on improving subprocesses or only on parts of the organization's processes, and not on the overall processes and problems across his organization.

CMMI took a synergistic approach that looked at his entire organization and how the different parts of his organization worked—or did not work—together.

Summary

Process improvement and change go hand in hand. You cannot have one without the other. Everyone must change, including technicians, practitioners, management, quality assurance, engineers, process improvement personnel, and even users and customers. Change is painful. If the pain of how you currently do your job is not high enough, then you probably will not change the way you do your job.

We don't usually tell jokes, and most people don't understand our jokes, but we are reminded of one. It's the old joke about changing light bulbs. Question: How many psychiatrists does it take to change a light bulb? Answer: One. But the light bulb has to really want to change. The same goes for process improvement.

If you are not really going to do process improvement, burn this book.

Good luck on your journey.

References and Further Reading

Florac, William, and Anita Carleton. *Measuring the Software Process*. Reading, MA: Addison Wesley, 1999.

Johnson, Kent, and Joe Dindo. "Expanding the Focus of Software Process Improvement to Include Systems Engineering." *Crosstalk*, October 1998.

Kan, Stephen. *Metrics and Models in Software Quality Engineering*. Reading, MA: Addison Wesley, 1995.

Kulpa, Margaret. "Ten Things Your Mother Never Told You about the Capability Maturity Model." *Crosstalk*, September 1998.

Kulpa, Margaret. "Why Should I Use the People CMM®?" *Crosstalk*, November 2007.

McGarry, John, David Card, Cheryl Jones, Beth Layman, Elizabeth Clark, Joseph Dean, and Fred Hall. *Practical Software Measurement*. Boston: Addison Wesley, 2002.

Software Engineering Institute. *Appraisal Requirements for CMMI®, Version 1.2 (ARC, V1.2)*. www.sei.cmu.edu.

Software Engineering Institute. *Handbook for Conducting Standard CMMI Appraisal Method for Process Improvement (SCAMPI) B and C Appraisals, Version 1.1*. www.sei.cmu.edu.

Software Engineering Institute. *Standard CMMI® Appraisal Method for Process Improvement (SCAMPI^SM) A, Version 1.2: Method Description Document (MDD)*. www.sei.cmu.edu.

Wheeler, Donald J. *Understanding Variation: The Key to Managing Chaos*. Knoxville, TN: SPC Press, 2000.

APPENDICES

Appendix A: Comparing CBI-IPI to SCE to SCAMPI

Once upon a time, there were three assessment types:

- Software Capability Evaluations (SCEs)
- CMM-Based Appraisals for Internal Process Improvement (CBA IPIs)
- Standard CMMI Appraisal Method for Process Improvement (SCAMPI)

Your organization may have heard of these assessments or even participated in one or more. The latest type is the SCAMPI. Because the SCAMPI is based on the techniques of its predecessors, we describe each in turn.

History

Previously, there were three families of SCEs:

- Acquisition
- Contract Monitoring/Process Monitoring
- Internal Evaluations

Compared to only one type of CBA IPI:

- Internal Process Improvement (IPI)

An Acquisition SCE was used by an organization to evaluate the capabilities of vendors vying for contracts; a Contract Monitoring SCE was used to monitor the performance of vendors or in-house units performing contracts; a Process Monitoring SCE was used to baseline current performance and then later to measure progress against that baseline; and an Internal Evaluation was used to baseline practices internal to an organization, begin internal process improvement activities, and measure progress. This last usage of the SCE maps to the functionality provided by the CBA-IPI, and corresponds to the Diagnosing phase of the IDEAL^{SM} model.

Historically, SCEs were first designed only for Acquisition SCEs, that is, for an organization or company to assess the capability of vendors vying for contracts to determine the risk associated with awarding the contract to the proposed vendors. This single application was later broadened. SCEs were used by organizations for software process improvement (a la CBA IPIs), as well as for acquisitions and contract monitoring. SCEs were originally designed to be applied against any of the existing CMMs, notably the CMM for Software and the Software Acquisition CMM.

Training

Some organizations would choose to do CBA IPIs because they thought they were saving money on training. During a CBA IPI, a Lead Assessor could only train his team in the fundamentals of the CMM (approximately three days), the basic steps in the CBA IPI (approximately two to four days), and then conduct the CBA IPI (on three to eight projects; this was tailorable). A team that was trained by the Lead Assessor could have been exposed to only the viewpoint and interpretation of that Lead Assessor. If team members chose to go on and become Lead Assessors, no matter how many times they had done CBA IPIs and completed the training for that CBA IPI, they were required to attend the Introduction to the CMM class conducted by a Software Engineering Institute (SEI)–authorized vendor before beginning Lead Assessor training.

For a SCE, the student had to take the Introduction to the CMM from an SEI-authorized vendor before SCE training. Some of the qualifications for an individual to get into SCE training were at least:

- 7 years of increasingly responsible software development experience (spread out among systems analysis, coding, testing, configuration management, quality assurance, systems programming, database administration and analysis, for example)
- 3 years of project management experience (costing, budgeting, tracking, scheduling)
- 2 years of acquisition experience (for federal acquisition/procurement SCEs only)

The 7-3-2 prerequisites were dropped as mandatory later on. The cost savings in training were that the student did not have to repeat the two courses (Introduction to CMM and SCE Training class) again in order to participate in more SCEs. By taking the courses before performing on the SCE team, the student also received the benefit of being instructed by several people who may have had different interpretations of the CMM.

Conduct

Both SCEs and IPIs were conducted by a "Lead"—either a Lead Evaluator (SCEs) or a Lead Assessor (IPIs). This lead must have participated in at least two previous SCEs (for the evaluator) or two previous IPIs (for the assessor) in order to qualify for training. (SCEs could not be substituted for IPIs; IPIs could not be substituted for SCEs). The training was mandatory and was only conducted by the SEI.

The SCE was led by the SEI-certified Lead Evaluator. The SCE usually did not include members of the organization on the team, depending on the type of SCE, and depending on whether financial remuneration or contract award was to be based on the outcome. For an internal evaluation, the team *must* have included members internal to the organization under review.

The IPI was led by an SEI-certified Lead Assessor. The Lead Assessor, as part of the method, had to train the members of the team (even if they had already participated on an IPI). The team had to consist of members of the organization being assessed.

Similarities and Differences

Both SCEs and IPIs sought to understand how an organization operated compared to the CMM. Both looked for strengths, weaknesses, and consistency across the organization by reviewing project activities. Both were used for software process improvement. Both conducted site visits and reviewed existing documentation. Both resulted in developing Action Plans (except for Acquisition SCEs; for Acquisition SCEs, Action Planning was left up to the vendor awarded the contract). For maturity-level ratings, both assessed organizations. Both methods had a trained leader, either an SEI-authorized Lead Assessor or an SEI-authorized Lead Evaluator.

Originally, SCEs only evaluated three to five projects in a five-day onsite visit, while CBA IPIs usually looked at four to eight projects in a five- to ten-day onsite period. Later, for SCEs, both the number of projects and the time spent onsite became tailorable to the organization's needs. The two prevailing misconceptions about SCEs are that they were only used for acquisitions, not improvement activities, and that they only looked at three projects within a five-day limitation.

One other difference existed, depending on the type of SCE (SCE family). If the SCE was done with financial incentives as a possible result of the rating (such as award fees), or if it was an acquisition SCE, members of the evaluated organization could not participate on the SCE team (conflict-of-interest rules applied to prevent predisposing the actions and results of the team). However, for improvement activities (the third SCE family listed), members of the organization were allowed to be part of the team and were an essential part of the team.

The final difference was a big one. SCE results were protestable in a court of law. Big bucks were involved with contract awards based on SCE results. Therefore, because the SCE team could have been sued, most SCEs were held to rigorous standards. The rigor of the SCE method was not tailorable depending on the SCE family invoked. In other words, the Internal SCE was conducted as rigorously as the Acquisition SCE.

SCAMPI and CMMI

The SEI generated a new model, the CMMI, and a new appraisal methodology, SCAMPI. The SCAMPI method now incorporates a number of the principles of the SCE and CBA-IPI. SCAMPI can be used for assessments (now called appraisals) on both the staged and continuous repsresentations of the CMMI. SCAMPI is an appraisal method for organizations that want to evaluate their own or another organization's processes using the CMMI as their reference model. SCAMPI consists of a structured set of team activities that include conducting interviews, reviewing documents, and receiving and giving presentations. Several projects, process areas, and maturity or capability levels may be investigated. SCAMPI results are ratings (although providing a rating is sometimes optional) and findings of strengths, weaknesses, and improvement activities using the CMMI. What are these results used for? To award contracts and to baseline processes for process improvement. Results are based on how the organization satisfies the goals for each process area. So, the steps in the SCAMPI are basically:

- Documentation is gathered and reviewed
- Interviews are conducted
- Deficiencies are discovered and documented
- Findings are presented

And the primary components of a SCAMPI are:

- Planning and preparing for the appraisal
- Collecting and consolidating data, both before and during the appraisal
- Making judgments
- Determining ratings (if requested by the organization and if allowed by the type of SCAMPI conducted)
- Reporting results

There are three types of appraisals: Class A, B, and C. Each class is distinguished by its degree of rigor. SCAMPI is discussed in greater detail in Chapters 20, 21, and 22.

Appendix B: Myths and Legends of the CMMI

These myths and legends have been gathered from the marketing of the CMMI, user perceptions, organizational implementations of the model, appraisals, public statements made during conferences, and conflicting statements in the CMMI itself. The authors of this book do not make any claims as to these arguments. We believe the reader should be able to make up his own mind.

1. CMM Maturity Level 2 is the same as CMMI Maturity Level 2.

   Because several of the process areas are named the same, uninitiated users feel that the two models are not significantly different. We disagree. For example, Requirements Management under the CMM only included requirements as they related to building your software. So while you may have had some systemwide requirements, the only responsibility you had toward them was to use them as the basis for initially deriving software-related requirements. You did not have to ensure that the higher-level requirements had been met. Now, Requirements Management under CMMI includes *all* requirements—from the systems engineering people, the hardware people, the software people, and any other requirements that need to be met. So the scope has been greatly expanded. In addition, a few more process areas have been added. For example, Measurement and Analysis is now its own process area (PA), and includes not only metrics to collect, but describes different activities recommended/required to be instituted. Most smaller organizations and less mature organizations have indicated that this is a good PA, but far too difficult to implement at Level 2. So with the increased scope of the model including the various disciplines (systems engineering, hardware engineering, etc.), plus the additional PAs, the two models and the two levels are dissimilar.

2. The process areas and practices for Levels 4 and 5 do not significantly raise the bar, as higher maturity organizations helped devise this model.

373

Reports from earlier appraisals done by the Ministry of Defence in Australia have specifically reported that the CMMI has made achieving Level 4 and 5 much more difficult. Whereas in the previous CMM for Software, the recommendation was to "keep it simple," now the implementation of these areas requires much more training and quantitative measurement techniques to be instituted in the organization. Responses heard at industry conferences have also mentioned that the CMMI focuses too heavily on sophisticated measurement techniques.

3. Transitioning from the CMM to the CMMI will be a trivial effort.

   Not if you read and understand points 1 and 2. There are also more procedures and training to be done, due to the additional process areas included in the model, and more people and groups to get involved. A presentation at the European SEPG Conference in Amsterdam described one organization's attempt to transition from the Systems Engineering Maturity Model, which it had been using for two to three years, to CMMI. The organization described its struggle as "significant."

4. The continuous representation allows you to select fewer process areas to institutionalize.

   Well, sort of. Yes, you can deselect PAs. But it doesn't really save an organization much in time, effort, and cost because the PAs are so interrelated and interdependent that you will soon discover that you must back up and include more and more PAs (or at least, several of the practices contained within the PAs) to be successful. For instance, in the continuous representation, how can you attempt Validation, or Verification, or practically any other process area without also tackling to some extent Project Planning, Project Monitoring and Control, and Process and Product Quality Assurance? Don't you need to plan, track, and ensure the quality of your product or process? And the generic goals and generic practices seem to enforce that you do so. So where do you go for guidance in structuring this effort? To those PAs that directly relate to them. So, those of you thinking of selecting the continuous representation so that you can select only a few process areas for improvement may be disappointed.

5. There are fewer procedures to write in the CMMI than in the CMM.

   Hahahahahahahahahaha. Big laugh there. The CMM specifically called out the phrase "according to a documented procedure." However, those of you who have done process improvement have noticed that just because the CMM did not specifically call out the use of a procedure, one was often required to enlighten your staff as to *how* to perform a function and *how* to perform this function consistently within a project or across many projects. The phrase "according to a documented procedure" is rarely if ever used in the CMMI. But, if you read what constitutes a "plan" in the CMMI, you will find that it includes a process description. So, just because the CMMI does not specifically reference the term *procedures* it does not mean that there don't need to be any. We also have found that most of the procedures an organization writes relate to how to implement the practices and subpractices within the process areas. Well, just looking at the CMMI demonstrates that there are an awful lot of PAs and practices included. So, better get cracking on those procedures.

6. CMMI is not prescriptive.

The CMMI consists of many process areas. Those process areas are so interrelated as to make them mandatory. While tailoring of the model is discussed in the body of the CMMI (with tailoring meaning "tailoring out" a process or practice) the resulting instructions or information describing tailoring options tend to disparage the tailoring out of anything. We feel that the process areas listed and their accompanying practices basically attempt to provide the steps that *must* be taken to achieve a level, or to be successful in improving your organization's process capability.

Where the model is not prescriptive is in the details describing the practices. This omission is unfortunate, as that is the area where more guidance is necessary but cannot really be found. Appraisal teams have reported that during SCAMPIs, it was difficult to not ask yes/no questions when trying to ascertain whether a practice had been implemented and how it had been implemented. And when more guidance was needed to understand the practice, there was none. To fix this problem, the new model has added additional Hints and Tips. While the information contained in these Hints and Tips is interesting and sometimes helpful, there is not a lot of interpretive guidance given.

7. CMMI is based on the best practices and lessons learned reported from usage of the CMM.

At the 2002 SEPG Conference in Phoenix, Arizona, this question was specifically asked of three of the authors of the original CMM for Software. Their presentation was about what they would have included in the CMM, based on what they now know many years later, having assessed or assisted in many implementations in many organizations. The question posed was, based on their discussion, were any of these lessons learned included in the CMMI? Their response was a moment of silence, and then a reference to Organizational Innovation and Deployment (OID at Level 5). Although CMMI purports to include the improvements devised under CMM version 2.0, that statement was also heatedly discussed during the same conference in a later presentation. (Buttons were handed out at this presentation that said, "Free version 2.0.") As a contributor to CMM version 2.0, one of the authors of this book does not see much of a resemblance. The newer version of the CMMI, version 1.2, is based on the previous version and has the same discrepancies.

8. CMMI was the result of overwhelming demand across the industry.

While there were some requests that we personally knew about (from DOD aerospace contractors), most organizations were busy using the CMM for Software, with a lesser number of organizations implementing the Systems Engineering Maturity Model. However, some organizations wishing to expand the sphere of influence of the CMM for Software to a more enterprise-wide application simply took the word *software* out of the CMM, and used the CMM across their enterprise. After all, the CMM was touted as being based on project management principles that could be expanded to include almost any type of project. Several presentations from organizations at the European SEPG Conference in Amsterdam described their efforts tailoring the CMM for more than software tasks, and these organizations seemed to have been quite effective in this deployment. While there may have been a DOD mandate for the generation of this model and the integration of all existing models, we know of no large outpouring of grief that an integrated model had not been created.

And is the CMMI really one integrated model? Well, if you can select the disciplines, and you can divide it up into systems engineering, software engineering, and IPPD, then no. While the areas are interrelated, they are not really integrated into one seamless model.

9. CMMI supports organizational business objectives.

One of the problems we often encounter is that most organizations (especially those new to process improvement) have no defined business objectives. They just want to "make money." So, CMMI support for your business objectives depends on what your organization's business objectives actually are and the extent to which you have defined them. Are they to save money? Well, maybe the CMMI will help and maybe not. Do you have the resources and funds to dedicate to process improvement using the CMMI? Do you have problems in your organization that can benefit from providing structure and documenting your processes? Maybe, maybe not. It all depends on your organization. And no, the CMMI—like the CMM—is *not* for every organization. We cannot find statistics that detail the number of organizations that begin this journey and then drop out. We can only find data on organizations that have achieved a level rating and been awarded contracts. How many of you have worked in organizations that needed to achieve Level 3 for contract awards, and once it was achieved, those organizations dropped out of the program? We know of several organizations like that. We also know of many organizations that drop out during the road to Level 2. There are many reasons, from not having the budget to not having enough people to not having the right people to being driven by time-to-market to not being able to support the time it takes to institute this path, and so on. Also, it takes a somewhat mature organization to actually have achievable business objectives that can be used to map to the CMMI. Most organizations simply say their business objective is Level 3 for contract awards so they can make money.

10. CMMI leads to consistent appraisal results and ratings.

The SCAMPI method using the CMMI has the same problems as the previous assessment methods using the CMM—that is, the makeup of the team members and their individual experiences will flavor their interpretations of the model, and their interpretations of the implementation of the model in the assessed organization. As discussed previously, SCAMPI teams are having trouble interpreting the practices. They refer to the explanations in the practices in the model and come up lacking enough explanatory information. So most teams have reported simply using their own experiences to interpret the meaning of the practices. While we do not want a book that mandates how to improve our organization, we still need more information on what the details mean. Without this guidance, we see no guarantee that this model supports more consistent results and ratings than the previous model. Any appraisal or assessment method that relies on people (their experiences, their knowledge, and their abilities to make unbiased, perhaps unpopular decisions) will always be prone to error.

Appendix C: Checklists for Pilot Projects

This appendix consists of checklists for pilots. The checklists presented include:

- Pilot Life-Cycle Phases
- Steps in the Pilot Process
- Checklist for Planning and Conducting Pilots
- Checklist for Evaluating the Effectiveness of the Pilot

These checklists are formatted according to pilot project phases. These checklists may be applied against almost any pilot—those that are process-improvement based and those that are not. An example of a nonprocess improvement pilot may be when an organization switches from a nonautomated system to an automated one. In that case, maybe only a few offices within a department may pilot the system or only portions of the new system may be tried. Process improvement pilots can work the same way, except that we focus on piloting processes, not developed systems.

These checklists were made for pilots that follow a "quasi-experimental design," not those that follow an "experimental design." Most of you in software or systems engineering won't really care. Those of you who are social scientists conducting blind and double-blind studies might take offense at some of the items left out of these checklists. For example, we do not impale ourselves over the integrity of raw data, and we do not draw intermediate and final conclusions that can be traced back to the raw data. We also do not assign accountability. For more information on quasi-experimental versus experimental design, we suggest you contact Charlie Weber, one of the original authors of the CMM for Software. It is one of his favorite subjects.

These checklists might also be considered to help structure several activities that reside in the CMMI process area Organizational Innovation and Deployment.

As a reminder, the phases of process improvement are:

- Set Up—Set up the EPG and infrastructure. Baseline and plan. Get funding and commitment.
- Design—Write policies, procedures, identify/write standards.
- Pilot—Train participants and try out the procedures in a few areas. Update the procedures as necessary.
- Implement—Follow the procedures on all projects.

The pilot life-cycle phases are somewhat similar to those of process improvement. They are the:

- Set Up Phase
- Design Phase
- Conduct Phase
- Evaluate Phase
- Implement Phase

Steps in the pilot process are to:

- Select pilot projects
- Document success criteria and measurement techniques
- Orient and train project members in process improvement concepts
- Orient pilot participants in the purpose, strategy, and plan for the pilot
- Orient and train members in procedures that will be piloted
- Orient and train members in their roles and responsibilities
- Conduct the pilots
- Monitor and measure results
- Provide lessons learned
- Refine the procedures and processes based on pilot results
- Plan for rollout
- Update the projects' processes and organizational processes as needed
- Train/retrain, replan, repilot, as needed

Checklist for Planning and Conducting Pilots

Set Up

1. Define the problem that is to be addressed.
2. Generate alternatives, if possible.
3. If alternatives exist, examine alternative solutions to the problem for technical feasibility and cost-benefit.
4. Choose at least one alternative solution for piloting.
5. Identify the key points to be measured.

6. Define the methods and techniques that will be used to draw conclusions about pilot results (e.g., committee of senior managers, EPG, survey of the pilot project members, definition of success/failure, supporting data to be collected), including technical, operational, and financial capability.

Design

7. Document the processes and procedures to be used on the pilot.
8. Define the pilot evaluation criteria. Include quality factors.
9. Define the methods, processes, roles, personnel, timing, report formats, and data collection activities needed to perform the evaluation.
10. Identify all affected parties whose input and ideas are beneficial to the pilot. Do not include "squeaky wheels" at this point.
11. Define ways of gathering and tracking cost and benefit data.
12. Derive a schedule and plan for the pilot. Include milestones for the pilot and associated deliverables.

Conduct

13. Conduct the pilot according to the plan generated during the Design phase:
    - Execute the processes
    - Contact all affected parties
    - Collect the necessary data
    - Achieve the milestones and deliverables
14. If the design could not be followed, log and explain all deviations.
15. Record all issues that occurred during the conduct of the pilot, important thoughts about those issues, and how the issues were resolved.
16. Save all data and intermediate and final results for evaluation and lessons learned.

Evaluate

17. Conduct the evaluation according to the Plan:
18. Use the evaluation methods and techniques
    - Investigate results
    - Analyze data
    - Achieve the milestones and deliverables
19. If the evaluation plan could not be followed, log and explain all deviations.

20. Record all issues encountered during the evaluation, important thoughts about those issues, and how the issue was resolved.
21. Save all data and intermediate and final results for lessons learned.
22. Draw conclusions about the workability and effectiveness of the approach that was the subject of the pilot, based on pilot results.
23. Conduct a cost-benefit analysis as part of the final decision to implement the results of this pilot.
24. Gather all of the lessons learned, refine them, and document them for future use and applicability on other pilots.
25. Make recommendations regarding future use.
26. Analyze the pilot itself in regard to how it was conducted, and for ways of improving future pilots.

Implement

27. Base implementation decisions on pilot evaluation results and recommendations, and not on personal or political biases.
28. Base implementation decisions on any ongoing alternatives analyses, comparing pilot findings with information from updated alternatives.
29. Base implementation decisions on any other pilots that may occur in the organization.
30. Continue to gather data to determine the effectiveness of the pilot results when implemented in the organization (costs-benefits, schedule improvement, quality improvement, etc.).
31. Continue to collect, document, and analyze lessons learned.

Checklist for Evaluating the Effectiveness of the Pilot

Set Up

1. Was this the first ever attempt to do a pilot? (Either the first attempt within the organization or the first attempt planned and administered by this group of people.)
2. Was this the first attempt to pilot this particular issue/process/approach?
3. Was the pilot project of small enough scope that its results could be meaningful for future implementation decisions?
4. Have personal or political biases (visions of success or failure of the pilot) been injected into the pilot process or the pilot plan?
5. Have costs and benefits been addressed in planning?

6. Have alternative approaches been taken into consideration?
7. Has planning for repiloting been addressed?

Design

8. Was an evaluation plan prepared?
9. Did the plan contain evaluation and measurement criteria?
10. Were key factors for evaluation identified?
11. Were all affected parties identified?
12. Were plans made to consider and include (as appropriate) the opinions and reactions of the affected parties pertaining to the results of the pilot?
13. Was provision made for collecting and analyzing cost-benefit information?
14. Was there an analysis identifying appropriate cost and benefit information?

Conduct

15. Was the primary focus of the pilot on evaluating the process/issue/ approach addressed in the pilot, or was the motivation for the pilot biased in any way?
16. Were pilot results documented?
17. Were lessons learned recorded?
18. Is associated documentation adequate?
19. Were feedback mechanisms implemented to foster proper evaluation of the pilot?
20. Were all affected parties/constituencies approached for their reactions?
21. Were these reactions documented and analyzed?
22. Was cost-benefit information collected and analyzed?

Evaluation

23. Was there a documented evaluation phase?
24. Was there a serious attempt to evaluate the pilot results?
25. Were the reactions of affected parties collected and analyzed?
26. Were recommendations resulting from the pilot based on lessons learned and not on personal/political biases?
27. Was there a formal decision-making process regarding the future use of the pilots in the organization?

28. Was there a formal decision-making process regarding the future use of the results of this pilot in the organization?
29. Were costs and benefits compared?
30. To what extent did the pilot work/not work?
31. Were cost and benefit data included as part of the decision-making process?
32. If the pilot did not work, are there any potentially beneficial results that can be drawn from this pilot?
33. Was there a plan for evaluation and was it followed?
34. Were evaluation and measurement criteria identified?
35. Was a methodology or tracking system for data collection defined?
36. Were the tasks involved in that methodology carefully defined?
37. Were evaluation conclusions clearly stated and well supported?
38. Is sufficient evidence presented to support the conclusions drawn?
39. How confident are you in *all* of the results of the pilot?
40. Do we need to repilot?

Implement

41. Were evaluation results used in a decision to implement?
42. Were alternatives to the pilot concept explored during planning for implementation?
43. In the decision making regarding implementation, are costs and benefits addressed?
44. Is there a discussion in the decision making of potential savings, or of monetary impact of implementation/nonimplementation?
45. In the decision-making process, were costs and benefits, and other insights gained during the conduct of the pilot, as well as possible alternatives, addressed?
46. Was implementation based on the original pilot methodology, or modifications to it?
47. Were cost-benefit and schedule considerations adjusted due to any such modifications?
48. Were accurate cost and benefit data kept during implementation and use?
49. Was a comparison made between estimated versus actual costs, benefits, schedule improvement, and quality?
50. What modifications to the product or process must be made to make this work?
51. What lessons learned can we draw?
52. Were the pilot tests true pilot efforts? (A true pilot will follow the phases of the pilot life cycle, especially concerning Set Up and planning.)

53. Are the pilots concerned only with technical feasibility, or do they also examine cost and schedule effectiveness of the proposed and alternate solutions? What, if any, cost and benefit measures were used?
54. Did pilot monitoring and control procedures follow the organization's standards and processes?
55. Did formal, documented evaluation processes exist for pilots? If so, did they yield valid results?
56. For pilots that led to system or process implementation, were the claimed/projected benefits actually realized?

Appendix D: Organizational In-Brief to SCAMPI Team

We have found that it is very beneficial for organizations being appraised to deliver an in-brief presentation to the appraisal team that explains what their organization does and who they really are. While this task may seem simple, you would not believe the types of presentations we (as the SCAMPI team) have been subjected to. One in-brief (and remember, it is called a "brief") took three hours where the director of software laboriously told us about the educational accomplishments of his managers (there were several PhDs) and how much revenue was generated by his division. We don't care. None of that has anything to do with the practices of the CMMI. So, here are a few items that you might want to consider when asked to present an overall description of what your organization does and how it does it. All of this helps an Appraisal Team (and especially, an external Lead Appraiser) understand the culture of your organization and why you made the process improvement decisions you made. It may also help the Lead Appraiser develop an accurate Appraisal Plan.

Roles

Discuss the skill sets in use and what the terms for those skill sets are. Do you use the terms *programmers* or *developers*? Are requirements analysts also system analysts? Does a project manager also code? What are the roles on each project? Who does requirements? Who codes? Who does planning? Who works the budget? Who does testing? Who plans and monitors acquisition of products and services? Who does security? What levels are all of these things done on (several levels of testing, several levels of planning, several levels of security planning and enforcement)?

Major Stakeholders

Who is the customer? What does the customer want? Are there different customers for each project selected? Do these customers demand special tailoring of the organization's processes?

Structure

What is the total number of people in the organization that are involved in project work—not secretaries or administrative staff, but including project managers and technical staff? How many people are on a project? How long is a project? What is a project? Are they really doing projects, or programs, or tasks? Briefly, what is the overall approach to developing systems? What is the life cycle? Explain the steps in the life cycle, not just name it. An incremental life cycle for one organization can be an evolutionary life cycle for another organization.

Communication Channels and Meetings

Describe how information is reported, to whom, when, and what gets reported. What management meetings take place, how often, and at what levels? This structure is usually followed throughout the organization and can help reduce the time it takes to conduct management interviews. Briefly, how does the organization track changes to plans, activities, requirements, and software?

Terminology

What special terms are used that might be confused with another definition? For example, at a nuclear facility where we once worked, the term *quality* did not mean "quality assurance" or even "testing." It meant "safety."

Process Assets

Where does the organization store documents and code? What tools are used? The Appraisal Team may request demonstrations of online tools and libraries. Demonstrations should only take 5 to 15 minutes for each of the selected products. And make sure during the demo that the tool actually works.

Rewards and Punishments

What is the reward structure in use? Who gets rewarded and for what? Has the EPG or project members been told they will receive a bonus if the SCAMPI A is successful? Will someone be fired if it is not?

Index

A

Acceptance criteria, 66
Acceptance Testing, 72
Achievement profile, 37
Acquisition, 147
    use of SCAMPI A for, 280–281
Acquisition SCE, 367–368
Action Plans, 158, 170, 184, 186
    template, 188t
Adaptive Software Development (ASD), 345
Additions, 39
Adherence, objective evaluation of, 75, 77
ADS, 316–318t
Advanced practices, 11, 35
Affirmations, 285
Affirmations, 308
Agent, 195
Agile
    CMMI and, 347–351
    documentation and, 346
    Manifesto, 344–345
    Methods, 345
    use of in high-maturity organizations, 351
AgileAlliance, website, 344
Alternative approach to process improvement, 165
Alternative practices, 311
Amplifications, 279
Appraisal classes, 281–283
    characteristics, 282t
    selecting appropriate method, 283–284
Appraisal Data Package, 319–320
Appraisal Disclosure Statement. *See* ADS
Appraisal Input, 300
    document outline, 301t
Appraisal Plan, 302t

Appraisal rating, definition of, 279
Appraisal Record, 319–320
Appraisal Requirements for CMMI, Version 1.2.
    See ARC, V1.2
Appraisal Team Leader, 303. *See also* Lead
    Appraisers
Appraisal Teams, 279
    selecting and preparing for SCAMPI A,
      303–305
Appraisals, 7, 26–27, 154–155, 164, 170. *See
    also* SCAMPI; SCAMPI A
    approach to CMMI, 10
    definition of, 278
    expected organizational participation
      during, 291t
    reuse of previous results, 287–288
    SEI guiding documents for, 277–278
    use of presentations in, 308
Approaches, staged *vs.* continuous, 54
ARC, V1.2, 277
Artifacts, 134, 305, 321
    categorization of in PIIDs, 323–324
AS IS processes, 165, 169–170, 194
Assessments. *See also* appraisals
    definition of, 278
Attribute data, 247
Audit, 75
    configuration, 78
    metrics related to, 221

B

Base measures, 135, 219, 257
Base practices, 11, 35
Baselines, 78–79